The Sounds of Silence

EUROPEAN EXPANSION AND GLOBAL INTERACTION

It may be said that the question of how the technology, languages, institutions, and even pastimes of Western Europe came to dominate global civilization – even came to create that civilization – is the greatest historical question of modern times. Yet scholars have paid relatively little attention to this veritable monumental phenomenon. This new series is designed to offer a forum for debate and bring new research to light.

VOLUME 1
The Language Encounter in the Americas, 1492–1800
Edited by Edward G. Gray and Norman Fiering

VOLUME 2
The Jews and the Expansion of Europe to the West, 1400–1800
Edited by Paolo Bernardini and Norman Fiering

VOLUME 3
The Dutch Munsee Encounter in America: The Struggle for Sovereignty in the Hudson Valley
Paul Otto

VOLUME 4
The Sounds of Silence: Nineteenth-century Portugal and the Abolition of the Slave Trade
João Pedro Marques
Translated by Richard Wall

The Sounds of Silence

Nineteenth-century Portugal and the Abolition of the Slave Trade

João Pedro Marques
Translated by:
Richard Wall

Berghahn Books
NEW YORK • OXFORD

Published in 2006 by

Berghahn Books

www.berghahnbooks.com

Library of Congress Cataloging-in-Publication Data

Marques, João Pedro.
[Sons do silêncio. English]
The sounds of silence : nineteenth-century Portugal and the abolition of the slave trade / João Pedro Marques; translated by Richard Wall.
p. cm. — (European expansion & global interaction ; v. 4)
Includes bibliographical references and index.
ISBN 1-57181-447-7
1. Antislavery movements—Portugal—History—19th century. 2. Slaves—Emancipation—Brazil—History—19th century. I. Title. II. European expansion and global interaction ; v. 4.

MT1223.M3713 2005
326'.8'094690934—dc22 2005048337

British Library Cataloguing in Publication Data
A catalogue record for this book is available from the British Library.

The Portuguese Institute for Books and Libraries supported the publication of this book.

MINISTÉRIO DA CULTURA

INSTITUTO PORTUGUÊS DO LIVRO E DAS BIBLIOTECAS

Printed in the United States on acid-free paper.

ISBN 1-57181-447-7 hardback

CONTENTS

ABBREVIATIONS USED IN THE NOTES

AGM	Arquivo Geral de Marinha, Lisboa—General Navy Archive, Lisbon
AHM	Arquivo Histórico Militar, Lisboa—Historical Military Archive, Lisbon
AHU	Arquivo Histórico Ultramarino, Lisboa—Historical Overseas Archive, Lisbon
AMNE	Arquivo do Ministério dos Negócios Estrangeiros, Lisboa—Foreign Ministry Archive, Lisbon
ANTT	Arquivo Nacional da Torre do Tombo, Lisboa—Torre do Tombo National Archives, Lisbon
BN	Biblioteca Nacional, Lisboa—National Library, Lisbon
BOGGPA	*Boletim Official do Governo-Geral da Provincia de Angola—Official Bulletin of the Office of the Governor-General of Angola*
DCD	*Diário da Câmara dos Deputados—Journal of the Chamber of Deputies*
DCP	*Diário da Câmara dos Pares—Journal of the Chamber of Peers*
DG	*Diário do Governo—Official Gazette*
DL	*Diário de Lisboa—Lisbon Daily Journal*
MNE	Ministério dos Negócios Estrangerios
PRO FO	Public Record Office (London), Foreign Office

cx.	*caixa* (a box of unbound documents)
liv.	*livro* (a book or a codex of bound documents)
ma.	*maço* (a bundle or an unbound set of papers)
proc.	*processo* (a case)

PREFACE

This book is about the Atlantic slave trade, which developed when the era of the discoveries opened up a black Africa that exported people, or had the potential to do so, and a New World that needed them. Between the fifteenth and nineteenth centuries, some 11 million Africans were transported to the American colonies, and also to Europe (albeit on a much smaller scale). The overall volume of this transport, its significance in the formation of the modern Atlantic world, and the distressing and even tragic conditions under which it was carried out have given it a special place in our memory. Nevertheless, when looked at more broadly, the Atlantic slave trade was not radically different from other trafficking in human beings, which was long known in the Old World and which it had come to accept without significant protest. It was not even the first occasion on which systematic and continuous transfers of slaves were being made over great distances, or even when Africa had taken on the role of being a major supplier of labour. If we go back a mere century or two before the Portuguese discoveries, the slave trade prospered on the shores of the Mediterranean and the Black Sea, was of major interest to Venice, Genoa and Majorca, and involved Europeans, Asians and those Africans who came into the loop through the Islamic world.[1] Nor should we forget that the Muslim world had since the eighth century imported large numbers of blacks from across the desert, the Red Sea and the Indian Ocean.[2] In addition to being propped up by strong political and economic interests, the transatlantic trade was just one variant of very ancient and planet-wide forms of trade, and was strongly underpinned by law, religion and custom. Few in the mid eighteenth century would therefore have foreseen its end. And yet, a few decades later, both the slave trade and slavery itself would start to be abolished as a result of a series of measures that the Western world decreed for itself and gradually imposed on others.

These anti-slavery reforms, which reconciled morality and material interests, seemed to many to be truly miraculous. For many nineteenth-century observers abolition was all the more unbelievable in that, in nearly all cases, it had been achieved not through bloody revolt by the slaves but, as Tocqueville said in 1843, by 'the enlightened will of the masters'.[3]

Astonishing as it was and continues to be, the 'will of the masters' has been the key issue in abolitionist historiography since the pioneering work of Thomas Clarkson.[4] Almost two centuries after the publication of his book, the debate on the origin, nature and political victory of the abolitionist 'will' remains open: it focuses mainly on Britain, which is understandable in the context of that country having been at the forefront of abolition and having persevered in its efforts throughout the nineteenth century. Whatever our view of the underlying logic of the event, whether we see it as the outcome of ideas or of material interests, or both, the abolition of the slave trade is above all British territory. This does not mean that the issue of 'the will of the masters' is confined to Britain. It is relevant, albeit with differing emphases, to all the countries of the Atlantic seaboard that had colonies or traded in slaves and that went through their own processes of abolition during the nineteenth century—in other words, it also applies to Portugal. It was the desire to examine and understand the Portuguese 'will' and the forces acting either for or against the Atlantic slave trade that led me to undertake specific research in this largely unexplored area.

Portuguese historians never paid much attention to the question of the 'will of the masters'—or indeed to any issue relating to the institutions of slaving. It is surprising, initially, to find that a country which was the first entrant to the transatlantic slave trade and administered Brazil and Angola, the main slave importing and exporting countries, respectively, either almost ignored this aspect of its history or, worse still, manipulated its truth with a popular version of the process of abolition based on a handful of episodes—nearly always the same ones—made to measure to provide an edifying view of Portuguese humanitarian zeal.

This self-image of the country enabled it to mystify its role as a pioneering anti-slavery nation. Here and there there were some dissenting views that stressed the Portuguese lack of interest in the subject and described the process of abolition as merely the personal struggle of the Viscount of Sá da Bandeira, and a lonely and misunderstood one at that. But, while the myth that the Portuguese were abolitionist pioneers was a complete distortion of the truth, focusing attention on the figure of one exceptional man had the same effect: by highlighting the most illustrious part of the story, it tended to generate darkness around it. Divided therefore between distortion and darkness, Portuguese historians generally satisfied their curiosity with oblique references, dispatching the issue of abolition to a minor compartment of nineteenth-century colonial and diplomatic history. Thus it was that until the 1970s the most reliable and detailed information on abolition in Portugal was to be found in foreign works that dealt with the subject at a tangent or as a side issue.

It was only from 1974 onwards, thanks to the work of José Capela and Valentim Alexandre, that the history of the abolition of the Portuguese slave trade began to acquire more solid foundations. These two historians produced no more than half a dozen articles in which they looked at aspects of the anti-slavery issue, sometimes in a subsidiary manner, but this small output was nevertheless sufficient to enhance the frame of reference on abolitionism in Portugal and to shatter many of the myths built up around it.[5] However, Capela and Alexandre's work did not definitively clarify the matter of the 'will of the masters', partly because they did not tackle the question of 'will' itself, as manifested in significant words and actions, or significant silence and inaction. Even though they looked at the activist aspects of the politics of abolition and at the positions adopted by the major personalities involved, neither of these historians studied in detail what the Portuguese thought of abolitionism, possibly because they may not have uncovered sufficient motives or material to do so.

In the 1970s both Capela and Alexandre were working within a Marxist conceptual framework. They saw the politics of abolition in the manner of Eric Williams, mainly as a by-product of economic development. In *Capitalism and Slavery* Williams had explained the abolition of the slave trade in the light of developments in the British imperial economy and the material interests of pressure groups within British society.[6] Currently it is difficult to accept this thesis in its classic form, especially following the excellent demolition job carried out by Seymour Drescher.[7] Nevertheless, at the time when Capela and Alexandre were taking the first steps towards an interpretation of abolition in Portugal, Williams's work was the true orthodoxy, and both writers followed its basic concepts, adapting them to the case in hand. In other words, they basically interpreted the Portuguese movement towards abolition in the light of an interest in the economic exploitation of Africa. The arguments they developed on the basis of this relationship of cause and effect were similar, and if they differed in some of their conclusions it was because they also made differing assessments of the economic factors involved.

For Capela, Portugal at the time of abolition was an obstructed society with no industrial bourgeoisie and in which, apart from some more enlightened minds, no one was interested in Africa's potential wealth. So it was a country which was incapable of generating genuine abolitionism and, in these circumstances, the abolitionist statute of 1836 was no more than a device aimed at deceiving the British and holding on for a while longer to the interests of the Portuguese slavers.[8] For Alexandre, in contrast, nearly all the sectors of the Portuguese bourgeoisie were potentially interested in exploiting Africa: that context would therefore explain why, once Brazil had become independent, liberal governments sought to abolish the slave trade, one of the 'prior conditions needed to strengthen the Portuguese economic presence in Africa'.[9] While not denying the significance of British pressures, the author did not see it as a decisive factor in shaping the Portuguese 'will' to abolish the slave trade. At the same time he made Sá da Bandeira, the man responsible for the 1836 statute, the promoter and architect of a policy based firmly on the 'colonial interests of the ruling classes'.[10]

Unlike Capela, who saw Sá da Bandeira's abolition statute as something which was substantially disconnected from the country's life and interests, Alexandre envisaged a scenario of national consensus and convergence, with everyone following—or letting themselves go—in the same pro-African and pro-abolitionist direction. Subsequently, however, he was to revise his initial interpretation, no longer insisting on the connection between the 1836 law and the bourgeoisie's African interests. In an article he wrote in 1991, he viewed abolitionism as something which was extremely rare in Portuguese society.[11] More recently still, and in response to some objections that I myself raised, Alexandre recognized that it was impossible to sustain the relationship he had sought to establish between Sá da Bandeira's abolitionism and the interests of the 'ruling classes'.[12] This progressive correction of his initial approach undermined the consistency of his thesis regarding the interest of the 'ruling classes' in Africa—an aspect to which I shall return below—and produced no evident gain in terms of understanding Portuguese attitudes to the abolition of the slave trade. In this area, Alexandre, like Capela, essentially characterized things in a negative way, arguing that abolitionism was rare or non-existent in Portugal but failing to fill the gap he had identified. Accordingly, and with the exception of a few isolated cases, historical knowledge was content to record a relative vacuum, and Portuguese society was seen as having been relatively neutral, neither favouring nor opposing abolition. In line with this approach, abolitionism was explained as being relatively foreign to the Portuguese, a process taking place in the upper spheres of diplomacy and government, which involved the British, some Portuguese ministers and the recalcitrant people of the colonies, but in which Portuguese society played little or no role.

This description was an accurate reflection of what was fairly obvious: in other words, the lack of pamphlets and books and the fact that there was no true public debate on the matter. It also reflected the lack of abolitionist or anti-abolitionist organizations that might have served as focal points for the opinions of the Portuguese nation. In my view however, the description was not satisfactory. In using terms like 'indifference' or 'lack of awareness', it virtually excluded the thoughts and feelings of the literate elements in Portuguese society regarding the new colonial philanthropy. And, because it excluded them, it could not assess their eventual role in the process of abolition. The possibility that the political and economic elites, writers and other members of Portuguese society had played a part in influencing the direction of events by either hindering or encouraging the end of the slave trade, whether in 1836 or before and after that date, was something which should at least have been given serious consideration. The theory that the Portuguese were broadly 'indifferent' to or 'unaware' of abolition cannot be accepted without reservation since, in purely logical terms, it seems inconceivable that a process that sought to put an end to 400 years of involvement with and tolerance of slavery, and which was taking place in a context of strong international pressure and conflict, should have operated, in Portugal, in a relative wasteland of ideas and emotions. The British had confronted Portugal with the dilemma of abolition since the beginning of the nineteenth century; even if they did not wish to think about it, even if no inner impulse drove them to it, the Portuguese could not avoid thinking about the issue.

There should therefore, in principle, have been some Portuguese thought in relation to abolitionism. Would the predominant attitude have been in favour of the slave trade? Would abolitionism have had low visibility because it was not a popular cause, or not a cause that attracted much militancy? Was there some other ideology at work that somehow was not clearly identifiable within our pro-slavery/abolitionism dichotomy? Or were all these factors present at the same time in varying measure? Expressed in these terms, the issue is no longer the irrelevance of abolitionism to the general public in Portugal, but rather the attempt to identify what lay beneath that irrelevance, in the place of open and active abolitionism (or anti-abolitionism). To put it in another way, the issue now became the reconstruction of the ideological frameworks that developed in Portugal in connection with the problem of abolishing the slave trade. To carry out that reconstruction seemed to me to be a worthwhile and significant task, not only because I could thereby plug gaps in our knowledge of the past, but also because more recent historiography pointed insistently to the key role of ideology in changing popular attitudes in the Western world to the problem of the transatlantic slave trade.

Theories that stress ideas as explanatory factors in the abolitionist movement have always been of fundamental significance for historians. From the time of Thomas Clarkson to the present day, the study of ideology has always been a significant part of the historiography of the antislavery movement, even in the period when Williams's conclusions, which had been generally recognized and accepted, tended to attribute to the explanatory power of ideas a secondary role in comparison with mechanisms of an economic nature. We should recall that it was during this period that David Brion Davis published a magisterial study on the religious and philosophical origins of abolitionism and the position of Western culture in relation to the problem of slavery.[13] Nevertheless, over the last twenty-five years, with the demolition of Williams's theory, this area of study has become doubly important: much recent work has tended to show how a convergence of economic and non-economic ideas produced the abolitionist crusade and made its ultimate victory possible.

Having acknowledged the importance of reconstructing the ideological framework, my problem then became one of rendering the task a viable one, given that, generally speaking, no one had properly identified arguments over the slave trade, whether for or against, because these had not acquired the public visibility in nineteenth-century Portugal which they had in the United States or in Britain. From the point of view of the historian, the most evident characteristic of the Portuguese attitude to abolitionism was indeed relative silence, which seemed to stand in the way of any desire to reconstruct it. But in my opinion it would have been premature to take the apparent lack of material on the slave trade as proof of its irrelevance or inconsistency, for two reasons. First, given the clandestine and morally anathematized nature of slaving practices in the nineteenth century, silence could be interpreted in a number of ways: it might represent not just neutral detachment but also a conscious strategy on the part of those who wished to see the slave trade continue. With the silence of the Portuguese having potentially different meanings, it could never be taken from the outset as equating to a vacuum or indifference. Secondly, even though the sum total of public statements on the problem of slavery seemed to be small, it might nonetheless be much larger than was generally thought. As I surmised when I started out, and as this study progressively confirmed, the non-existence of an abolitionist movement in Portugal did not necessarily imply that ideas on abolition were lacking, but only that it was more difficult to capture them, in that they were diffuse and scattered. However, if it were possible to uncover and put together a sufficiently large number of expressions of opinion on abolition, it would, in principle, also be possible to dissipate and decode the relative silence. That was the target I set out to achieve—hence the title I have chosen. Both the target and the path to be followed were new, because my concern was not so much to describe the various arguments, as to reconstruct the underlying systems of mental representation in each of them, as well as to analyse whether those systems persisted, changed or died out over time and in the light of events in the political, economic and social spheres.

To the extent that I regarded it as the core element in understanding Portuguese attitudes to the abolition of the slave trade, the study of ideas constitutes the main itinerary of this book, but it is not the only one. As I mentioned above, the ultimate purpose of my work was to explain nineteenth-century Portugal's abolitionist or non-abolitionist 'will'. This means that alongside the study of ideas I also sought to take into account practices, actions and inactions. I did not do this merely to provide a context, on the grounds that practice influenced the production of ideas, but because I assumed that actions were in themselves a manifestation of values and that the 'will' of parliamentarians, ministers, colonial governors and other persons in authority in Portugal was to be found as much in what they said as in what they did (or did not do).

The incipient historiography of abolitionism in Portugal had hitherto focused more on practices than on ideas. This was particularly true in connection with legislative and diplomatic activity, which had traditionally been the object of a certain amount of attention. But there were some aspects of action which earlier research had barely touched upon and which needed to be explored if one wanted to achieve a broader knowledge of Portuguese attitudes to abolitionism. In particular, this was what had happened with the issue of suppression, that is to say, with the Portuguese naval and other police authorities' efforts to rein in the slave trade, which had not been studied systematically until now; and with the reverberations of abolitionism in the Portuguese Cortes, which none had yet mapped out, from identifying the champions of abolition and their adversaries, to defining the moments of confrontation and the political manoeuvrings used in order to prevail. Alongside these and other aspects that had remained almost untouched, there were a number of other problems that had been dealt with but that needed to be reassessed or examined in greater depth. To paraphrase Paul Veyne, no historian is obliged to shut off any issue prematurely; on the contrary, he should seek to take it as far as he can go, because the progress of historical explanation depends, in essence, on deeper enquiry.[14] It was on the basis of this epistemological approach that I felt that the explanation of certain instances of pro- or anti-abolitionist activity in Portugal should not be left in the state in which earlier research had left them.

The need to study ideas and actions obliged me to take in a much broader and more varied range of sources. As a general rule I tried, in connection with my work on the ideological framework, to analyse all the material on abolitionism written in Portugal at the time, ranging from fictional literature to legislation, from specific books and pamphlets to parliamentary speeches and, most of all, newspapers. By virtue of the huge volume of documentation they make available, but also because they do so frequently, newspapers are the main path to the currents of opinion that existed in Portuguese society. I examined the huge collection in the Biblioteca Nacional (National Library) up to the year 1851, which was when the slave trade declined in importance with the closing off of the Brazilian import markets. From 1851 onwards, I narrowed my choice of materials down to a few titles, selected on the basis of the relevance of specific items within them or their editorial content.

I also studied at length the vast collection of parliamentary *Diários* (Daily Record) from the date it started out at the beginning of the 1820s up to the mid-1860s. But, as is to be expected, the main basis for the study of the political and diplomatic process is the documentation held in the Ministério dos Negócios Estrangeiros (Ministry of Foreign Affairs), in the papers of Sá da Bandeira and in the specific documentation of the Arquivo Geral de Marinha (Navy General Records) and the Biblioteca Nacional. I naturally paid special attention to those documents that related to the struggle against the slave trade and those concerning relations between Britain and Portugal. Whenever I found it necessary I examined the exchanges of correspondence with other countries' legations and other documentary sources. For the period between 1820 and 1850 I also used the documentation in the British Public Record Office (Foreign Office 84 series), not only to complement the information I had already obtained in Portuguese sources, but also to view the Portuguese 'will' from the outside, as it was seen and felt by the British.

The work I carried out on this extensive documentation resulted in a text that is deliberately close to the documents. There are two main reasons for this. First, it was absolutely necessary to explain the past when, as in this case, I was dealing with issues on which silence had generally been maintained, or about which little was known. Secondly, staying close to the document brings a healthy discipline to the work of writing history, preventing the historian from imagining the facts in the light of his own desires and projections, or from mentioning them without having studied them carefully.[15] Inevitably, this had consequences in terms of the type of history I would write. Because it deals simultaneously with ideas and practice, because it seeks to remain close to the document but to be more than mere description, this is historiography on two levels. On one level it puts information first: given that a narrative in chronological order seemed to me the best form of giving an account of ideas, policies and even interests, whether pro- or anti-slavery, in nineteenth-century Portugal, with the necessary amount of detail, narrative is the book's matrix. It is on the foundation of that matrix that I then move up to a second historiographic level, one that seeks above all to provide explanations.

This book is a study of the abolition of the slave trade in Portugal. It covers the period from the end of the eighteenth century to the mid-1860s, in other words from the beginning of the political movement against slave trading up to the American civil war and the closure of the Cuban import markets, the two events that finally ended the transatlantic slave trade. Within this time frame it is easy to identify the stages of abolition in Portugal. Certain moments, such as the start of British political pressure, the loss of Brazil and the decline of the transatlantic trade with the end of Brazilian imports, are clear linkages between periods when different issues and abolitionist targets prevailed. The narrative accordingly seeks to accompany these chronological stages, reconciling them as far as possible with the main phases of Portuguese political history.

Chapter 1 deals with the final years of the eighteenth century and the beginning of the nineteenth—the phase during which abolitionism was still an issue external to Portugal—and in it I have sought to define as closely as possible the interlocking ideas and political achievements that were leading to the abolition of the slave trade outside Portugal. In fact it is precisely on account of the international aspects of the question that I have endeavoured in every chapter, however succinctly, to sum up the objectives, the obstacles and the results of suppression in each stage of the struggle against the slave trade. Following the introduction, the second part of the chapter examines how Portugal maintained a certain distance in relation to an issue that had enormous implications for the life of the Euro-African-Brazilian empire. Subsequently, and because maintaining a distance does not imply that there was an ideological vacuum, this chapter looks at the prevailing systems of reference in Portugal in connection with the slave trade and its abolition.

Chapters 2 and 3 cover the period from 1811 to 1834, more or less from the beginning of the British police action against Portuguese slave ships up to the victory of the Liberals in the Portuguese civil war, and including the Brazilian secession. The persistent backdrop of these chapters is British pressure for abolition, and in them I seek to explain how the Portuguese resisted this pressure, the points where there was friction and the points where they yielded. Having defined this historical framework, these two chapters examine the development of various ideological trends during that period, from the emergence of a universal defence of gradualism up to the time, towards the end of the 1820s, when the issue was once again forgotten and remained dormant for a time.

Chapter 4 is the core of the work, both by reason of its length and because it deals with the most controversial and most heavily documented period in the history of abolition in Portugal. It covers the period from 1834 to 1842, a time of turmoil as the liberal regime sought to settle down, the September revolution took place and the Constitutional Charter was restored. In terms of abolitionism, there was an increase in British pressure, Sá da Bandeira's decree was published, Palmerston's bill was passed and finally the much-awaited Anglo-Portuguese treaty on abolition was signed. Throughout this chapter I have followed in detail the paths taken by different governments in Lisbon in relation to the British pressure, attempting to relate them to the prevailing currents of thought and political interests in Portuguese society at the time, which were plentifully revealed both in the press and in the Cortes.

Chapter 5 studies the period from 1842 up to the closure of the Cuban import markets, with a point of linkage in the year 1851, when the Brazilian transatlantic trade came to an end and the *Regeneração* (Regeneration) movement triumphed in Portugal: this event reconciled the warring liberal factions, and ended the period of revolutions and political turmoil that had lasted since 1834. In line with the explanatory model that I followed from the beginning, this chapter summarizes the final phase of the slave trade, as well as the ups and downs of the struggle to end the trade, studying Portuguese abolitionist moves in this context and seeking to demonstrate the importance of the idea of national honour as the driving force behind these moves.

Finally, in chapter 6, I break the chronological sequence in order to assess the significance of Africa in the life and imagination of liberal Portugal from 1820 to 1865, seeking to establish possible connections between that significance and Portuguese attitudes to abolition of the slave trade.

This book is an abridged version of a work published in Lisbon in 1999. Its translation into English would not have been possible without the support of Professors Pieter C. Emmer and Seymour Drescher, who from the outset showed enormous interest in my work. I am equally grateful to Professors Joseph C. Miller, David Birmingham, António Barreto and David Brion Davis, who gave me a wealth of advice and who, in various ways, sustained my efforts at publication. I must also thank the Calouste Gulbenkian Foundation and the Instituto Português do Livro e das Bibliotecas for their generous support in funding the cost of translating this book. Finally, enormous thanks are due to my wife, Paula, for the patience with which she read and commented on both the Portuguese and the English versions.

Notes

1. See Charles Verlinden, *L'Esclavage dans l'Europe Médiévale,* De Temple, Brugge, 1955; idem, *The Beginnings of Modern Colonization. Eleven Essays with an Introduction,* Cornell University Press, Ithaca, NY, 1970.
2. See Ralph A. Austen, 'The Trans-Saharan Slave Trade: a Tentative Census', in H. Gemery and J. Hogendorn (eds), *The Uncommon Market. Essays in the Economic History of the Atlantic Slave Trade,* Academic Press, New York, 1979, pp. 23–76; idem, 'The Mediterranean Islamic Slave Trade Out of Africa', *Slavery and Abolition,* 13, 1, 1992, pp. 214–48.
3. Alexis de Tocqueville, 'On the Emancipation of Slaves' (1843), in Seymour Drescher (ed.), *Tocqueville and Beaumont on Social Reform,* Harper & Row, New York, 1968, p. 138.
4. Thomas Clarkson, *History of the Rise, Progress, and Accomplishment of the Abolition of the African Slave Trade by the British Parliament,* London, 1839 (1st edition 1808).
5. José Capela, *Escravatura: a empresa do saque. O abolicionismo, 1810–1875,* Afrontamento, Porto, 1974; idem, *A burguesia mercantil do Porto e as colónias (1834–1900),* Afrontamento, Porto, 1975; idem, *As burguesias portuguesas e a abolição do tráfico da escravatura,* Afrontamento, Porto, 1979; idem, 'Abolicion y abolicionismo en Portugal y sus colonias', in Francisco de Solano and Agustín Guimerá (eds), *Esclavitud y derechos humanos. La lucha por la libertad del negro en el siglo XIX,* CSIC, Madrid, 1986, pp. 577–603; Valentim Alexandre, *Origens do colonialismo português moderno (1822–1891),* Sá da Costa, Lisbon, 1979; idem, 'O liberalismo português e as colónias de África, 1820–1839', *Análise Social,* 16, 61–62, 1980, pp. 319–40; idem, 'Portugal e a abolição do tráfico de escravos (1834–51)', *Análise Social,* 26, 111, 1991, pp. 293–333.
6. Eric Williams, *Capitalism and Slavery,* Andre Deutsch, London, 1964 (1st edition 1944).
7. Seymour Drescher, *Econocide: British Slavery in the Era of Abolition,* University of Pittsburgh Press, Pittsburgh, 1977. For an outline of the subsequent debate, see Seymour Drescher, 'The Decline Thesis of British Slavery Since Econocide', and Selwyn Carrington, 'The State of the Debate on the Role of Capitalism in the Ending of the Slave Trade', in H. Beckles and V. Shepherd (eds), *Caribbean Slave Society and Economy,* IRP, Kingston, 1991, pp. 136–49 and 435–45, respectively; see also Thomas Bender (ed.), *The Antislavery Debate: Capitalism and Abolitionism as a Problem in Historical Interpretation,* University of California Press, Berkeley, 1992; and Seymour Drescher, 'Capitalism and Slavery after Fifty Years', *Slavery and Abolition,* 18, 3, 1997, pp. 212–27.
8. Capela, *A burguesia mercantil,* pp. 11–13; see also idem, *Escravatura,* pp. 181 ff. and 231–32; idem, *As burguesias portuguesas,* pp. 209–10.

9. Alexandre, 'O liberalismo', p. 335.
10. Alexandre, *Origens*, pp. 14–21 and 45–46.
11. Alexandre, 'Portugal e a abolição', p. 301 ff.
12. Valentim Alexandre, 'Projecto colonial e abolicionismo', *Penélope*, 14, 1994, p. 125; for the article which gave rise to Alexandre's new writing, see João Pedro Marques, 'Uma revisão crítica das teorias sobre a abolição do tráfico de escravos português', *Penélope*, 14, 1994, pp. 95–118, especially pp. 108–10.
13. David B. Davis, *The Problem of Slavery in Western Culture*, Cornell University Press, Ithaca, NY, 1966.
14. Paul Veyne, *Comment on écrit l'histoire. Éssai d'épistémologie*, Ed. du Seuil, Paris, 1971 (Spanish translation by Mariano M. Alonso, *Como se escribe la historia. Ensayo de epistemologia*, Fragua, Madrid, 1972, pp. 123–24, 128–29).
15. Raymond Aron, 'Comment l'historien écrit l'épistémologie: a propos du livre de Paul Veyne', *Annales*, 26, 1971, p. 1332.

List of Illustrations

Figures

Maps

– Chapter 1 –

PORTUGAL AND ABOLITIONISM AT THE END OF THE EIGHTEENTH CENTURY AND BEGINNING OF THE NINETEENTH CENTURY: FROM DETACHMENT TO POLITICAL COMMITMENT

In 1792, in his dispatches to Lisbon, the Portuguese ambassador in London mentioned that 'universal benevolence' was surprisingly taking over from material interests and that the party of those who were demanding the end of the slave trade was growing 'at a pace which nothing had led one to expect'.[1] The ambassador's surprise was fully justified. If truth be told, criticism of the institutions of slavery was not new, far from it. At least since the beginning of the eighteenth century, fictional literature, moral philosophy and political economy had all contributed directly or indirectly to developing feelings of aversion to the slave trade and slavery itself. However, the extent of that aversion in the closing years of the eighteenth century, the scope and direction of the changes being demanded, and the aspect of a religious crusade that threatened to submerge not only the British system of slavery but all others as well undoubtedly represented sudden and unexpected changes to the status quo.

1.1 Tolerationism and Abolitionism

The educated man at the time of the Enlightenment could acknowledge the iniquity of the system of slavery, but he understood and accepted the reasons why it existed in the world as it then was. That is why the philosophers did not harbour any great illusions as to the viability of abolition. They knew that generous and sensitive souls would support the idea of freeing the slaves, but they also knew that greed, which ruled the world, would be deaf to their appeals. It was undoubtedly for this reason that Condorcet acknowledged that the voices of those philosophers who from time to time advocated the end of the slave trade and slavery did not flourish within governments, and were quickly forgotten by society.[2]

As a rule, the response of Enlightenment humanitarianism to the problem of slavery followed three paths, none of which led to abolitionism. The most common one was to design plans that would enable the system to be improved. Another method was based on the tranquillizing belief that progress would slowly straighten out the injustices of the institution and that relief would gradually come to its victims. A third—and more explosive—route appealed purely and simply for a revolt by the slaves.[3] In other words, the learned gentleman of 1770 was not an abolitionist. He simply disapproved of or criticized the institutions of slavery in differing degrees. His was an attitude of sentimental sympathy for the slave, of complacent lamentation at the injustice done to the African, and of hope that happier times might bring the end of institutions that were so evidently barbarous. It was clear that there was a current of thought that was increasingly incompatible with slavery and that inclined many to accept appropriate reforms. Such reforms might extend to gradual abolition, but nothing more. As Davis accurately observed, for a time the critique of slavery appeared to be a harmless philanthropic fashion of the late Enlightenment.[4]

However, in the final quarter of the century a substantially new approach emerged. Blending historical interpretation, biblical exegesis, political economy and ethnography, several North American and British writers started to disseminate three central and convergent ideas: that Europeans were guilty of the existence of the traffic (and of Africa's consequent barbarity); that divine punishment was imminent for the continuation of an inhuman practice; and that major political and economic advantages were to be obtained by prohibiting it. This new approach, spurred by religious zeal and by the mirage of material reward, incited an activist attitude, the aim of which was an immediate or almost immediate end to the slave trade and, shortly after that, of slavery itself.

It is this attitude—and only this attitude—which is entitled to the label abolitionism, in order better to differentiate it from that other attitude which, around 1770, represented the commonest position among the learned elites, and which I will label generally as tolerationism. Abolitionism accordingly has a precise and restrictive meaning, while tolerationism, which refers to the attitude of those who, while in some way condemning the traffic, were not (or not yet) abolitionists, inevitably has a broader and more imprecise meaning. In the absence of a better term, tolerationism has the advantage that it retains something of a coeval flavour—the verb to tolerate was used frequently in this era and in this context—and emphasizes a key distinction: for the abolitionist, the traffic encapsulated practices that were abhorrent to such a degree that it should immediately be swept from the face of the earth; for the tolerationist, even if the slave trade was regarded as immoral and unjust, it could nonetheless be maintained for political or other reasons.

To the extent that the word tolerationism covers differing positions, some of them quite close to abolitionism, the distinction I am suggesting should not be seen as implying that there was an irreconcilable gulf between them. The basic distinction between a mental attitude of disapproval of the slave trade which, at times, was prepared to admit that it would end in the medium to long term and another attitude that saw it as execrable and sought its immediate extinction is just one among the different possible ways of looking at and classifying the spectrum of positions that Western culture adopted in the eighteenth century in relation to the 'odious commerce'. But it is a form which is useful from the analytical point of view in that, as we shall see below when dealing with the Portuguese case, it makes it possible to carry out a preliminary breakdown of the always murky realm of political and journalistic discussion of slavery. Abolitionism sought the immediate end of the slave trade; tolerationism could accept abolition, but only gradually. Because it allowed for an element of inaction, or delayed action, tolerationism was a current of opinion that was open to contamination, and would frequently be appropriated by those who defended the institutions of slavery. That was not the case of abolitionism pure and simple, which fought for immediatism. Gradualism and immediatism were therefore the agendas for action—or inaction—according to the intentions of those who promoted them, and the surest identifier of genuine abolitionism lies in the type of action suggested by the ideology. It was for that very reason that abolitionists themselves made immediatism the preferred criterion for assessing the moral sincerity of those who said they supported their cause.[5]

It should be noted that, initially, immediatism applied only to the abolition of the slave trade, because the early abolitionists assumed that cutting off the supply of African slaves would automatically lead to the introduction of compensating mechanisms in the American colonies, which would induce the plantation owners themselves to free those blacks they still held in captivity. However, in order for all this fantastic social engineering to take place, the slave trade would have to stop immediately. That is the reason why the true abolitionists were immediatists on the issue of the slave trade.

Apologists for immediate action to abolish the slave trade began to make their views known in the last thirty years of the eighteenth century, mainly in the form of religiously inspired messages. The frontal attack on slavery had been started by some of the Quakers in the North American colonies. Their anti-slavery message was directed at their own congregations and, understandably, had a limited impact. However, in the 1770s, once prohibition on trading and owning slaves had been achieved at the sectarian level, the Quakers turned their attention to broader objectives, applying pressure on the colonial legislative assemblies and then on the government itself. It was as part of that political effort that their philanthropic message began to spread to wider audiences, even if this did require a broadening of the early arguments. A line of thinking which, as a rule, perceived the traffic and ownership of men to be demonic practices now combined that notion with facts brought to light by travel literature and with ideas recently developed by political and moral philosophy, economics and theology.[6]

Anthony Benezet was the pioneer of this all-embracing approach. Basing himself on the information collected in the writings of travellers and slavers—which at the time were the only authorities on Africa—Benezet built up what was almost an ethnographic anthology and, alongside it, developed a convincing argument in favour of abolition. His book *Some Historical Account of Guinea* described in some detail an Africa that was fertile, albeit unhealthy for Europeans, populated by simple, innocent people who were capable of progress and able to live happily.[7] For Benezet there were no intellectual hindrances in the way of civilizing the Africans. The true obstacles were the slave trade and colonial slavery. His analysis of their origins and consequences led him to the conclusion that the West was entirely guilty of both evils. Towards the end of the book the writer crowned his rational edifice with the intervention of a justice-wielding God. What would happen, he asked, when the cries of the Negroes reached the heavens, 'what shall we do when God riseth up?'[8] In order that the divine scourge should not fall inexorably on the sinful nations, the traffic would have to cease at once and the existing slaves would shortly have to be freed. These measures would placate the celestial wrath and bring benefits both in terms of public safety in the colonies and for the British nation as a whole, which would then be able to access the riches of Africa through a civilizing and more Christian trade.

Benezet influenced several leading opinion-makers and people of other Protestant denominations, and his work led to a series of further developments of the subject matter, the most significant of which was the work of Thomas Clarkson. To all those who opposed abolition on the grounds that the slave trade was the mainstay for the British merchant navy Clarkson responded with the argument that mortality rates among the slave ship crews were clearly higher than those recorded in any other type of seafaring; that is to say, the sailors, like the Africans, were martyrs to an inhuman trade.[9] In order to contradict the common adage that, with abolition, production in the American colonies would inevitably fall, Clarkson cited the example of plantations that had remained viable while managing the work of their slaves in an enlightened manner, giving them reasonable conditions for living and reproducing. Provided that such an arrangement became universal, the colonies would suffer little from the interruption of the slave trade. However, even if this were not so, the wider interests of the British nation demanded a new policy towards Africa. Negroes had commercial flair, the African soil was more fertile than any other, and it was therefore imperative to suppress the slave trade so that the whole continent could open up to harmless trade. Perceiving that merely religious or humanitarian arguments would not be sufficient to draw people into the abolitionist cause, Clarkson appealed to the national interest by showing that it would be of great advantage to the British state and the British people to prohibit the 'odious commerce'.[10] The association between abolition and the economic development of Africa was systematically exploited by the abolitionists, and all the more convincingly in that some of its advocates seemed to know what they were talking about. Cugoano and Equiano, two former slaves who had devoted themselves to the 'cause of humanity', assured their readers that the African continent had much to give England if its inhabitants were to be seen as consumers and not merely as animate objects.[11]

In overall terms, the message conveyed by the many religion-inspired abolitionist writings which circulated in Britain in the last quarter of the eighteenth century was clear and simple. The Europeans were shown to be the instigators of the slave trade, a sin from which humanity would have to free itself in short order. First, the suggested view made the reader conscious of the 'crime'; secondly, it provoked feelings of guilt and remorse; finally, it demanded action to right the situation. This basic triangular design—awareness, remorse and purification—seemed all the more acceptable to the extent that, at a more practical level, the moral and religious curse which hung over the institutions of slavery was reinforced by a conviction that abolition was the proper national policy.

The appeals of the abolitionists coincided, moreover, with an upsurge of interest in African colonization. From early on in the eighteenth century some of their forerunners had advocated reorienting British activity in the tropics away from the Americas and to the African coast.[12] The idea therefore went back quite a long way, and did not necessarily imply an attack on the institutions of slavery. However, towards the end of the eighteenth century, arguments had begun to proliferate in favour of both the ending of the slave trade and the use of voluntary paid labour, in order to develop agriculture along various parts of the African coast. Some of these utopian colonial planners published their plans for social and economic engineering, making them available to the general reader. Most of them shared an idyllic view of Africa and an aversion to the 'odious commerce'.[13]

The idea of abolition also spread through travellers and naturalists. Since the beginning of the European expansion some visitors to the coast of Africa had written down their views on slavery and on the slave trade. In general, these writers recognized that the trade in human beings seemed to partake of something barbarous and unnatural. The trade was at the same time sad for humanity and traumatizing for the Negro (who was usually described as a poor unfortunate who was worthy of pity). Nevertheless, the descriptions by Bosman, Labat, Snelgrave and other travellers of the time also conveyed the belief that everything surrounding the operations of slaving, from food to ships' hygiene, was an improvement in comparison with the conditions Africans had to bear in their own lands, where they would be dead if white men would not buy them. At the same time, they all stressed the vital need for the traffic if the

American colonies were to prosper and survive.[14] Nevertheless, in the final quarter of the eighteenth century, some travellers and former slave traders began to publish accounts that broke with the usual tone of prior writings and introduced critical judgements on the inexpedient nature and inhumanity of the system of slavery, and suggested ways of ending it. It is true that some of the accounts were still very ambivalent regarding the slave trade and slavery (and some still adopted the old pro-slavery point of view). Despite this, in the new context of philanthropy at the close of the century, these accounts became overwhelmingly abolitionist in tone, even if only on account of the detailed descriptions they gave of a world and of doings which were, paradoxically, little known in Europe. The intrinsic violence of slavery was such that, as the abolitionists understood early on, the mere setting out of the facts could itself become a powerful weapon in pursuit of the cause. A work such as that of Stedman, for example, might help to promote the new humanitarian message despite the author's reservations regarding abolitionist methods and intentions.[15]

Some books were widely disseminated and had a clear impact. Stedman's work was translated into Dutch, French, German, Swedish and Italian, and new editions were published in London in 1801 and 1813. Clarkson was read closely in Western Europe, from Bordeaux to Scandinavia. Abbé Raynal's *Histoire philosophique* circulated quite widely outside his country of origin: from 1776 to 1806, which is roughly the period that concerns us, it went to fifteen editions in Britain, as many as Adam Smith's *Wealth of Nations* in the same period and in the same country.[16] But even books by lesser-known authors were publishing successes. Nine editions of the autobiography of Olaudah Equiano, for example, were published in Britain between 1789 and 1794: during that time it was translated into Dutch, German and Russian.[17]

In Britain, the widening of the scope of the pro-abolitionist bibliography was accompanied by remarkable militant efforts to spread the message. In 1783 the British Quakers organized a committee that sought to compile and republish an abolitionist bibliography and to channel some articles to the periodicals.[18] In the years that followed this propaganda activity increased because, as Clarkson said, 'a general circulation of knowledge on this subject was absolutely necessary'.[19] In 1787, the recently-constituted London Abolition Committee gained the support of the major newspapers and invested heavily in the publication and distribution of abolitionist texts. Some 78,000 books and reports were published up to the middle of the following year. The period of the first major assault on the slave trade gave rise to something like 109 abolitionist pamphlets—to these we should add other forms of propaganda, such as medallions, tea services and prints that showed the suffering of the Africans in the sugar mills or in the hold of a slave ship.[20]

A propaganda campaign was also launched in the United States. In Rhode Island, for example, the Quakers saturated the local press with essays, poems and articles illustrating the evils of the slave trade and the institution of slavery.[21] In continental Europe the number of abolitionist publications was lower, but, nonetheless, here too images and ideas were disseminated, and in France, for example, some of the English abolitionist texts were translated and distributed.[22] Of course, some publications in favour of slavery also circulated alongside works directly or indirectly opposing it, especially in England, where the controversy reached its highest point.[23] In a sense, however, these publications helped to heat up the debate on the problem of Negro slavery.

To sum up, at the end of the eighteenth century the West witnessed the birth of a new way of looking at the problem of slavery. In its commonest form the abolitionist ideology was decidedly forward-looking and universalist, with strong millennialist overtones, pointing the way to a different and better world, to a freer America, an Africa that could be civilized and a Europe that would be richer thanks to African trade. Like all ideologies of struggle, it had created its own myths and its own heroes and victims, spreading the image of the poor and peaceful black man crushed by the limitless greed of the European. Likewise, it had classified the traffic as a crime against humanity and had stigmatized the criminals. At the same time, and in addition to condemning the 'odious commerce' on religious and moral grounds, it argued that it was immediately dispensable on grounds of material and national interest. While in the rest of Europe anti-slavery continued to be seen from an essentially Enlightenment point of view—that is, a tolerationist point of view—in Britain there was popular support for the body of abolitionist ideas, and abolition was felt to be something that touched on key religious principles. As Temperley recently said, the British believed that the world could and should do without the slave trade.[24] And it was precisely that which the world began to do at the end of the eighteenth and the beginning of the nineteenth centuries, albeit on occasion somewhat timidly and spasmodically.

The United States had started to move towards the abolition of the slave trade in the 1780s, even if progress was uneven, reflecting the different interests of each state. Rhode Island—which at the time was the main slaving centre in North America—was the first state to decree abolition, in 1787. In the following year similar measures were adopted by Connecticut, Massachusetts, New York and Pennsylvania, and in 1789 by Delaware. Abolition of the transatlantic slave trade at the national level was slower because of opposition from several quarters, particularly South Carolina and Georgia. In anticipation of the opening up of lands further west, and certain that these new lands would require labour, these states sought to avoid making any permanent commitment on the issue. A federal law prohibiting North American involvement in foreign slave trade was approved in 1794, but it was only on 2 March 1807 that the importation of slaves would be totally prohibited in the United States. The prohibition was to enter into force at the beginning of 1808, even if in a mild form, since Congress did not give its authority for naval action to suppress slave trading (it would only do this in 1819).[25]

In France, the process of abolition was entwined with the revolution and followed its erratic and explosive path. The abolition of the slave trade was first promoted by the Société des Amis des Noirs, an association founded in 1788, at the urging of the English Quakers. Mainly encouraged by Protestants, and not having a national network of contacts, the association sought above all to engage influential personalities. But the conservative political attitudes of many of the Amis des Noirs, and their close ties to the British abolitionists, were factors that worked against it at a time of national convulsion, and the appeal for abolition foundered on the rock of revolutionary upheaval. A wave of rumours of treason, as early as 1789, and alleged conspiracies on the part of the Amis to incite the slaves in the colonies to revolt made the abolitionist cause extremely unpopular. Then, in 1791, the great rebellion in Saint Domingue brought matters to a head, confusing the issue and causing the abolitionist core to crumble in the revolutionary whirlwind, with many of its top leaders leaving the kingdom, while others—like Brissot, for example—were executed. The association still revived sporadically in 1798, but then ceased its activities altogether.[26] Meanwhile, and somewhat paradoxically, the Convention decreed the end of slavery itself on 4 February 1794. This was not because there was any strong social pressure to do so, but only to provide post facto legitimacy for what was happening in Saint Domingue, in the hope of not completely losing their footing in the face of the insurrection. In 1802–3, when the French armies sought to retake the island, Napoleon restored the slave trade and slavery.[27]

Anti-slavery policy in Denmark was more consistent. The Danish government appointed a commission to investigate the slave trade in 1791. In the following year, based on the commission's report, it decreed the abolition of the slave trade, creating a ten-year transitional period, during which it encouraged the importation of African women to help maintain the slave population of the Antilles colonies by increasing its rate of reproduction. At the end of that period, from 1 January 1803 onwards, the Danish traffic would end.[28]

It was in Britain, however, that political moves towards abolition took on the greatest significance, not only on account of the size of the British slave trade—the largest of all—but because it openly sought to end this trade at a world level. In terms of principles, the humanitarians were as much opposed to the slave trade as to slavery itself, but for reasons of strategy they made a clear distinction between the two issues, because it appeared to be politically easier to attack a branch of British trade rather than the private property of the plantation owners.[29] Moreover, and as we have already seen, many abolitionists thought the suppression of the slave trade would necessarily mean the end of the whole system of slavery.

In the early years of the campaign, in the throng of local committees, conferences, parliamentary committees of inquiry, petitions signed by hundreds of thousands of people, abolition seemed imminent, and the House of Commons eventually approved it (the measure would not, however, be approved by the House of Lords).[30] Yet, from 1793 onwards, and particularly from 1796, abolitionism lost some of its force.[31] Wilberforce continued to move forward religiously with his parliamentary motion almost every year, but was defeated every time. Discouraged, some firm abolitionists were ready to fall in with their enemies' tactics and accept palliative measures and delays such as gradual abolition, when international circumstances changed in their favour. From 1803 onwards, in large measure on account of the rekindling of the Napoleonic wars, suppression of the slave trade could be put forward as a way of debilitating the enemy, and British abolitionism acquired a second wind, on the way to rapid political victory: in 1805 the government prohibited the importation of slaves into the colonies captured since 1802; in the following year Parliament forbade the export of slaves from the old possessions, such as Jamaica, to recently acquired territories, and also forbade the transportation of slaves to all the foreign colonies. This meant in practice outlawing over 75 per cent of Britain's slave trade; and, on 25 March 1807, the *Abolition Act* legally put an end to what remained of that trade.[32]

The two years 1806 and 1807 are a key period for the abolitionist movement, not so much because anti-slave trade laws were approved in England, but because they marked the moment when government took over, thus promoting the internationalization of the issue. The novelty lay in the fact that Britain was prepared to apply the law—something neither France nor the United States had done—and, above all, sought to drag the other colonial powers along with it. It was as a result of British pressure that Portugal was dragged to centre stage on the issue of abolition.

1.2 Portugal, a Country Aloof

According to late eighteenth-century estimates Portugal accounted for some 25 per cent of the transatlantic slave trade at the time. It was, however, feared that with the war and the temporary removal of the French slavers that percentage would rise, and would continue to rise after the departure of the British slavers.[33] In April 1807 the Foreign Office took the precaution of sounding out the Lisbon government as to its intentions regarding the abolition of the slave trade. In his reply the then Foreign Minister of Portugal, Araújo de Azevedo, said that any measure to discourage the slave trade, which was vital for Brazil, was simply impracticable, and accordingly there were even stronger arguments against abolishing it.[34]

When Araújo de Azevedo rejected the first British abolitionist approaches, Portugal was still neutral in a world at war. But, when

French troops invaded Portugal on 19 November 1807, this narrowed the government's range of political options in its attempts to avoid British pressure on the slave trade.[35] The government and the royal family withdrew to Brazil, escorted by the Royal Navy, while Portugal was delivered up to the invaders and later on to counter-attack by the British allies. As Strangford, the British ambassador in Lisbon, had already noted, the stage was set for obtaining certain concessions from the Portuguese. At the strictly political level, Britain succeeded in replacing Francophile ministers in Lisbon with people who unambiguously inclined towards mutual Luso-British interests (in particular, Rodrigo de Sousa Coutinho, the future Count of Linhares). Significant economic and political concessions would follow, when, as early as 2 January 1808, the Brazilian ports were opened up to foreign shipping and later on, in 1810, when two treaties were signed. In that period of time, the new Rio de Janeiro government borrowed 600,000 pounds sterling in Britain to fund the costs of war in Europe.[36]

It was in this context of the extreme vulnerability of the Portuguese government, and at a time when conditions seemed to favour an increase in the slave trade to Brazil, that the British government once more raised the issue of abolition. On 17 April 1808, Strangford, who had gone to Rio de Janeiro with the royal court, received orders to include in any treaty which might be negotiated with Portugal a clause providing for the abolition of the slave trade. This result was achieved in article 10 of the treaty of alliance and friendship signed on 19 February 1810. In it, the Portuguese government acknowledged that it was 'fully convinced of the injustice and mistaken policy of the trade in slaves' and undertook to cooperate with Britain in the 'cause of humanity', by 'adopting the most effective means of achieving a gradual abolition in all its domains'. However, the Portuguese would retain the right to pursue the slave trade in areas of the African coast belonging to Portugal (or to which Portugal laid claim).[37]

1.2.1 Factors in Portugal's Detachment

In 1807 Portugal was profoundly unaware of the issue of abolition. Throughout the eighteenth century enlightened minds had been able to follow tolerationist currents abroad, but they knew practically nothing of what was going on in the abolitionist camp. It is certainly hard to follow and prove the flow of ideas. Such movements do not depend on the circulation of books and periodicals alone (nor are these the only places where ideas are revealed). Nevertheless, contemporary as well as later accounts indicate that abolitionist ideas had not reached Portugal by the end of the eighteenth century and that there was at that time, even amongst the more enlightened members of society, a substantial lack of awareness of the arguments, methods and objectives of the British abolitionists.

Censorship, which was strong at the time, could well have had an influence on the Portuguese lack of awareness. A special court, the Real Mesa Censória (the King's Censorship Court), had privative and exclusive jurisdiction over all matters relating to the inspection and approval of books and written manuscripts or printed materials. In addition to examining all works, its job was to inspect all bookshops in the kingdom (even those privately owned), all printing workshops and book warehouses, and all ships coming from foreign ports. Any work coming from abroad had to be placed in a depository immediately, where it would remain stored. The recipient would then ask the censor for the work to be delivered to him, once it had passed inspection. As a rule, he would submit the list of titles that had been sent for inspection, stressing the harmless nature of their content, if such were the case, or other factors likely to help it be viewed favourably by the censor. One element that was frequently highlighted was the fact that the books were by Catholic writers.[38] Here it should be recalled that the more specifically abolitionist writings were associated with ideas of sedition and Jacobinism. Moreover, even in France they were mainly the work of Protestants; and the reading of Protestant writers, while not entirely forbidden, was reserved for learned men who were regarded as being immune to the ideological dangers conveyed by those writers.[39]

A rapid overview of the documentation of the Real Mesa Censória is sufficient to suggest that almost nothing passed the censor and, more importantly, to show that there was not even a potential readership for writings on the slavery issue. The lists submitted show that arithmetical tables, grammars, dictionaries and medical books were easily imported, as were some historical works, military memoirs and sermons, but little that might question the established social order. Works such as Rousseau's *Du Contrat social,* Raynal's *Histoire philosophique* and Voltaire's *Candide* were suppressed, and permission to read Adam Smith's *Wealth of Nations* (in a French translation) was restricted to 'privileged persons'.[40] Generally speaking, any inveighing against the slave trade was a sufficient motive for the circulation of a work to be made difficult. In 1790, a book which, amongst other Protestant signs of disrespect, protested at the Pope for allowing the slave trade was, very naturally, restricted to 'privileged persons'.[41] And specifically abolitionist writings such as those of Benezet and Clarkson, for example, are not on the banned books list, possibly because they may never have been submitted to the censor.

There were, of course, breaches in the system of repression. The Academia Real das Ciências de Lisboa (Lisbon Royal Academy of Sciences) was exempt from censorship but, to judge by the works currently in its library, did not use that exemption to acquire the major works of British abolitionism. Momentarily, towards the end of the century, there was a loosening of the censor's grip so that, in theory, one can argue that some of the main abolitionist works may have secretly entered Portugal both at that time and in earlier or later years. But even if this did happen—and I have not been able to confirm this—they were certainly not disseminated, if only because they were mostly written in English, a language that was not familiar, even to the upper classes.

The censorship was certainly responsible for the involuntary lack of awareness that was imposed from above and was the result of the most basic lack of information. There is no assurance, however, that things would have been radically different even had there been no censorship. Portuguese lack of awareness on the slavery issue also derived from the conviction that, given the specific position of the empire and its interests, it would be better not to touch on something which was potentially embarrassing and disturbing to the existing order. For the literate and ruling strata of society the detachment was a precaution based on a defensive ideological position on the issue of slavery. This led to an attitude of relative lack of interest and even of carelessness: this was sometimes evident amongst those who were abroad on a diplomatic or other mission, and in direct contact with the abolitionist culture. A study of the correspondence of Portuguese ambassadors in London from 1788 to 1807 shows that the abolitionist agitation that pervaded British society at that time was not monitored consistently, and that the British abolitionists' publicly known methods and objectives were not sufficiently analysed and appreciated.

Initially there may have been apprehension regarding the number of dissenters. The ambassador in London in mid-1788, Luís de Sousa Coutinho, reported that Pitt had asked the House of Commons to take the matter into serious consideration, 'in the light of the immense number of petitions made … against the slave trade'.[42] The following year Cipriano Ribeiro Freire, the new chargé d'affaires, reported moves by the British abolitionists seeking to involve other colonial nations in universal antislavery cooperation, but expressed the hope that recent measures introduced in Parliament to regulate and humanize the transport of slaves might dampen the impetus of Wilberforce and his peers. In fact, Freire doubted whether humanity could ever triumph 'over commercial greed'.[43] For a moment, in 1792, there was a mild commotion when it was perceived that abolition would be approved by the House of Commons. Diplomatic notes filled with frequent and detailed information on the vitality of British abolitionism:

> New petitions came from various trading places and cities of England, but also one from the Common Council of the city of London, hurriedly voted on on the same day, petitioning for the abolition of this trade in Negroes. Mr. Wilberforce opened the debate … and began his long speech with the most vivid and horrible portrait of the cruelties and injustice with which this trade was practised …. Several prominent members of both parties followed along the same path and it could be said that on this day the interests of all private individuals, and even national interests, have given way to the grand purpose of an unprecedented universal benevolence, and that no other voices were heard save those of justice and humanity.[44]

However, as has been mentioned above, abolitionism lost momentum from the mid-1790s onwards. Portuguese diplomats do not seem to have believed sufficiently in its progress, which was less evident from then on. Domingos de Sousa Coutinho had followed parliamentary matters since 1803, but in his official reports to Lisbon he rarely mentioned abolitionist moves. Whenever he did, he invariably played down their importance. On 3 July 1804, for example, he reported that the abolitionist bill had been passed in the House of Commons, but added straight away that he did not expect it to be passed by the House of Lords. He saw the whole abolitionist agitation as nothing more than 'a kind of stage-play', with well-known actors and stereotyped roles. It was true that Pitt and Fox voted against the trade, but they did so more as a 'habit and for a kind of honour' than for any other reason.[45] In the following year the ambassador was reporting that the House of Commons had finally 'lost its patience' with the abolitionists and that it had rejected the bill for the abolition of the trade in slaves which the tireless Wilberforce had submitted once again.[46]

In Lisbon, with the country facing serious political threats, few regarded British abolitionism as a delicate issue. The European–African–Brazilian empire was self-sufficient as far as slaves were concerned: it was not dependent on foreign transports. Only when the Abolition Act was finally passed and Domingos de Sousa Coutinho reported that diplomatic enquiries were being made as to the Portuguese position on the matter did the Ministry react, but still without any major concern. Araújo de Azevedo, Foreign Minister at the time, stressed that both Denmark and Britain had operated in a gradual way, allowing time for the colonists to adjust to the new measures and for an abolitionist party to form in public opinion. This had not occurred in Portugal, and everything came together to prevent the country from immediately following the British example. Moreover, since the issue seemed to be one of humaneness, Portugal could easily 'ameliorate' the transport of slaves to Brazil; this was an area in which, according to the Minister, the Portuguese were already superior, ensuring conditions of carriage and protection for the slaves unequalled by any other nation.[47] In any case, the head of Portuguese foreign policy did not see London putting any barriers in the way of the Portuguese slave trade. In his view, British abolitionist policy was to be applied only to British slave traders.[48]

In Brazil, when the Anglo-Portuguese treaties of 1810 came to be negotiated, not many objections were raised to the abolitionist clause suggested by Strangford. The draft treaties were discussed at innumerable conferences, and several written opinions were given. Only one of those opinions, by judge Luís José de Melo, raised open objections to the commitment to abolition which would be ratified in 1810. It seemed to the objecting judge that the Portuguese government should not agree to any limitation of its slave trade because it was essential to populate Brazil and also to supply the Spaniards.[49] Another counsellor, António da Silva

Lisboa, recalled that the Costa da Mina, that is the coast running from Cape Palmas to the Cameroons, which was of such key importance for Bahia's trade, was one of the areas where the British were seeking to prevent the trade in slaves and, for that reason, it would be sensible to safeguard in the body of the treaty that Portugal would retain the right to acquire slaves in the ports which it habitually used on that part of the coast.[50] Most of the counsellors, however, did not even touch on the issue of abolition, no doubt because they thought that the commitment, being entirely theoretical, was not worthy of any particular comment. One of the counsellors even made this view explicitly:

> Our promise to cooperate in the abolition of the trade in slaves, and all the other condescensions we make to the British, are not significant, and we need not deal with them here because they do not require any sacrifice of us: our trade in slaves, despite what is stated at the beginning of the article, will not only remain as it is at present, but will actually be increased with the trade from the port of Cabinda.[51]

Nevertheless, Linhares, who negotiated the treaty, took the precaution of handing Strangford a memorandum that set out the Portuguese government's understanding of what had been agreed, reminding him that the article in question was nothing more than 'the expression of the humane sentiments of the … royal heart'. In fact, the Portuguese government could not do without importing slaves, something which he detested but which was indispensable; for that reason, and to avoid future doubts and complaints, it would be a good thing if the British government were to state unequivocally that it would not obstruct the slave trade in those ports where the Portuguese usually operated.[52] The minister's care shows the concern that the vague phraseology article 10 had acquired might be both a defence and a danger at the same time. In any event, his apprehension was not sufficient to stop the whole process, and the treaty was signed (even though Britain never supplied any reassuring statement). Sometime later, Linhares was able to assure the Bahia traders that the slave trade on the Costa da Mina could be carried on freely and that the government, far from seeking to restrict such trade, had in mind to promote it as the only means of increasing the population of Brazil.[53]

To sum up, at the start of the nineteenth century there was a lack of awareness in Portugal regarding the issue of abolition, not only because it remained impervious to the new spirit of philanthropy that was flourishing abroad, but also because there was no internal pressure in that direction. Almost hermetically sealed off from information and the circulation of ideas that demanded the end of the traffic, strangely deaf to the growing volume of disturbing signs that pointed to the destabilization of its empire, the Portuguese government stumbled almost blindfold into the first bilateral agreement for the abolition of the 'odious commerce'. But to be blindfolded does not mean an absence of ideas. In conceptual terms the Portuguese did not fall into abolitionism from a zero starting point. Over the centuries, they had generated and preserved a system of concepts and images regarding slavery and, as the eighteenth century turned into the nineteenth, they had an ideological frame of reference in which pro-slavery and tolerationist viewpoints overlapped.

1.2.2 The Ideology of Slavery

David Brion Davis has provided a magnificent overview of the key elements of the ideology of slavery. Let us follow his lead for a quick reminder of its basic features.

For Plato and Aristotle slavery was conceivable in the light of the general principles of order and authority, and as such could be located on the same level as any other relationship of subordination in the domestic sphere. The institution had a natural and rational foundation, which, quite simply, lay in the slave's inferiority, whether that inferiority was intellectual, as Plato maintained, or whether it was the result of an innate deficiency in the intrinsic virtue of the soul, as for Aristotle, for whom some were destined to subjection and others to domination from the moment of their birth.[54] Aristotle was, however, sensitive to the potential injustice inherent in his conception of natural slavery. Since no outward sign made it possible to distinguish the natural slave from other men, it was always to be admitted that war and other vicissitudes might lead to intrinsically free people becoming slaves. The system of slavery thus carried within it a potential for injustice which the philosopher recognized, but which he did not solve rationally.

The Stoics had a different view. They saw slavery as a simple social convention that was basically contrary to nature. However, the potential for dissent, that such a view implied was diluted by way of the Stoics' relativistic notion of liberty. For this school of thought, true liberty lay in the ability of each man to rise above social limitations, material passions and the sorrows of life. In this view, an individual's role in society was irrelevant, and the slave was as well positioned at the outset as any powerful man in the world. Beyond appearances, the captive could be a truly free man, while the citizen who was legally free might be nothing more than a wretched slave to his instincts and appetites. Following this line of thought, Seneca would argue that only the slave's physical body could belong to his master, given that the soul was free—or, rather, potentially free. The Stoics thought that true liberty was attained only by a small number of philosophers, who achieved it through their individual effort; the vast majority of the population, whatever their social status, were slaves to vice, desire and wrongdoing.

Although several issues were left unresolved, Antiquity produced rationalizations for the existence of slavery in which there were both convergence and conflict. While the main currents of thought tied the slave to some form of inferiority, ideas differed as to the rational foundation for slavery: it was natural for the Aristotelians and purely conventional for the Stoics. The issue of the potential injustice of the act of enslavement remained unresolved. This was a relatively minor issue for the Stoics, who tended to allow it to dissolve in their overall devaluation of the concrete circumstances of life.

The early Fathers of the Church, finding themselves forced to reconcile Christ with the realities of the Roman world, absorbed the Aristotelian and Stoic ideas into the Christian message, strengthened their points of convergence, harmonized their differences and settled the unanswered questions by means of new ideological solutions to the dilemmas of slavery. They adopted in full the Stoic dichotomies between the apparent and the real slave and between the captive body and the free soul, and the idea of the natural inferiority of the slave was absorbed into the concept of sin. For the Fathers of the Church, true liberty was the absence or the remission of sin. This particular, but truly essential, form of freedom was within everyone's reach—not just of an elite, as the Stoics maintained—and was to be obtained through entry into the Christian community. Christianity thus offered collective access to true freedom and, in that sense, democratized the liberty of the Stoics. Moreover, the notion of sin made it possible to solve the Aristotelian question of the potential injustice of the act of enslavement, at least in part. In so far as all of humanity was marked by sin, no one was innocent, and it fell to God to indicate who should command and who should obey.[55]

Thus it came about that, because slavery was included in the divine order of things and conformed to a divine purpose, it was natural, but not because it was part of the creation or because it was in itself good. Slavery had been created as a consequence of sin, as an instrument of punishment, and represented a secondary intention of nature, more suited to man's abilities. In other words, slavery was contrary to the ideal kingdom of nature, but it was an indispensable part of the concrete world of sinful acts. It was therefore a useful and necessary form—albeit a painful one—of realizing nature's aims.

It was along these lines that an intellectual endeavour that lasted for centuries melded and harmonized the thought of the main authorities of Antiquity with that of the Christian theologians. After Thomas Aquinas the ideological edifice that justified slavery was fully stabilized and consecrated. It was for this reason that, as Davis emphasizes, any questioning of the moral basis of slavery was equivalent to contesting the fundamental notions of divine purpose and human destiny.[56] It was no surprise that the edifice remained practically untouched throughout the Middle Ages and much of the Modern Era. During that time discussions on the question of slavery were limited to practical issues such as ascertaining whether baptism would or would not liberate the slave, or discussing the situation of Christians who were captives of non-Christians (Jews or Muslims).[57] But the tensions between slavery and Christian ideas did not disappear. They were inherent in the fact of perceiving the slave as both man and object, and so persisted within Western culture and became more pronounced when the discoveries and the colonization of the New World once again brought the major issue of the slave—this time, the black slave—to the forefront of European perceptions. However, the main contradictions had, in a sense, been tamed by the doctrines of the Church: they amalgamated in a consistent mental construct which even acquired some ideological ballast from the fifteenth century onwards, based on the purely lay arguments of utility and custom.[58]

For centuries the Christian nations resorted to this theoretical construct whenever there was a need to justify the slave trade and the enslavement of Africans. The few wider studies made of this subject in Portugal between the fifteenth and eighteenth centuries invariably harked back to the ideology of slavery. In mentioning the arrival of the first load of African slaves in Portugal in 1444, Zurara waxed emotional regarding the luck of the captives and 'wept piously on account of their suffering'.[59] But he hastened to add that, as time passed, and once over the pain of the initial separation, the slaves became socially integrated, became Christian, learned how to do their jobs and sometimes even became free men. The salvation of souls and the introduction to Christian civility gave legitimacy to the act of enslavement:

> Thus it is that where before they lived in perdition of their souls and bodies, they came to receive in all the opposite: for their souls which, while they were pagan, had not the light and fire of the holy Faith; and for their bodies, because they lived as wild beasts, with none of the order of reasonable creatures, where they knew not what was wine nor bread, nor covering of cloth, nor lodging in a house.[60]

In 1633, in one of his sermons to Negro slaves in Bahia, Father António Vieira resorted to the whole panoply of pro-slavery ideology: he did so not to provide justification for the slavers, but rather to convince the victims. Recognizing that the enslavement of the African was, in certain cases, 'just', Vieira admitted that he was disturbed by the severity and unfairness of the treatment inflicted on the slaves. He was saddened at the spectacle of the ships which arrived from Angola laden with Negroes; he was angered by the contrast between the humility of the wretched captives, hungry and naked, and the arrogance and brutality of their masters. But these sentiments were countered by the deeply held conviction that this apparently unjust situation was in line with a hidden divine purpose: a purpose that revealed itself from the outset in the crossing of the Atlantic, over which, Vieira reflected, the hand of God was undoubtedly watching:

> Some great mystery is contained right in this very transmigration; and moreover if we note that it is singularly favoured and assisted by God, with there being in the whole ocean no navigation without danger and adverse wind, only that which takes these [African] peoples from their lands and brings them to the exercise of captivity is always blessed with a wind astern and with no change of sail.[61]

There could be no doubt that the captivity of the first transmigration —the passage from Africa to America—was ordained by divine mercy 'for the freedom' of the second transmigration, that is, the passing from the material world to life eternal. Through a series of biblical examples, Vieira demonstrated to his assembly of slaves that the path to God was necessarily to be found through suffering and redemption, captivity and freedom. The first transmigration was the one of earthly vicissitudes, but the captivity required by that transmigration was the preparation for eternal freedom. That was why the first transmigration was advantageous for the African: it permitted the liberation of his soul. Basing himself on Seneca, the speaker expounded at length on the dualities of captive body/liberated soul and apparent slave/real slave to conclude that 'the best part of man, which is the soul ... cannot remain captive; the body, and only the body, can'.[62]

The enslavement of the Negro in Brazil was therefore only 'semi-slavery'. The soul of the slave was potentially free, and it would be the height of disgrace if Africans, who were already captive in body, were to end up also captive in their souls, if they sold them to the Devil. If the slave, once landed in Brazil and admitted to the bosom of the Church, should relinquish sin, he would be free 'of the greater and more burdensome captivity'. He would, of course, remain physically captive, but it was up to him to see that state as a mercy and not as a punishment. Consequently, the Negroes should not rise up against their present situation, because it was the divine will that they should live so, in order that, through this 'temporal captivity', they should 'very easily attain eternal freedom'. They should indeed suffer patiently the labours of their day-to-day lives, praise God 'for the moderation of the captivity' to which He had brought them, and serve their earthly masters well, in the certainty that in the heavenly life, everything would be reversed and reconciled.[63]

The practice of enslaving Africans, which started with the discoveries, did not dismantle the ideology of slavery. On the contrary, and as the example of Zurara shows, it actually reinforced the edifice with a new justification in the idea of civilizing action. It is true that from the sixteenth century onwards the conditions under which the traffic took place led people to question the ways in which slaves were obtained and held. In the Iberian peninsula thinkers such as Luis Molina, Tomás de Mercado, Fernando Oliveira and others raised various objections of this sort. In their eyes the purchase of Negro slaves on the African coast carried grave moral risks, since it was practically impossible for the buyer to ensure that the human beings he was purchasing came from lawful capture.[64] But these were casuistic arguments and objections. They related to the underlying good or evil resulting from the application of a rule in this or that case, and generally they did not question the legitimacy of slavery. Since the act of enslavement was accepted in the Bible, in philosophy and by the Fathers of the Church, the problem lay in establishing whether or not the slaves had been acquired by legitimate means.

It is in that old and sturdy ideological edifice, which has been summarily touched on here, that we should place the thought of Father Ribeiro da Rocha. His *Ethiope resgatado* (The Redeemed Ethiopian) is not an abolitionist treatise—as some Portuguese writers claim—but a very long-drawn-out effort to reconcile the slave trade and slavery with a good Christian conscience. Ribeiro da Rocha did not contest the legitimacy of enslaving the pagan, provided that he had been 'captured in a public, just and true war' or because he had committed 'some serious crime', or yet again if he had been sold by his father 'in the absence of any other remedy for the sustenance of the breath of life'. Undoubtedly the fate of the poor people thus enslaved would be a bitter one, but it could not be said that it was unjust. Nevertheless, the good Christian should not remain blind to reality. Ribeiro da Rocha regarded the conditions under which slaves were obtained in Africa generally not as being legitimate but, on the contrary, as those of kidnap and robbery. Consequently, any person who purchased captives without first establishing the circumstances of their captivity ran a grave risk of sinning. It seemed an established principle of jurisprudence that only those who knew of the illegitimate circumstances under which the slaves had been obtained would be faced with problems. Those who were unaware of them could unconcernedly buy and hold slaves, because their lack of knowledge meant that they were 'acting in good faith'. But the souls of all others were under serious threat: the slave traders who travelled to the African coast were in a state of eternal damnation, and were obliged to indemnify all the captives they might have traded and to cease that form of trading forthwith; other persons who might later purchase those slaves for their service were obliged to restore their freedom to them, together with the profits which the captives might have obtained if they had been free and with restitution of those services they had performed while in slavery. Faced with such 'horrendous burdens', the potential purchasers of slaves would most certainly become 'worried and anxious'. Ribeiro da Rocha worked on a solution for this very problem: that is to say, he sought a reassuring solution that would both safeguard the slave trade and the souls of those who owned slaves, concluding that there was 'another kind of contract', by which Christians might hold on to the slaves they already owned and, in the future, acquire more slaves without committing any sin that implied a risk of damnation.[65]

Most of the *Ethiope* is precisely the explanation of that 'other contract', the basic recipe for which was summed up by the writer himself in a simple formula: the Negro should be progressively 'redeemed' from an unjust enslavement to which his brothers in Africa had subjected him; 'committed' to respecting, obeying and serving his master for as long as he could not pay the value of his redemption; 'maintained', without this being a charitable act; his vices should be 'corrected' through kindness and tolerance, and he should be 'taught' the Christian doctrine and good living habits; finally, he should be 'freed'—if he were still alive—by one of the methods provided for by law. In sum, Ribeiro da Rocha contested a certain form of slavery, not its essence. Nothing in his work sought to end the slave trade. Quite the opposite: that possibility was specifically excluded.[66]

1.2.3 The Ideology of Slavery Brought Up to Date: the Theory of the Lesser Evil

In 1794, Azeredo Coutinho, the bishop of Pernambuco and later of Elvas, a prominent figure of the Enlightenment in Portugal, argued that the lack of hands in Brazil could only be overcome by importing slaves, and suggested that special ships be built to transport them under better and safer conditions.[67] This was a type of argument that justified the slave trade on the grounds of necessity and which, as frequently occurred at the time, drew up plans to improve the conditions of that trade. Azeredo Coutinho was not, however, a tolerationist. In 1808 he had occasion to expound at length on this matter, and what emerged was the ideology of slavery combined with a series of reactive arguments expressly aimed at the philanthropic suggestions then starting to appear on the horizon.

Following the lines drawn by Christian theologians since the Middle Ages, Azeredo Coutinho did not claim that slavery obeyed absolute, primary natural law; he spoke only of 'secondary natural law', which required of man in society that he should always choose between the lesser of two evils, 'that which was least harmful to his life and his existence'. Natural law, in human society, was that which provided for the greatest good and the lesser evil. In order for laws to be just, it was merely necessary that they should be based on relative justice —and that was why nations should constantly change their laws, because justice depended on circumstances and these were constantly changing.[68]

The slave trade was without a doubt a law dictated by circumstances for the greater good, or the lesser evil, of the barbarous nations and the colonial world. Africa was a land of cannibalism, arbitrariness and cruelty. Hence what the slave traders were bringing the Africans was the chance to opt for a lesser evil. And since the black nations, in accordance with their own rules, had the opportunity of commuting sentences of death or life imprisonment to slavery and exile, the Europeans were merely taking advantage of that fact to acquire the condemned men. Traffic and slavery were therefore the greater good, or the lesser evil, for all involved: for the slave, who would prefer being sold to being put to death; for the African societies which in this way ensured regular trading contacts with the Europeans, acquiring goods they needed (at the same time as they sweetened their customs); for the Europeans, who in this way acquired hands to cultivate their plantations and work their mines; and, finally, for souls, since slavery was the means of introducing these barbarians to the true religion.[69] Of course, there was always a risk that the slave traders would buy people who had been illegally enslaved. But how could one know? It was also clear that it would be much better if the slave traders, in a gesture of Christian charity, bought slaves to save them from death and then freed them. Yet what traders would have the means and the power to buy Negroes on the coast of Africa without receiving at least an amount equivalent to that which they spent and to cover their risks? Would it be better to 'let the poor wretches be killed than to save their lives, even if that meant that they would become slaves?'.[70]

The traffic was not pleasant, but it was far from being what was portrayed in the 'implausible tales' told by the *Nouvels Philosophes*.[71] The bishop acknowledged that in Brazil several slave owners treated their slaves in an inhuman way. One of his objectives was therefore to persuade them that it was in their own interest to improve the captives' circumstances. To that end he suggested the drafting of a law that would protect slaves: in essence that law took up concerns that were dear to the Church and which had been propounded by several ecclesiastical writers.[72]

This overview of Portuguese authors from Zurara to Azeredo Coutinho shows how persistent the ideology of slavery was in Portugal, and how it could mould and adapt itself to different circumstances. Even though the arguments analysed differ in their historical background and in their objectives, there is a common foundation to all of them: the theory of the salvation of souls, generally complemented by the notion that the traffic was indispensable for Brazil's prosperity, and the idea of the lesser evil—implicit in the picture of the barbarity and inferiority of African civilization. In any event it is very possible that, at the end of the eighteenth century, a change of emphasis occurred within that ideology, as the theory of the salvation of souls, which was crucial for António Vieira, lost out to more secular approaches such as the lesser evil and African barbarity. It is important to stress that the idea of African barbarity was practically universal, being shared by both slavers and abolitionists. For the latter, however, the barbarity was caused, or at least exacerbated, by the slave trade. For the supporters of slavery, on the other hand, the barbarity was something innate, originating in the wild character of the African and having no causal connection to the slave trade. The pro-slavery attitude of Azeredo Coutinho was constructed around this latter conception of innate barbarity.

Composed at a time when the institutions of slavery were under attack, the bishop's writings brought new ideological factors into play. These gave a new cast to the ideology of slavery, drawing on strategies, images and ideas that were to have a long future. The most significant of these factors was the need to disparage abolitionism. The philanthropists were equated to the Anabaptists, in an obvious attempt to take advantage of the messianic nature of the abolitionist movement and thereby sustain an ideological counter-attack that would belittle it by association with a sect that was anathematized. As his work was published in 1808, the bishop was also able to take advantage of the tragic example of the slave rebellions in Saint Domingue, and even of recent events in France itself, which had gone back on its abolitionist policy.[73] He was also able to raise the bogey of the Revolution, diluting the issue of slavery by tying abolitionism to Jacobinism. As Azeredo Coutinho stated, he wrote more to counter-attack the 'sectarian supporters' of Brissot and Robespierre than to defend the institutions of slavery as such. Opposition to the slave trade was, according to him, a sideways and camouflaged manner of targeting deeper and more serious objectives. In order to confront this threat, the bishop had gone along 'the same road', thereby tying the question of the slave trade into a broader and more menacing set of issues.[74] It should be mentioned in passing that it was current practice to make the connection between abolitionism and Jacobinism during the period of the French Revolution—even in Britain—and this had indeed been suggested by the revolutionaries themselves.[75]

A third way of disparaging abolitionism was what we might call the critique of telescopic philanthropy—in other words to criticize those who bemoaned the evils of distant Africa while at the same time ignoring the misfortunes before their very eyes. In Azeredo Coutinho the supporters of abolition were systematically confronted with their own silence and apathy in the face of other kinds of injustice that were as serious as the slave trade and much closer to home.[76] Moreover, the critique of telescopic philanthropy, or of abolitionist hypocrisy, opened up another line of defence (which was barely visible in the bishop's work): the favourable comparison of the life of the slave in the Americas with the life of the working classes in Europe, who were supposedly more unhappy and wretched.

Another defensive notion put forward by Azeredo Coutinho was that the end of the slave trade would necessarily mean the downfall of Portugal. With the exception of wine, and some salt, oil and fruit, the country's wealth was derived entirely from colonial trade, which in turn was based on Brazil's fertile agriculture. Now if that agriculture were to fade away for lack of slave labour, how could Portugal survive?[77]

1.2.4 Tolerationism and Silence

At the beginning of the nineteenth century the ideology of slavery was alive and well and had adapted, reactively, to the emergence of new abolitionist ideas. But it was not the only ideological framework that arose in connection with the slave trade. Another way of looking at the issue was also evident in the Portuguese empire at the end of the eighteenth and the beginning of the nineteenth century.

António Ribeiro Sanches was a doctor by profession who was suspected of being a Jew. He left Portugal in the 1720s, and lived first in London and Leyden, and then for many years in Russia, and finally in Paris, where he was part of the local intellectual circle and where he remained until he died in 1782. In his *Cartas sobre a educação da mocidade* (Letters on the Education of Youth) he rebelled against the Catholic Church's position on the issue of slavery, and especially against the fact that the ecclesiastics allowed slaves born and baptized in Brazil to remain enslaved. As a pedagogue, Ribeiro Sanches desired that young people should be inculcated with notions of humaneness, in addition to receiving a good education. He thought it would be impossible for such notions to be imparted while each rich child had his own little slave.[78]

The point of view of Luís dos Santos Vilhena was very similar. He was a modest teacher of Greek who spent part of his life in Bahia. In 1802 he wrote a series of epistles that described this Brazilian city, its people and its problems, and in them he naturally referred to the slaves. Vilhena doubted that the slave trade was as useful as was generally presumed. It seemed obvious to him that it was not a means of Christianizing the Negroes, who were reluctant to abandon their ancestral practices and beliefs. On the other hand, the unchecked importation of slaves was filling Brazil with a 'multitude of infections', of murderous, insolent and lascivious people, who corrupted the catholic family and represented a threat to the masters.[79]

Another writer who stressed the negative aspects of the slave trade was Luís António de Oliveira Mendes, a man born in Bahia who had taken a law degree at the University of Coimbra. Concerned with the fate of the Negroes, but also with that of the planters, who tied up capital to buy them, Mendes presented a memoir to the Lisbon Royal Academy of Sciences in 1793, in which he argued for various measures to optimize and humanize the slave trade. Starting out from the principle that a better knowledge of Africans would help to adapt the slave trade to their specific physical and cultural characteristics and alleviate their suffering, the writer focused closely on Africa and its peoples and on the physical and psychic illnesses that affected the slaves, suggesting ways in which they could be diminished or eliminated.[80]

In private letters written at the end of the eighteenth century António Ribeiro dos Santos also came out against the institutions of slavery. Ribeiro dos Santos had grown up in Brazil, returning later to Coimbra, where he completed a degree in law. After a career as a judge and university lecturer, he was appointed commissioner of the Inquisition and censor, before taking charge of the Royal Public Library in 1796.[81] A sensitive man, he shuddered in his heart at the horrors of the world, whether they were the tyrannies of the Marquis of Pombal, of still recent memory, or the stories of the heroes of India in the distant past told by the chroniclers in books that were inventories of 'infinite cruelties' and 'thousands of mounds of dead bodies'.[82] Ribeiro dos Santos's aversion to slavery was based on the horror of violence, but it also had a very solid rational grounding in Montesquieu, Adam Smith, the Quakers and their followers. It was this rational structure that led him to believe that slavery could not be justified on grounds of law, religion or politics, or even on economic grounds, because slave labour turned out to be 'more expensive than that done by free men'.[83]

Similar views were held by João Rodrigues de Brito, a native of Évora, who was to become a judge in Bahia, and who in 1807 wrote a series of Letters on the political economy of that city. Brito was concerned with the condition of the souls of the wretched slaves, beings who were distressed by the perpetuity of slavery, which depressed their mind and body. He suggested that they should be granted their freedom as a reward for significant service or for the work they carried out on their days of rest. The suggestion was based not only on humane grounds, but also on grounds of economic advantage, in that the judge believed free labour to be necessarily more productive than slave labour. As far as the traffic itself was concerned, he regretted that the laws on the capacity of slave ships were brazenly evaded, and that the government did not do something about the cruel circumstances under which the transatlantic slave trade was carried out.[84]

Teodoro Biancardi's *Cartas americanas* (American Letters) are writings of a moral nature consciously influenced by Montesquieu's *Lettres persanes*. In one of these letters, written in Lisbon in 1808, probably as a reply to Azeredo Coutinho's apologetics for slavery, Biancardi admitted his philosophical and emotional aversion to slavery, and his objections to the purchasing of men in Africa to be exploited in the Americas: 'the memory of the barbarian who thought to ordain the scheme of so odious a commerce shall forever be abominable to me, for I know not for what singular reason that which is dispensed with everywhere else is necessary for the cultivation of the lands of America'.[85]

José Agostinho de Macedo probably wrote the short play *O Preto Sensível* (The Sensitive Black) during the Napoleonic wars. The action of the play took place in Brazil and began with Catul, a slave, who awaited the break of day while contemplating his sleeping son and lamenting the sad fate of both of them. Sorely troubled, the slave anticipated the moment when that son would be torn from him to be sold to another master, just as his wife had already been. Finally the day dawned and the owner of the sugar mill woke the slaves with beatings, forcing them into work. As fate would have it, however, on that day Inácia, a lady born in Europe, visited the place just before starting out on her return journey to Portugal. Inácia did not go to the sugar mill to defend the slaves, but only to 'enjoy the view of the pleasant fields'. However, her 'sensitive' heart felt pity for the fate of the blacks.[86] Through a series of chance occurrences, Inácia would successively acquire Bunga (the wife), the little black boy and Catul, reuniting the family that had earlier been broken up. In an action of pure kindness, she freed them all and took them to Portugal, a country which, in Catul's words, appeared as a province of redemption: the 'fortunate land which is the home of sensitive souls'.[87]

Here, in seven different testimonies—as many as I could find—is the position of the tolerationist, the man who could theoretically accept (and desire) the abolition of the slave trade and of slavery itself, but who, restricted by the laws of necessity and the public good, thrust such an event into a distant and indeterminate future. His view of the issue was critical and more or less compassionate, but it was not part of a campaign in favour of abolition.

There was nothing new or particularly challenging in Ribeiro Sanches's argument. The idea that contact between master and slave could be harmful harked back to Aristotle, and the question of knowing whether baptism freed the slave was, basically, a medieval issue. Actually, while Ribeiro Sanches waxed indignant because the sacrament of baptism did not free the slave born in Brazil, for political reasons he tolerated the fact that the adult slave purchased in Africa should remain a slave even after being baptized.[88] The opposition to slavery in the memoir submitted to the Academy of Sciences by Oliveira Mendes was even milder. Despite criticizing some aspects of the way the slave trade operated and regretting the fate of the Negro, the memoir did not openly challenge the existence of that trade, nor did it make any appeal for its abolition. There was, moreover, a short passage in which, in relation to what he called 'moral considerations' on the slave trade, the writer explicitly recommended the reading of Father António Vieira's sermons, which, as we have seen, justified the transport of slaves from Africa in terms of divine purpose.[89]

Vilhena too had no alternative proposals that would have allowed him to do without the importation of slaves. This is why he did not bother to ascertain whether it was 'just and decent' to go to Africa to buy men to work in the colonies of Brazil.[90] João Rodrigues de Brito nourished the hope that the incentives for Asians to emigrate to Brazil would supply 'working hands' that would supplement or even replace the imported African, but he did not speak of abolition.[91] Nor did Biancardi mention it. His diatribe against the slavers was essentially a sensitive man letting off steam—'I took up the pen to relieve my heart'—and, while he interrogated himself with bitter irony as to the 'singular circumstance' which apparently made slavery necessary in the Americas, he did not offer any practical alternatives that might end or replace it.[92]

Agostinho de Macedo's short play revealed two basic concerns: to describe the slave as a human being, with fears and feelings that were identical to those of the European; and to establish a clear dividing line between two physical and cultural areas, Brazil and Portugal, which were respectively lands of oppression and freedom; the stereotypes of the sugar mill owner's brutality and the cultivated sentimentalism of Inácia corresponded to those two worlds. But the work made not the slightest concession to abolitionism or to the desire to put an end to institutions one might question but which were accepted by reason of the need for the 'immense work' that produced 'the delight of Europe'.[93] All the play did was to advocate ad hoc action, the Christian humanitarianism of the European, who, in passing, guided by chance and by a good heart, crossed his cultured sentimentalism with the suffering of the slave and felt pity for the spectacle he witnessed.

Apart from the fact that criticism of slavery was not very incisive, it also did not achieve very wide circulation (at least in printed form) and, as far as we can see, it was only exhibited in somewhat restricted circles. Ribeiro Sanches's book was published in Paris in 1760, but only a tiny number of copies were produced: fifty. The letters of Biancardi and Rodrigues de Brito were published only at the beginning of the 1820s, many years after they had been written. The same goes for the play by Agostinho de Macedo, which would appear only in 1836, five years after its author's passing, and also for the letters of Ribeiro dos Santos, published very recently. It can safely be stated that the press of the day did not help to disseminate any opposition to the institutions of slavery. Although many new publications appeared towards the end of the century, periodical journals were still very few in number and, of course, heavily gagged by the censor. It was only by way of exception that they touched on the question of the slave trade and, when they did so, it was merely to convey an item of news.[94]

There are only a few indirect pointers to the relative importance of the pro-slavery and tolerationist positions amongst the educated elite. They suggest that there was greater acceptance of tolerationism, but do not enable us to reach a definite conclusion. The near non-existence of writings in defence of the slave trade and of slavery may not mean, necessarily, a lack of interest or ideas in defence of slaving practice, but simply the lack of any direct motive to fight for institutions which, in general, were assumed to be indispensable. Whatever the case may be, it seems unlikely that, at the time, and among the leading Portuguese intellectuals, there were many people who espoused the pro-slavery ideas of Azeredo Coutinho. Coutinho himself admitted that he had few followers, said that his work was addressed specifically to the Brazilians, and noted the attacks to which his writings had been subjected.[95]

One of those attacks was let loose by Ribeiro dos Santos, who, as censor, was called upon to deliver a verdict on the bishop's writings. He concluded that they should not be published. What most upset his censor's sensibility was the 'apologetic and declamatory' style used by Coutinho in a cause that it was difficult to defend. In his view the problem of slavery was a controversial matter on which it was better to 'remain silent rather than to talk'. Even if circumstances obliged governments to 'tolerate' the traffic, it was desirable that 'no more obstacles and motives' for perpetuating it should be brought into play.[96]

It is quite possible that this type of tolerationism was common among the educated elites. It is known that the work of Azeredo Coutinho was initially submitted to the Lisbon Royal Academy of Sciences and that, according to Ribeiro dos Santos, it had offended 'the feelings of the audience' (the reason why it was not accepted for publication).[97] But it is highly unlikely that the more critical side of tolerationism, that which was closest to abolitionism and which, for the sake of convenience, I shall call para-abolitionism, had been very widely disseminated beyond a very small circle of educated people, if only because its supporters generally adopted a strategy of silence. The most significant aspect of the excerpt from Ribeiro dos Santos quoted above is the exhortation to mutism: he recommended that it was better 'to remain silent rather than to talk'. For new ideas to circulate in opposition to slavery, it was essential that its intrinsic horrors should have the widest possible exposure. In the Western world at the end of the eighteenth century, the well-informed man knew that the slave trade would have trouble surviving a wider public debate.[98] A similar conviction existed in Portugal and accounted for the fact that potential supporters of abolitionist ideas preferred to keep quiet on the subject, bearing in mind the interests of the empire. A scholar and bibliophile like Ribeiro dos Santos would have been relatively well informed about the progress of abolitionism in the United States, France and Britain. He might not have read Benezet, but he was acquainted with British parliamentary debates, with various articles by the Quakers and with the anti-slavery arguments of Montesquieu, Adam Smith and Brissot. In his private correspondence, he was concerned to point out in minute detail the pages of books and periodicals that were required reading for anyone who wished to oppose slavery.[99] However, for a man who was one of the most respected and prolific Portuguese writers in the eighteenth century, he did not use that information to support his confessed desire to put an end to the slave trade.

From the outset, omission and silence were key elements in the history of abolitionism in Portugal, which led to persistent confusion of those who opposed and those who supported the so-called 'cause of humanity', since silence was a tactic used by almost all supporters of slavery: it was used in Liverpool at the time of the great popular campaign against the British slave trade;[100] it was used in France in 1789 when the large plantation owners of Saint Domingue concluded that they should keep as quiet as possible (while at the same time doing everything possible to ensure that the issue of abolition was not debated in the Assembly);[101] and it was also used in the United States where the matter was strangely forgotten following independence.[102]

The veil of silence, which served to obfuscate matters at the time, hinders the efforts of those who today seek to understand mental attitudes on the basis of a dozen or so outward expressions of opinion. Strictly speaking, this means it is impossible, using the few occasions when this subject was broached in Portugal, to establish how significant the two ways of seeing the problem of the slave trade were in Portuguese society at the time. Nevertheless, the analysis reveals that abolitionism did not exist in Portugal. Apart from the underground writings of Ribeiro dos Santos, there is no visible outline of any current of opinion viewing the problems in the manner of the British abolitionists or which was even aware of their thinking, their actions and their universal plan.

Having little or no access to the rivers of ideas which were flowing outside Portugal, the nation was also not in a position to generate its own abolitionist waters. During the eighteenth century and at the start of the nineteenth, there was sporadic opposition to slavery and to the forms the slave trade took, but this was never something that could serve as the basis for a theoretical change of attitude regarding the practices established in the past. There were two different conceptions in Portugal, and there could be tension or convergence between them. They were not, as a rule, diametrically opposed, but merely different forms, more or less recent, more or less flexible, of dealing ideologically with the ancient question of how to accommodate slavery in the Christian culture. For immediate purposes, they both sought to maintain the status quo, either expressly or by omission and silence. It was this tacit consent to remain silent, in a state of slumber and detachment, which helps to explain not only the ease with which the Portuguese government accepted being tagged on to the British abolitionist locomotive, but also the national feeling of having been deceived that emerged when, in 1811, the British moved from words to action. This feeling of having been tricked was to affect the manner in which the problem of slavery would thereafter be addressed in Portugal, both politically and ideologically.

Notes

1. Cipriano R. Freire to Luís de Sousa Coutinho, 4 April 1792, ANTT, MNE, *cx.* 710.
2. See David B. Davis, *The Problem of Slavery in Western Culture,* Cornell University Press, Ithaca, NY, 1966, p. 421.
3. Ibid., chaps. 13 and 14.
4. David B. Davis, *The Problem of Slavery in the Age of Revolution, 1770–1823,* Cornell University Press, Ithaca, NY, and London, 1975, p. 92.
5. David B. Davis, 'The Emergence of Immediatism in British and American Anti-Slavery Thought', *Mississipi Valley Historical Review,* 49, 2, 1962, pp. 218–19.
6. For the theological roots of Anglo-American abolitionism and the role played by the Quakers, see Roger Anstey, *The Atlantic Slave Trade and British Abolition, 1760–1810,* Macmillan Press, London, 1975, chaps. 5, 7, 8 and 9; Davis, *Western Culture,* chap. 12; and idem, *Age of Revolution,* chap. 5.
7. Anthony Benezet, *Some Historical Account of Guinea, Its Situation, Produce, and the General Disposition of Its Inhabitants with an Inquiry into the Rise and Progress of the Slave Trade, Its Nature and Lamentable Effects,* Philadelphia, 1771 (republished in London in 1788; this is the edition I used); Benezet also produced some other significant works, in particular *A Caution to Great Britain and Her Colonies in a Short Representation of the Calamitous State of the Enslaved Negroes in the British Dominions,* Philadelphia, 1766 (republished in London in 1784).
8. Benezet, *Some Historical Account,* p. 109.
9. Thomas Clarkson, *An Essay on the Impolicy of the African Slave Trade,* London, 1788 (I worked with the French translation, *Essai sur les désavantages politiques de la traite des Nègres,* Neufchatel, 1789, p. 156 ff.); for a recent study on mortality rates among the slave ship crews, see Stephen D. Behrendt, 'Crew

Mortality in the Transatlantic Slave Trade in the Eighteenth Century', *Slavery and Abolition*, 18, 1, 1997, pp. 49–71.

10. Clarkson, *Essai*, pp. 317–18.
11. Olaudah Equiano, *The Interesting Narrative of the Life of Olaudah Equiano, or Gustavus Vassa, the African: Written by Himself*, London, 1789; Ottobah Cugoano, *Thoughts and Sentiments on the Evil and Wicked Traffic of the Slavery and Commerce of Human Species*, London, 1797.
12. Philip D. Curtin, *The Image of Africa: British Ideas and Action, 1780–1850*, University of Wisconsin Press, Madison, 1964, p. 60 ff.; and C. Duncan Rice, 'Literary Sources and the Revolution in British Attitudes to Slavery', in Christine Bolt and Seymour Drescher (eds), *Anti-slavery, Religion, and Reform. Essays in Memory of Roger Anstey*, Dawson, Folkestone, 1980, pp. 322–23.
13. Curtin, *The Image of Africa*, pp. 88–119. Many British plans of the time opposed the continuation of the slave trade even if at times such aversion to the trade did not extend to an abolitionist position: Beaver, who colonized Bulama, for example, was a typical tolerationist who, while expressing his repugnance for the institutions of slavery—'no man is a greater enemy to slavery than I am'—saw an immediate abolition of the slave trade as something undesirable (Philip Beaver, *African Memoranda: Relative to an Attempt to Establish a British Settlement on the Island of Bulama, on the Western Coast of Africa, in the Year 1792*, London, 1805, p. 399).
14. See, for example, William Bosman, *Voyage en Guinée, contenant une description nouvelle et très exacte de cette côte, ou l'on trouve et où l'on trafique l'or, les dents d'éléphants et les esclaves*, Utrecht, 1705; Jean-Baptiste Labat, *Voyage du Chevalier Des Marchais en Guinée, iles voisines et à Cayenne fait en 1725, 1726, 1727*, Paris, 1730; William Snelgrave, *Nouvelle relation de quelques endroits de Guinée et du commerce d'esclaves…*, Amsterdam, 1735 (published in London in the previous year).
15. John Gabriel Stedman, *Narrative of a Five Years' Expedition against the Revolted Negroes of Surinam*, London, 1796 (I used the part of the text which is included in I. and J.L. Vissière, *La traite des noirs au siècle des Lumières*, A.M. Métaillé, Paris, 1982, pp. 133–44); Gert Oostindie, 'Voltaire, Stedman and Suriname Slavery', *Slavery and Abolition*, 14, 2, 1993, p. 9.
16. Anstey, *Atlantic Slave Trade*, p. 123. Up to 1822, the *Histoire philosophique* went to 37 editions in France (see Hugh Honour, *L'image du Noir dans l'Europe occidental. De la Révolution américaine à la Première Guerre Mondiale*, vol. 1, Gallimard, Paris, 1989, p. 53).
17. James Green, 'The Publishing History of Olaudah Equiano's Interesting Narrative', *Slavery and Abolition*, 16, 3, 1995, p. 363.
18. Judith Jennings, 'Joseph Woods, Merchant and Philosopher: the Making of the British Anti-Slave Trade Ethic', *Slavery and Abolition*, 14, 3, 1993, p. 164 ff.; for the first committee of Quakers see also Davis, *Age of Revolution*, pp. 218–19; and Anstey, *Atlantic Slave Trade*, pp. 230–31.
19. Thomas Clarkson, *History of the Rise, Progress, and Accomplishment of the Abolition of the African Slave Trade by the British Parliament*, London, 1839 (1st edition 1808), pp. 172–23.
20. Ibid., p. 571; Anstey, *Atlantic Slave Trade*, pp. 222–30 and 256 ff.; on the dissemination of the abolitionist bibliography, see also Davis, *Age of Revolution*, p. 224; and Jennings, 'Joseph Woods', p. 163 ff..; for the dissemination of abolitionist imagery on typically feminine objects and in the arts, see Clare Midgley, 'Slave Sugar Boycotts, Female Activism and the Domestic Base of British Anti-Slavery Culture', *Slavery and Abolition*, 17, 3, 1996, p. 142 ff.; and Honour, *L'Image*, p. 27 ff., respectively.

21. Jay Coughtry, *The Notorious Triangle. Rhode Island and the African Slave Trade, 1700–1807*, Temple University Press, Philadelphia, 1981, p. 205.
22. Marcel Chatillon, 'La diffusion de la gravure du Brooks par la Société des Amis des Noirs et son impact', in S. Daget (ed.), *De la traite à l'esclavage*, vol. 2, Centre de Recherches sur l'Histoire du Monde Atlantique/Société Française d'Histoire d'Outre-Mer, Nantes, 1988, pp. 135–47; and Serge Daget, 'A Model of the French Abolitionist Movement and its Variations', in Bolt and Drescher (eds), *Anti-Slavery*, p. 65 ff.
23. For apologies for slavery, see Davis, *Age of Revolution*, p. 542 ff.; Larry E. Tise, *Proslavery. A History of the Defense of Slavery in America, 1701–1840*, University of Georgia Press, Athens, Georgia, 1987, p. 79; Anstey, *Atlantic Slave Trade*, pp. 292–95; Seymour Drescher, 'The Slaving Capital of the World. Liverpool and National Opinion in the Age of Abolition', *Slavery and Abolition*, 9, 2, 1988, p. 133; David Turley, *The Culture of English Antislavery, 1780–1860*, Routledge, London, 1991, pp. 23–24 and 53 ff.; James A. Rawley, 'London's Defense of the Slave Trade', *Slavery and Abolition*, 14, 2, 1993, pp. 50 and 56.
24. Howard Temperley, 'The Ideology of Anti-Slavery', in David Eltis and James Walvin (eds), *The Abolition of the Atlantic Slave Trade. Origins and Effects in Europe, Africa, and the Americas*, University of Wisconsin Press, Madison, 1981, pp. 28–29.
25. Davis, *Age of Revolution*, pp. 119–37; Coughtry, *Notorious Triangle*, p. 203 ff.
26. Davis, *Age of Revolution*, p. 95 ff.; Daget, 'A Model', pp. 65–67; Chatillon, 'La diffusion', p. 135.
27. Chatillon, 'La diffusion', p. 146; Lawrence C. Jennings, *French Anti-Slavery. The Movement for the Abolition of Slavery in France, 1802–1848*, Cambridge University Press, Cambridge, 2000, pp. 1–4.
28. Svend E. Green-Pedersen, 'Slave Demography in the Danish West Indies and the Abolition of the Danish Slave Trade', and Hans Christian Johansen, 'The Reality behind the Demographic Arguments to Abolish the Danish Slave Trade', in Eltis and Walvin (eds), *Abolition*, pp. 231–57 and 221–23, respectively.
29. Anstey, *Atlantic Slave Trade*, pp. 255–56.
30. For a detailed description of this first period of political agitation in England in favour of abolition, see ibid., chap. 11. See also Davis, *Age of Revolution*, p. 101 ff.; James Walvin, 'The Rise of British Popular Sentiment for Abolition, 1787–1832', in Bolt and Drescher (eds), *Anti-Slavery*, pp. 151–59; idem, 'The Public Campaign in England Against Slavery, 1787–1834', in Eltis and Walvin (eds), *Abolition*; Turley, *Culture*, p. 63 ff.
31. For a countervailing point of view, which states that abolitionism remained alive and well in British public opinion after 1793, see Seymour Drescher, 'Whose Abolition? Popular Pressure and the Ending of the British Slave Trade', *Past and Present*, 143, 1994, pp. 136–66.
32. For the whole of the final phase that led to the abolition of the British slave trade, see Anstey, *Atlantic Slave Trade*, chaps. 14 to 16; Seymour Drescher, *Econocide: British Slavery in the Era of Abolition*, University of Pittsburgh Press. Pittsburgh, 1977 (the whole work).
33. See James Bandinel, *Some Account of the Trade in Slaves from Africa, as Connected with Europe and America. From the Introduction of the Trade into Modern Europe, down to Present Time, especially with Reference to the Efforts made by the British Government for its Extinction*, Frank Cass, London, 1968 (1st edition 1842), pp. 85–86 and 105; and Christopher Lloyd, *The Navy and the Slave Trade. The Suppression of the African Slave Trade in the Nineteenth Century*, Frank Cass, London, 1968 (1st edition 1949), p. 5. According to recent historical data, the Portuguese accounted for close to 38% of the transatlantic slave trade in the final decade of the eighteenth century (Philip D. Curtin,

The Atlantic Slave Trade: a Census, University of Wisconsin Press, Madison, 1969, p. 211).

34. Strangford to Canning, 4 June 1807, quoted in Bandinel, *Some Account*, p. 6.
35. For Portuguese diplomatic manoeuvres in 1807, see Valentim Alexandre, *Os sentidos do Império. Questão nacional e questão colonial na crise do Antigo Regime Português*, Afrontamento, Porto, 1993, p. 147 ff.
36. Ibid., p. 167 ff.; Jorge Borges de Macedo, *História diplomática portuguesa. Constantes e linhas de força. Estudo de geopolítica*, Instituto de Defesa Nacional, Lisbon, 1987.
37. José F. Borges de Castro, *Collecção dos tratados, convenções, contratos e actos públicos celebrados entre a Coroa de Portugal e as mais Potências desde 1640 até ao presente*, vol. IV, Imprensa Nacional, Lisbon, 1857, pp. 412–23.
38. José Timóteo da Silva Bastos, *História da censura intelectual em Portugal*, Imprensa da Universidade, Coimbra, 1926, p. 116 ff.; Jorge Borges de Macedo, 'Real Mesa Censória', in Joel Serrão (ed.), *Dicionário de História de Portugal*, vol. IV, Figueirinhas, Porto, 1981, pp. 276–67; for an example of the application for approval, see application by Guilherme Nassau, 12 October 1796, Rolls of books of British origin for entry into the kingdom, ANTT, Real Mesa Censória, *cx.* 142.
39. Bastos, *História*, p. 207.
40. Catálogo de Livros Defezos Neste Reyno desde o dia da Criação da Real Meza Cençória athé ao presente, ANTT, Real Mesa Censória, *liv.* 12; Bastos, *História*, pp. 63 and 162.
41. Bastos, *História*, p. 252.
42. Luís de Sousa Coutinho to Melo e Castro, 14 May 1788, ANTT, MNE, *cx.* 707.
43. Cipriano R. Freire to Luís de Sousa Coutinho, 8 and 15 April and 24 June 1789, ANTT, MNE, *cx.* 708.
44. Cipriano R. Freire to Luís de Sousa Coutinho, 4 April 1792, ANTT, MNE, *cx.* 710; see also, in the same *cx.*, official letters dated 11 April, 2 and 9 May of that year.
45. Letters of Domingos de Sousa Coutinho, 3 July 1804, BN, Restricted documents, *liv.* 9052.
46. Letters of Domingos de Sousa Coutinho, 5 March 1805, BN, Restricted documents, *liv.* 9055.
47. Araújo de Azevedo to Domingos de Sousa Coutinho (restricted despatches), 18 March 1807, ANTT, MNE, *liv.* 113.
48. Araújo de Azevedo to Domingos de Sousa Coutinho (reserved despatches), 11 April 1807, ANTT, MNE, *liv.* 113.
49. Opinion of Luís José de Melo, 14 January 1809, ANTT, MNE, *cx.* 35, *ma.* 10 (part of metal filing cabinet).
50. Opinion of António da Silva Lisboa, 14 January 1809, ANTT, MNE, *cx.* 35, *ma.* 10 (part of metal filing cabinet).
51. Opinion of Manuel Jacinto, undated, ANTT, MNE, *cx.* 53, *ma.* 2 (part of metal filing cabinet).
52. Linhares to Strangford, 4 March 1809, in Júlio Firmino Júdice Biker, *Suplemento à Colecção de Tratados, Convenções, Contractos e Actos Públicos, celebrados entre a Coroa de Portugal e as mais Potências desde 1640 até ao presente*, vol. XVII, Lisbon, 1879, pp. 21–22.
53. Pierre Verger, *Flux et reflux de la traite des nègres entre le golfe de Bénin et Bahia de Todos os Santos du XVIIe au XIXe siècles*, Mouton, Paris, 1968, pp. 274–75.
54. *Politics*, I, 1254a.
55. Augustine, *City of God*, XIX, XV.
56. Davis, *Western Culture*, p. 91. Much of what I have summarized above concerning the ideology of slavery can be found in chaps. 3 and 4 of Davis's work.

57. For an example of discussion of these practical issues in the sixteenth century, and in the context of the Portuguese empire, see Luís Filipe Thomaz, 'A escravatura em Malaca no século XVI', *Studia*, 53, 1994, p. 291 ff.
58. See Davis, *Western Culture*, pp. 109–15.
59. *Crónica de Guiné*, XXV.
60. Ibid., XXVI.
61. António Vieira, 'Sermão vigésimo sétimo', in *Sermões, problemas raciais e políticos do Brasil*, Ed. Cultrix, São Paulo, 1975, pp. 57–58.
62. Ibid., pp. 59–61.
63. Ibid., pp. 62, 75 and 83.
64. Scc, in particular, Fernando Oliveira, *Arte de guerra do mar*, Arquivo Histórico da Marinha, Lisbon, 1937, chap. IV, pp. 23–25 (original version 1555). For an analysis of most of these writers, see Davis, *Western Culture*, pp. 106–21 and 165–96; and Vitorino Magalhães Godinho, *Os descobrimentos e a economia mundial*, vol. IV, Ed. Presença, Lisbon, 1983 (2nd edition), chap. 9 (in particular, p. 181 ff.).
65. Manoel Ribeiro da Rocha, *Ethiope resgatado, empenhado, sustentado, corregido, instruido e libertado. Discurso theologico-juridico em que se propoem o modo de comerciar, haver e possuir validamente, quanto a hum e outro foro, os Pretos cativos africanos, e as principais obrigações que correm a quem deles se servir*, Lisbon, 1758, pp. 3, 26–27 and 62–63.
66. Ibid., introduction and pp. 99–100.
67. D. José Joaquim da Cunha de Azeredo Coutinho, *Ensaio económico sobre o comércio de Portugal e suas colónias*, Lisbon, 1794, pp. 95–96 and 98 (note). For the bibliography on Azeredo Coutinho, see Innocêncio Francisco da Silva, *Diccionario Bibliographico Portuguez*, vol. IV, Imprensa Nacional, Lisbon, 1860, pp. 384–86; the *Diccionario* contains information on nearly all the Portuguese and Brazilian writers referenced in this book. Since I have used it for this purpose, I have refrained from citing the Diccionario for each writer.
68. D. José Joaquim da Cunha de Azeredo Coutinho, *Analyse sobre a justiça do commercio do Resgate dos Escravos da Costa de Africa, novamente revista e acrescentada por seu author*, Lisbon, 1808, pp. 1–16.
69. Ibid., p. 33 ff.
70. Ibid., pp. 49–50.
71. Ibid., p. 43.
72. Ibid., p. 107 ff..; for similar suggestions from other elements in the Catholic Church, see, for example, J. Benci, *Economia cristã dos senhores no governo dos escravos*, Livraria Apostolado da Imprensa, Porto, 1954 (1st edition 1700).
73. Coutinho, *Analyse sobre*, pp. VI–IX and 52–53.
74. Ibid., dedication, pp. IX–XI and 50; idem, *Concordância das leis de Portugal e das Bullas Pontificias, das quaes humas permittem a escravidão dos pretos d'Africa, e outras prohibem a escravidão dos Indios do Brazil*, Lisbon, 1808, p. 39 (note 1).
75. Davis, *Western Culture*, p. 415; idem, *Age of Revolution*, p. 99 (note 21).
76. Coutinho, *Analyse sobre*, p. 29 (note 1); idem, *Concordância*, pp. 3–5.
77. Idem, *Analyse sobre*, pp. 73–74.
78. António Ribeiro Sanches, *Cartas sobre a educação da mocidade*, parte XIII, Imprensa da Universidade, Coimbra, 1922 (1st edition 1760), pp. 88–90.
79. Luís dos Santos Vilhena, *Recopilação de notícias soteropolitanas e brasílicas, contidas em vinte cartas…*, Bahia, 1921, pp. 136–37.
80. Luís António de Oliveira Mendes, *Memória a respeito dos escravos e tráfico da escravatura entre a costa d'Africa e o Brasil, apresentada à Real Academia das Ciências de Lisboa em 1793*, Pub. Escorpião, Porto, 1977.
81. For a succinct autobiography, see L.F. Carvalho Dias, *Algumas cartas do Doutor António Ribeiro dos Santos aos seus contemporâneos*, Coimbra, 1975, pp. 417–20.

82. 'Cartas sobre Pombal e sobre os escritores das nossas coisas da Índia', in ibid., pp. 444 and 455.
83. Carta sobre a escravatura, BN, Reserved, *liv.* 4710, pp. 77–79.
84. João Rodrigues de Brito, *Cartas económico-políticas sobre a agricultura e commercio da Bahia*, Lisbon, 1821, pp. 34–35 and 39.
85. Theodoro José Biancardi, *Cartas americanas*, Lisbon, 1820, p. 80.
86. José Agostinho de Macedo, 'O Preto Sensível', in *Minerva*, Lisbon, II, 1836, pp. 100 and 103–05.
87. Ibid., p. 115.
88. Sanches, *Cartas*, p. 88.
89. Mendes, *Memória*, p. 88, note 28.
90. Vilhena, *Recopilação*, p. 136.
91. Brito, *Cartas*, p. 35.
92. Biancardi, *Cartas*, p. 80.
93. Macedo, 'O Preto Sensível', p. 104. The notion that the pleasures and delights of Europe were bought at the expense of the blood of Negroes was one of the commonplaces of the literature of the time: 'Femmes sensibles, vous pleurez aux tragédies, et ce qui sert à vos plaisirs est mouillé des pleurs et teint du sang des hommes!' (Jacques-Henri Bernardin de Saint-Pierre, *Voyage à l'Isle de France, à l'Isle de Bourbon, au Cap de Bonne Espérance, ... par un officier du Roi*, 2 vols., Paris, 1773, pp. 121–22).
94. See, for example, *Gazeta de Lisboa*, 15 March 1796 (news report on Wilberforce's speech in the Commons).
95. Coutinho, *Analyse sobre*, preface (p. V).
96. Bastos, *História*, pp. 296–97.
97. Ibid.; it should be noted that, despite the Academy's refusal and the censorship decreed by Ribeiro dos Santos in 1806, Coutinho's work was eventually printed and published in Lisbon two years later, by command of a higher authority.
98. Davis, *Age of Revolution*, p. 425.
99. Carta de Ribeiro dos Santos sobre a escravatura, BN, Reserved documents, *liv.* 4710 (pp. 75–76).
100. Drescher, 'The Slaving Capital', p. 132.
101. Chatillon, 'La diffusion', p. 142.
102. Tise, *Proslavery*, pp. 16 and 33; and Coughtry, *Notorious Triangle*, pp. 205–07.

– *Chapter 2* –

THE MAINTENANCE OF THE SLAVE TRADE IN AN ABOLITIONIST CONTEXT: FROM THE BEGINNING OF BRITISH PRESSURE TO BRAZILIAN SECESSION

When the Abolition Act came into force in 1808, the Royal Navy began a systematic assault on the slave trade, deploying two ships to the African coast (where they also provided support for British involvement in Sierra Leone, an area of paramount interest to the recently formed African Institution, the organization that sought to consolidate abolitionism and encourage legitimate trade with Africa).[1]

To begin with the British navy did not interfere with Portuguese shipping on the African coast. First, this was because, as Portugal was an allied power, there was as yet no legal basis for the arrest of the *tumbeiros,* a word sometimes used to refer to the slave ships and which literally means 'that which leads to the grave'.[2] Secondly, it did not then have enough ships to patrol the whole of the coast, and the Brazil slaving ships were not particularly active in the area that was effectively patrolled. The British commissioners' first report on the state of the slave trade is revealing of the desire to confine the struggle against the slavers. Given that the main arena in which the 'odious commerce' took place was on the coastline between Whydah and Angola and that the cruisers then available were not of a sufficient number to operate over such a large area, it was judged preferable that they should focus their efforts on Sierra Leone and its surroundings (see Map 2.1), so as to stem the flow of slaves from that region. Within this restricted geographical area, the major threat seemed to come from the North Americans who had become involved in the trade, in violation of the laws of their country, disguising their ships with false flags and false papers (generally Spanish). As far as Portugal was concerned, only the traffic emanating from the so-called Rivers of Guinea was to be feared, and the commissioners

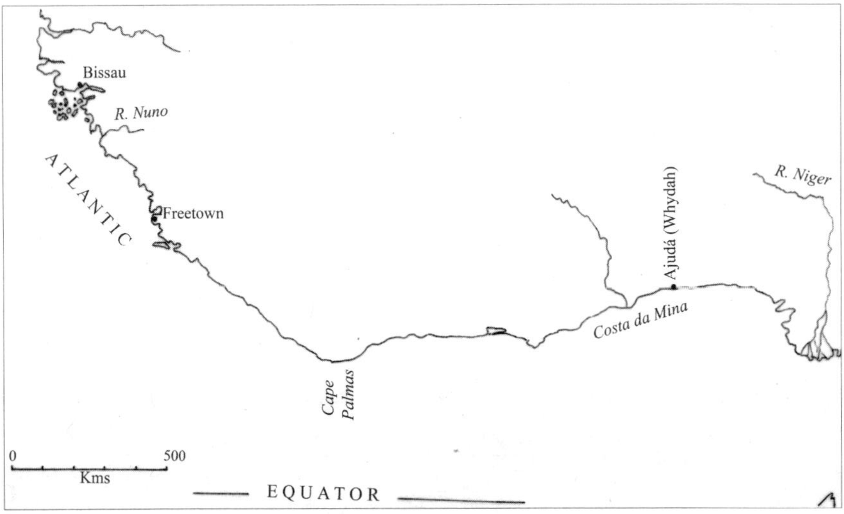

MAP 2.1. The west coast of Africa north of the equator.

asked merely that 'a strict prohibition' of the slave trade from Bissau and its dependencies be enforced. The report even suggested that, in order to seal off the Sierra Leone area to the slavers, foreign powers should be compensated by being allowed to carry on the trade east of Whydah (Ajuda, in Portuguese).[3]

The British government did not adopt its commissioners' suggestions for restricting the slave trade. But both the Royal Navy and British diplomacy acted in accordance with the information coming from Freetown. For this reason, in a secret article of the Anglo-Portuguese treaty of 1810, Portugal was persuaded to agree to prohibit the slave trade in the settlements of Cacheu and Bissau. The article even stipulated that, under certain conditions, these settlements would be ceded to Britain for a period of fifty years.[4]

The conditions provided for in the treaty's secret article were never fulfilled, so Bissau and Cacheu remained under the dominion of the Portuguese Crown. However, the abolitionist undertakings of the Rio de Janeiro government given in article 10 of the 1810 treaty of alliance and friendship became a powerful lever in the hands of the British abolitionists. The article restricted the trade to the Portuguese dominions, but it did not require the promulgation of any specific measures, nor did it give the British cruisers any right to intervene. The text was so vague that William Scott, one of the most respected judges in the British Admiralty, would later admit that he was unable to provide any explanation for it, 'involved as it is by its own obscure and equivocal phraseology, and by its application to the geography of a coast very superficially known here, and to Portuguese claims of sovereignty, not at all understood'.[5] Nonetheless, and even though they were aware of the ambiguities of the article in question, the abolitionists were determined to use it, and they deliberately interpreted it in a broader and more concrete sense, giving the Royal Navy the excuse to start policing the Portuguese slavers in transit on the Atlantic Ocean. In 1811 the captains of the anti-slave trade cruisers (which were by then already four in number) received orders to intervene on the coast between Cape Verde and Angola and to seize Portuguese ships found to be trading slaves outside the settlements effectively occupied by the Portuguese Crown.[6]

2.1 The British Pincer

From the middle of 1811 to January of the following year British cruisers, in addition to driving away from the African coast some of the *tumbeiros* that were preparing to load up with slaves, seized at least eighteen of them, thirteen of which were in the ports of the Costa da Mina; the other five were seized in the Antilles, in Cabinda and on the high seas.[7] At the end of 1812 the number of Portuguese-flag slave ships seized had risen to twenty-four.[8]

These actions raised a chorus of protest in Brazil, particularly in Bahia. Insurance company directors and Bahian merchants protested immediately at the British intervention, deconstructing what they called, with reason, the 'cabalistic excuses' used by the British to justify the arrests.[9] In theory, it would have been desirable for the government in Rio de Janeiro if Britain had recognized the arbitrary nature of its police action and had corrected it accordingly. Only in this way would it be possible to safeguard national prestige and obtain swift compensation for damages. In practice, however, the first priority was to ensure the continued supply of slaves to Brazil. That was the Portuguese government's first objective, and early results were obtained: on 6 May 1813 the Foreign Office instructed the Admiralty to stop interfering with the Portuguese slave ships operating bona fide under the treaty provisions and, in that year, only four ships were seized (and only two in the following year).[10] More difficult to solve was the problem of compensation for wrongful arrest. London was not sure that its actions had complied with the law. The expression used at the beginning of 1812 was that the seizing of Portuguese ships 'could not be considered to be unlawful'.[11] In any event, the British government stalled on admitting that the Portuguese were in the right and, in response to insistent demands for compensation for the affected slavers, it suggested that they should first submit to the Admiralty courts proof of the illegality of the Royal Navy's actions.[12] The British strategy seemed to be based on the supposition, which was correct, that most of the injured parties would rather avoid the lengthy delays involved in making submissions to the courts and would prefer rapidly to reach agreements and changes to the law which would ensure that the maritime routes were disencumbered.

The British position was interpreted and absorbed differently in Rio de Janeiro and in the Portuguese embassy in London, and those differences of interpretation and acceptance reflected differing perceptions of the nature and significance of the British abolitionist movement.

The Count of Funchal (Domingos de Sousa Coutinho) had been living in England for many years and, even if not always accurately, was able to make a direct personal assessment of the importance that abolition had acquired in British cultural life. Consequently he drew the attention of the Portuguese government to the need to pacify the 'philanthropists' by means of spontaneously adopted measures against the slave trade. The ambassador insisted that the question of slavery required serious attention, and reminded the government that the opposition in England was 'always attentive to this matter', as was 'the party of the Methodists, which is very strong in this country'; their influence in abolitionist policy in Britain was substantial and Wilberforce, whom Funchal described as 'the patriarch of this sort of fanatics', had allegedly even been called to Downing Street to examine the articles of the Anglo-Portuguese treaty relating to the trade in slaves. It was therefore important, he said, to pay attention to an issue that could 'cause some trouble to His Royal Majesty'.[13]

Another aspect that came out consistently in Funchal's dispatches was the criticism of the Rio government's lack of abolitionist cooperation with the government in London. Portuguese inaction was particularly damaging, he wrote, not only because it harmed the image of the Portuguese rulers, but also because it adversely predisposed the public mind in Britain. Funchal therefore took the liberty of making criticisms and suggesting solutions, reminding the government that Wilberforce was accusing the Portuguese slavers of 'piling up the blacks without any consideration for the ships' capacity', thereby violating the older Portuguese law of 1684, and that, for this reason, Castlereagh was threatening to deny assistance to the Portuguese slaving ships. Funchal also recalled that accusations were not just being made in Britain: Luís Oliveira Mendes's *Memória* expressly acknowledged that the law of 1684 was not being observed. The ambassador pointed out as well that the Portuguese law in question should be improved, because it allowed traders to load twice as many slaves as the British law of 1789. He also suggested that a tax on urban or luxury slaves should be imposed in Brazil. In his opinion, the British would be 'more docile' if they could see that Portugal was taking some steps towards gradual abolition. Mindful perhaps of the example of the inquiries carried out by the British Parliament, Funchal thought that 'the Religion and Devotion of His Royal Highness alone, and without foreign influence, made it a worthwhile cause to undertake an investigation *on their own account*, to remedy the evil, if necessary' and recommended that this 'Glorious Investigation' should be carried out with all gravity and solemnity, because this would reflect great honour on the sovereign.[14]

From this critical view of Portuguese action—or inaction—and with his conciliatory approach to British interests, Funchal was, of course, open to compromise in order to resolve the differences. At the beginning of 1813 he was already discussing the need for a bilateral convention on slave trading that would, in article 1, stipulate the amount of compensation the government in London would pay for ships seized on the African coast and, in article 2, that the trade in slaves should be banned in Cacheu and Bissau to meet 'the chimera of Mr. Wilberforce and others enamoured of the system of free colonization of blacks in Sierra Leone'.[15] Giving up the trade in these two trading posts was a necessary sacrifice, according to Funchal, in order to persuade Wilberforce and Stephen, 'the two most influential members of the fanatical society called the African Institution, and who had caused so much uproar in Parliament', to abandon the Costa da Mina and be content with what was being offered in relation to Bissau.[16] Funchal accordingly drew up a plan under which Portugal, in exchange for compensation, would place a total ban on trade north of Cape Palmas and would accept that Bissau would be governed by a British officer, in order to ensure that the commitment to abolition was observed in practice.[17]

These suggestions found no approval in Rio de Janeiro. The proposals partially to abolish the trade and to hand over supervision of the arrangements to a British officer were seen as implying a loss of sovereignty and bringing on the losses that would automatically ensue from the shutting down of a branch of business activity, and were therefore regarded as being entirely out of the question.[18] Of all the suggestions made by its ambassador in London, the Portuguese government retained only one, the rules setting out the full complement of the slaving ships, while at the same time making clear that there would be no further concessions to Britain.[19]

Moreover, in the preceding months the relationship between Portugal and Britain had deteriorated. Apart from the problem of arrests of the slaving ships—which had reached a complete impasse—there was also British opposition to the Iberian union and the desire of the Rio de Janeiro government to expand its Brazilian domain southwards, as well as a growing wave of recriminations over the manner in which the commercial treaty of 1810 was being applied.[20] The end of the entente between Portugal and Britain was to have an impact on the composition of the Portuguese government itself: following the death of Linhares at the beginning of 1812, the Foreign Ministry was given to Aguiar and, later, Galveias, ministers who where still acceptable to London, but in January 1814 Araújo de Azevedo was once again brought into the government. Even though Aguiar remained at the Foreign Ministry, in practice the direction of foreign policy was in the hands of Araújo de Azevedo, who would oppose Britain from that moment on. Strangford's protests and his efforts to prevent the appointment of the Francophile Araújo de Azevedo and to make the royal family come back to Lisbon were all to no avail.

This was the turning point. On the issue of the slave trade Aguiar and Araújo de Azevedo voluntarily confined themselves to the tactics of defiance, which were unproductive in the short term, given that to be properly effective they would have required economic, political and ideological retaliation, in other words, total diplomacy, which Rio de Janeiro could not countenance. In an adverse political climate, because the war in Europe had pushed mere legal conflicts into the background, all the Rio government could do was to wait for the end of hostilities in Europe and for the treaties and adjustments that would stem from them.

The new government naturally withdrew all backing from Funchal. Judged to be incompetent and an Anglophile, he was sidelined from the delegation to the Congress of Vienna and from the London embassy itself. Before leaving, however, the ambassador had one more chance to repeat his warnings on the 'obstinacy' with which Wilberforce and the Parliament were persisting in the plan to equate the slave trade with piracy, and to warn that Portugal would not be able to resist the commitment to abolition in Britain. It should therefore make concessions or give up the slave trade completely—something which in his view would actually not be a bad thing at all. Anticipating the end of the 'odious commerce', Funchal was even of the opinion that thought should be given to what to ask for from Britain by way of compensation for abolition.[21]

2.2 A Time for Concessions: from Vienna to the Convention of 1817

Rio de Janeiro's ability to resist British pressure implied taking advantage of a dialectical reversal that might take place during the realignment of forces in the post-war period if, alarmed at the extent of Britain's power, some of the allies should move to a position of neutrality and the neutrals to opposition. That was the drift of the instructions given to the Portuguese representatives at the Congress of Vienna (Palmela, Saldanha da Gama and Lobo da Silveira). Those instructions, after an overview of the history of ship seizures and a brief analysis of the British 'false veneer of philanthropy', insisted on the key notion that the slave trade could only be ended 'slowly and gradually'. Since Britain was resorting to force to end it 'at once', the plenipotentiaries to the Congress should seek to ally themselves with nations that were in a similar situation, in particular Russia, and should refuse to sign any declaration that provided for immediate abolition.[22]

The nature of these instructions shows the extent to which the Rio government's diplomacy on the slave trade question was divorced from European political and ideological realities. To the British abolitionists, whose only objective at the time was the end of the maritime trade in slaves, the issue of Russian serfdom had little to do with the Portuguese slave trade. Geographically distant from the centres of decision-making and with little awareness of the abolitionists' motives and aims, the Portuguese rulers tended to confuse different issues and to choose the wrong interlocutors.

The end of the war therefore found the Portuguese government obdurate in terms of principle and hoping to avoid the problems of abolition altogether. Its position had not improved. In actual fact, the chances of keeping the Portuguese traffic going on a legal basis, which were already low, had declined even further with the manoeuvres that took place in 1814, the year in which popular pressure on the British government for abolition was stepped up. Britain had emerged from the Napoleonic wars in a position of dominance, and Wilberforce and his peers were relying on that superiority to put a rapid end to the 'infamous commerce'. France had been defeated and the Iberian countries were in such a precarious state that—as they thought—it would be relatively easy to force them into abolition.[23] The British government had a somewhat less maximalist view of its strategic advantages: while it had succeeded in getting the major continental powers to agree, in principle, to support all the measures relating to abolition that it might submit to the Congress of Vienna, in the Treaty of Paris of 30 May 1814 it had restored the French colonies to France and agreed to the continuation of the French slave trade for a further five years.

This concession was extremely unpopular in Britain, where the abolitionists stirred up public opinion against what they described as a revival of the 'odious commerce'. In little over one month over 770 petitions—containing some 1 million signatures[24]—were submitted to Parliament, and there was a new wave of anti-slavery publications. Wellington received orders to try to renegotiate what had been agreed with the French, while Macaulay and Clarkson went to Paris to try to influence the French government.[25] Under these circumstances the Foreign Office would have to achieve something in Vienna to pacify domestic public opinion. For this reason, as Liverpool said to Castlereagh, its targets were the total abolition of the slave trade within a period of five years or, at the very least, its prohibition north of Cape Formoso.[26]

The Congress began in September 1814 and focused on re-establishing political equilibrium in Europe and on maintaining peace. A new generalized conflict would certainly imply fresh revolutions and the destruction of the *anciens régimes*. At the end of that year it looked as if the anti-revolutionary alliance would break down as a result of Russian territorial demands, and at the beginning of 1815 Britain, France and Austria actually established a secret defensive alliance in order to oppose the Russo-Polish plan. But Russia resigned itself to circumstances, and no realignment of forces took place that might have been favourable to the slaving objectives of the Portuguese Crown.

In its negotiations with Castlereagh, the Portuguese delegation adopted a negotiating philosophy and tactics that were the opposite to what had been established by the government in Rio. In fact, Palmela chose to negotiate above all with Britain—as he himself said, it was essential 'to deal directly and only with the British'.[27] He was conciliatory and made some significant concessions. The agreement with Britain gave rise to two documents: the convention of 21 January 1815 and the Anglo-Portuguese Treaty dated the following day. In the convention the British government undertook to pay the sum of 300,000 pounds sterling in compensation, as a way of ending the disputes over ship seizures up to 31 May 1814 (in a secret additional article, Britain undertook to return the ships that had been seized after 1 June 1814). Under the 22 January treaty, Portugal promised to abolish the slave trade north of the equator, and it was stipulated that henceforth there would be no such trade in the southern hemisphere other than to supply slaves to the 'transatlantic possessions of the Crown of Portugal'. The Portuguese government also undertook to adopt, in concert with Britain, measures that would best contribute to the suppression of the traffic in slaves in the northern hemisphere. In return, the Treaty of Alliance and Friendship of 1810, including its secret articles, was annulled, and the loan of 600,000 pounds sterling made in 1809 was considered settled (the Portuguese government having already repaid some 25 per cent).[28]

This was a total defeat of the strategy outlined at Rio and the affirmation of Funchal's Anglophile approach. Funchal saw some of his ideas being implemented by Palmela, his nephew. Palmela had been in London from January 1813 until the middle of the following year, when he left for France. And it is significant that from Paris, at the beginning of 1814, he should have written to his uncle asking him, amongst other things, for the documents relating to the seizures of slave ships on the African coast and for a map on which he might trace 'the line to the north of which we promised to cease the slave trade'.[29] A month and half later, as he was leaving for Vienna, Palmela asked his uncle if he should request from Britain 'the cancellation of the commercial treaty [of 1810] or of just some of its articles', if there were to be total abolition.[30] These two letters show not only how Funchal gave advice and guided his nephew, but also that Palmela took it for granted that there would be partial abolition—something that was 'promised'—and that total abolition could be seen as something that would be implemented in exchange for compensation, as Funchal had already advocated. In Vienna, having received instructions from Rio, Palmela almost certainly succeeded in demonstrating to his Portuguese fellow diplomats the impossibility of carrying them out. So the three decided to distance themselves from what the government had laid down and to accept a new basis for negotiations with Castlereagh.

While the bilateral discussions were taking place, the start of a general conference on the slave trade was subjected to successive delays. The conference would finally begin on 16 January 1815, with plenipotentiaries from Britain, France, Spain, Portugal, Sweden, Russia, Austria and Prussia. This in itself was an early setback for the Iberian representatives, who had sought to limit participation to nations with overseas interests. Nevertheless, when Castlereagh proposed immediate abolition, he came up against a cautious French position alongside strong opposition from Spain and Portugal.[31] The discussion was to end on 8 February with an ambiguous declaration that described the slave trade as 'repellent to the principles of humanity and universal morality' and spoke exaggeratedly of the 'public outcry in all civilized countries' for the slave trade to be suppressed 'as soon as possible', but ended up accepting the principle of gradual abolition because it recognized 'the difficulty of suddenly putting a stop to its course'.[32] In any event, and even though Portugal was able to hold on to most of its flow of slaves to Brazil—because it came from its African colonies in the southern hemisphere—the Anglo-Portuguese Treaty of 1815 was to have a severe impact on the interests of the merchants and planters of Bahia, Pernambuco, Pará and Maranhão, who had traditionally had close ties to the trading posts on the Costa da Mina and in Guinea.

Apparently resigned to these facts, the government in Rio sought to minimize the impact of something inevitable. Persisting with his policy of muddying the waters, Aguiar congratulated himself on the fact that the Final Act of the Congress contained no clause relating to the slave trade for, as he said, 'the less is agreed on this topic, the easier it will be to rebut the legal measures which the British government will no doubt undertake to speed up the total elimination of the slave trade'.[33] The minister had already instructed the embassy in London to hurry up and collect the 300,000 pounds sterling from the British government, and to try to obtain an exemption for the islands of São Tomé and Príncipe, which lay almost on the equator and which, in a strict interpretation of the letter of the law, would be prevented from importing slaves for the continuation of their trade and agriculture. Anticipating possible problems that might arise from the obligation contracted in Vienna to adopt, in concert with Britain, concrete measures to end the slave trade, the government in Rio sought to retain for itself the exclusive right to control Portuguese shipping (to be carried out by Portuguese cruisers).[34] On another level, and in a bid to gain time, it refrained from moving forward with a law which would punish any violations of the treaty of 22 January 1815.

Despite the fact that the Rio de Janeiro government had yielded ground, the Vienna agreements did not bring to an end the state of conflict that prevailed between Britain and Portugal on the issue of the slave trade. With the advent of peace, and in the light of the law, the seamen of the Royal Navy had no authority to search, let alone to detain, another nation's ships, even where that nation had already outlawed the slave trade through a treaty with Britain. At the precise moment when it seemed to have the conditions and the means to smash the trade, the British government necessarily had to start giving up practices that were, to say the least, debatable. In this context, the right of search became more important, in practice, than achieving full abolition, which was a difficult objective in the short term and something it was practically impossible to control.[35] This is why the harassment of Portugal (and other slaving nations) continued after Vienna.

At the beginning of 1816, the Foreign Office put the Portuguese government on notice that it would block the payments it had promised to make until such time as the Portuguese government, complying with what had been agreed, should promulgate legislation to combat the slave trade.[36] At sea, the Royal Navy had already started chasing Portuguese slave ships, which continued to put in on the Costa da Mina, which was now illegal. From April to July 1815, five Bahia slavers were seized. Since the Rio de Janeiro government did nothing about this, some Bahian merchants armed their ships with the firm intention of continuing with the slave trade, in any shape or form. In September 1815 the brig *Leal Portuguez* was sunk by British cruisers. In the following year, the owner of the brig *Temerário* openly announced in Bahia that he was disposed to continue with the slave trade and to do battle with the British if necessary; the brig was to be seized in April as it prepared to load 600 slaves in Whydah, but only after a fierce fight, 'with great slaughter on each side'.[37] Up to the end of that year the British navy seized six more Bahia ships and the state of irritation in Brazil was such that it was feared war 'might start before the respective governments declared it', as Saldanha da Gama stated in a memoir delivered to the Russian government.[38]

To make matters worse, Portugal did not obtain the desired support of a great power. However receptive it might be to Saldanha da Gama's arguments, Russia—which was a continental power with little or no involvement in Atlantic issues—did not seem to be willing to jeopardize its recent alliances for reasons that were as morally dubious as those of the slave trade. The same was true of the Austrian and Prussian courts, which were not very receptive to the advances of Lobo da Silveira. France, meanwhile, was no longer a potential supporter: one of Napoleon's first acts on his return was the re-abolition of the slave trade (hoping thereby to gain favour with British public opinion); British diplomacy naturally took advantage of the precedent that had been set and, after Waterloo, forced Louis XVIII to sanction abolition through an additional article to the Treaty of Paris. Only Spain was left, a kingdom that depended on slave labour for economic growth in Cuba. In 1815, Palmela may have considered the possibility of making an alliance with the Spanish government in order, amongst other things, better to resist British abolitionist pressure. But that option was turned down by Rio, which was interested in territorial expansion in the River Plate region at the expense of former Spanish colonies. This was obviously incompatible with an Iberian alliance.[39]

Thus at the close of 1816, and since there had been no breakthrough, Aguiar was already contemplating the possibility of breaking the Vienna accords. But Palmela, the new ambassador in London, advised against such a step. Since the Portuguese objective was 'to prolong for as long as possible' the traffic south of the equator, it was 'indispensable' that it should rapidly comply (and demand compliance) with the treaty of 22 January 1815, because, if it did not do so, the British government could

FIGURE 2.1. D. Pedro de Sousa Holstein, 1st Count, 1st Marquis and 1st Duke of Palmela (1781–1850).

declare it null and void, and then demand other and even more damaging terms.[40] Starting out from a philosophy that was diametrically opposed to that of the government in Rio, Palmela (Fig. 2.1) argued that the more extensive and detailed the agreements were with Britain, the easier it would be to protect Portuguese shipping and the legal trade in slaves. He also drew his government's attention to the fact that there was continuing abolitionist pressure from Britain on other nations. He thought there was 'grave cause for concern' that in a possible political crisis those nations would no longer line up with the Portuguese position.[41]

The opportunity which the diplomat feared quickly arose. The expansionist plans of Brazil became clearer with the increasing Americanization of the Rio government's political priorities. Brazil was elevated to the status of a kingdom at the end of 1815. In the following year Portuguese troops started a move to attack the so-called Banda Oriental (Eastern Flank), and Montevideo fell on 20 January of the following year. In-as-much as Spain still claimed sovereignty over the region, the conquest of the city was an aggressive act by Portugal against its Iberian neighbour, and the conflict clearly had repercussions in Europe, jeopardizing the delicate equilibrium that had just recently been reinstated. At the beginning of 1817 Palmela reported that the great powers were aligning themselves with Spain's cause, and that even Russia was talking about reprisals and the immediate use of force against Portugal.[42] The British government made no secret of its sharp criticism of the taking of Montevideo, and even threatened Portugal with breaking off the guarantee of military protection. In the summer of 1817 Portuguese military chiefs were extremely apprehensive at the prospect of losing British military support, especially because Spain had concentrated troops near the Portuguese border.

These unfavourable international circumstances meant that the slave trade took second place to the primordial need to preserve Britain's support, and opened the way to the policy of conciliation that Palmela sought to apply. This led to the convention of 28 July 1817, which instituted the right of search and established two mixed Anglo-Portuguese commissions for a rapid handing down of sentences, with no right of appeal, for violations of anti-slave trade laws. One of the commissions was to be based in Brazil, the other in a British possession on the African coast—which turned out to be Sierra Leone. There was to be a third, interim mixed commission in London, which would review the cases of Portuguese slavers who had already been sentenced.[43] On 26 January 1818, to give effect to what had been agreed three years earlier, the Brazilian government finally published a law prohibiting the slave trade north of the equator and imposing heavy penalties on those who broke it.[44] But the Rio cabinet took away with one hand what it had given with the other, since the new law revoked the 1813 charter, which had placed limits on the number of slaves transported in accordance with ships' tonnage; as the editor of *O Portuguez* trenchantly observed, this was a way of bringing the maximum number of slaves into Brazil while the British did not oblige the Portuguese to end that trade all together.[45]

The 1817 convention was a significant surrender of political sovereignty. The Portuguese government was the first to acquiesce in this regard, and the fact that Spain did so on 23 September 1817 and Holland on 4 May 1818 did nothing to mitigate the convention's negative image. France refused the right of search until 1830, and the United States until the 1860s. Fully aware of the discrediting aspect of the concessions, Palmela asserted that the reciprocity of the agreement safeguarded decorum and national independence.[46] Everyone was aware, however, that the rights were mutual in theory only, especially if, as was foreseen—and as effectively did happen—they were not exercised by the Portuguese government.

Nevertheless, the convention was inescapable, and it brought Portugal some gains. In the first place, it offered the political guarantee that Britain would remain faithful to its commitment to defend the integrity of the kingdom of Portugal. Secondly, it ensured that the money still due would be paid. But the main benefit lay in the diplomatic field. Realizing that not much more could be expected of a nation as strong as the British than 'good words and indirect satisfactions', the Portuguese ambassador stole a march on all the others powers in the regulation of the cruisers and the right of search, thereby placing himself in the vanguard of negotiations. This protected Rio de Janeiro from having to accede to more demands for the time being.[47] When in the autumn of 1818, at the Conference of Aix-la-Chapelle, Britain once again insisted on setting a final date for the abolition of the Portuguese slave trade, and also for the extension of the right of search to France, Austria, Russia and Prussia, Palmela had little difficulty in defending the status quo. Even if it did so reluctantly, Portugal subjected its merchant ships to inspection by the Royal Navy, something none of the great powers was prepared to do. The inclusion of abolition issues in the same negotiating block as the right of search embarrassed the powers and weakened the British position. At Aix-la-Chapelle the issue seemed to be stalled.[48]

Certainly Britain continued to insist through diplomatic channels that Portugal should abolish the traffic south of the equator, but it was less incisive than before. The British abolitionists had nonetheless achieved a significant partial objective, since they believed at the time that the right of search was equivalent to 'practical abolition'.[49] This confirmed the optimism shown by Palmela in the final assessment of the convention of 1817: 'It seems beyond doubt that the execution of this convention will enable us to continue the legal trade in slaves quietly until such time as His Majesty should see fit to abolish it entirely'.[50]

In the decade of 1810 Portugal was obliged to face up to the first wave of British abolitionist pressure and to make its first concessions. Over a period of seven years it went from a vague concession to abolitionism to giving up a substantial part of its slave trade. More important still: in allowing the British navy and British judges to intervene in controlling and trying offenders, the Portuguese government gave up the chance to retain for an indefinite period the 'system of doing nothing', which, in the suggestive words of the British chargé d'affaires in Rio, had been its typical attitude to the suppression of the slave trade.[51]

Even so, as the 1820s began, Portugal was the only colonial nation to maintain a legal slave trade south of the equator, an exceptional situation that was mainly the result of the game of political concessions and balancing acts in which Palmela had played a key role. In the light of the physical and political distance of a government that had set its sights firmly on its South American objectives (to the detriment of the home country), it fell almost entirely to Palmela to define the diplomatic strategy that would finally prevail. In Vienna and, more clearly, in London, with the convention of 1817, Palmela wove a legal web that it was difficult to disentangle except by force. But what should be stressed in the context of this study is that the long-drawn-out conflict between the governments of London and Rio de Janeiro over the issue of slavery, the mesh of recriminations and concessions which in this respect was the hallmark of the whole of the 1810s, finally had a marked effect on the way the question of abolition came to be viewed in Portugal.

2.3 In the Realm of Ideas: Defending Gradualism

It was in the context of British pressure, and as a result of it, that the issue of abolition began to emerge and acquire some importance in Portuguese culture. The main instruments for that expression were periodical journals, especially those that were published abroad and escaped the censor.

The *Correio Braziliense* (Brazilian Courier), launched in 1808 and published continuously in London until 1822, was the first uncensored organ of the liberal press to be distributed.[52] The editor was Hipólito da Costa, a Freemason of Brazilian origin who had emigrated to Britain and there became 'the most well-known, feared and influential Portuguese publicist of the time'.[53] The *Investigador Portuguez em Inglaterra* (the Portuguese Investigator in England) was established in 1811, sponsored and financed by the embassy in London to combat Hipólito da Costa's increasingly 'pernicious' influence on public opinion.[54] The journal's expenses were covered by the Portuguese ambassador, who, in theory, also supervised the editorial content, but it was much more open than that permitted in the censored press in Portugal and Brazil. At the end of 1813 José Liberato Freire de Carvalho—who was also a Freemason persecuted by the Inquisition—took on the editorship, pursuing a more radical liberal line (which would account for later disagreements with Palmela).[55] Liberato abandoned the *Investigador*—which would cease publication for lack of government funds—at the end of 1818, and founded the *Campeão Portuguez* (the Portuguese Champion), which came out in London until 1821 and in Lisbon in the following two years.[56] Another important outlet for liberal ideas was *O Portuguez* (The Portuguese), a journal published in London between 1814 and 1825 by the radical João Bernardo da Rocha Loureiro.

There were other, less important journals: the *Microscópio de Verdades* (the Microscope of Truths) was a title that started in London in 1814 but closed down in the following year; the *Observador Luzitano em Paris* (Lusitanian Observer in Paris), which went to only four issues in 1815, was owned and run by the economist Solano Constâncio, who would later join other editors in the publication *Annaes das Sciencias, das Artes e das Letras* (Annals of the Sciences, Arts and Letters), also published in Paris, between 1818 and 1822. Of the journals that were subject to censorship and still extant in the Biblioteca Nacional in Lisbon, only *Idade d'Ouro do Brazil* (Golden Age of Brazil) discussed the issue of the slave trade. The journal was published in Bahia between 1811 and 1821 by Father Inácio de Macedo and seems to have had a considerable impact on the local population.

Liberal pamphlets had few subscribers—around 500 for the best-known ones—but they were passed from hand to hand, were read in Portugal and Brazil and were of prime importance in shaping the opinions of the educated elites. The impact of these publications can be gauged by the concern they raised in government circles. As Palmela said, titles such as the *Correio Braziliense* and *O Portuguez* had 'an influence and a public importance which it would be useless to deny'.[57] Palmela even managed to have Castlereagh boycott the *Correio Braziliense*, and tried unsuccessfully to get the British authorities to expel the editor of *O Portuguez*.[58] These and other journals were confiscated on several occasions by the Portuguese authorities.

An analysis of the press at the beginning of the century shows no change in relation to the earlier pattern of silence. Until 1812, with occasional exceptions, the question of slavery was voluntarily censored: editors understood, more or less, the sensitive nature of the issue. This stands out plainly from a study of the uncensored overseas press: neither the *Correio Braziliense* nor the *Investigador Portuguez em Inglaterra*, the only publications at the time, contained any substantive coverage of the issue of abolition before the seizing of Portuguese slaving ships off the African coast. The *Correio Braziliense* itself recognized that its initial lack of interest was deliberate, and explained it by the sensitivity and difficulty of the subject matter.[59]

In so far as the discussion emerged as a result of outside pressure and subsequently fluctuated according to variations in that pressure, nationalism immediately and strongly permeated most opinions, giving them a generally uniform tone. Behind the veil of nationalist rhetoric, however, it is possible to glimpse not only two different ways of viewing abolition, but also the fact that a kind of contraction of the ideological spectrum enabled those two viewpoints to come together, giving rise to an almost uniform view.

2.3.1 A Time of Contraction

Bishop Azeredo Coutinho's pamphlets were the last unabashed apologies for the slave trade. In the realm of ideas, the most interesting characteristic of the decade of 1810 is the disappearance of the ideology of slavery, or, rather, its dissimulation in tolerationist arguments. That dissimulation is proved by the persistence of pro-slavery concepts, in particular those of the lesser evil and the inherent barbarity of the African, in much of the decade's tolerationist discourse. This dissimulation produced two varieties of tolerationism: the sincere and the dissembled.

The notion that the ideology of slavery merged into tolerationism is essential for understanding attitudes in the 1810s and after. We should not lose sight of the fact that, with the rise of the theory of natural rights, there were few in Europe who dared to postulate the justice of slavery and, because of this, pro-slavery ideology tended to be dissembled in tolerationism. This happened throughout the Western world, and of course in Portugal as well, as we shall see in more detail below.

In 1819, in the journal *Annaes das Sciencias, das Artes e das Letras*, Solano Constâncio made some remarks on a work called *From Cape Coast to Ashantee*, by T. E. Bowditch, a British naturalist who had recently visited the African interior. Constâncio began by postulating the existence of a Portuguese system of relating to the Negro, a system he summed up as the 'spirit of gentleness and fraternity' with which Portugal generally treated indigenous peoples. While some writers regarded Africans as animals whom nature had destined for slavery, the age-old Portuguese system accepted as a principle that Negroes were 'men like the white men', and could be educated.[60] The writer then sought to show that the right way to abolition lay precisely in the application of the Portuguese system, and not in abolition in the British style. And why? First, there was the state of barbarism and superstition of the inhabitants of Africa (a condition that had existed long before the development of the slave trade). Basing himself on Bowditch's accounts, Constâncio stated that in the kingdom of Ashanti there were frequent human sacrifices. From here, he engaged with the issue of abolition, deeming most of the prisoners to be of no use to the Negro kingdoms. Since it was not possible to channel them to the Americas, they were therefore barbarically murdered. He thus concluded that there was no gain for humanity to be achieved by suppressing the traffic, which Britain was trying so hard to do under the pretext of philanthropy:

> If then, instead of stopping the purchase of Negroes on the coast of Africa, a system were to be established whereby, in saving them from a certain death, or a possibly even worse fate, we were to reconcile the need which America has for hands with the duty of humanity, and all nations were to adopt a system suited to the character and habits of the Negro, getting him used to a not excessive burden of work and giving him the means one day to improve his condition, then in that case the extraction of men from Africa could be a remarkable benefit for the men thus sold, and for the industry and commerce of the countries to which they had been transported. ... it would be easier for Britain to persuade, or even oblige other nations to treat their slaves better, and to give them a certain portion of liberty little by little ... than to prevent the horrible slaughter which the black nations of Africa have since time immemorial inflicted on their fellow-creatures—a slaughter which, although much older than the commerce of slaves itself, would grow even more with the abolition of this trade.[61]

There were three fundamental aspects to Constâncio's tolerationism—the inherent barbarity of the Negro, the failure of the British abolitionist method and the appropriateness of the Portuguese civilizing system. Alongside improvement in the institutions of slavery, he argued for the continuation of the traffic as the lesser evil. He was an apologist for a progressive methodology, as against the abrupt British method. If we ignore the idea of the failure of British suppression—something that could be diagnosed in 1819, but which naturally was not yet known in the early years of the struggle against the slave trade, we can see that this line of reasoning was also adopted by journals such as *Idade d'Ouro do Brazil, Observador Luzitano em Paris, Microscópio de Verdades* and, on occasion, the *Investigador Portuguez em Inglaterra*. As a general rule, this basic pattern of support for maintaining the institutions of slavery emerged out of a range of mental associations that sought to reinforce it, and not only drew on ideas that were already present in Azeredo Coutinho, but also accepted indefinite gradualism and sought to safeguard national honour—and this was a novelty.

The tolerationist press disparaged British abolitionism in various ways. One of them was to classify it as a passing fad, something which, by definition, was ephemeral.[62] Another way of belittling it, which converged with the critique of telescopic philanthropy, involved portraying abolitionism as excessive and misplaced social concern; to achieve this effect it was sufficient to relativize the inhumanity of the traffic, comparing it with other situations of oppression judged to be equally distressing. The slaves in Brazil were said to be 'much happier' than British sailors or Bonaparte's soldiers.[63] At their worst, comparisons of this sort could degenerate into manoeuvres of ideological reversal. The *Idade d'Ouro do Brazil*, for example, published a very detailed description of the captivity of Christian prisoners in Algiers, setting out the inhuman conditions under which they lived, worked and died. The editor accordingly called on all Christian nations to attack Algiers and put an end to the slavery of the whites. It is significant that a journal which had made the appeal to the emotions seem ridiculous in the case of the Negro slave should resort to tragic tones to give a detailed portrait of the captivity of Christians in North Africa. But it was even more significant that, in his remarks about reports on the situation in Algiers, the editor should refer to the Moors repeatedly as just 'Africans'.[64] Beyond a diversionary manoeuvre or a simple dilution by means of comparison, this was a true inverting of positions, by which Africa was shown to be enslaving the Christians, and so the scales were even. *O Investigador Portuguez em Inglaterra* (now under the direction of José Liberato) made this scheme clearer still: 'From the south of Africa the Europeans transport numberless *Negro* slaves; the Africans transport numberless *white* slaves to North Africa. The first cause British humanity to grieve; the second, despite the fact that they are white as they are ..., evoke not even one tear of commiseration'.[65] The Algerian theme was exploited by all the journals reviewed here, until such time as the British and Dutch squadrons attacked Algiers and imposed a treaty aimed at ending the slavery of whites.

The most frequent and the most effective way to disparage abolitionism was through an appeal to the idea of 'suspect philanthropy', an idea that was full of negative connotations regarding British political deception and manipulation and evoked a whole recent past history of Anglo-

Portuguese disagreements (and, more remotely, the old idea that foreigners were progressively weakening the empire). It was conventional wisdom for all Portuguese publicists that the diplomatic manoeuvrings of the Foreign Office aimed at ending the export of slaves from Africa were due to false humanity, and were a cover for other, shameful purposes. By imposing the abolition of the slave trade on all colonial nations, the British were seeking nothing more than to ensure their own profit, their dominion over Africa and the ruin of rival colonial powers.[66]

It was, of course, argued that it was necessary to resist such false philanthropy. First of all, it was necessary on strictly economic grounds: a shortage of Negroes would be the ruin of Brazil, it would deprive Portugal, which was so dependent on Brazilian prosperity, it would lead to the collapse of industry and trade, to the decline of the navy and, in short order, to hunger for thousands of families. But, in addition to all the economic considerations, it was also necessary to resist the British false philanthropy for reasons of honour and patriotism. The persistent view was that it would be deeply humiliating to yield to foreign demands. The Portuguese government knew the laws of humanity and would know precisely how to reconcile them with the national interest without moral tutelage from Britain.[67]

Resistance was therefore based on economic reasons and on national pride. But what resistance could be offered in practical terms? Even if some publicists suggested resorting to arms, such proposals were rare in contemporary notions regarding the abolition of the slave trade. In general terms, not only was Britain's power acknowledged, but so was the moral force of the new philanthropic ideas and the corresponding difficulty of facing up to them directly. A vague gradualism, postponing the solution to a future and undefined date, therefore emerged as a suitable defensive strategy, capable of professing allegiance to the new philanthropy, safeguarding national honour and avoiding upsets to the colonial system. As was said in the *Microscópio de Verdades*, it was necessary 'to abolish very gradually' and in accordance with the Portuguese will and at Portugal's convenience, and never at the pace imposed by the British.[68]

The gradualist option was unanimously promoted in the press in the first half of the decade of 1810. But even more revealing was the fact that the whole ideological scheme put forward by the press was adopted by the slave merchants themselves (or by those who spoke for them). While publicly proclaiming their philanthropic feelings, which dubbed the traffic 'unseemly' and 'offensive to natural law and to the rights of Man', and at the same time seeing that abolition would be a 'healthy result of the century's enlightenment', the slave traders of Bahia, for example, protested against the suspect philanthropy of the British and, taking shelter behind the national interest and national honour, asked for another 'twenty years' for their business, 'a slow and lingering pace' for abolitionist policies, rather than the 'mutilating and subversive blow' of the established rules.[69]

To sum up, those who wanted to continue the slave trade had totally abandoned the straight defence of slavery and, having accepted the principle of abolition in theory, became apologists of gradualism. Their arguments came closest to the boldest version of tolerationism, draining it of its pro-abolitionist virtues. In fact, and because it was a complacent and ambiguous modus operandi, gradualism was able to operate both as a cautious guarantee of abolition and as an attempt to tame the abolitionist pressure coming from abroad: that is, as a strategy for the perpetuation of slavery. It was an open invitation to duplicity, and through it tolerationism entered into a realm of misunderstandings where there was room for all, from the closet slaver to the cautious anti-slavery campaigner. These two positions coexisted in the camouflage of an ideology that covered them both, in such a way that, if one were to base oneself solely on the press of the first half of the decade of 1810, it would be extremely difficult to make the distinction between those who sincerely wished for the gradual shutting down of the traffic and those who held on to that banner merely in order to procrastinate. It is highly significant that until 1815 tolerationist thinking had been accepted and carried by all the journals that broached the issue. Of course, the opinions expressed in the *Correio Braziliense* and in *O Portuguez* were not always in point-by-point agreement with the chain of ideas outlined above. But, even if one element were missing, they provided all the rest of the ideological panoply.

In effect, and like their fellow journalists, both Hipólito da Costa and Rocha Loureiro saw in British abolitionist pressure an interference that was offensive to national dignity and derived from a hypocritical philanthropy; on the basis of that assessment, they at various times expressed an opinion on the absolute need to resist Britain's hidden interests, in order to preserve the colonies and safeguard national honour. The *Correio Braziliense* even advocated reprisals against the actions of the Royal Navy.[70] The *Correio Braziliense* and *O Portuguez* likewise supported the idea that abolition would imply the collapse of Brazil, and that it should therefore be resisted. It is true that neither of these journals argued in favour of the slave trade as the lesser evil for the African. Both regarded the activity of slaving as inhuman and unjust. However, they rarely explained how inhuman the conditions of slavery were, and they almost never made any emotional appeal on behalf of the slave. The lack of an emotional appeal is, moreover, a hallmark of all the Portuguese press at the time. The type of argument held dear by the philanthropists of the age, with the use of negative adjectives and a strong appeal to the reader's sensitivities, was rare in Portugal at the beginning of the nineteenth century: as a rule, the issue was broached in a general way, without going into detail. While such discursive omission is not surprising in *Idade d'Ouro do Brazil* and the *Microscópio de Verdades*—for which the slave trade was not exactly an evil—it is significant that in journals that were supposedly hostile to the slave trade, like the *Correio Braziliense* and *O Portuguez*, appeals to the emotions and negative references, where they existed, tended to be attenuated by means of comparisons to other cases that were held to be equally horrible.[71]

We should note once again that, at the time, comparativism and the critique of telescopic philanthropy were two of the methods used everywhere by those who favoured the continuation of the slave trade. As one of them wrote, 'humanity has no need to visit distant regions'.[72] There was therefore a tendency, even among journalists who argued on the basis of the iniquity of the traffic, to dilute the problem of the slave's suffering and indirectly therefore to devalue abolitionism. *O Portuguez* even managed to devalue it directly by describing it as merely quixotic.[73]

In sum, up to 1815 there were nuances in the ideological framework conveyed by all the periodicals analysed: tendencies varied according to the stressing of certain ideas. But there was no fundamental opposition between those tendencies, which all converged in a defence of gradualism. Up to the mid-1810s no journal sought the immediate or even short-term abolition of the slave trade, which was judged vital for the survival of Brazil. As the *Correio Braziliense* stated, 'slaves are a fictitious people, of little value, and dangerous; but even so, they are better than nothing'.[74] In the same vein, the journal refrained from criticizing the Rio government for its indecision over the slave trade, and simply hoped that progress would bring about 'a gradual and prudent reform in this area'.[75] The uniformity of positions in the Portuguese press at the time suggests that the British pressure had narrowed the ideological spectrum, the result not only of the dissimulation of the ideology of slavery in tolerationism, but also of a certain convergence in the different forms of tolerationism, giving rise to an almost unanimous pattern of argument. National honour and gradualism were its warhorses.

2.3.2 *A Time of Distension*

The narrowing of the ideological spectrum eased only in the second half of the 1810s, when the *Correio Braziliense*, *O Portuguez* and later the *Investigador Portuguez em Inglaterra* began to adopt a different line, one that was clearly para-abolitionist: it advocated a direct condemnation of the traffic and of slavery itself, on philosophical, economic, social and political grounds.

In mid-1814, around the time when the Treaty of Paris was signed, the *Correio Braziliense* touched lightly on some ideas that pointed to the end of the traffic and to the gradual emancipation of the slaves. It was to develop these ideas more fully late in 1815.[76] A similar and progressively stronger argument appeared in *O Portuguez* from March 1815 onwards, and *O Investigador Portuguez em Inglaterra* moved along similar lines in a memoir published in January 1817 (when Palmela was installed in the London embassy).[77] Other frankly anti-slavery views appeared in 1820 in pamphlets by António Sequeira, a Coimbra student, and by Francisco Soares Franco, professor of medicine at the University of Coimbra.[78] In general terms, the arguments which emerged clearly and publicly from these texts were based on the idea that the prohibition of the 'odious commerce' would inevitably be imposed from abroad. It was therefore necessary to adapt to the new realities.

Late in 1815, the *Correio Braziliense* acknowledged that, in the light of France having recently decreed the abolition of the slave trade and the fact that Spain would almost certainly yield to British humanitarian pressure, the Portuguese government would be isolated on the international stage and so had to prepare for the 'inevitable blow'. Hipólito da Costa therefore dared to address his fellow citizens in terms that he himself described as 'quite strong', encouraging them to abolish the slave trade and to bring about the gradual emancipation of the slaves.[79] *O Portuguez* also repeatedly underlined the unavoidable nature of abolition. Portugal still retained the right to trade in slaves, but the British would not rest in their fight to put an end to the institutions of slavery and there was no way out of this. Consequently, the Rio government was advised to prepare for the inevitable: the slave trade could not last much longer.[80]

The recognition and acceptance of the fact that abolition was inevitable contributed widely to removing the negative connotations attached to 'suspect philanthropy' which all journalists had associated with British abolitionism. In specific cases, para-abolitionist proposals might even seem to be entirely devoid of references to outside political pressure. But even when they continued to mention it and when the idea of 'suspect philanthropy' persisted in the new patterns of discourse, the stressing now lay not on the need to resist it but on accepting it: British actions were perhaps self-interested, but they would have a beneficial effect.[81]

With the laying to rest of the British ghost, there was also a reversal of the ideological role of defending national honour. Given the inevitability of abolition by the decision of a concert of nations, it was imperative to act in order to preserve Portuguese dignity. The sentiment now was, at times, one of shame and embarrassment at the protection the Rio government gave the slave trade.[82]

The theory that the prohibition of the slave trade would inevitably cause the collapse of Brazil—which the tolerationism of 1812–15 had so insisted upon—was also toned down in the columns of the *Correio Braziliense* and *O Portuguez* after the Congress of Vienna. In some cases it was even overturned, the notion of economic disaster being associated with the continuation of the traffic in slaves rather than its end. Hipólito da Costa gave a clear warning towards the end of 1815: if Brazil tried to oppose the anti-slave trade opinion of all the powers or if it were to fail to provide in good time for the effects of abolition, industry and settlement would fall off everywhere.[83] The writer of the memoir published in the *Investigador Portuguez em Inglaterra* went even further, condemning the importation of Africans not only because he believed in the superiority of free labour, but because he judged the purchase of slaves to be equivalent to a lottery. The capital tied up with the purchase of a Negro was lost when he died, so the operation could only be profitable if each slave left descendants. But in this case there would be a disproportionate increase in the number of blacks, and white insecurity would grow. The memoir added that, contrary to what was widely propagated, the economic effects of abolition would be far from catastrophic.[84]

As an alternative to the slaves coming from Africa, these writers invariably advocated the importation of machines, and encouraged the immigration of Europeans. The *Correio Braziliense,* which in June 1814 had argued for the continuation of the traffic as being 'better than nothing', now envisaged 'no difficulty' in transferring from Europe to Brazil entire colonies of useful and already civilized people.[85] The argument for European immigration as an alternative to the transport of Africans was often reinforced by feelings of social discord between black and white. Unlike slaving, which had traditionally claimed for the trade in Negroes a civilizing function, which would integrate the barbarian African people into civilized society—a function that would in part provide ideological justification for its continuation—para-abolitionism sought to connect its political programme to a plan for the whitening of Brazilian society:

> Let us suppose … that Brazil needs to import men; does it not have fine men in Europe, and industrious men in China? Does barbarous, uneducated, depopulated Africa have to be the market where we supply ourselves? Black colour and the hideous, or anti-European, features will perhaps be the only attractions and the only recommendations of the caste we wish to amalgamate with ourselves.[86]

The *Correio Braziliense,* expressing satisfaction at the anticipated arrival of some Swiss immigrants in Brazil, argued in similar fashion: colour was an 'insurmountable obstacle' to the assimilation of Negroes, whereas miscegenation among Europeans was easy, and would form 'a truly Brazilian people in every sense'.[87] In the second half of the 1810s acceptance that the slave trade would be abolished thus seemed to be closely tied to the idea of racial uniformity, an idea which, it should be said, did not necessarily lead to segregationism. António Sequeira, who was also in favour of European immigration and of providing incentives for the local inhabitants to work, as ways of overcoming the foreseeable lack of manpower, and who also sought to purify the racial spectrum, argued for miscegenation as a way of diluting people's blackness:

> If there is a mixture of the black race with the white, in the second or third generation they will become whites, then Brazil in less than 100 years will have all white inhabitants, because if also there are marriages of whites with natives, the copper colour will come to an end; so if it is desired to hasten the extinction of the two races, why not give prizes to white men who marry black women or natives in the first or second generation.

In his sociological and genetic folly Sequeira went as far as to suggest that men over twenty-five should not enjoy citizenship rights if they were not married, and to recommend that permission be sought from Rome for priests to marry in the Portuguese dominions.[88]

Soares Franco's approach was very similar. The doctor held that Negroes suffered and were to be pitied, but they were also dangerous people against whose evil-doings it would be necessary to provide, taking measures 'to reduce the Portuguese nation in America to a single nation'. The main problem lay in Negroes and their descendants and, in order to deal with it, it would be necessary to resort to European immigration and to wipe out 'half-breeds', through administrative control of biological reproduction. Like Sequeira, Soares Franco assumed that racial blending would progressively dissolve the dark tone of the skin. Given that the 'half-breeds'—who, in his terminology, were merely those who had one African ancestor—would retain 'only half, or less than half, of the African stamp', if subsequently they were to marry into the white race, they would produce children of a less 'tarnished' colour, and if the third generation were the product of marriage with whites, the 'African stamp' would be lost altogether. There was therefore a need to stop the slave trade and enforce strict prohibition of marriage between 'half-breeds' and Africans, so that all Negroes would be 'decanted into the white race'. Soares Franco regarded the option of celibacy as a dangerous liberty, and accordingly desired that during the first fifty years of what he called 'the re-establishment of Brazil', men should not be allowed to have jobs or receive honours unless they were first married.[89]

But the radical, indeed almost despotic, nature of the demographic policies advocated by Sequeira and Soares Franco went counter to the apparent trend among para-abolitionists of the time, for whom the promotion of European immigration was in no way compatible with despotism. On the contrary, such immigration would be a solution to the problem of Brazilian settlement only if it were accompanied by firm guarantees of civil and religious freedom, which would persuade the world that the authorities and institutions of Brazil were welcoming and liberal. It is important to note that one of the engines of this first awakening of abolitionism and para-abolitionism in Portugal was political liberalism. In the second half of the 1810s, slavery began frequently to be portrayed in the liberal periodicals published in London—except for the *Investigador Portuguez em Inglaterra*, the embassy's journal—as being in fundamental opposition to the then dawning social and political freedoms. That theory was, as it were, the pinnacle of an argument that, in simplified form, can be summed up as follows: the abolition of the slave trade was inevitable (being imposed from abroad); the solution for mitigating the consequences of that abolition lay in large part in encouraging white immigration; and this in turn required that the political system be liberalized. For *O Portuguez*, for example, immigration could only be encouraged if Brazil attracted the people of Europe, 'who are afraid to settle there by reason of their hatred and fear of the despotism of the government'.[90] The central message was therefore clear: the end of the slave trade would not be a catastrophe for Brazil, the solution was at hand, and involved, as a last resort, the liberalization of the political system.

To reinforce these ideas all newspapers resorted on occasion to the usual stock of moral principles against slavery, invoking the philosophers and seeking to demonstrate that slavery could not be of use either to the slave, who did not work by reason of virtue, or to the master, who in contact with slaves acquired all their inherent vices.[91] At the beginning of the 1820s the *Correio Braziliense* even argued for the abolition of slavery itself, because it was thought to set a bad example to children.[92] The memoir, published in the *Investigador Portuguez em Inglaterra* some years before, had condemned slavery in religious terms, bringing in the threat of divine punishment in the manner of the early North American and British abolitionists like Benezet and Granville Sharp: 'can a nation consider itself free when it daily sets aside the firm conviction that freedom is a gift of God, and that it cannot be violated without arousing his indignation? That is why I tremble for my motherland when I remember that God is just and that his justice never sleeps'.[93]

The para-abolitionist arguments of the second half of the 1810s were meant to reassure the slavers and planters facing change, and were designed to help them accept, in the short term, what everyone knew to be inevitable. But they were in essence borderline arguments, halfway between tolerationism and abolitionism. *O Portuguez* even recommended to the government that, at some time in the future, it should abolish the slave trade 'of its own accord', but such encouragement of independent initiative was rare.[94] As a rule, proponents of abolition adopted a passive attitude, hoping that the measure would be forced upon them by Britain. The only openly abolitionist texts of this whole period are the pamphlets by António Sequeira and Soares Franco. Sequeira even wished for slavery itself to be abolished 'forthwith', with compensation being given to the masters and subsidies to the freed Negroes so that they could marry and settle down.[95] Soares Franco, having shown that the slave trade ran counter to religion and politics, asked that the importation of any more slaves be rigorously forbidden, the sole exception being for continued imports of those required for work in the mines (such imports being limited to just one Brazilian port).[96]

For Portugal in the second half of the 1810s, the arguments advanced by Sequeira and Soares Franco seemed extreme. In addition, para-abolitionist ideas in journals and diplomatic notes were rarely consistent, and even less insistent. Only two months after it had first argued in favour of abolition, *O Portuguez* protested at the fact that the Portuguese plenipotentiaries in Vienna had negotiated an immediate ban on the slave trade north of the equator instead of stipulating 'only a gradual abolition'.[97] In 1818 the *Correio Braziliense* issued a violent diatribe against the concession of rights of search and the setting up of mixed commissions for trying the slavers quickly.[98] Such contradictions show the fickle nature of para-abolitionism, which contracted and distended according to the degree of foreign interference, and tended to revert to a position close to obstruction when confronted with concrete measures. Portuguese abolitionism was also inconsistent: Soares Franco himself, who some months after publishing his pamphlet was elected a deputy to the Cortes Constituintes (Constituent Assembly) of 1821, and later to the Câmara dos Deputados (Chamber of Deputies) of 1826, took no advantage of this opportunity to give material form to his confessed opposition to slavery—on the contrary, he made a point of remaining silent when this issue was discussed. It should be added that there were only a limited number of writings in favour of abolishing the slave trade. While newspapers did give significant space to these arguments, they only did so for a limited time and, in the final analysis, those who actually expressed their opinion and feelings about 'the cause of all humanity' in public were few. At the end of 1822 Hipólito da Costa expressed surprise that 'all the writers of Brazil' were still silent on an 'issue of such importance'.[99] But the explanation was clear: mutism was still the best strategy for maintaining the status quo.

In any event, and despite the inconsistencies and hesitations, the second half of the 1810s saw the public dissemination of abolitionist or quasi-abolitionist ideas. They emerged at this specific time because sincere tolerationism adjusted to the changes resulting from Vienna and the changeable nature of British pressure. Vienna had established the universal principle of abolition, but it had also stipulated that it would fall to each state to determine when the 'infamous commerce' should cease. In this way it established a break in the pace of abolition imposed by Britain, and it was this hiatus, which was expected to be a short one, that those who effectively accepted abolition sought to take advantage of. The arguments found in some journals after 1815 were the public version of what, in restricted form, we find in Palmela's notes, advising the government to start preparing 'the minds' for the 'final and indispensable end to that trade'.[100]

Because the change was not a radical one, the new arguments put forward in *O Portuguez* and in the *Correio Braziliense* did not raise insuperable barriers between tolerationism and abolitionism, all the more so because ideologies, being adaptable and elastic, made it possible continuously to dissemble one's intentions by adopting the propositions and imagery cherished by opposing ideologies. At the beginning of the 1820s the timid para-abolitionist programme of the London-based journalists was partially incorporated into an obstructive tolerationism, which was constantly being revised and updated. This much was already clear in a pamphlet by Maciel da Costa, a future minister of independent Brazil, which was published in Coimbra in 1821. As with the writings of the *Correio Braziliense*, the article was aimed at reassuring the planters, who were concerned at the news of the coming end of the slave trade to Brazil, but that was not its only purpose. It was also aimed at telling leaders and constitutionalists who had emerged from the recent Portuguese liberal revolution, and who might entertain abolitionist whims, what were the acceptable limits of their future reforms.

Maciel da Costa argued in favour of gradual abolition only and, in doing so, he once again updated the obstructive aspect of tolerationism, adapting it to the most recent para-abolitionist proposals. He began by stating that the traffic was beneficial to the Africans, despite the fact that this went contrary to European notions of humanity: they would gain from being transferred 'from their burning sands' to the 'wonderful climate of Brazil', where they would be employed in the 'gentle labour of agriculture'. It was also advantageous in that it allowed Negroes to be instructed in the duties of religion, an undeniable mark of progress for them. The philanthropists tended to exaggerate the evils faced by slaves on the American plantations and to tone down or forget how they suffered in Africa. As a general rule the masters exercised paternal care in the handling of their slaves, they did not require them to work beyond their strength, and rewarded them with freedom if they behaved well.[101] In the final part of his work, in a chapter which argued that Portuguese Africa should become a Brazilian agricultural colony as soon as the slave trade was abolished, Maciel da Costa recommended that care should be taken to prevent the colonial authorities from becoming so enthusiastic for the new philanthropic ideas that they liberated the Africans:

> Is it not of precious benefit to these miserable savages, who have no safe haven, no personal safety, who are the victims of the whims of their black rulers and continuously involved in bloody wars of human carnage, to bring them together, teach them, dress them, feed them? It is here that we should start out on the grand task of civilizing them, and not treat them as if they were European peasants .... There is a huge gap between the Polish serfs and the barbarous Africans and Americans. *Medio tutissimus ibis*.[102]

Within this rationale, which was broadly pro-slavery, the author proceeded to plant ideas that had recently been put forward by the para-abolitionists, from the argument in favour of free labour to the idea that slaves were a threat to the security of the state. For all these reasons, the slave trade should cease, but not 'without preparation and within a reasonable time frame', under pain of ruining agriculture and business. On this particular point, Maciel da Costa was vague: he did not say when the importation of Negroes should cease, but implicitly he pointed to the long term. The expression 'twenty years'—a number that was dear to nineteenth-century supporters of slavery—appears on several occasions in his pamphlet as the minimum period of time countenanced. Meanwhile, and whatever the time frame set, the number of slaves imported annually should be in the range of 25,000 to 30,000 so as to avoid irreparable disequilibrium in Brazil.[103]

Throughout the 1810s, and under British political pressure, ideas on the issue of the abolition of the slave trade came out of the silence and changed as a result of that pressure. But abolitionism did not establish itself in Portugal during this decade. The fact that partial abolition of the 'odious commerce' had been imposed through external political pressure did allow a nationalist discourse to emerge, in which both pro-slavery and tolerationist arguments were interwoven, minimizing their differences under the cover of a defence of national honour and the national interest. The linkages between pro-slavery and tolerationist arguments produced channels of extreme ambiguity, mental bridges over which it was easy to pass from one position to the other. At times of greater external pressure, those who were closer to abolitionism, and whom I have called para-abolitionists, tended to fall back on defensive positions, adopting at least in part the obstructivist tolerationist way of thinking in which the two positions merged into one. Slippage was encouraged, not just by the similarities in the phraseology, but also by the infrequent moral condemnation of the trafficker. Slavers were commonly just called 'merchants', and there was no thought that there was anything shameful in being involved in practices that had not yet been anathematized: 'what is shameful about carrying on a trade which is judged necessary for the cultivation of the kingdom of Brazil?' the *Investigador Portuguez em Inglaterra* asked (at the time it was managed by Liberato).[104]

On the other hand there was still the adaptability of the old pro-slavery ideology, now camouflaged in tolerationist garb. This mimetic ability of pro-slavery thinking and the corresponding inability of sincere tolerationists to shake it off by unequivocally promoting abolition account for the placid, almost homoeostatic, nature of the ideological climate in Portugal. With the exception of an isolated disagreement, there is not one trace in the Portuguese written record of the 1810s of an ideological struggle over the issue of abolition, because everyone basically shared a set of ideas that almost always culminated in a defence of gradualism. And gradualism, especially when propped up by a strong sense of national honour, was a powerful barrier to the advance of abolitionist ideas and, above all, abolitionist practice.

Notes

1. Christopher Lloyd, *The Navy and the Slave Trade. The Suppression of the African Slave Trade in the Nineteenth Century*, Frank Cass, London, 1968 (1st edition 1949), p. 61; Philip D. Curtin, *The Image of Africa. British Ideas and Action, 1780–1850*, University of Wisconsin Press, Madison, 1964, pp. 157–58. On the beginnings of the colonization of Sierra Leone and the colony's relationship with the African Institution, see Christopher Fyfe, *A History of Sierra Leone*, Oxford University Press, London, 1962, chaps. I–V.
2. In Angola, the word tumbeiro was also used to refer to the Africans who brought slaves to the coast from the interior (Joseph C. Miller, *Way of Death. Merchant Capitalism and the Angolan Slave Trade, 1730–1830*, University of Wisconsin Press, Madison, 1988, p. 314).

3. Report of the Commissioners Appointed for Investigating the State of Settlements and Governments on the Coast of Africa (Appendix A), *Parliamentary Papers*, 1811 (I used the Portuguese translation 'Relação dos Comissários Nomeados para Investigar o estado dos Estabelecimentos e Governos na Costa de Africa que têm Relação com a Escravatura', *O Investigador Portuguez em Inglaterra*, September and October 1812, pp. 393–401 and 599–605, respectively); see also Fyfe, *Sierra Leone*, pp. 105–14.
4. Linhares to Funchal, 6 March 1809, ANTT, MNE, *liv.* 566. For the complete text of the article, see José F. Borges de Castro, *Collecção dos tratados, convenções, contratos e actos públicos celebrados entre a Coroa de Portugal e as mais Potências desde 1640 até ao presente*, Imprensa Nacional, Lisbon, 1857–58, pp. 413–15.
5. Scott to the Admiralty, 4 August 1814, quoted in David Eltis, *Economic Growth and the Ending of the Transatlantic Slave Trade*, Oxford University Press, New York, 1987, p. 107.
6. Lloyd, *The Navy*, p. 62; see memorandum from John Barlow (secretary to the Admiralty) to the captains of the cruisers, 2 May 1811, in *Correio Braziliense*, September 1815, pp. 384–85.
7. Bahia was the market most affected, with 15 ships seized (see Pierre Verger, *Flux et reflux de la traite des nègres entre le golfe de Bénin et Bahia de Todos os Santos du XVIIe au XIXe siècles*, Mouton, Paris and The Hague, 1968, pp. 295–97, 321–22 and 637). For the full list of arrests in 1811–12, see *Correio Braziliense*, June 1812, p. 746.
8. Eltis, *Economic Growth*, p. 108.
9. Representations of the merchants of Bahia to the Prince Regent D. João, *O Investigador Portuguez em Inglaterra*, May 1813, p. 363.
10. Castlereagh to the Admiralty, 6 May 1813, *Correio Braziliense*, September 1815, pp. 385–86; Eltis, *Economic Growth*, p. 108. According to the list held at the Portuguese Consulate-General in London, at the beginning of 1815 the number of Portuguese slaving ships seized or otherwise harmed by the Royal Navy had risen to 34 (see *O Investigador Portuguez em Inglaterra*, March 1815, p. 141).
11. Liverpool to Funchal, 27 February 1812, ANTT, MNE, *liv.* 535.
12. Castlereagh to Funchal, 20 April 1813, ANTT, MNE, *liv.* 535.
13. Dispatch of 7 April 1812, BN, Reserved documents, *liv.* 9073.
14. Dispatch of 27 September 1813 (top secret), BN, Reserved documents, *liv.* 9074 (italics in the original).
15. Dispatch of 10 March 1813, BN, Reserved documents, *liv.* 9073.
16. Dispatch of 27 September 1813, BN, Reserved documents, *liv.* 9074.
17. Funchal to Galveias, 26 August 1813, ANTT, MNE, *cx.* 733.
18. Galveias to Funchal, 7 January 1814, in Julio Firmino Júdice Biker, *Suplemento à colecção de Tratados, Convenções, Contratos e Actos Públicos celebrados entre a Coroa de Portugal e as mais Potências desde 1640 até ao presente*, vol. XVIII, pp. 26–30.
19. Charter of 24 November 1813, in *Correio Braziliense*, March 1814, pp. 478–90.
20. See Valentim Alexandre, *Os Sentidos do Império Questão nacional e questão colonial na crise do Antigo Regime português*, Afrontamento, Porto, 1993, pp. 243–85.
21. Dispatch of 4 July 1814, BN, Reserved documents, *liv.* 9075.
22. Aguiar to Palmela, 16 June 1814, ANTT, MNE, *liv.* 47.
23. David R. Murray, *Odious Commerce: Britain, Spain and the Abolition of the Cuban Slave Trade*, Cambridge University Press, Cambridge, 1980, p. 50. It should be noted that in the meantime Sweden, under pressure from Britain, had already forbidden the trafficking of slaves on 3 March 1813, that Denmark undertook by a treaty of 14 January 1814 to cooperate with the British

in suppressing the traffic worldwide, and that Holland would ban the slave trade by an edict of 17 June 1814 (see James Bandinel, *Some Account of the Trade in Slaves from Africa, as Connected with Europe and America. From the Introduction of the Trade into Modern Europe, down to Present Time, especially with Reference to the Efforts made by the British Government for its Extinction,* Frank Cass, London, 1968, First edition 1842, pp. 132–35).

24. Reginald Coupland, *The British Anti-Slavery Movement*, Frank Cass, London, 1964 (1st edition 1933), p. 154; Murray, *Odious Commerce*, pp. 49–50; James Walvin, 'The Public Campaign in England against Slavery', in David Eltis and James Walvin (eds), *The Abolition of the Atlantic Slave Trade. Origins and Effects in Europe, Africa, and the Americas*, University of Wisconsin Press, Madison, 1981, p. 68; Seymour Drescher, 'Whose Abolition? Popular Pressure and the Ending of the British Slave Trade', *Past and Present*, 143, 1994, pp. 159 ff.
25. Drescher, 'Whose Abolition', p. 162; David Geggus, 'Haiti and the Abolitionists: Opinion, Propaganda and International Politics in Britain and France, 1804–1838', in David Richardson (ed.), *Abolition and its Aftermath. The Historical Context, 1790–1916*, Frank Cass, London, 1985, pp. 118–19.
26. See Murray, *Odious Commerce*, pp. 54–55.
27. Palmela to Aguiar, 12 November 1814, in Biker, *Suplemento*, vol. XVIII, pp. 195–96.
28. For the texts of the convention and the treaty, see Castro, *Collecção*.
29. Palmela to Funchal, 6 August 1814, ANTT, MNE, *cx.* 961 (my italics).
30. Palmela to Funchal, 17 September 1814, ANTT, MNE, *cx.* 961.
31. Palmela to Aguiar, 16 January 1815, ANTT, MNE, *liv.* 47.
32. Castro, *Collecção*, vol. V, pp. 195–201. Spain did not sign the declaration of Vienna.
33. Aguiar to the Portuguese plenipotentiaries, 15 September 1815, ANTT, MNE, *liv.* 47.
34. Aguiar to Cipriano R. Freire, 15 June 1815, in Biker, *Suplemento*, vol. XVIII, pp. 134–37.
35. On the problem of the right of search, see Serge Daget, 'Tactiques, stratégies et effets du droit de visite', in Serge Daget (ed.), *De la traite à l'esclavage*, Tome II, CRHMA/Société Française d'Histoire d'Outre-Mer, Nantes, 1988, pp. 343–58; see also Leslie Bethell, *The Abolition of the Brazilian Slave Trade. Britain, Brazil and the Slave Trade Question (1807–1869)*, Cambridge University Press, Cambridge, 1970, pp. 17–19.
36. Castlereagh to Cipriano R. Freire, 9 January 1816, ANTT, MNE, *liv.* 536.
37. *O Investigador Portuguez em Inglaterra*, March and July 1816, pp. 71 and 115, respectively.
38. António Saldanha da Gama, *Memoria historica e política sobre o commercio da escravatura, entregue no dia 2 de Novembro de 1816 ao Conde Capo d'Istria, Ministro do Imperador da Russia*, Imprensa Nacional, Lisbon, 1880, p. 37. On the seizing of the Bahia ships see Verger, *Flux et reflux*, p. 638.
39. Alexandre, *Os Sentidos do império*, p. 331 ff.
40. Palmela to Aguiar, 10 October 1816, ANTT, MNE, *cx.* 464.
41. Ibid.
42. Palmela to Barca (Araújo de Azevedo), 11 and 19 February 1817, ANTT, MNE, *cx.* 464.
43. On the manner in which the commissions operated, see Leslie Bethell, 'The Mixed Commissions for the Suppression of the Transatlantic Slave Trade in the Nineteenth Century', *Journal of African History*, 7, 1, 1966, pp. 79–93.
44. J.J. de Andrade e Silva, *Collecção Chronologica da legislação portuguesa*, Lisbon, 1859, pp. 607–09.
45. *O Portuguez*, February 1818, p. 278.
46. Palmela to Barca, 10 January 1817, ANTT, MNE, *cx.* 464.

47. Palmela to Barca, 10 February 1817, ANTT, MNE, *cx.* 464.
48. Castlereagh to Bathurst, 23 November 1818, *Correio Braziliense*, April 1819, p. 364.
49. Lloyd, *The Navy*, p. 45.
50. Palmela to Barca, 29 July 1817, ANTT, MNE, *cx.* 464.
51. See Bethell, *The Abolition of the Brazilian*, p. 15.
52. For useful references on journals published in Portugal, see Innocêncio Francisco da Silva, *Diccionario Bibliographico Portuguez*, various volumes, Imprensa Nacional, Lisbon, 1860, and the manuscript of J. Silva Pereira, 'Diccionário jornalístico Portuguez', which is to be found in the Lisbon Academy of Sciences; J. Silva Pereira also published a list of periodical publications, *O jornalismo portuguez. Resenha chronológica de todos os periódicos portuguezes impressos e publicados no Reino e no estrangeiro, desde o meiado do século XVII até à morte do saudoso Rei Senhor D. Luis I, bem como dos jornais em língua estrangeira publicados em Portugal durante o mesmo tempo*, Lisbon, 1895. For a description of some publications and for an assessment of the significance of the periodicals, see José Tengarrinha, *História da imprensa periódica portuguesa*, Lisbon, undated; specifically for the titles of the period under study, see also C. Rizzini, *Hipólito da Costa e o Correio Braziliense*, Companhia Editora Nacional, São Paulo, 1957.
53. Rizzini, *Hipólito*, p. 26.
54. Funchal to Linhares, 5 January 1812 (top secret), BN, Reserved documents, *liv.* 9072.
55. Palmela to Aguiar, 5 January 1817, ANTT, MNE, *cx.* 464.
56. For information on José Liberato Freire de Carvalho see his *Memórias da vida de José Liberato Freire de Carvalho*, Assírio e Alvim, Lisbon, 1982 (1st edition 1855).
57. Palmela to Aguiar, 5 January 1817, 16 July 1817, ANTT, MNE, *cx.* 464.
58. Palmela to Barca, 16 July 1817, ANTT, MNE, *cx.* 464; see also Rizzini, *Hipólito*, p. 30.
59. *Correio Braziliense*, March 1814, pp. 607–08.
60. *Annaes das Sciencias, das Artes e das Letras*, V, 1819, pp. 157–58.
61. Ibid., pp. 161–62.
62. *Idade d'Ouro do Brazil*, 1 November 1814. For similar observations see *Microscópio de Verdades*, no. 2, 1814, p. 85; *Observador Luzitano em Paris*, March 1815, p. 410; *O Investigador Portuguez em Inglaterra*, September 1813, pp. 381 ff.
63. *Microscópio de Verdades*, no. 2, 1814, pp. 84–85.
64. *Idade d'Ouro do Brazil*, 1 October 1816.
65. *O Investigador Potuguez em Inglaterra*, July 1814, pp. 145–46 (italics in the original); see also the edition of July 1816, pp. 117–18.
66. *Idade d'Ouro do Brazil*, 6 December 1814; for identical articles see *Microscópio de Verdades*, no. 7, 1815, p. 105; *Observador Luzitano em Paris*, February 1815, pp. 176–77; *O Investigador Portuguez em Inglaterra*, July 1814, p. 147.
67. See, for example, *Observador Luzitano em Paris*, February 1815, pp. 188–89.
68. *Microscópio de Verdades*, no. 2, 1814, p. 87; see also *Idade d'Ouro do Brazil*, 1 November 1814.
69. First representation by the merchants of Bahia, *O Investigador Portuguez em Inglaterra*, May 1813, pp. 370–71.
70. *Correio Braziliense*, July 1814, p. 914. *O Investigador Portuguez em Inglaterra* was the only journal to get close to the British abolitionist position at this time, probably on account of Funchal, who, as Liberato put it, 'entertained himself writing his articles on things Portuguese and on politics, under assumed names' (Carvalho, *Memórias*, p. 81).
71. See, for example, *O Portuguez*, June 1814, pp. 149–51 (for a comparison of the trade with certain habits of rural England).

72. See Roger Anstey, *The Atlantic Slave Trade and British Abolition, 1760–1810*, Macmillan Press, London, 1975, p. 294.
73. *O Portuguez*, July 1814, p. 239; see also *O Investigador Portuguez em Inglaterra*, July 1814, p. 144.
74. *Correio Braziliense*, June 1814, p. 914.
75. Ibid., March 1814, p. 609.
76. Ibid., December 1815, pp. 735–39.
77. *O Portuguez*, March 1815, pp. 398–448. *O Investigador Portuguez em Inglaterra*, January 1817, p. 245 ff.; all indications point to Palmela as having encouraged the publication of the article (supposedly written in Rio de Janeiro in mid-1815), given the similarity of some of the opinions expressed in it and those which he himself was putting forward in his official correspondence.
78. António d'Oliva de Sousa Sequeira, *Projecto para o estabelecimento político do Reino-Unido de Portugal, Brasil e Algarves*, Coimbra, 1821; and Francisco Soares Franco, *Ensaio sobre os melhoramentos de Portugal e Brazil*, book 4, Lisbon, 1820.
79. *Correio Braziliense*, December 1815, pp. 735–39.
80. *O Portuguez*, December 1817, pp. 121–22.
81. Ibid., June 1817, p. 840.
82. Ibid., March 1815, p. 405.
83. *Correio Braziliense*, December 1815, p. 738.
84. *O Investigador Portuguez em Inglaterra*, January 1817, p. 252.
85. *Correio Braziliense*, December 1815, pp. 737–38.
86. *O Investigador Portuguez em Inglaterra*, p. 260. For the relationship between abolitionism and hostility to Negroes, and for the rarity of that hostility in Europe (in contrast to its frequency in the Americas), see Seymour Drescher, 'The Ending of the Slave Trade and the Evolution of European Scientific Racism', *Social Science History*, 14, 3, 1990, p. 416 ff.
87. *Correio Braziliense*, April 1819, p. 429 (my italics).
88. Sequeira, *Projecto*, pp. 51–53.
89. Franco, *Ensaio*, pp. 8, 18–19 and 21.
90. *O Portuguez*, February 1818, p. 278.
91. *Correio Braziliense*, December 1815, p. 738.
92. Ibid., November 1822, pp. 574–76.
93. *O Investigador Portuguez em Inglaterra*, January 1817, p. 254.
94. *O Portuguez*, June 1817, p. 840.
95. Sequeira, *Projecto*, pp. 50–51.
96. Franco, *Ensaio*, pp. 14–16.
97. *O Portuguez*, May 1815, p. 71.
98. *Correio Braziliense*, January and March 1818, pp. 91–94 and 311–12, respectively.
99. Ibid., November 1822, p. 574.
100. Palmela to Minister of Foreign Affairs, 13 February 1818, ANTT, MNE, *cx.* 464.
101. João S. Maciel da Costa, *Memória sobre a necessidade de abolir a introdução dos escravos africanos no Brasil: sobre o modo e condições com que esta abolição se deve fazer, e sobre os meios de remediar a falta de braços que ella pode occasionar*, Coimbra, 1821, pp. 11 and 13.
102. Ibid., pp. 86–87 (italics in the original).
103. Ibid., pp. 8, 35 and 38.
104. *O Investigador Portuguez em Inglaterra*, July 1816, p. 113.

– *Chapter 3* –

FROM THE LOSS OF BRAZIL TO THE LIBERAL WARS: EARLY ABOLITIONIST PROPOSALS AND THE RETURN OF SILENCE

Despite the profusion of abolitionist treaties and laws, the transatlantic slave trade once again grew to high levels from the mid-1810s onwards. Slavers had found ways of circumventing the measures to suppress the slave trade which governments, one by one, had decreed. One of their tactics was the so-called practice of *embandeiramento* (flagging), that is to say, the sale of the ship to a real or imaginary partner in a country where the slave trade was still legal or tolerated by compliant authorities. In this way papers and flags were obtained to protect the slave ships from the British anti-traffic squadrons. But there were other methods too, which were particularly fertile in the Portuguese case, since the slave trade in the southern hemisphere was still legal: slavers acquired dual passports, for example, one for the slave trade in the south, and another for the legal trade in animal and vegetable products to the north of the line (which would justify the presence of the vessel in those latitudes).[1]

Such stratagems were the more fanciful, but not necessarily the most significant, side of the pro-slavery iceberg. They were only successful—or rather, so successful—because they took advantage of many omissions, weaknesses and connivances on the part of the authorities involved.

3.1 The Deadlocks in the Search for Abolitionist Consensus

Paradoxically, the transatlantic slave trade flourished indirectly on account of the economic vitality of Britain itself. In fact—and this was one of the great contradictions of the new abolitionist and liberal era—London's struggle against the slave trade took place at the same time as the new markets in Latin America were being conquered. Less than a year after the British Parliament approved the Abolition Act, Portugal opened up its Brazilian ports to foreign shipping. This measure enabled some one hundred British trading companies to set up in Brazil.[2] And, while the Bahia slave trade was basically supported by the products of local agriculture, British manufactures began to take on a fundamental role in the typical stock of Rio de Janeiro exports to Africa—as in Cuba.[3] But the British trading companies meant much more than large quantities of cheap products. They also opened up a channel to the largest financial centre in the world, and to its insurers and investors. On the African coast, as in America, the slave trade was an economic activity, in which settlement was made more or less long-term. Credit was therefore a key mechanism of the slaving enterprise, and it was credit which the British trading companies came prodigally to dispense, advancing merchandise to the slavers and agreeing to wait sometimes up to two years for payment. As Eltis shows, there is a positive correlation between exports of British products to Cuba and Brazil and the flow of slaves to those regions.[4] Ironically, at the precise moment when the abolitionists were trying to put an end to the 'infamous commerce' throughout the world, the slave trade to Brazil and Cuba was being reorganized with the indirect support of British merchants and capitalists. This involvement seemed unavoidable unless one of the main channels of British economic life were to be blockaded and stifled.

The contradictory nature of British intervention in the Atlantic basin was ancillary to the problem, not the main problem in itself. The main reason why the slave trade persisted from 1820 onwards was the reluctance of the various countries involved to enforce their laws or to allocate stronger coercive means to the British navy so that it might suppress the slave trade universally and more effectively. At the beginning of the 1820s it was generally acknowledged that the 'odious commerce' could only be fought effectively through the concerted action of all the nations involved in it. Nevertheless, despite the fact that they had all legally abolished the trade, except for Portugal, concerted action was proving practically impossible to achieve.

The slave trade of Britain and small transporting countries like Holland and Denmark practically ceased. The transportation of slaves to the United States also declined significantly as North American plantations began to meet supply needs through an internal system of breeding and selling.[5] Nevertheless, there were United States citizens directly involved in transporting slaves to the colonies of other countries that were beyond the reach of the British naval warships. The federal government sought to prevent such involvement, and even established a small squadron that operated on the African coast from 1820 onwards and seized a total of eleven ships. But this was transitory. The captains of the warships were told quite early on not to engage except in cases that were beyond all doubt, and in 1824 the patrol came to an end.[6] In March of that year an Anglo-American agreement was signed, granting rights of search and seizure to ships of either nation, but it was never ratified.

The French slave trade, which re-emerged in 1814 after the long interval of war, not only persisted despite the abolition imposed in 1815, but actually grew noticeably from 1818 onwards. France followed a highly ambiguous policy, which was abolitionist in form but non-functional in practice. It did promulgate an anti-traffic law on 15 April 1818, and it also set up a patrol of three warships, which were supposed to operate in African waters in the French sphere of influence, but until 1821 these warships did not make a single arrest.[7] Since, in addition, France obstinately refused to grant rights of search to foreign nations or to join an anti-slave trade league, the traffic in slaves carried on under the French flag remained entirely out of reach of the Royal Navy.

French slaving helped in part to supply slaves to Cuba, which remained open to the importation of Africans, despite the fact that the Anglo-Spanish abolition treaty had entered into force. At the beginning of the 1820s the Cuban traffic was not a major problem, since it had fallen off greatly in comparison with the large numbers imported in earlier years. However, from 1828 onwards imports again rose to very high levels.[8]

The Portuguese slave trade also persisted, on a large scale, both legally, in the southern hemisphere, and illegally, based on the Costa da Mina and the areas of the so-called Rivers of Guinea.[9] The Portuguese government took practically no part in the job of suppressing the slave trade, since it had not sent ships to the African coast. The attendance of Altavila and Figanière, the two Portuguese representatives at the Sierra Leone mixed commission, was brief and without glory. The inhospitable climate, illness and shortage of funds obliged them to leave their posts and return to Europe, leaving behind correspondence that was full of complaints about British high-handedness, disease and, above all, remuneration that never arrived.[10] At the beginning of the 1820s, Lisbon made insistent attempts to transfer the seat of the commission from Sierra Leone to the archipelago of Cape Verde. The seizure of slaving ships helped to populate the territories where those ships were tried, as the freed slaves would remain there, completing a period of apprenticeship for several years. Thanks to this system, which, as usual with British abolitionism, established close ties between humanity and material interest, in 1811 Freetown absorbed some 2,000 freed men. The continuing seizures of ships helped to meet the colony's demographic needs.[11] From the Portuguese point of view the British system made it possible to 'recruit blacks … at no cost and with little inconvenience', which was why they sought to divert the population flow from Freetown to the islands of Cape Verde, thereby effortlessly reaping the fruits of British labours. Naturally, London refused.[12] In 1824 Palmela stated his intention of ending Portuguese participation in the mixed commission, and two years later the Portuguese government formally announced that no new commissioners would be appointed to Sierra Leone. This was no more than an acknowledgement of the facts: since 1821 the trials had been conducted entirely by British officials.[13]

It was thus that, after several years of political effort and pressure on the governments of other colonial nations, British suppression policies seemed to have reached a dead end. In overall terms the traffic had grown, and all indications were that it would continue to grow unless Britain were able to obtain the active collaboration of other nations. Some governments had indeed conceded the right of search and had agreed to the establishment of mixed commissions for the trial of ships that had been apprehended. But it soon became apparent that these concessions were insufficient. With limited means and a vast area to patrol, the Royal Navy allowed most of the *tumbeiros* to slip through its fingers. In addition, those it did intercept and inspect could only be apprehended in flagrante delicto. For this reason, the London government wanted Portugal, as well as Holland and Spain, to accept the principle that any ship could be apprehended and condemned which, even if it had no slaves on board, was manifestly equipped to transport them. It also wished to be allowed to dismantle the vessels that had been condemned, so as to avoid them being bought by traffickers and once again used in the slave trade. But only Holland accepted the equipment clause. Spain (on 10 December 1822) and Portugal (on 15 March 1823) merely consented to the vague principle that ships could be apprehended without slaves on board provided that they showed unmistakable signs of having unloaded them very recently.[14]

From 1823 onwards, and even though it had not obtained any significant concessions from the Portuguese government, London surprisingly eased the abolitionist pressure on Lisbon. This probably had to do with changes in the abolitionist context both within and outside Britain.

In Britain, after the setbacks and deadlocks they had faced in trying to suppress the foreign traffic, the abolitionists focused on the more tangible objective of emancipating the slaves in the West Indies.[15] In 1823 they founded the Society for the Amelioration and Gradual Abolition of Slavery Throughout the British Dominions (or Anti-Slavery Society) and embarked on a national campaign for the gradual abolition of slavery. Despite his sixty-three years, Clarkson lent his name to the cause and again travelled up and down the country, forming local committees, giving speeches, and agitating. Specialized journals were published, and once again there was a spurt of intensive propaganda and freely disseminated specialized literature (the Anti-Slavery Society issued some 3 million publications between 1823 and 1831).[16] In its wake, and after several advances and retreats, came massive public pressure, and with it new waves of petitioners. These reached their highest point in 1833, when Parliament received around 5,000 petitions, signed by millions of people.[17] In the same year, Britain started emancipating some of the 780,000 slaves in its American colonies, paying 20 million pounds in compensation to their owners.[18] It was laid down that slavery would legally end on 1 August 1834, and that the former slaves would become apprentices for a period of not more than six years, at the end of which they would be entirely free. Subsequently the date for full emancipation was brought forward to 1838.

The British law of 1833 was a strong reason for collective pride: it gave rise to a period of great national enthusiasm. It was also profoundly admired by rival nations. But it is important to note that for most of the 1820s and 1830s the energies of the main British abolitionist leaders were mostly engaged in the question of the West Indies. The concern with suppressing the traffic had not gone away—far from it—but it had become an essentially diplomatic affair, which the London government was able to manage in more elastic fashion, according to its strategic convenience and without the compulsion that derived from popular philanthropic pressure.

Elasticity and strategy were what was needed in the case of Portugal: the revolution of 1820, political agitation and, almost simultaneously, the disintegration of the Luso-Brazilian empire brought about substantial changes to the issues of suppression. The Portuguese liberal revolution, which began in Oporto on 24 August 1820, sought, amongst other things, to bring Brazil back into the more or less mercantilist fold of the empire. This aim was subverted by the revolution itself. After months of hesitation, D. João VI did return to Lisbon, accepting the role which the Cortes Constituintes (Constituent Assembly) had assigned to him. But on the other side of the Atlantic, Brazil, where the liberal principles proclaimed in Oporto had found an echo early on, was not disposed to accept the restoration of the old imperial system, nor its status as a colonial dependency, nor even a double-headed system of two united kingdoms.[19] At the beginning of 1822 the prince D. Pedro, who had remained in Rio as regent, refused to come back to the mother country, choosing instead to head up the burgeoning independence movement. In September the Brazilians became de facto independent. The emergence of the new state put in jeopardy the legal anti-slave trade network which had been so laboriously and persistently put together by the Foreign Office, especially because the new state—which naturally had no commitment with Britain to implement abolition—was the largest importer of African labour, 'the very child and champion of the slave trade', in Wilberforce's words.[20] Nevertheless, while Brazilian independence was a threat to the enemies of the slave trade, it was also an unexpected gift in so far as, to the extent the new country needed Britain's good offices to succeed in its claims against the metropole, it might be possible to obtain from it significant abolitionist concessions. At the Congress of Verona, in 1822, Britain had made clear that no new state would be acknowledged unless it abolished the 'odious commerce'. It is therefore not surprising that Canning, at the end of the year, maintained that it was through Brazil that the slave trade might be ended and that, correspondingly, the bulk of British abolitionist pressure had fallen on Rio de Janeiro.[21]

From this moment on an intense diplomatic game of advances and retreats took place, during which the Brazilian government moved back and forth between promises of swift abolition (within four years) and silence and reticence. Its political position was extremely difficult: it could not yield on abolition without having the main economic forces in Brazil—farmers and merchants—turn against it and without a strong risk of the political break-up of the whole country. Despite these many problems, the Anglo-Brazilian treaty for the total abolition of the slave trade was concluded in October 1825 and, following renegotiation to cater for a few British objections, was finally signed on 23 November 1826. The agreement provided for the final end of the slave trade carried on in Brazilian ships three years after ratification—which would take place on 13 May 1827—and heavily stigmatized slave trading, equating it to piracy.[22]

With British abolitionist attentions focused mainly elsewhere, Portugal's role diminished significantly. Portuguese governments had always alleged that only their transatlantic interests had been in the way of an immediate and complete end to the slave trade, and it seemed clear that the empire's split into two blocks would change its attitude to the problem for good, if only from a legal standpoint. As a result of Brazilian secession, and in the light of the laws and treaties then in force, the Portuguese slave trade would become illegal *ipso facto*, since the provisions of successive bilateral agreements in 1815 and 1817 and the charter of 26 January 1818 had forbidden the export of slaves to foreign territories—something the Foreign Office noted immediately, at the end of 1822.[23] In spite of all this, the Portuguese government, in the person of successive ministers, reacted to British claims in a zigzag fashion. In 1822–23, a time of great harassment by the Foreign Office, it resisted these claims by threatening to break all the treaties.[24] Later, at the beginning of 1824, and through Palmela, it stated its openness to the possibility of abolishing the slave trade as a way of obtaining British collaboration for future imperial reunification or in exchange for financial compensation.[25] Some months later Palmela would refuse immediate abolition, not only because that would mean, implicitly, recognition of Brazilian independence, but also because there was a risk that abolition would be interpreted as a hostile act towards Brazil and invite retaliation against the Portuguese living there.[26] At the beginning of 1825, in the person of the Count of Porto Santo (Saldanha da Gama), Lisbon went back openly to a policy of obstructing abolition of the slave trade. It was only in October 1826, a year after the Luso-Brazilian treaty sanctioning Brazilian independence—and with Porto Santo already out of the government—that Portugal admitted it was time to put an end to the issue:

> The Portuguese government acknowledges that the moment has come to bring to an end the inhuman traffic of slaves, and therefore there can be no doubt about inserting into the trade-treaty ... an article in which His Most Faithful Majesty undertakes not only to abolish the slave trade in its entirety in the states belonging to the Crown of Portugal, but also to join with His British Majesty in the total extinction of so barbarous a commerce in the countries where unhappily it still exists.[27]

Britain's efforts to obtain 'a written pledge' that would formally commit the Lisbon government to abolition had been crowned with success.[28] The necessary agreement would follow with no major urgency given that, in any event, it would be necessary to maintain a supply of slaves to Brazil until 1830 (to comply with an article in the abolitionist Anglo-Brazilian treaty, which had meanwhile been signed). Twenty years after the start of abolitionist pressure, the Portuguese problem seemed finally on the way to a satisfactory outcome. Nevertheless, the formal commitment of the Lisbon government was a long way from reflecting the feelings of the Portuguese elites on this question.

3.2 The Pathways to Abolitionism in Portugal

The Lisbon government's zigzags were the result not just of internal political upheavals, the complexity of the situation following Brazilian secession—in which abolition weighed considerably, whether as a medium of exchange or as an element of pressure or conciliation—or greater or lesser insistence on Britain's part. There was also the supremacy of tolerationism among the Portuguese elites. This was not immediately visible only because its specific manifestations were relatively rare. If we exclude older publications—like the *Correio Braziliense*, for example—the subject was broached only sporadically in the periodicals during the first liberal period. For the new press, liberty was a burning issue, but one that was basically polarized into political concepts, and this justifies the common analogy made in the eighteenth and nineteenth centuries between slavery and peoples' subjection to authoritarian regimes. In the whirlwind of social strife that followed the revolution of 1820, there was tireless debate on standards of living and the rights of the disadvantaged classes or on the slavery of nations, but it was not often that there was discussion of the slave trade and slavery of Africans. However, this did not mean there was a vacuum: even though the problems of slavery had been underestimated by the new liberal era, there were some commentaries on the subject, both in the columns of the newspapers and in the Cortes, the new platform the revolution had opened up to the voice of the people. These commentaries show that arguments for abolition did in fact emerge in the 1820s, but that those who advocated them were in a minority and were inconsistent. They also show that tolerationism persisted and adapted to the new circumstances following the loss of Brazil. Finally, they show that the events of the time shifted the debate, which now entered a new orbit: driven by the libertarian spirit of the time and, above all, by Brazilian secession, the issue of abolition became partially disconnected from its traditional locus, Brazil, and began rather to revolve around Africa. And, on this new chosen ground, budding abolitionism surprisingly encountered new obstacles and soon fell silent once more.

3.2.1 *The Abolition Issue in the Cortes*

In the Cortes's sessions of 1821–22 the issue of abolition was raised, basically in the context of the article of the Constitution that laid down the rules for acquiring Portuguese nationality. The first draft worked on by the members of the constituent assembly granted the right of nationality and citizenship to free men (implicitly excluding those who were not free) and in general the discussion did not provide major cause to question the existence of slavery. Initially only Braancamp found it morally disturbing, and serious, that the basic law implicitly sanctioned the continuation of slavery:

> All free men, the article states, [and] I believe the word free should be struck from this article. I see that we are obliged to retain slavery in our overseas possessions, but I would wish that this sad necessity should appear as the exception and not as the general rule, which will have to govern all those who come after us.[29]

Braancamp's concerns were not immediately echoed in the chamber. Only Margiochi, a little later on, sought to bring the matter up again, requesting that the meeting should pay heed to Braancamp's proposal for the striking of the word 'free' from that article of the Constitution. The Lisbon deputy went further, seeking to have all slaves in the overseas possessions regarded as citizens and stating, in connection with the 'rights of man', that measures should be established to prevent their sale. Margiochi promised that he would subsequently put forward draft bills for the abolition of the slave trade, but he sought to impose from the outset the suspension of the rights of citizenship for any man who continued to deal in slaves; he even proposed that the Brazilian delegation—which was still absent—should be prevented from taking its seat in the Cortes if it did not subscribe to the anti-slavery principles he had just set out.[30] The chamber was not receptive to so radical a position, nor was Braancamp himself, whose intentions were merely to draw up a plan for a gradual end to the slave trade and for partial measures against slavery, such as the freedom of the womb—that is to say, the freedom of all slaves born in the future. In any case Braancamp thought that any decision on these matters would require the Brazilian deputies to be present.[31] This was, moreover, an almost unanimous view. The vast majority of the deputies decided to take no decision until the Brazilian delegation arrived, on the basis that any measure, even freedom of the womb, could be upsetting—'let us not talk of such questions now'[32]—and even harmful for the slaves thus liberated, who would presumably be abandoned to their fate.

Margiochi never did submit his draft bills for the abolition of the slave trade. When the Brazilian deputies arrived a few weeks later, and in the light of political developments in Brazil, the few abolitionist intentions manifested in the Cortes in the summer of 1821 evaporated, or receded into positions of extreme caution. To preserve the unity of the

Portuguese of both hemispheres it was necessary to minimize the differences: the majority in the chamber sought to adjust to the prevailing circumstances, in a desperate effort to avoid tearing the empire apart. It should be mentioned that Margiochi belonged to the faction that is sometimes called the 'integrationists', a group of deputies that had a relatively firm political attitude to the Brazilian rebels. They naturally sought the unity of the Portuguese empire, but with Brazil as the junior partner. As the Brazilian rebellion proceeded, and based on the principle that Portugal did not have the military means to become involved in a prolonged conflict in Brazil—particularly given the limited chances of military victory—the 'integrationists' argued that it would be better to accept secession than to have to prolong the union with an insubordinate partner.[33] As Fernandes Tomás, the head of the 'integrationists' stated in a speech that would become famous, 'if Brazil ... does not wish to unite with Portugal as it has always been united, let us put an end to this: let Mr. Brazil go his own way, and we will look after ourselves here'.[34] It is possible he was bluffing. The 'integrationists' were in any case in a minority in the Cortes, where the moderates prevailed. For the latter, the slavery issue was one to be avoided as much as possible.

Thus the issue of abolition tended to remain in the limbo to which the Brazilian delegation wished to consign it. The draft bill submitted by the deputy for Bahia, Borges de Barros, is a perfect example of this approach. The draft, which sought to settle colonists in the unpopulated parts of Brazil, made any measure that might eventually be vaguely favourable to slaves contingent on the eventual success of that colonization: 'if the number of foreign immigrants to Brazil is large in these early days, the slave trade between that kingdom and Angola will end within 6 years'; as for slavery, the draft acknowledged only ad hoc emancipation, as a form of reward for some 'virtuous action' or 'good service' rendered to their masters. It also provided that 'the son and the slave woman who should bear him of the master' should be free, together with 'the slaves who in sickness are abandoned by their masters'; and, to encourage biological reproduction, the bill promoted marriage between slaves, granting enfranchisement to 'the married female slave who could exhibit six live children'.[35] A draft of this sort was the confirmation of the institutions of slavery, not their end. As the deputy Girão said sadly, if two Congresses were to be established—one in the mother country, the other in Brazil, which was a possibility being discussed at the time—all hope would be lost of ever being able to ease the miserable situation of the colonial slave by means of the Portuguese Constitution.[36]

The issue of abolition of the institutions of slavery was not raised exclusively from the point of view of Brazilian interests. Although the Cortes paid little attention to the rest of the overseas empire and particularly to Africa, even so they did now and then refer to the possibilities for African economic development. Strictly speaking, the idea was not entirely new. In 1814, anticipating the time when Portugal would be deprived of its American colony, Saldanha da Gama drew up a Memoir in which he set out in detail the economic potential of Portuguese Africa.[37] In the following year the *Observador Luzitano em Paris* published a similar report on Angola.[38] The *Investigador Portuguez em Inglaterra* had also published letters and reports on the development of the French and British colonies in Africa, stressing the point that, if Portugal wasted time and failed to understand 'the new order of things', it might be prevented from 'taking part in the advantages of the system [of colonization]' which the other nations had started to adopt.[39] But it was with the dawning of the Constitution and, above all, after the Brazil crisis began that arguments for the colonization of Africa began to emerge again with a measure of consistency.

These arguments did not generate much enthusiasm in Portugal in the first half of the nineteenth century, as we shall see in chapter 6. For now it should just be emphasized that some of these proposals accepted or advocated the possibility of changes to the institutions of slavery—for example, the opinion on the provinces of Angola and São Tomé and Príncipe, submitted to the Cortes on 19 April 1822. This contained a survey of the potential wealth of the Angolan territory and considered the usefulness of cultivating 'bountiful plants', amongst other measures, as a way of helping the Portuguese establishments on the coast to prosper. While this opinion did not go so far as to ask for the abolition of the slave trade, it made some tentative suggestions: 'would it not be more appropriate to a free and generous Nation, to try rather to civilize these pagans little by little, teaching them to cultivate their lands and work their mines …?'As a subsidiary question it suggested that the 'cruel and unjust trade of slavery' should be ended or obstructed and that, as an alternative, black slave labourers should be used for African development.[40]

It is likely that the main inspiration behind this opinion was Alexandre de Morais Sarmento, a man who on a number of occasions came out against the existence of the slave trade, and whose attitudes were close to those of the British abolitionists. He had no hesitation in speaking publicly about the horrors caused by the traffic.[41] His aversion to the slave trade would even translate into a draft bill, if only four years later. In effect, the Cortes were disbanded on 3 June 1823, following the *Vilafrancada*, the first showing of the Absolutist reaction, and it was only in 1826, after the death of D. João VI and the replacement of the suspended Constitution of 1822 by the Constitutional Charter proclaimed by D. Pedro, the first born son of the late king, that the legislative assemblies started to operate again, divided now into the Chamber of Peers and the Chamber of Deputies. Morais Sarmento submitted to the Chamber of Deputies, at the end of that year, the proposal that would become the first Portuguese draft bill for the abolition of the 'odious commerce':

> Gentlemen, … I propose the abolition of the infamous commerce in slaves, that traffic which has taken terror and desolation to Africa …, and which has

> already condemned millions of human lives to the greatest miseries and torments. The Religion and Glory of the name of Portugal demand that we put an end to such commerce because, apart from its iniquity, its immediate effect is the death of all those virtuous sentiments which may arise in the human heart.

The draft bill forbade the export of Africans from the ports of Africa, and allocated to the Portuguese navy the duty to suppress the traffic (it envisaged a bonus system, in the British manner, for the crew of the arresting ship). The penalties intended included fines, the arrest and possible forfeiture of the slaving ship, and exile for a period of five to ten years for authorities conniving with the enterprise.[42] Submitted three days before the closure of the extraordinary session of 1826, the proposal died. In the months following, the difficult balance between Absolutists and Liberals that D. João VI had been able to maintain, despite military confrontation and rebellion, fell apart for good, and Portugal slid into widespread conflict. With the Absolutists' return to power in 1828, the country sank into a period of terror that would only end with the civil war of 1832–34.

We should not, however, succumb to the temptation of attributing final responsibility for the failure of Morais Sarmento's proposals to the political crisis. Despite all the upheavals, the Cortes of 1827 and 1828 held a total of 117 sessions, to which dozens of draft bills were submitted. Morais Sarmento himself submitted in 1827 a draft for the founding of a Royal African Institute, and this was swiftly approved in the Chamber of Deputies.[43] Therefore it was not just for lack of time that the draft for the abolition of the slave trade did not progress. There are other signs that abolitionism was far from being close to the parliamentarians' hearts, even amongst those who openly defended the African option. It should be recalled that, a few days before Morais Sarmento submitted his draft abolitionist bill to the Cortes, deputy Braklami had moved to submit a draft bill encouraging colonial development. This bill did not envisage the abolition of the slave trade, but only the granting of compensation to the owners of African undertakings over 50 per cent of whose employees were free men.[44] Later draft bills for Africa, in 1827 and 1828, either did not mention the problem of the slave trade or, while recognizing its importance for the overseas provinces, adopted a passive stance on the question, preferring to put forward economic adjustment measures for the time when abolition would come into effect as a result of international treaties.[45] There is nothing to suggest therefore that Morais Sarmento's proposals were likely to garner wide-ranging support. On the contrary, and with the exception of sporadic cases, which I shall come to at the end of this chapter, all indications point to tolerationism continuing to be the dominant way of thinking among the Portuguese political elites.

3.2.2 *Tolerationism—Staying Power and Adaptation*

Brazilian independence might have taken the wind out of tolerationism. Clearly that ideology was still relevant, and useful in a defensive role in relation to Brazil, as we have seen in the context of the pamphlet by Maciel da Costa. But, in the Portuguese portion of the empire, and with the division of national interest into two parts, which were not only different but, in theory, antagonistic, reservations regarding abolition of the slave trade might have ceased to be justified.

In practice, however, it was not so. Even though Brazil had been lost, tolerationism persisted and continued to develop in liberal Portugal. The key concept now was that abolition would do irreparable harm to the remaining colonies. This idea was not entirely new, even if, during the 1810s, when concerns with preserving the institutions of slavery were understandably focused on Brazil, it had become practically submerged in the second to third line of ideological defence. In any event, in 1815 judge Diogo Tovar e Albuquerque drew up a memoir on the situation in the *Estado da Índia* (the Portuguese colonies in India), in which he considered that, since the cloth exported from Goa for the slave trade in Africa was the only trade that brought in customs duties for the Portuguese possessions in India, those possessions could not survive if the slave trade were to come to an end.[46] Saldanha da Gama also drew up his own memoir in 1814, in which he recommended that certain changes be made in the economic organization of the African colonies, in order that the end of the slave trade as a result of British pressure should not lead to the loss of those colonies.[47] And it was thus that, when the time had come to stop appealing to Brazilian interests as the reason for delaying abolition, tolerationism persisted in Portuguese life. Now that the Brazilian obstacle, which had previously been used to demand—and obtain—a moratorium from the British, had disappeared, there was a new hindrance in the form of the issue of survival of the remaining possessions. There is evidence of these ideological changes in Portugal during the 1820s, both in the politicians' arguments and in the press and literature of the decade.

Portuguese tolerationism in its new form appeared for the first time towards the end of 1822, in an important note from Silvestre Pinheiro Ferreira, the Minister of Foreign Affairs, who argued that Portuguese reluctance to abolish the slave trade had always been due to consideration of the interests of the African and Asiatic colonies rather than to a concern with Brazil:

> It was not principally on behalf of Brazil's interests that we chose to delay the abolition of the slave trade .... Certainly, immediate abolition of the slave trade would cause Brazil grave harm, but in the very considerable number of slaves already there, and in the best advantage that their masters would seek to take of their service, ... Brazil would find an abundance of resources to sustain and even to improve its agriculture, its rural arts and its mines. However ... the countries which would be irreparably ruined by the immediate aboli-

tion of the slave trade, were all the dominions of Portugal on the Coast of Africa, and all those in Asia principally involved in trade with Africa.[48]

In line with this approach, the intention of the Lisbon government was to hold back British abolitionist haste as much as possible, so that it might later on, at its own pace, abolish the slave trade 'imperceptibly'.[49] Temporarily overtaken in the year and a half that Palmela held the office of Minister of Foreign Affairs, that political philosophy reappeared with his successor, the Count of Porto Santo. The former governor of Angola, who had attended the Congress of Vienna, had many occasions to tell his friend Palmela—who was then ambassador in London—the reasons why the banning of the slave trade would cause irretrievable losses to Portuguese Africa. From his point of view, despite the Brazilian secession, the issue of the slave trade was still of major importance not only as 'a trade matter' and on account of the 'removal of slaves from one lot of colonies to other colonies on the Coast of Africa', but also because it affected 'the largest movement of funds in Angola and Mozambique, which are the duties on the slaves which they export'. The Portuguese government could therefore only contemplate examining this matter after the question of Brazilian independence had been resolved and if, in compensation for what it would lose, it were to receive in exchange 'certain advantages'.[50]

It was not only Porto Santo who was resisting the end of the slave trade. As the date approached for the end of the commercial treaty of 1810, requiring negotiation of a new agreement, several organizations and personalities—among them the Attorney General and the Minister of the Treasury—were called upon to express their opinion on the changes to be made. All the opinions received contained new objections to the idea of abolishing the slave trade, some of them tied to Brazilian interests. Lisbon could not make any hasty decision, so as not to deprive Brazil 'of the hands it still needs'. Accordingly, and since it would not be fair to grant the Brazilians privileges which the Portuguese did not enjoy, the government could not outlaw the 'barbarous commerce' while Brazil did not do likewise. To proceed in any other fashion would be unjust and would raise severe practical problems, since it would be extremely difficult to identify the nationality of the vessels involved.[51]

Porto Santo's despatches reveal the perennial nature of some forms of the Portuguese resistance to the policy of abolition, starting with those relating to the transportation of slaves between colonies. Since 1815, one of the doors the Portuguese administration had wanted to keep open was the supply of labour to São Tomé and Príncipe, and some of the disputes between London and Lisbon related to these islands.[52] In 1825 Porto Santo was still of the opinion that Portugal should under no circumstances give up the traffic entirely, not even after eventual abolition in Brazil, so as to keep open the possibility of transporting people to the islands of São Tomé, Príncipe and Cape Verde—something which, curiously, had been prohibited since 1815, even if the Portuguese government frequently sought to circumvent this prohibition.[53] The Portuguese minister's despatches also stressed concerns with the loss of income from the overseas customs posts, and made quite clear the fear of the shock which prohibition of the slave trade would give to the Portuguese whose lives were in some shape or form tied to the institutions of slavery, both in Portugal and, above all, in Brazil.

There were thus a number of objections that Palmela in the London embassy naturally had to consider. At the beginning of 1824, the then Marquis had confided to Edward Thornton, the British representative in Lisbon, that, if Brazil were to become independent, Portugal would be inclined to abolish the slave trade entirely. But two years later, and in the light of the instructions he had received from Lisbon, he had to distance himself from that statement, which he described as a merely private opinion that he had 'allowed to come out' in conversation with Thornton. He went on to say that it 'would not be suitable' for Brazil's interests to be set aside by the Portuguese government when the matter in hand was the issue of the slave trade.[54]

After the death of D. João VI, Porto Santo left the government in July 1826, and was replaced by D. Francisco de Almeida (the future Count of Lavradio). It was through his good offices that Portugal now emerged with an official willingness to sign a treaty abolishing the slave trade in its entirety, as mentioned above. But his anti-slavery policy went no further than this expression of willingness. In April 1827 the Portuguese government even asserted that it had given orders for two warships to patrol the Cape Verde area in order to act against the slave trade, but these vessels were never sent there.[55] Around the same time Palmela, still in London, was insisting on the urgent need for something to be done to prepare Portugal for the end of the slave trade:

> Your Excellency will permit me to suggest the need to take into account that the legal slave trade to Brazil will cease within three years, and that the Portuguese government will in my opinion find itself in an awkward position if it wishes to keep open, so to speak, a market in slaves which it will only be possible to sell from then on by smuggling. … It seems to me that legislative action should properly be taken to prohibit the sale of slaves outside the Portuguese dominions after a certain time.[56]

But nothing was done: no treaties, no statutes and, as it was already mentioned, no naval actions against the slave trade.

The strong dose of tolerationism in the Lisbon government's policies, which accounted for its zigzagging and hesitations, was also present in civil society, both in newspaper commentary and in lengthier writings. José Acúrsio das Neves, one of the key figures in Portuguese economic thought, was the author of one of the most interesting examples of tolerationist thought at the time. In a piece published in 1830, the year in which, according to the Anglo-Brazilian treaty of 1826, the slave trade to Brazil should by law have come to its end, Acúrsio gave a detailed description of the Portuguese overseas possessions, their climate, their produce and the outlook for their economic development. In amongst these he expounded on the slave trade: looked at in overall terms, his comments outlined a tolerationism that had already adjusted to prevailing circumstances.

There were two main aspects to this tolerationism. The first was the notion of the barbarity of the Negro, an intrinsic barbarity that was fostered and consolidated by the slave trade, though it was not its principal cause. Civilization had started in the East, whence it had spread in all directions. But because the rays of civilization gradually lost their power as they moved away from their point of origin, the kingdoms of Western and Southern Africa ended up being 'buried in the darkness of their ancient barbarism'. It was not the fault of the European slavers that African civilization had retreated or died: it had never existed, and the Europeans had not been able or had not known how to introduce it.[57] As usual, the idea of intrinsic barbarity served, amongst other things, to relativize the day-to-day violence of the American plantations and of the slave trade. In Acúrsio's view, these practices were no more barbarous than 'the treatment which the wretched captives endure in the power of the cruel Africans'.[58]

The second key notion in Acúrsio das Neves's tolerationism was that there would be an inevitable collapse of the Portuguese colonies as a result of the abolitionist policy imposed by Britain. The 'big trade centres' at Bissau and Cacheu, whence were extracted 'the finest slaves in the whole of Africa', had already been reduced to 'miserable establishments', which would be totally wiped out if precautionary measures were not taken; Angola, which in the distant future might become a 'new Brazil', was about to collapse into 'the greatest poverty, following the prohibition of the trade in slaves'.[59] However, Acúrsio das Neves made no appeal to resounding and active anti-abolitionist resistance, or even to the concept of gradual abolition, in order to prevent the imminent or already heralded collapse of the African colonies. In 1830 any one of those strategies seemed meaningless, since the decision to go for abolition had already been taken elsewhere, by the British and Brazilian governments, and the process seemed to have a life of its own completely outside Portuguese jurisdiction. Given that the slave trade had been made completely illegal, Acúrsio was suggesting the adoption of an operationally polyvalent position.

He did so because he had serious reservations about the suitability of the British abolitionist method. It did not properly take into account the intrinsic barbarity of the African and tended to 'deprive the rulers of the main source of their income', thus setting them against British philanthropy. For the British to succeed in their abolitionist aims, it would be necessary for them to 'assuage the ferocity of the Africans', which they would only succeed in doing through the slow medium of civilization—

in other words, by means of what the tolerationists of the previous decade had called the 'Portuguese system'. There was no guarantee at all that, despite its great economic and military might, Britain would have sufficient strength to put an end once and for all to the 'iniquitous commerce' and, given the resistance to abolition everywhere, in Europe, America and Africa, it would only require that a less active British government should moderate its coercive measures for the slave trade to be revived. Accordingly the European nations—and especially Portugal, because it had the largest and most important African colonies—should seek to adopt a wait-and-see approach, which, in practice, would allow them to operate and adapt to the two possible outcomes—that is, the end or the revival of the slave trade.[60]

Because its proposals were functionally polyvalent, Acúrsio das Neves's tolerationism was not a simple form of obstruction but a forward-looking argument that sought to overcome the problems created by a supposed fait accompli. Since the main revenue of the colonial customs was the duties on the export of slaves, and those exports were going to cease, there would inevitably be a huge fiscal deficit. It was unthinkable that the mother country should bankrupt itself in order to subsidize its colonies, so that deficit would have to be equalized by developing other forms of income, the most obvious of which was legal trade. However, as only a well-developed trade could provide gains as significant as those assured by the traffic in slaves, and since that legal trade was not likely to start up immediately, the Negroes being entirely focused on the export of men, it would be necessary to develop agriculture. In other words, abolition as imposed by the British could be favourable for the African colonies if it allowed them to develop their agriculture to the point where they would rival Brazil. But all this needed time and a willingness to invest, which Portugal lacked.[61] And this in turn meant that suppressing the slave trade could be the end of the Portuguese colonies: if they did not die of the disease, they would die of the cure. In order to avoid this outcome, carefully measured doses of therapy would have to be administered so as to achieve equilibrium, making the slave trade coexist with legal trade: 'what might suit us is a goods warehouse on our islands [São Tomé and Príncipe] which could be despatched in small ships to Portugal, as they were used up ...; but this plan would have been better carried out when the slave trade so favoured it, rather than now when that foundation is lacking'.[62] This passage contains an implicit trace of gradualism, which was only not expressly suggested now because it was apparently useless once the Brazilian slave trade had legally come to an end. But the new form of tolerationist thinking put forward by Acúrsio das Neves coincided in several ways with the old chain of defensive ideas on abolition developed in the 1810s, namely its core concept: the intrinsic barbarity of the African, the collapse of the colonies, the unsuitability of the British anti-slavery method and the appropriateness of the Portuguese civilizing method.

Tolerationism seems to have been the commonest way of thinking in Portugal during the 1820s. It is true that slavery seemed to be something that was incompatible with a nation that sought to be free. However, the humanitarian and libertarian drive had to be reconciled with the circumstances of the world, with Brazilian interests and then with those of Portuguese Africa (as the decade progressed, and since Brazil was lost, the firm conviction spread in Portugal that abolition of the slave trade would lead to the loss of the African colonies).

However, despite the persistence and apparently greater prevalence of tolerationist ideas, there were some voices in Portuguese society in favour of abolition. They came from different parts and did not always come together in their assumptions and objectives. Some came from abroad; others, being Portuguese, were generally circumstantial.

3.2.3 British-inspired Abolitionism

The liberal revolution opened the door to the publication of abolitionist books and pamphlets in Portuguese but, except for the works of Sequeira and Soares Franco, which were discussed in the previous chapter, these publications were all of British origin.

The indications are that it was probably Quaker donations that substantially funded abolitionist propaganda efforts in Europe in the 1820s and 1830s.[63] As part of this campaign, taking advantage of the end of the Inquisition and the censorship, the first publication to come out, in 1821, was *Breve resumo sobre a natureza do commercio da escravatura e das atrocidades que dele resultam* (A brief summary of the nature of the trade in slaves and of the atrocities resulting therefrom).[64] *Bosquejo sobre o commercio em escravos* (An outline of the trade in slaves) was published in the same year. It was a translation into Portuguese of a book that had initially been directed at the Spanish and had been written anonymously by Blanco White, editor of *El Español*, a liberal journal published in London.[65] A few months later the Portuguese version of a booklet by Clarkson appeared, called *Os gemidos dos Africanos* (The Cry of the Africans). It sought to disseminate the information gathered by Mungo Park in his journey through the interior of Africa, and described in detail the way captives were obtained, how they were driven to the *tumbeiros*, and the conditions under which they were transported to the Americas. The text had illustrations, including a print of a ship called *The Brooks* (Fig. 3.1), which since the end of the eighteenth century had been used for propaganda purposes, showing how slaves were loaded into the tiny spaces between decks.[66] A little while later, in 1824, *Memorial aos habitantes da Europa* (Memorial to the inhabitants of Europe) appeared, a Portuguese translation of a Quaker text published in London two years earlier. In its preface it was recommended that it should be read by all those who spoke Portuguese and who lived in lands where such an 'iniquitous and detestable' traffic continued to exist.[67]

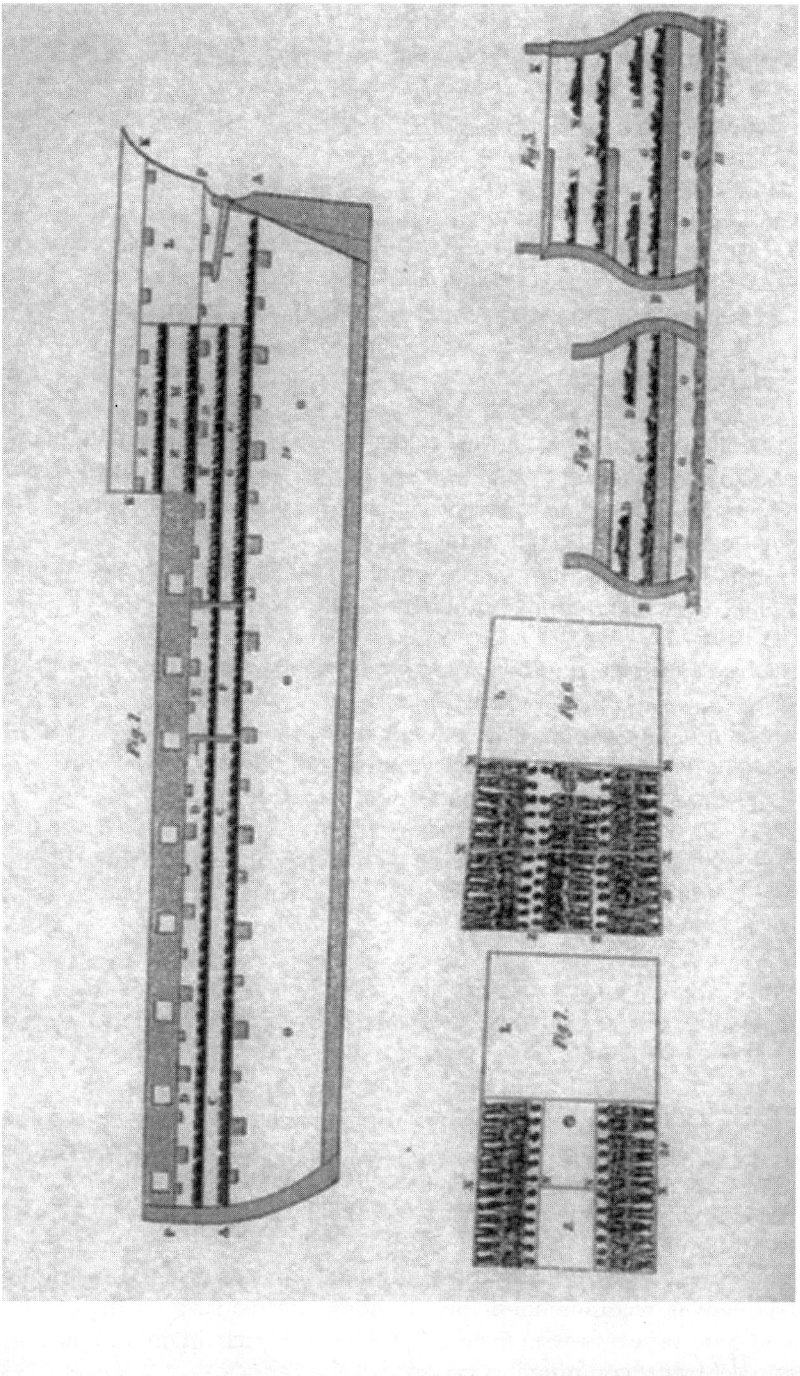

FIGURE 3.1. Plans of the slave ship *The Brooks*.

Taken as a whole these works, as was usual with British abolitionism, sought to make evil explicit, presenting the issue as a struggle between civilized man and the sordid trafficker or the selfish planter. They generally used extensive and detailed descriptions of the miseries and torments caused by the traffic, from Africa to the colonial plantations, because the authors believed that portraying these horrors would convince enlightened and just minds, provided that care was taken to oppose the 'more subtle artifices' the opponents of abolition used to muddy the issue for public opinion.[68] Blanco White, for example, was concerned to point out and dismantle such artifices: the belittling of abolitionism; the catastrophic visions of the consequences of abolition; the idea that slavery was a good thing for Negroes, when compared to their state in Africa; the legitimizing of modern slavery on the basis of the Greek and Roman examples; the defence of gradualism. For the author of the *Bosquejo*, the argument for gradualism was possibly the most insidious of the anti-abolitionists' stratagems, but also the one that was most revealing of how wrong they were: the political pretexts on which the slave trade was based were so abominable that its protectors did not dare to defend it without limitation; all they asked of governments was that they should allow it to continue for a few more years.[69]

Taking advantage of the freedom of the press that was becoming widespread in the continental monarchies, the British abolitionists sought to include propaganda materials in some foreign journals. That was at least in part why the abolitionist message appeared now and then in the pages of some Portuguese newspapers. In some cases British influence was direct and transparent. In 1820 *O Templo da Memória* (The Temple of Memory), an occasional political and literary journal, published the translation of several British poems that evoked scenes in which blaks were seized, homes destroyed and slaves transported, separated and subjected daily to violence by their masters.[70] In other cases, the Portuguese journalist played a more important role and British influence was more discreet. This was the case of the *Correio da Tarde* (the Evening Post) and especially of *O Compilador* (The Compiler) and the *Gazeta de Portugal* (Portugal Gazette), two journals edited by the lawyer José Baptista Gastão. In a long article published in 1822 Baptista Gastão started out by showing that, in economic terms, both the traffic and slavery itself were harmful to Brazil. In addition to not being very productive, slave labour stifled the development potential of the Brazilian economy because the planter relied on Negro labour and felt no need to adopt modern and much more profitable agricultural methods. Moreover, the continued purchase of Africans was inappropriate on social, safety and public morality grounds. If Brazil were not to cease importing slaves, it would soon become 'a new Africa, entirely peopled by blacks'. As an alternative to the traffic—which had to cease—Baptista Gastão argued for European immigration, which in his opinion could be encouraged by the liberal nature of the constitutional system that was then being established in the empire. But, even if there were a shortage of immigrants, it was always possible to improve the reproduction of existing slaves and even divert into agriculture many Negroes who were assigned to domestic service through the 'rank idleness' of Brazilian women.[71]

This was, roughly speaking, the kernel of the para-abolitionist argument, which we have already seen in journals such as the *Correio Braziliense* and *O Portuguez*. But now, in the manner of militant abolitionism, room was made for detailed descriptions of the horrors of the traffic and emphasis was placed on the moral, sentimental and religious aspects of the slavery issue.

The best example of this new approach is to be found in *O Compilador*. Seeking to open up 'avenues to sensibility', Baptista Gastão asked his readers to feel the 'affliction and pain' of the slave on board the slaving ship, to try out the 'sensations' of those who were enclosed in a small space which just allowed them to breathe.[72] Having stressed the violence and anguish inherent in the transatlantic transports, *O Compilador* followed the African's journey through markets and colonial plantations, where he would toil laboriously under the scourge of his master.[73] To complete his detailed picture, he told of the horror of two recent cases that were typical of the criminal and piratical activity. The first of these was the saga of *Le Rodeur*, a French slaving ship on which serious cases of ophthalmia broke out among both slaves and crew. The number of those who had gone blind grew every day, until there was just one sailor left with sufficiently good eyesight to manoeuvre the ship. In its half-blinded progress the slaver came across the *San Leon*, a Spanish ship affected by the same epidemic and on which all had already lost their sight, and to whom the French were obviously unable to give any help. *Le Rodeur* was luckier than the *San Leon*—which was lost at sea—and finally reached a safe haven, but twelve of its twenty-two crew members had gone permanently blind and another five had lost one eye; of the 160 slaves loaded in Africa only twenty-six retained their sight. It came to light subsequently, to crown this macabre episode, that some of the Africans who had gone blind had been thrown overboard during the trip, to save on the costs of maintenance and ensure that the insurers would pay up for the loss of cargo. The second case described by *O Compilador* also involved a French ship, which, with a British cruiser in pursuit, hurriedly threw some barrels overboard, apparently to lighten its load. When it was captured it emerged—but too late to do anything whatsoever about it—that the slaver ship's captain, in seeking to jettison incriminating evidence, had shut into those barrels some of the slave children he was carrying, leaving them to drift to their fate.[74]

Allocating space to these descriptions of the inherent violence and inhumanity of slavery was, as we have seen, one of the main strategies of abolitionism—the explanation of evil—and opened up the way to introducing something new in the Portuguese context: the open branding of those who took part in and encouraged slavery, from the 'criminal crews' of the slave ships to the 'despotic' and 'tyrannical' planter.[75] At the same time, in his sentimental journey on the routes of slavery, Baptista Gastão sought to sharpen feelings of guilt and to establish a strong contrast between the violence and power of the master and the innocence of the Negro:

> How much more virtuous and more innocent the uneducated Africans are than we who boast of being enlightened by the beacon of Revelation .... In their quiet deserts they never forged heavy chains with which to manacle beings of their own species .... Back in their woods and hovels their most fervent desires were probably that no ship of white men should ever touch their shores to tear them away forever from their families, their homes and their country.[76]

With their powerfully emotional roots, these new abolitionist arguments also carried a strong religious connotation, which, as we have seen in the memoir published in 1817 by the *Investigador Portuguez em Inglaterra*, called on a just and punishing God to condemn the criminal actions of the white man. Baptista Gastão interpreted the blindness of the *Le Rodeur* crew as the 'clear revenge of Providence ... against these enormous transgressions'.[77] The masters were 'monsters' whom Heaven would punish through idleness and debauchery, practices that would lead to a life of disease and unhappiness.[78]

This was, of course, a compilation of the basic triangular system of British abolitionism—awareness of the crime, remorse and reparation—which culminated in a clear argument for immediate abolition of the traffic, or even of the whole system of slavery, within a maximum of twenty years, as the journalist suggested in the *Gazeta de Portugal*[79]—and immediate abolition of the traffic for economic, social and political reasons but, above all, because it was an absolute evil, which no reason could justify. That was why the abolitionist campaigns of the British politicians were generally applauded—or at least not opposed. In any case, how was it possible to oppose British abolitionism on grounds of economic self-interest and at the same time argue for the continuation of the slave trade for similar reasons of self-interest?[80]

In sum, at the beginning of the 1820s, a few short and specific writings, and articles in the newspapers spread an unambiguously abolitionist message in Portugal for the first time. This message viewed the slave trade as a crime—thereby attaching negative connotations to those who encouraged it—and demanded an immediate or swift end to it. With substantial foundation in the moral and sentimental aspects of the issue, the message called for total opposition to the old rationale for slavery, and put forward, as an alternative, a system of mental representations that reversed it. Inasmuch as most of these articles had their origin in Britain, and the particular forms taken by Portuguese pro-slavery or tolerationist thought were unknown to their authors, opposition to that line of thinking generally took the form of an appeal to philosophical and sentimental principles that were judged to be universal, or of examples taken from the history of the anti-slavery struggle in Britain. However, in writings produced in Portugal, the abolitionist message tended to refer to the real background identified by local journalists and ideologues. It is therefore not surprising that Baptista Gastão should have taken the trouble to rebut bishop Azeredo Coutinho directly or that he should have been concerned to demolish the religious and philosophical ideas and associations that had until then been used in Portugal to argue for the continuation of the slave trade.[81]

3.2.4 The Inconsistent Abolitionism of Retaliation

Alongside the British-inspired abolitionist arguments, which came largely from outside the country, there came a time when some of the Portuguese press developed a second line of argument that was abolitionist in form but of a more specific nature. In 1822–23 these arguments were emerging against the backdrop of Brazilian separatism, a matter that, understandably, was of interest to all the journals, and which was therefore more frequent, or at any rate less infrequent, than the abolitionist propaganda, which appeared sporadically in the pages of four or five journals or pamphlets subsidized by the Quakers.

In the first years of the 1820s, the Portuguese press was almost unanimous in stating that, for various reasons, an independent Brazil would be unable to stand on its own two feet. One of those reasons, the one perhaps most often repeated, was that there was slavery in its midst. For this reason alone, given the nature of the master/slave relationship, cataclysmic outcomes were foreseen in the event of the Brazilians foregoing Portuguese tutelage. For José Liberato's *Campeão Portuguez em Lisboa* (Portuguese Champion in Lisbon), for example, Brazil could only contain the slaves if it was backed by the 'power of Portugal'; if the Brazilians should choose to live in independence and isolation, they would soon fall under the 'blows, or the barbarous dominion' of the African race.[82] The *Campeão Lisbonense* (Lisbon Champion) estimated that there were twenty Negroes for every white person in Brazil, and foresaw the worst:

> The cruel treatment inflicted by the masters on their slaves is a memorial imprinted on their souls. It sows the seed of revenge and motivates them to break the iron chains of their slavery .... The master who calls for independence brings on the moment of his downfall, for if he should seek independence from the mother country, the slaves will seek independence from their tyrant masters, and they will seek it all the more because their dependency is much heavier than the other.[83]

Those who argued that the internal state of Brazil as a result of slavery, amongst other things, prevented it from becoming independent, were not necessarily abolitionists. On the contrary, they were not generally opposed to the perpetuation of (or very gradual change in) the prevailing social conditions in Brazil because, in the circumstances of the time, they were a powerful brake on notions of independence. It is therefore no surprise that some of the press should have wished to maintain the status quo of slavery and were not opposed to the slave trade. The *Astro da Lusitania* (Lusitanian Star), the journal with the highest readership of the day, even published part of Maciel da Costa's memoir and made its columns available to an 'Oporto patriot' who asked for protection for the slave trade because it was a significant source of revenue for the national treasury.[84]

As in the Cortes, the position most often taken by the Portuguese press of the time was one of tolerance of the slave trade. As a general rule it was held that, because of the sensitive nature of Brazilian problems, it would not be suitable to force the consciences of the American brothers with hasty measures; the slaves would have to be freed little by little, in a manner compatible with 'the prosperity of our brothers in Brazil' and the survival of those slaves.[85] However, from the spring of 1822, and with the Brazilian breakaway, some journalists—and not only those who favoured political theories of 'integrationism'—began to consider abolition of the slave trade as a possible form of retaliation or a posteriori adjustment to Brazil's new seditious status. In the Cortes, at a particularly bitter point in the debate, Borges Carneiro mentioned the possibility of blackmailing the Brazilian rebels by cutting off the supply of slaves directly on the African coast.[86] But this was an excess for a moderate, and it was not taken up by his peers. In the press, however, the retaliation argument could be advocated with less subterfuge, and some journalists therefore started to argue for, or accept, the total and immediate abolition of the slave trade. Among them we find José Liberato and Solano Constâncio, which should not surprise us. Since both of them had in the past foreseen the end of the slave trade as unfailingly bringing on the collapse of Brazil, they could now argue for such an outcome precisely on the basis of that equivalence. For Liberato and Constâncio abolition was a weapon in the counter-attack, something which, although not desired, it might be necessary to put into practice.

This retaliation approach was closely tied to arguments for the development of the African colonies. Admittedly not all favoured this option. *O Compilador*, for example, was explicitly hostile to new efforts in the colonies.[87] The *Annaes das Sciências, das Artes e das Letras*, adopting a less drastic attitude, called for the abandonment of 'disastrous plans' to govern distant colonies, and suggested that, along with Brazil, Portugal should also let go of its Asian territories.[88] Nevertheless, the *Annaes* and other journals argued in favour of the idea that Portugal could easily create 'new Brazils' in its African possessions. Seen in this light, the imperial divorce could become 'a major benefit' if it made the country industrious and active, if it forced Portugal to create in the Atlantic islands and in

Africa 'a power so solid and so wealthy' that it might cause 'belated regrets' to form in the Brazilians' minds.[89] The retaliationists, who brandished abolitionism as a weapon, evidently assumed that the whole system of slavery could be diverted from its traditional destination and easily converted, and imagined a list of tropical products to be cultivated intensively in Africa, where the over-abundant Negro labour would immediately be employed. With its African option, Portugal could then do without imports from Brazil, compete with Brazil in international markets and, what is more, deprive it of the extraordinary resource that slave labour represented—a deprivation that would give a serious jolt to the Brazilian economy, which did not really have any alternative to the slave trade. Brazil could have no hope of 'seeing the hard-working Swiss, the constant German, the active and ingenious Frenchman, the robust Irishman, or the skilful and prudent Scotsman work the earth alongside the Negro, and have to partake of the disdain to which the poor slave is constantly subjected'.[90]

The retaliatory abolitionism that had just emerged seemed to be making a common front with the abolitionism of British origin, which, as we have seen, was beginning to achieve a degree of dissemination in public life. But that common front was weak, for two reasons. First, the total number of abolitionist manifestations was limited, and short-lived. The counter-revolution, which began in 1823, led to the closing down of the main organs of the liberal press, and resulted in the flight or the exile of several journalists (such as José Liberato, for example).[91] The number of journals in circulation would increase again in 1826–28, but that increase did not bring with it a resumption of debate on abolition. From 1823 onwards, it was once again submerged in Portuguese culture and was touched upon only sporadically when foreign news items were transcribed.[92] This eclipse occurred because—and this is the second reason—retaliatory abolitionism was circumstantial and intermittent in nature. To succeed, it required a number of improbable factors to come together. In 1822 the commitment to the African colonies as an alternative to Brazil represented an outpouring of temporary annoyance and of ideas put together in the heat of the moment. The formally abolitionist rhetoric that came out of that process was an element in the arguments of those who, feeling betrayed by the jewel of the crown and seeking to put a shine on other gems of the old empire, sought to strangle the slave trade and thereby prevent rivals profiting from it. This last motivation was in a sense a reproduction on the Portuguese scene of what had occurred with the planters in the West Indies. When faced with the fait accompli of abolition in 1807, they moved from defending the slave trade to arguing for its universal suppression. This was the only way they had of mitigating their defeat and of trying to cancel out the future advantages of their colonial competitors. In both cases material interest was the true motive for their change of heart. But, in the Portuguese case, it was a form of abolitionism that few believed in, because there was no agreement, even among the enthusiasts for the development of a 'new Brazil', that such a development would require the abolition of the slave trade; in addition, it was also a conditional form of abolitionism, which in a way remained marooned because it was strictly dependent on the cutting of the Luso-Brazilian umbilical cord and the simultaneous interest of Portuguese politicians and capitalists in African mirages.

The first few months after Brazilian secession soon showed how unreal that scenario was. Despite the efforts of the pro-colonization propaganda, the idea that the African colonies might replace Brazil was viewed with reticence, with disdain or with profound irony by many observers—particularly by the Brazilians—for whom it seemed that the proposal to exchange the gentle breezes of South America for the deserts of Africa was like the dog in the fable that let go of 'the cheese it had in its mouth to grab another one it sees reflected in the water'.[93] In Portugal, projections of optimistic and fantasized scenarios involving Africa's potential were scarcely credible. Portuguese society had been in contact with the realities of Africa for a long time, and with its promise and drawbacks. The margin for dreaming and fantasizing was relatively thin, tempered by centuries of misfortune and a knowledge born of experience. How could anyone believe, the *Gazeta Universal* (Universal Gazette) asked, 'that the Portuguese, not having advanced the colonies of Africa until now, despite having been lords and masters of them for nearly 400 years, will now succeed in making enormous strides in production and wealth?'[94]

That long experience of Africa and the depressing outlook that derived from it—aspects we shall look at in detail in chapter 6—help in large measure to explain why there was no turning to Africa, despite the very unfavourable circumstances that affected Portuguese external trade when the colonial monopoly was broken (1808) and later with the secession of Brazil. In fact, recognizing Brazilian independence did not mean the Portuguese had to abandon the American dream for ever, but rather a successive redefinition of economic objectives along ever more modest lines. At times there might have been a fear that, following secession, Portuguese trade might be completely swept from Brazilian ports. And it was in this context that, in 1823, and in the narrow logic of retaliatory abolitionism, the governor of Angola, Avelino Dias, tried to ban the slave trade from the colony he governed.[95] But this retaliatory approach was soon dropped in favour of trade treaty negotiations whereby, in exchange for political recognition, assurances were sought that, amongst other things, there would be total duty and tax exemption on Portuguese wine in Brazil.[96]

Even if the latter aim was not achieved in the Luso-Brazilian treaty of 29 August 1825, the efforts of the Lisbon government were not directed to the African colonies but to the attempts to improve the terms that had just been agreed with Brazil. Significantly, it was even willing to grant exclusive access to the Portuguese market for Brazilian articles that might compete directly with African products (a proposal Brazil rejected). Better trade terms were just being obtained, with a reduction of duties to 10 per cent, when the death of D. João VI in 1826 interrupted and postponed the negotiations *sine die*.[97] For the merchants, on the other hand, the collapse of Brazilian trade did not bring on a rush to Africa: first, because that collapse was uneven in its impact on the country, affecting Lisbon especially;[98] and, secondly, because in Portugal in 1825–35 a collapsed Brazil trade that had difficulty competing seemed all the same to be preferable to very risky dealings with Africa. With the agrarian and mercantile bourgeoisie's persistent attachment to what remained of the Brazilian market, the imaginary enthusiasm for Africa evaporated, and with it retaliatory abolitionism. Liberato did not take advantage of the time he was to spend at the *Gazeta de Lisboa* in 1827 to unearth his abolitionist proposals of 1822.[99] Only Morais Sarmento—who was not in favour of retaliation in the strict sense of the term—remained remarkably persistent for a few years, but even he would bend, as we shall see in the next chapter.

Retaliatory abolitionism had been born at the time of a colonial split, and it reflected the pains of that birth. Genetically tied to the loss of an empire and to the idea of building another, it fluctuated and would continue to fluctuate in the following years, according to the viability of that idea. This means it was a circumstantial abolitionism: the common front it seemed to form with British-inspired abolitionism was unstable. To the extent that it depended on the position taken in relation to Brazil and on what was considered useful for the African colonies at any given moment, it was a wavering approach that easily slid into a more or less obstructive tolerationism.

Tolerationists sought to prolong the life of the transatlantic slave trade because they thought that abolishing it in a hurry would lead to the loss of the African colonies unless, as Acúrsio das Neves explained, there were to be a clear commitment to the development of those colonies—precisely the scenario which the retaliatory abolitionists optimistically imagined was within their grasp. The degree of convergence of the two approaches depended therefore on the greater or lesser viability of plans for Africa. It should be emphasized that the anti-slave trade proposals of José Liberato, Solano Constâncio and other retaliators were the result of the adaptation of the tolerationism of the 1810s to the new historical circumstances, but they were not diametrically opposed to that form of tolerationism and retained some of its key concepts. In particular, *et pour cause*, the idea that the end of the slave trade would mean the collapse of Brazil, the notion of the intrinsic barbarity of the African (and the relative humaneness of slavery) and the desire to improve the 'Portuguese system', through which Negroes could attain the major benefit of progressively becoming more civilized.[100] Even if it favoured political and economic arguments, retaliatory abolitionism was not unaware of arguments of a philosophical and moral nature; however, it was not underlain with any truly radical sentimental or ethical condemnation of the practice of slavery, which was not seen as a crime. Unlike the British-inspired abolitionists, the aim of the retaliators was not to end slavery—because its own outcome continued to be seen as the lesser evil for the Negro. José Liberato's and Solano Constâncio's articles did not suggest putting an end to slavery but merely diverting the demographic flow, redirecting a slave trade that until then had flowed unhampered to the Americas.

Some of the basic assumptions of the ideology of slavery and of the obstructive tolerationism that succeeded it were thus preserved in the inconsistent abolitionism of retaliation, albeit now applied to new situations. This was not just something residual, nor was it without its consequences. On the contrary, it contributed to the versatility and lability of that kind of abolitionism, allowing it to slide along the spectrum according to circumstances. Rather than stressing the sporadic and transitory nature of pro-abolitionist manifestations in Portugal in the 1820s, it is more important to underline the fact that the bifocal framework of Portuguese pro-abolitionism in that period carried the potential for convergence—of which Morais Sarmento would be the best personification at the time—but it also contained significant divergences. While these were not always immediately obvious, they would come into the light of day and be of major importance fifteen years later, in the *Septembrista* era.

To sum up, the period from 1820 to 1834 was one of the most troubled periods in Portuguese history. In those years of great transformations and break-ups, revolutions and uprisings, of the loss of an empire, of constitutional advances and retreats, the issue of slavery was very low down on the list of Portuguese concerns. In spite of everything, there were men who came out openly against the slave trade and, for a time, there seemed to be a common approach favourable to abolition, adopted by journalists such as Baptista Gastão and José Liberato, by deputies such as Margiochi and Morais Sarmento and by ministers like Palmela and the future Count of Lavradio. However, that approach was the result of two divergent lines of thinking, one of which was not unequivocally distant from tolerationism. Thus, despite Brazil's secession, the period in question did not even see a reduction in the widespread mimicry and promiscuity of argument between those against and those who were deceptively in favour of the institutions of slavery. On the contrary, the ideological backdrop took on new tonalities and layers, and became overloaded with the idea of African interests, which made it more difficult to abandon the half-tints of the tolerationist approach.

With no internal pressure, and lost now in the whirlwind of serious political crisis and military conflict, the abolitionist intentions that had surfaced intermittently between 1820 and 1827 withered away, and the decade came to an end with the issue sliding once more into obscurity and silence. This was made even easier by the fact that British pressure also declined. It can never be overemphasized how important that pressure was in motivating abolitionist discussion in Portugal. Between 1823 and 1827 British diplomats were not particularly insistent in their dealings with the Portuguese government, preferring to focus their attentions on Brazil. Subsequently, given the 'peculiar circumstances' in which the Portuguese Crown found itself, as Palmerston would say, London refrained from 'squeezing too hard' for the conclusion of the desired treaty.[101]

Notes

1. For the stratagems used by the Portuguese slavers, see Pierre Verger, *Flux et reflux de la traite des nègres entre le golfe de Bénin et Bahia de Todos os Santos du XVIIe au XIXe siècles*, Mouton, Paris and The Hague, 1968, pp. 403–05, and the various cases recorded by British sources (PRO FO 84/10).
2. David Eltis, 'The British Contribution to the Nineteenth-Century Transatlantic Slave Trade', *Economic History Review*, 32, 2, 1979, p. 220 (especially note 3).
3. Textiles produced in Manchester rapidly replaced Indian textiles, which had been an important prop for the Portuguese slave trade—including the trade in Mozambique, where English cloth arrived via Bombay. Eltis reckons that by around 1820 products of British origin represented most of the manufactures transported by Portuguese and Brazilian slave ships to the African coast (ibid., pp. 219–20). For Bahia's tobacco trade with the Costa da Mina, see Verger, *Flux et reflux*, p. 28 ff.
4. Eltis, 'The British Contribution', p. 214 ff.
5. Since there is no reliable information on the volume of traffic of North American slaves after 1807, Eltis projected average imports of one thousand slaves per year up to 1822 (David Eltis, 'The Nineteenth-Century Transatlantic Slave Trade: An Annual Time Series of Imports into the Americas, Broken Down by Region', *The Hispanic American Historical Review*, 67, 1987, p. 135, note 67).
6. A.R. Booth, 'The United States African Squadron, 1843–1861', in *Boston University Papers on Africa*, vol. 1, Boston, 1964, p. 83 (note 20).
7. Serge Daget, 'Armateurs Nantais et trafic négrier illégal: une histoire sans petite boîte verte', *Enquêtes et Documents*, XIII, 1987, pp. 74–75; and idem, 'Les croisières françaises de répression de la traite des noirs sur les côtes occidentales de l'Afrique (1817–1850)', *Enquêtes et Documents*, XIV, 1988, p. 31.
8. Between 1816 and 1820 Cuba is said to have imported an average of over 25,500 slaves per year; from 1821 to 1823 that average fell to 3,600 slaves per year, and the Cuban traffic was held to moderate levels before it revived towards the end of the decade: from 1828 to 1830 Cuba would import some 14,000 slaves per year, an average that rose in subsequent years (see Eltis, 'The Nineteenth-Century', p. 122).
9. António Carreira, *O tráfico de escravos nos rios de Guiné e ilhas de Cabo Verde, 1810–1850. Subsídios para o seu estudo*, Junta de Investigação Científica do Ultramar, Lisbon, 1981, pp. 24–38; G.E. Brooks, 'A Nhara of the Guinea-Bissau Region: Mãe Aurélia Correia', in C.C. Robertson and M. Klein (eds), *Women and Slavery in Africa*, University of Wisconsin Press, Madison, 1983, p. 312. For the ways in which the illegal trade on the Costa da Mina was organized, see Verger, *Flux et reflux*, chapter 15.
10. For the complaints of the Portuguese commissioners, see ANTT, MNE, *cx.* 224; and J. César de Figanière e Morão, *Descripção de Serra Leoa e seus contornos. Escripta em doze cartas à qual se ajuntão os trabalhos da Commissão-Mixta portugueza e inglesa estabelecida naquela colónia*, Lisbon, 1822.

11. Christopher Fyfe, *A History of Sierra Leone*, Oxford University Press, London, 1962, p. 114 ff.
12. Silvestre P. Ferreira to Cristóvão Morais Sarmento, 5 April 1823, ANTT, MNE, *liv.* 571.
13. Thornton to Canning, 8 March 1824, PRO FO 84/31; Palmela to Porto Santo, 9 January 1826, in J.J. Reis e Vasconcellos, *Despachos e Correspondência do Duque de Palmela*, vol. 2, Imprensa Nacional, Lisbon, 1851, p. 204; Palmela to Canning, 9 August 1826, ANTT, MNE, *cx.* 481.
14. Julio Firmino Júdice Biker, *Suplemento à colecção de Tratados, Convenções, Contratos e Actos Públicos celebrados entre a Coroa de Portugal e as mais Potências desde 1640 até ao presente*, vol. XX, Lisbon, 1879, p. 24. For the text of the supplementary Anglo-Portuguese agreement of 1823, see José F. Borges de Castro, *Collecção dos tratados, convenções, contratos e actos públicos celebrados entre a Coroa de Portugal e as mais Potências desde 1640 até ao presente*, vols. IV and V, Imprensa Nacional, Lisbon, 1857–58.
15. W.A. Green, *British Slave Emancipation. The Sugar Colonies and the Great Experiment, 1830–1865*, Clarendon Press, Oxford, 1976, pp. 100–01; David B. Davis, *The Problem of Slavery in the Age of Revolution, 1770–1823*, Cornell University Press, Ithaca, NY, and London, 1975, p. 160 ff.; idem, *Slavery and Human Progress*, Oxford University Press, Oxford, 1984, pp. 176–77; Roger Anstey, 'Religion and British Slave Emancipation', in David Eltis and James Walvin (eds), *The Abolition of the Atlantic Slave Trade. Origins and Effects in Europe, Africa and the Americas*, University of Wisconsin Press, Madison, 1981, p. 38 ff.
16. David Turley, *The Culture of English Antislavery, 1780–1860*, Routledge, London, 1991, p. 48.
17. Ibid., pp. 63 ff.; James Walvin, 'The Public Campaign in England Against Slavery', in Eltis and Walvin (eds), *Abolition*, p. 73.
18. Davis, *Slavery and Human*, p. 108; Green, *British*, pp. 119 ff.
19. For the impact of the Portuguese revolution in Brazil, see Maria Beatriz Nizza da Silva, 'A repercussão da Revolução de 1820 no Brasil. Eventos e ideologias', *Revista de História das Ideias*, 2, 1978–79, pp. 1–52; and Valentim Alexandre, *Os sentidos do Império. Questão nacional e questão colonial na crise do Antigo Regime português*, Afrontamento, Porto, 1993, p. 490 ff.
20. Quoted in Leslie Bethell, *The Abolition of the Brazilian Slave Trade. Britain, Brazil and the Slave Trade Question (1807–1869)*, Cambridge University Press, Cambridge, 1970, p. 31.
21. Ibid., p. 31 ff.
22. Ibid., pp. 28–61.
23. Ward to Silvestre P. Ferreira, 13 November 1822, ANTT, MNE, *cx.* 485.
24. Silvestre P. Ferreira to Ward, 12 December 1822, in Biker, *Suplemento*, vol. XX, pp. 242–45.
25. Palmela to Vila Real, 13 January 1824, in Biker, *Suplemento*, vol. XXI, p. 315.
26. Thornton to Canning and Palmela to Thornton, 18 June and 14 September 1824, respectively, PRO FO 84/31.
27. Francisco de Almeida to A'Court, 2 October 1826, ANTT, MNE, *liv.* 180.
28. Canning to A'Court, September 1826, PRO FO 84/54.
29. *Diário das Cortes*, session of 2 August 1821, p. 1768.
30. Ibid., p. 1770.
31. Ibid.
32. Ibid., p. 1771 (speech by the abbot of Medrões).
33. Alexandre, *Os sentidos do império*, pp. 594–95 and 618 ff.
34. *Diário das Cortes*, session of 22 March 1822, pp. 582–83.
35. Ibid., session of 18 March 1822, p. 541.
36. Ibid., session of 26 June 1822, p. 565.

37. António Saldanha da Gama, *Memória sobre as colónias de Portugal situadas na costa Ocidental d'Africa, mandada ao governo pelo antigo Governador e Capitão-Geral do Reino de Angola... em 1814, precedida de um discurso preliminar, augmentada de alguns additamentos e notas,...,* Paris, 1839.
38. *Observador Luzitano em Paris,* March 1815, pp. 407–18.
39. See, for example, the letter published in *O Investigador Portuguez em Inglaterra,* September 1812, pp. 402–07.
40. *Diário das Cortes,* session of 19 April 1822, pp. 884–85.
41. See, for example, the reference by Morais Sarmento to the case of the ship *Le Rodeur, Diário das Cortes,* session of 8 June 1822, p. 388.
42. Chamber of Deputies, session of 20 December 1826, *Gazeta de Lisboa,* 21 December 1826.
43. J. Albuquerque, *Indice Alphabetico e Remissivo dos trabalhos Parlamentares das Cortes Geraes da Nação Portuguesa,* vol. II, Lisbon, 1901, p. 47.
44. *DCD,* session of 11 December 1826, p. 157.
45. *DCD,* session of 8 March 1828, p. 732.
46. Memoir of Diogo Tovar e Albuquerque (1815), *Annaes do Conselho Ultramarino,* April 1854, pp. 42–44.
47. Saldanha da Gama, *Memória sobre as colónias.*
48. Silvestre P. Ferreira to Ward, 12 December 1822, in Biker, *Suplemento,* vol. XX, pp. 242–45.
49. Instruction given to José Basílio Rademaker (who negotiated on behalf of Portugal the supplementary article to the convention of 28 July 1817), 18 February 1823, in Biker, *Suplemento,* vol. XX, p. 248.
50. Porto Santo to Palmela, 25 June and 20 October 1825, ANTT, MNE, *liv.* 571.
51. Porto Santo to Palmela, 15 December 1825, ANTT, MNE, *liv.* 583.
52. See, for example, A'Court to Porto Santo, 24 December 1825, PRO FO 84/41 and Palmela to Canning, 17 June 1826, ANTT, MNE, *cx.* 481.
53. Porto Santo to Palmela, 15 December 1825, ANTT, MNE, *liv.* 583; Porto Santo to A'Court, 23 February 1826, and Palmela to Canning (and the latter's reply), 14 and 30 June 1826, PRO FO 84/54.
54. Palmela to Canning, 5 July 1826, ANTT, MNE, *cx.* 481.
55. D. Francisco de Almeida to A'Court, 24 April 1827, PRO FO 84/72. For the missions undertaken during this period by the vessels in question—the brig *Constituição* and schooner *Conceição*—see António Esparteiro, *Três séculos no mar (1640–1910),* 32 vols., Ministério da Marinha, Lisbon, 1974–86.
56. Palmela to D. Francisco de Almeida, 28 April 1827, in Vasconcellos, *Despachos,* vol. 3, pp. 123–24.
57. José Acúrsio das Neves, *Considerações Politicas e Commerciais sobre os descobrimentos e Possessões dos Portuguezes na África e na Asia,* Lisbon, 1830, p. 135.
58. Ibid., pp. 129–30.
59. Ibid., pp. 122–23, 129, 145 and 229.
60. Ibid., pp. 130–31 and 138.
61. Ibid., pp. 153–154, 234–35 and 238.
62. Ibid., pp. 160–61.
63. Turley, *Culture,* pp. 48–51.
64. *Breve Resumo sobre a Natureza do commercio da escravatura e das atrocidades que dele resultam,* London, 1821.
65. (Blanco White), *Bosquejo sobre o commercio em escravos. Reflexões sobre este tráfico, considerado moral, política and christãmente,* London, 1821. On the identity of the author, see David R. Murray, *Odious Commerce: Britain, Spain and the Abolition of the Cuban Slave Trade,* Cambridge University Press, Cambridge, 1980, p. 61.
66. Thomas Clarkson, *Os gemidos dos africanos por causa do trafico da Escravatura, ou breve exposição das injurias e dos horrores que accompanham este traffico homicida,* London, 1823.

67. *Memorial aos habitantes da Europa sobre a iniquidade do Commercio da Escravatura*, London, 1824.
68. (Blanco White), *Bosquejo*, p. 88.
69. Ibid., pp. 60–61 and 85.
70. Poem by James Montgomery, 'The West Indies', 1807, *O Templo da Memória*, 4 and 6, 1820, pp. 7–11 and 5–11, respectively.
71. *Gazeta de Portugal*, 30 September and 3 October 1822.
72. *O Compilador*, March 1822, pp. 380–81.
73. Ibid.
74. Ibid., pp. 390–91. For further examples of abolitionist approaches that appealed to the reader's sensibility, see the *Gazeta de Portugal* of 3 October 1822, and *Correio da Tarde*, 11 April 1823.
75. *O Compilador*, March 1822, pp. 381 and 387.
76. Ibid., p. 383.
77. Ibid., pp. 384–90.
78. *Gazeta de Portugal*, 3 October 1822.
79. Ibid., 5 October 1822.
80. Ibid., 3 October 1822. For other favourable views of British philanthropy see *Correio da Tarde*, 11 April 1823.
81. *Gazeta de Portugal*, 3 October 1822.
82. *Campeão Portuguez em Lisboa*, 11 May 1822, pp. 84–86.
83. *Campeão Lisbonense*, 21 May and 4 June 1822. For similar conclusions see *O Amigo do Povo*, 2 June 1821; *Annaes das Sciências das Artes e das Letras*, April 1822, p. 99, and *Jornal da Sociedade Literária e Patriótica*, April 1822, p. 26. The dire prognostications for Brazil's future naturally persisted right up to the moment of independence (see, for example, *Gazeta de Lisboa*, 10 January and 28 February 1824).
84. *Astro da Lusitania*, 26 October 1821 and 23 and 24 April 1822.
85. *O Amigo do Povo*, 2 June 1821.
86. *Diário das Cortes*, session of 27 April 1822, p. 979.
87. *O Compilador*, May 1822, pp. 15–16.
88. *Annaes das Sciências, das Artes e das Letras*, April 1822, p. 93.
89. *Campeão Portuguez em Lisboa*, 11 May 1822, pp. 92–93.
90. *Annaes das Sciências, das Artes e das Letras*, April 1822, pp. 97 and 101.
91. José Liberato Freire de Carvalho, *Memórias da vida de José Liberato Freire de Carvalho*, Assírio e Alvim, Lisbon, 1982 (1st edition 1855), p. 167 ff.; for the drop in the number of newspapers, see the list provided by J. Silva Pereira, *O jornalismo Portuguez. Resenha chronológica de todos os periódicos portuguezes impressos e publicados no Reino e no estrangeiro, desde o meiado do século XVII até à morte do saudoso Rei Senhor D. Luís I, bem como dos jornais em língua estrangeira publicados em Portugal durante o mesmo tempo*, Lisbon, 1895, and José Tengarrinha, *História da imprensa periódica portuguesa*, Lisbon, undated, pp. 89–90.
92. See, by way of example, *Gazeta de Lisboa*, 12 February 1824, 28 February and 12 March 1825.
93. *Campeão Lisbonense*, 5 August 1822.
94. *Gazeta Universal*, 29 March 1822.
95. Valentim Alexandre, *Origens do colonialismo português moderno (1822–1891)*, Sá da Costa, Lisboa, 1979, pp. 32–33; idem, 'O liberalismo português e as colónias de África, 1820–1839', *Análise Social*, 16, 61–62, 1980, p. 326.
96. Valentim Alexandre, 'A desagregação do império: Portugal e o reconhecimento do Estado brasileiro (1824–1826)', *Análise Social*, 28, 121, 1993, p. 328.
97. Ibid., pp. 339–41. For the dispatches of Charles Stuart (who negotiated on behalf of Portugal) to Porto Santo (minister of Foreign Affairs), see Biker, *Suplemento*, vol. XXIII, pp. 424–32.

98. Maria de Fátima Bonifácio, 'Comércio externo e política pautal na 1ª metade do século XIX', *Ler História*, 10, 1987, p. 81.
99. On Liberato's time at the *Gazeta de Lisboa*, see his own references in Carvalho, *Memórias*, pp. 176–77.
100. *Annaes das Sciências, das Artes e das Letras*, April 1822, pp. 95–96.
101. Palmerston to Howard de Walden, 8 September 1834, in *Documentos àcerca do tráfico da escravatura extrahidos dos papéis relativos a Portugal apresentados ao Parlamento Britannico*, Lisbon, 1840, p. 1.

– *Chapter 4* –

PLANS AND STRATAGEMS: THE *SEPTEMBRISTAS* AND THE PROBLEM OF THE SUPPRESSION OF THE SLAVE TRADE

The French slave trade ended at the beginning of the 1830s, partly on account of the efforts of the Société de la Morale Chrétienne, a small group of enlightened personages, many of them Protestant, who sought to persuade selected individuals and whose favourite method, in the British manner, was the publication of articles and petitions to Parliament.[1] Although modest compared with the British, the French abolitionists' campaign was instrumental in producing more forceful action against the illegal slave trade. Naval efforts intensified, and from 1826 to 1831 French warships apprehended thirty-five slave ships. The French Parliament approved new abolitionist laws, and on 30 November 1831 the Paris government finally acknowledged the right of search, in a new treaty with Britain, which would be reinforced by the additional protocol of 22 March 1833. From that year on, the French trade ceased for all practical purposes.[2]

The situation of the slave trade to Cuba was the complete opposite, as that trade grew and came close to the high levels it had attained in the second half of the 1810s.[3] The abolitionist zeal of the Spanish authorities, who were generally more interested in encouraging the slave trade than in enforcing the law, was virtually nil. From 1820 to 1842 the Spanish navy apprehended only two slave ships, both flying the Portuguese flag.[4] The Foreign Office had great hopes of a new treaty containing a clause that would allow for the seizure of vessels equipped for the slave trade—even if there were no slaves on board. After much toing and froing this treaty was finally signed on 28 June 1835.[5]

The biggest problem at the start of the decade was, however, the resurgence of the Brazilian trade. Abolitionist agreements with Britain had been concocted without taking the interests of the traders and planters into account and without regard for the prevailing currents of opinion in Brazil. An abolitionist law imposing bodily punishment and fines on importers of slaves was passed on 7 November 1831, but this was a false alarm.[6] It is true that, for a time, the slave trade to Brazil seemed to be in decline, but this was due to uncertainty as to how strictly the Brazilian authorities would apply the law and also to the momentary saturation of the labour markets following the surge in imports at the end of the 1820s. With the coffee boom and a perception that the law was not being applied, the Brazilian trade resumed in full. It was reorganized on a completely illegal basis, which was highly profitable. By the middle of the decade import figures were once again extremely high.[7]

With the revival of the Brazilian slave trade Portugal once again took on the central role on the abolitionist stage, not only because the main slavers resident in Brazil were Portuguese—according to obviously exaggerated statements of the British consul in Rio, there were said to be 30,000 Portuguese there, all of them involved in that trade[8]—but also, and above all, because most of the undertakings were carried on with the connivance of the Portuguese authorities. In fact, with the effective French ban and the uncertainty as to how strict Brazilian policing would be, the Portuguese flag was once again much sought after both north and, more troublingly, south of the equator.

4.1 Pressures and Procrastinations

When the Portuguese civil war ended, with the triumph of the liberals, Britain resumed its diplomatic pressure for Lisbon to sign a treaty that would totally ban the trade in slaves, and which would enable the Royal Navy cruisers to intervene much more broadly and effectively. Strictly speaking, British pressure re-emerged even before the war had ended.[9] But it was after the liberal regime had settled down that the pressure became more intense and systematic. In September 1834, Palmerston, thinking that Portugal should be 'anxious' to comply with the abolitionist obligations it had taken on, sent a draft of a treaty to his ambassador in Lisbon, Howard de Walden, to be submitted to the Portuguese government and negotiated 'with the least possible delay'.[10] From the end of that year, London began to bombard the Ministry of Foreign Affairs with dispatches, reports and communiqués that drew attention to the widespread involvement of Portuguese in the 'odious commerce'.

Both Vila Real and Palmela, and even Loulé, the liberal Ministers of Foreign Affairs between October 1834 and September 1836, sought to demonstrate that they in no way encouraged or consented to the continuation of the slave trade. Confronted with one denunciation after another, they gave repeated orders and instructions for inquiries to be held. Whenever those involved were positively identified, they duly informed the competent authorities so that the offenders might be punished under prevailing laws. They also addressed dispatches to successive Navy Ministers, requesting them to investigate and to renew their instructions to the colonial authorities to prevent the export of slaves from Portuguese Africa. Inspections and inquiries would follow, but they were always inconclusive.[11]

At the time it was clear that there were policy differences between the Navy and Foreign Ministers. The Foreign Ministers held the view that the transatlantic slave trade had been completely prohibited since Brazilian independence and that there were laws which, however limited and imperfect they might be, enabled them to act in some way against the slavers.[12] However, because Portuguese anti-slave trade legislation had too many holes and grey areas in it, the Foreign Ministry's interpretations were rarely in accord with those of the Navy, for whom there was nothing illegal about allowing Brazilian ships, for example, to call on the Angolan coast to buy slaves.[13] We should add that the Navy was generally annoyed by the British accusations, not only because they showed up the variety of tricks the Portuguese authorities used in order to perpetuate the trade, but also because they made it obvious that Portugal did not comply with its own legislation, in particular the charter of 26 January 1818, which had banned the slave trade north of the equator. As Howard de Walden emphasized, ships were apprehended in the northern hemisphere and were condemned by the mixed commission in Sierra Leone and the cases were notified to the Lisbon government, which made repeated promises to apply the law, but nothing ever came of it. More serious was the situation south of the equator, where the Royal Navy frequently sighted *tumbeiros* flying the Portuguese flag. Despite the fact that they were clearly operating illegally, they could not be seized and prosecuted under the treaties then in force. In these circumstances, the warnings given by the British embassy were justified: 'if the government of Portugal denies to others the power to detain, in particular latitudes, Portuguese vessels in a trade which is now confessedly illegal, surely a heavy obligation rests upon that government to put a stop themselves … to the prosecution of Portuguese slave trade in those latitudes.'[14]

In a word, British pressure was making it urgent that new legislation be passed and, above all, that it be applied vigorously and without ambiguities. Even though Portugal was bound, by the treaty of 22 January 1815, jointly with Britain to set the date when the slave trade in its dominions would cease in its entirety, there was no reason why it could not take other measures on its own initiative. In political terms it even seemed appropriate that it should do so, to safeguard the country's image. The British would not object: quite the contrary, since it had always been an expressed desire of the various British administrations that successive abolitionist laws should be seen as the emanation of each country's will, and not the result of outside interference.[15] It was in this context, and at Palmela's insistence, that the Council of Ministers instructed the Minister of Justice at the beginning of 1835, Barreto Ferraz, to draw up a law prohibiting the trade in slaves and to make it equivalent to piracy. Shortly afterwards, Barreto Ferraz submitted his draft law to the cabinet, and at the end of March it was decided that it should be submitted 'as soon as possible' to the Cortes.[16]

This was never done. Palmela, whose government fell on 28 April, attributed the setback to the very unstable political climate of the day.[17] The government did not have a firm majority in the Cortes, where it faced tenacious opposition from the more or less radical left and the threatening agitation of the audience that filled the galleries. With no popular support, under constant pressure from the armed populace of the cities, whom nobody had yet been able to disarm, governments had a precarious existence and their members were lonely men. Palmela, in particular, was seen by large segments of the urban population as a mere agent of British interests in Portugal, and was hated accordingly. In March 1835 he even suffered the supreme humiliation of having to flee through the back gardens to escape the mob, which had surrounded his house and had threatened to lynch him (and which did in fact assault and assassinate some passers-by).[18] Accused of being responsible for nearly everything bad that was happening in Portuguese society, Palmela could naturally do without further grounds for his unpopularity. Even if, as he said, he had wished to move forward with the abolition law and was ready to start negotiating the treaty with Britain, he put off such moves.

In any event, in 1835, Palmela, in his official correspondence with the British ambassador, while regretting the delay in the negotiations, declared that he was fully receptive to London's demands. In his view, and in line with the position he had adopted many times in earlier years, the trade in slaves between the African colonies and Brazil was totally illegal. He therefore accepted that, until a new agreement was made, the Royal Navy should be free to extend the provisions of the 1817 convention to the southern hemisphere.[19] In an attempt to demonstrate good faith and improve suppression within the existing legal framework, Palmela, who returned to government at the end of May, issued a government order that, by reference to existing anti-slave trade legislation, authorized the consular and colonial authorities to take any measures required to ensure that offenders would not go unpunished and to prevent the fitting out of slave ships in Portuguese ports.[20] But these instructions had no practical effect: the authorities in question ignored them, and they were irrelevant for the British, because the Royal Navy continued to have no legal cover for its intervention against Portuguese slavers in the southern hemisphere—and would only acquire it if the Lisbon government were to grant it expressly by way of a treaty.[21]

Anglo-Portuguese negotiations over abolition only began in earnest in October 1835, but were interrupted shortly thereafter by another political crisis, which brought the left into power (with Loulé as Minister of Foreign Affairs and Sá da Bandeira as Navy Minister). In March 1836, in response to the constant British pressure, Loulé promised that a law making the slave trade an act of piracy would shortly be submitted to the Cortes.[22] The draft law which his fellow minister Sá da Bandeira actually submitted to the Chamber of Peers on 26 March 1836 made no mention of piracy. Even so, it was an ambitious plan that not only sought to ban the slave trade but also laid down the freedom of the womb and provided for the setting up of a registration mechanism that would require all owners to submit a list of the slaves they owned, on pain of forfeiting them.[23] The draft was referred to a special committee for evaluation, and there it stayed. However, in the brief remarks made in the Chamber, voices immediately made themselves heard arguing that the proposed measures were inopportune and unworkable. For Xavier Botelho—an ex-governor of Mozambique who, as Sá da Bandeira himself mentioned in his *Diário* (Diary), was said to have been involved in the slave trade[24]—the state of the colonies and the lack of strong authority meant that it would be unwise to pass such a law. Morais Sarmento was of a similar opinion, something that illustrates how volatile pro-abolition positions in Portugal were at the time, for Sarmento was, it will be recalled, the father of the first draft law in Portugal on the abolition of the slave trade and a conspicuous admirer of British anti-slavery.[25] Nobody argued at any length in favour of the draft law. Only Loulé and Taipa sought to counter the objections raised in the Chamber, with the argument that the proposed legislation was only directed at the trade in slaves. Apart from the fact that this was not entirely true, it did not disarm the draft legislation's opponents.[26]

The left-wing government fell shortly afterwards and was replaced by a more moderate administration (with Vila Real at the Ministry of Foreign Affairs). With the way through the Cortes blocked, there was still an opening in an abolition treaty with Great Britain, which, towards the end of April, was almost negotiated, apparently putting an end to what had been, in Palmerston's words, 'a long and painful recital of Portuguese bad faith on the slave trade question going back 30 years'.[27] Since it was an extension of what had been set down by Palmela in the agreements of 1815 and 1817, the treaty naturally followed the same philosophy: it totally abolished the slave trade conducted from Portuguese possessions; it obliged Lisbon to issue anti-slave trade laws similar to the British ones; and it maintained the right of search and created more mixed commissions for trying the arrested ships. In addition, it met an old British demand by including clauses on equipment and on the dismantling of condemned slave ships.[28] The only point on which there was not yet total agreement was the number of domestic slaves who would be permitted to accompany their masters on sea voyages between Portuguese possessions, which Britain sought to restrict tightly and to which Vila Real was opposed, arguing that such a restriction would be unacceptable and would clash with the right freely to move one's property.[29] Even so, at the beginning of September it seemed that this obstacle was well on its way to being overcome: both Palmerston and the Portuguese minister were willing to withdraw the controversial article from the treaty so as to avoid any further delay in its signing.[30] And that was the state of play when the September Revolution brought the left into power, this time with hegemony.

4.2 The *Septembrista* Ambiguity on Abolition

On 10 December 1836 the *Septembrista* government approved a law drawn up by Sá da Bandeira (Fig. 4.1), the new Minister of Foreign Affairs, prohibiting the export of slaves in all the Portuguese dominions without exception. The law would enter into effect in Africa from its date of publication in the various Portuguese possessions. In comparison with the draft law that had been submitted to the Chamber of Peers nine months earlier, Sá dropped everything relating to freedom of the womb and most of the subject matter relating to registration of slaves. He also reduced the penalties to be applied to offenders and left open the possibility of a small number of slaves being transported by colonists moving from one Portuguese possession to another. Despite this, the law seemed to be a significant step forward and was praised by both Howard de Walden and Palmerston.[31]

4.2.1 One Step Forward, Two Steps Back

Very quickly, however, the British government began to perceive that the law of 10 December was not the embodiment of ancient promises but the starting point for a strategy designed to keep it largely removed from the action. In this respect the law was not so much a step forward as two steps backwards in the struggle to suppress the slave trade in Portugal.

Despite being constantly pressed to put the promised treaty in motion, Sá put off negotiations. When he did finally resume them, he did it with a counter-project which, as Howard de Walden said, was far removed 'in principle, spirit and effectiveness' from what had earlier been agreed.[32] Amongst other changes, the Portuguese minister sought to put an end to the mixed commissions, granting Portuguese political and legal bodies the right to restrain and try offenders; he also sought to limit the geographical scope of search rights and to insist that slaves recaptured on board Portuguese slavers be disembarked in Portuguese Africa (where slavery persisted). More significantly, the counter-project was accompanied by remarks that were almost an ultimatum: if the British government should turn down the new basis for negotiations now proposed, then there would be no possibility of agreement and the convention of 1817—which allowed British cruisers to arrest slavers only north of the equator—would remain in force until December 1851.[33]

In other words, the Portuguese government was resorting to the recently published law of 1836 and to a distorted interpretation of a separate article of the 1817 convention. This article provided for the convention to be prolonged for a further period of fifteen years from the date on which Portugal abolished the slave trade, unless the parties agreed otherwise. In this way it drew up a legalistic shield that Palmerston would be unable to penetrate. It is important to mention that Britain had already used the separate article of the convention to its own benefit in negotiations with Brazil, to increase its capacity to intervene against the Brazilian slave trade.[34] Sá was proposing to do the opposite, restricting British intervention and sacrificing efficient suppression of that trade to benefit his political image. Knowing the abolitionist sentiments of the Portuguese minister, Howard de Walden saw his attitude as an act of pure demagoguery, worthy of the most celebrated radicals of the day.[35] The *Septembrista* objections, which had emerged *ab initio* and had nothing to do with the difficulties of applying the abolition law in the colonies, made 'perfectly clear' the state of mind in which the Portuguese minister had embarked on this question.[36] In London's eyes the Portuguese counter-

FIGURE 4.1. Bernardo de Sá Nogueira de Figueiredo, only Baron, 1st Viscount and 1st Marquis of Sá da Bandeira (1795–1876).

project was an intolerable backward move after years and years of insistence and negotiation, a document which, if it were accepted, would convert the treaty into a ream of paper as ineffective as Portuguese laws, giving legitimacy to the continuation of the old circus of orders, instructions and government decrees, a method Portugal had been using for decades and which succeeded in avoiding the key issue: effective repression of the slavers.[37]

The *Septembrista* minister's move was, and continues to be, the object of differing historical interpretations. Capela viewed it and subsequent policies as a set of ruses designed to prolong the slave trade for a few more years; Alexandre, by contrast, interpreted it as a serious attempt to abolish that trade, and one that failed basically on account of resistance from the colonies.[38] In fact, Sá da Bandeira's manoeuvres were both these things, a duplicitous step that has to be seen as a latticework of good intentions and subterfuge. At certain times good intentions and goodwill were to the fore; at other times, it was the trickery that prevailed. This means that there were different periods and trends in Sá's abolitionist action. The basic strategy, however, was clear: to abolish the slave trade at a Portuguese pace, keeping Britain as much as possible on the outside or on the edge of the action.

Sá da Bandeira took an interest in the issue of abolition relatively early on, possibly during a stay in England in the 1820s. Later on he travelled to Brazil, where he was able to see the world of slavery in operation. Sá was not a militant abolitionist in the British mould. He was a nationalist politician and a utopian colonial planner, for whom the abolition of the slave trade was an indispensable condition for the colonial design. This eminently pragmatic side of his can be seen in the pages of his *Diário*, where references to the problem of the slave trade tend to be short and unsentimental. This in no way prevented him from having a firm notion of the need for abolition, viewed as a precondition for the development and civilization of Africa.[39]

In February 1836, when he was already Minister for the Navy, Sá da Bandeira had an opportunity to make his views known through a report submitted to the Cortes. In it he anticipated the excellent results Portugal might rapidly obtain from the African colonies if it were to undertake a reform of the colonial legislation and encourage the settlement of men and capital investment. But such arrangements would be of no use if they were not accompanied by the abolition of the slave trade. The report recalled that the slave trade was already banned, but that the traders' 'avarice' and the 'connivance' of the authorities had sabotaged the ban. For this reason, the slave trade continued, bleeding Portuguese Africa every year of many thousands of human beings. It was therefore imperative to abolish it, even at the cost of an 'outcry' from speculators and venal authorities.[40]

In line with this approach, he submitted a draft abolition law to the Chamber of Peers and subsequently had the decree of 10 December 1836 published, as mentioned above. However, his desire to abolish the slave trade was not written on a blank piece of paper. In the background there was the intense British pressure and, on paper already, all the commitments Portugal had made over the years. Consequently, his colonial plan came up against a difficult dilemma: while on the one hand the 'odious commerce' would destroy whatever improvements could be undertaken in Africa, on the other hand the African plan needed time to mature before it could take off, time Britain did not seem minded to concede. To carry out his policy it would therefore be necessary for the Portuguese to subscribe to abolitionist aims, to allow themselves to be seduced by new overseas adventures and, at the same time, to protect the burgeoning African colonial plan from Britain's fearsome grasp, by means of legal safety valves.

This was the task the *Septembristas* sought to undertake from December 1836. As we saw earlier, the safety valve lay in the letter of the supplementary article to the convention of 1817. The *Septembristas* seized on this to create a legal cushion which, if the worst came to the worst, might drastically limit British intervention in the Portuguese colonial sphere for a period of at least fifteen years. The promotion of anti-slavery ideas among the Portuguese was contained in the preamble to the decree of 10 December 1836, a text that had strong nationalist connotations, recalled that the Portuguese had been the first in Africa, established a connection between abolitionism and the greatness of the past, and proclaimed the idea that the Portuguese government had banned the slave trade of its own volition. The theory of spontaneity naturally gave legitimacy to the claim that, in the new agreement to be made with London, Portugal would be negotiating from a completely new starting point. The claim was based on the idea of honour and was as simple as a four-sided geometrical figure: it was acknowledged that in 1836 an agreement had already been negotiated with Britain to abolish the slave trade; however, abolition through a treaty with a foreign nation would be an affront to national dignity; for this reason a law had been passed beforehand, 'spontaneously' to safeguard that dignity; but the existence of that 'spontaneous' law made it necessary to review the whole basis of the agreement which had already been negotiated with Britain in 1836.[41] Thus were the ideological pretext and justification created, and there was even a touch of provocation mixed in. As the preamble to the 10 December law stated, the Portuguese were not 'the only or the worst offenders' in the trade in slaves: 'accomplices who so accused us subsequently, sinned more and more seriously'.[42] With this allusion to Britain, the Lisbon government set the tone for the defiance that was to follow.

In blending the issue of abolition with history, national honour and anti-British nationalism—one of the strongest sentiments at the time—Sá was seeking to involve the nation in a subject it viewed as foreign or with a certain amount of indifference. There were two reasons why this was a risky strategy. First, it crossed abolitionism with anti-British nationalism, an ideological connection which, as we have seen in chapter 2, was already contaminated in Portuguese culture, since it had been appropriated by those who opposed abolition. Secondly, the possible set-backs of *Septembrista* abolitionism would have instant repercussions on national dignity. But, in addition to these risks over time, Sá's whole plan for abolition faced another, much more immediate, practical difficulty: how to achieve the total suppression of the slave trade without British support. Britain was the only power that had the means and, above all, the political will to mount a frontal assault on the institutions of slavery and to persevere with it. Was Sá convinced that he could do it with only Portuguese means and with the Portuguese will?

No Portuguese government official had at his disposal an organization like the Slave Trade Department—a specialized section of the Foreign Office, established in 1819, the job of which was to analyse all the information gathered on the slave trade. It is therefore understandable that Sá should have been unaware of all the ins and outs of the slave trade. However, the Portuguese minister was in touch with what was being published about Africa and the problem of slavery: he received books on these specific topics through private channels or through the Portuguese embassy in London.[43] In addition it should be recalled that he headed the Navy Ministry in 1835–36 and was aware of naval weaknesses; he was fully aware of British complaints of Portuguese connivance with the slave trade and the difficulty of putting an end to them; he also knew the potential cost of applying impromptu measures in the colonies—that was the main argument that had been used in the Chamber of Peers by those who opposed his plans of March 1836—and he certainly did not expect that his decree could be applied painlessly, for he himself anticipated that it would provoke a strong 'outcry' from speculators and the corrupt authorities.

Paradoxically, despite being aware of all this—or, rather, precisely because he was aware of it—Sá turned down the British anti-trafficking methods, choosing to base his suppression policy on the action of the colonial governors—that is to say, choosing a weak method that had already been tried unsuccessfully by earlier governments and that made everything dependent on a single man posted in the heart of the volcano. Nevertheless, the method did have the advantage of managing the enforcement of the law from the inside and according to prevailing circumstances. It made it possible to carry out the suppression according to the needs, possibilities and desires of the Portuguese. In other words, while it was not credible that the choice made in 1836 derived from complete ignorance of the difficulties action against the slave trade would be likely to face, it is highly plausible to suggest that in 1836–37 Sá was trying to take moderate action to suppress the slave trade, preferring to adopt a mild and progressive method of abolition by which he might obtain the results he sought for his colonial plans without complete disruption of the life of the colonies, but a method that was still sufficient to legitimize an attitude of resistance to future British abolitionist pressure. There is no document that shows that Sá da Bandeira had gradualist plans. But that intention can be inferred from his actions and from the exchange of correspondence at the time with the Minister of the Navy and with the British embassy. There is only one discordant element in all this—the fact that, at a given moment, the minister gave orders for the navy to proceed to apprehend slave ships. This merits more detailed analysis.

From December 1836 onwards, Sá wrote to the Minister for the Navy several times, recommending that he should insist with the colonial authorities that they enforce compliance with the decree of 10 December 1836 and related legislation. During that time he never requested any other type of intervention, and accordingly the ships that sailed for Africa had no instructions to take action against the slavers.[44] This type of directive was maintained until 13 April 1837, inclusive. On the following day, Sá requested for the first time that orders be given to warships to apprehend ships found to be flouting the abolition law.[45] The Navy Minister did not respond to Sá's letter, and the warships that sailed for Africa two days later had no instructions to take action against the slave trade. Later on, specific orders were in fact given to captains of ships travelling to India and which passed by Mozambique in the autumn of 1837, but they made no arrests. But what is significant, apart from the apparent lack of communication between ministries, is the timing and scope of Sá da Bandeira's new orders. In effect, captains of warships were called upon to carry out the law of 1836 prematurely, at a time when the law had not been published in the colonies and was therefore not in force. In other words, if the navy had carried out the orders of 14 April 1837, it would have arrested and detained ships illegally.

How are we to interpret these hasty orders, which were apparently inconsistent with the type of action Sá had ordered up to 13 April? At the time these orders were given, the Portuguese minister was under strong pressure from Howard de Walden to sign the treaty that had been negotiated earlier, in 1836.[46] In fact, in the letter in which he asked for the navy's intervention for the first time, Sá justified this request as being the result of British pressure.[47] Spring 1837 was also the time when the *Septembrista* government was getting ready to up the stakes by submitting the counter-project for an abolition treaty, which might well be badly received in London—as indeed it was. From that moment on, the mild abolitionism of September could only prevail if it were to produce tangible results—and nothing was more tangible than the seizure of some *tumbeiros*. But let us have no illusions. The impromptu orders of 14 April 1837 were basically intended as a demonstration of good faith and to give some visibility to Portuguese abolitionist policies. But the heart of action against the slave trade would continue to be with the colonial governors. Moreover, in 1837, ships' captains were directly answerable to the governors: they were required to patrol the areas designated by them at the times set by them. This meant that their action might be of no use at all if the said governors were not vigorous in pursuit of the slave trade. It was only later on, in 1842, and when he had already left government, that Sá da Bandeira acknowledged his personal error in having gambled on action by the colonial governors to abolish the slave trade: 'I was to blame, but it was due to ignorance, on account of lack of experience, when I had the Naval Stations put under the command of the governors'.[48]

4.2.2 *The Plot Thickens*

The first *Septembrista* government fell in May 1837 and gave way to an even more radical executive. Some weeks later Sá was sent north to fight the so-called Revolt of the Marshals. The country was suffering severe internal unrest, with the military revolt in the north, absolutist guerrillas fighting in the south and the now chronic gangs of highwaymen all over the country. Anti-British feelings increased after the failed attempt at a palace coup at the beginning of November 1836—in which the British embassy was known to have played a part—and reached its height soon afterwards, with the newspapers publishing constant slanders and threats against British citizens resident in Portugal.[49]

Sá da Bandeira came back to the Ministry of Foreign Affairs (and to be head of the government) in November 1837. During his absence the matter of abolition had been forgotten—it was clearly not a passionate concern of the then minister, Castro Pereira. Seeing that nothing had been done, Sá immediately wrote to Bonfim, the Navy Minister, once again tying his insistence on it to British pressure, and, in mid-December, he gave orders that captains of warships should carry on board a copy of the anti-slavery legislation so that they would be unable to claim ignorance of it.[50] Bonfim responded with a request for a firm hand: 'everything has been said, everything is presumed, and no-one can now claim to do wrong by reason of ignorance .... As far as I am concerned, we have no other option but to give some significant example, punishing offenders as harshly as the law allows, particularly authorities who connive in the offence'.[51]

But actual punishments were few and far between, applied late and selectively, despite constant British complaints and the fact that several offenders were well known. One of the accused was Cardoso de Melo, who acted as Danish vice-consul in Cape Verde.[52] Grave accusations were also made against João Baptista Moreira, the Portuguese consul general in Brazil. Moreira, who had been an active slaver prior to 1830, had succeeded in devising a series of pretexts for continuing to provide a Portuguese flag and Portuguese papers for traders operating in Brazil.[53] There was also blatant Portuguese involvement in Cuba. Contrary to the Foreign Office's hopes, the Anglo-Spanish treaty of 1835 had not solved the problem of the illegal trade. It did, however, give the Royal Navy the

TABLE 4.1 Nationality of ships unloading slaves in Cuba (1834–40).

Year	Spanish	Portuguese	Other
1834	29	3	1
1835	42	8	—
1836	29	14	—
1837	3	48	—
1838	4	44	2
1839	2	29	6
1840	7	29	5

Source: James Bandinel, *Some Account of the Trade in Slaves from Africa, as Connected with Europe and America. From the Introduction of the Trade into Modern Europe, down to Present Time, especially with Reference to the Efforts made by the British Government for its Extinction*, Frank Cass, London, 1968, First edition 1842, pp. 232–33.

power to detain slave ships that had no slaves on board, and the British fleet in 1836 captured thirty-seven vessels flying the Spanish flag—compared to an annual average of only ten between 1830 and 1835.[54] But there was no corresponding drop in imports of slaves into Cuba. What was happening now was that slavers rarely used the Spanish flag (Table 4.1). They preferred to use the Portuguese one instead, thanks to the good offices of the Portuguese consul in Havana, José Miguel Fernandes.[55] Accusations were also levelled at other consular and port authorities, and at the masters and crews of slave ships (some of whom were resident in Lisbon). Nevertheless, the most unfavourable winds were blowing in from Africa.

Colonel Vidal had left for Angola in April 1837, on board the corvette *Galateia*, with instructions to apply the abolition law. When he arrived in Luanda to be faced by local opposition, Vidal not only failed to publish the law—deliberately making it known that he had decided not to publish it—but is said to have started drawing personal monetary benefit from the protection afforded to slavers. The captain of the *Galateia* was to recount later how the captains or consignees of the slave ships acquired passports in the governor's palace and the shamelessness with which they loaded slaves in sight of everyone in the port of Luanda.[56]

The Marquis of Aracaty arrived in Mozambique in October 1837 and had Sá da Bandeira's law published. But, a few days later, 'driven and subjugated by the imperious law of necessity, which is above all other laws', he issued a circular which reauthorized the export of slaves and established a tax to be levied on those exports. The Marquis justified this step in the text of the circular. It would be 'an absurd procedure' to suppress the slave trade, thereby 'stupidly' (*sic*) cutting off every means of subsistence available to the Mozambican population.[57]

Only in Cape Verde were there some signs that abolitionist measures were being applied, for in 1837 governor Joaquim Pereira Marinho arrested four schooners judged to be slavers.[58] Despite this action Marinho would later be accused by his detractors of protecting slave traders.

In the crossfire of accusations and counter-accusations that followed, it emerged that the governor had effectively granted Portuguese passports to a number of slave ships because he had no orders to turn them down and because the funds thus obtained were his main source of revenue for the province.[59]

Despite the information and indeed mounting proof that his strategy for abolition was a total failure, Sá never concluded an abolition treaty with Britain. On the contrary, he became entangled in a complex web of objections and stratagems, which dragged the country into an untenable position on the international stage.

At the beginning of April 1838, Sá da Bandeira was disposed to reopen negotiations with Britain over abolition. In mid-1837 Palmerston had already made it known that the continuation of an obstructionist policy by Portugal would lead to its flag no longer being respected. Now, roughly a year since anything positive had been obtained, and with the Portuguese trade growing after it had been legally abolished, the British minister went ahead with a kind of ultimatum, submitting a draft of a treaty with Lisbon that was no longer to be negotiated but was to be signed on the spot, just as it was. The Portuguese government should say clearly, once and for all, if it wanted to sign the convention or not. It was certain that, if it did not wish to do so, Britain would proceed of its own accord.[60]

It was as a result of this pressure that Sá da Bandeira made himself available to sign an agreement on abolition that would 'really'—that was the word he used—stop the Portuguese trade in slaves.[61] Even though Gomes de Oliveira, a senior official at the Ministry of Foreign Affairs, had given a very negative opinion of Palmerston's draft, Sá gave up his counter-project of 1837 and gradually accepted, almost in its entirety what he had earlier refused (in particular, the existence of mixed commissions and the possibility of the right of search being exercised over a wide geographical area).[62] On 7 May, convinced that everything had already been comprehensively discussed, Howard de Walden told London that full agreement had been reached even if, as far as he himself was concerned, he had gone slightly beyond his instructions in accepting certain minor changes intended to make it 'more agreeable to the Portuguese public'.[63] But on the following day everything was back to square one: the British ambassador received a note from Sá—to which Aracaty's circular was attached—informing him that on account of the risk of rebellion in the colonies, the deterioration of the Portuguese Navy and the lack of funds, the Portuguese government could only keep in force the abolition law of 1836 and sign the treaty demanded by the British government if the latter would provide 'formal and explicit guarantees that the African dominions would remain subject to the Portuguese Crown'. Britain was also called on to provide possible extensive military assistance, which was to be discussed in a new round of negotiations.[64] This was the admission of defeat for the *Septembrista* abolition option, and the beginning of a new stratagem.

Howard de Walden saw in this note, which was submitted precisely on the eve of his planned departure from Lisbon, the desire to prolong the negotiations indefinitely.[65] London had already promised some specific, limited military aid in the event of disturbances or attempts at secession by the Portuguese colonies. In addition, Sá da Bandeira's note contained nothing really new. Howard de Walden, naturally, set little store by it, and he even took the opportunity to recall that Aracaty's accompanying announcement—of which the ambassador was already aware—was nothing more than the confirmation of what had long been known, namely, that the Portuguese authorities were not applying their abolitionist legislation.[66] Aware of the serious political implications of the Portuguese reversal, Howard delayed his departure to London and tried for almost two weeks to persuade Sá da Bandeira to sign the treaty. On a number of occasions he pointed out to him the risks he was running and expressed his regret that the consequences of the misunderstanding with Britain should fall precisely on him, 'the only Portuguese minister' who was 'truly' interested in abolition.[67] But his efforts were in vain: Sá not only failed to drop his conditions but actually hardened them, demanding possible additional military aid, for an indefinite period of time, which might amount to five warships and 1,300 soldiers, to rescue Mozambique and Angola, with proportional assistance to rescue the other colonies and secure all the African possessions—even those north of the equator, where the slave trade was already prohibited by the treaty of 1815 (which had given Portugal compensation of over 450,000 pounds sterling).[68] He classified it as 'modest aid', which London could easily concede.[69]

The Portuguese government also refused to equate trading in slaves to piracy. British harassment over this issue was long established, even if intermittent. Some countries had classified the slave trade as an act of piracy. If that classification were to be recognized in international law, any trafficker in slaves could be tried by the courts of the arresting country. But no authority wanted the measure to go as far as this, and even Britain never exercised that right, apparently because it feared that British merchants would suffer retaliation in foreign courts.[70] The issue of piracy therefore had an essentially psychological value, and would emerge from time to time when the British government or Parliament—as now—insisted on this solution. As Palmerston said, the British government attached 'great importance to the moral effect' that would be produced in Portuguese public opinion if those involved in the crime of trafficking slaves were to be branded ignominiously as pirates.[71] Sá da Bandeira refused, however, to acquiesce in the British request, arguing that, under Portuguese legislation, the crime of piracy was punishable by death, when in truth what Britain was asking was merely that Portuguese law should be made equivalent to British law, which since 1837 had applied the penalty of deportation to pirates, but not death.[72]

With the issue having reached a complete impasse, Howard de Walden returned to Britain on 22 May. One week later, Sá tried to revive the negotiations with Jerningham, the chargé d'affaires, who had remained in Lisbon, alleging that the only reason the treaty had not been concluded was that the ambassador had had to leave.[73] However, Jerningham had received no instructions from his government to negotiate, but only to submit a new and even harsher draft, together with a formal ultimatum: 'any further delay in concluding this treaty, or any further proposal to change this draft, shall be regarded by Great Britain as being equivalent to a refusal by Portugal to comply with the obligations to which it is bound in this regard'.[74] As Howard de Walden had predicted, the British position had hardened and Portugal was heading towards a major political crisis.

The *Septembristas* sought to excuse the renewed backtracking by their government on the basis of justifiable reasons of a patriotic nature—the imminent loss of the colonies—and several Portuguese historians have accepted this excuse. In the most recent and detailed version of this theory, it is said that Sá da Bandeira was ready to sign the treaty with Britain at the end of April but that he had stepped back at the last moment when faced with the content of Aracaty's circular (which had been received in Lisbon on 28 or 29 April) and a subsequent opinion of Gomes de Oliveira (dated 1 May), which alerted him to the risk of losing the African possessions. It was when faced with these documents that the head of the Portuguese government had decided to demand guarantees and military aid from Britain, and only the denial of this request had prevented the agreement from being concluded.[75] The origins of the Portuguese volte-face lay in a somewhat fortuitous event—the arrival in Lisbon of Aracaty's circular just prior to signature by Sá da Bandeira—which had put in jeopardy the whole of an already concluded agreement. But this theory is superficial and unsatisfactory. Too aware of the obvious—colonial resistance—it fails to take into account the degree of opposition to suppression of the slave trade in Portuguese society itself. In addition, there is no proof that Sá went back on his intention to sign the treaty only when he became aware of the Aracaty circular; on the contrary, the available data cast serious doubt on this hypothesis.

As has already been mentioned, the Marquis of Aracaty's circular was received in Lisbon at the end of April and gave rise to a lengthy official opinion by Gomes de Oliveira. The first surprising aspect in this opinion is the complete and uncritical acceptance of the circular's arguments and the veneration given to its author. Aracaty—who in the meantime had died from tropical fever, a fact that was not yet known in Lisbon—was described therein as someone who was above all suspicion. Now, if a man who was solid, wise and loyal had yielded to the interests of the slavers and to the voice of necessity, then there were strong grounds to fear that his example might be followed in the other African colonies involved in the slave trade. For this reason, Gomes de Oliveira recommended that careful thought should be given as to how to proceed, because 'any rushed or premature measure' might lead to the loss of the colonies. Portugal might yet 'become a wealthy nation' from the ownership of its colonies; without them it would forever be reduced to insignificance.[76]

In stressing the risk of national collapse, the opinion placed a heavy responsibility on the head of the government. For this reason it advised him to protect himself by seeking the counsel of men who were known for their familiarity with the overseas dominions—such as Saldanha da Gama, Xavier Botelho and others—who were to be expressly summoned to a meeting in order to give their opinions on a number of concrete issues. Amongst other things, Gomes de Oliveira suggested that they should answer the following:

- Given that in the treaty to be signed Britain sought a declaration abolishing the slave trade in perpetuity, was it convenient to demand of that country a formal and explicit guarantee for the Portuguese overseas dominions against possible rebellions that might arise there?
- In addition to this guarantee, should Britain be obliged to make two warships and a thousand men available to cover any possible appeal for help by Portuguese colonial governors?
- Bearing in mind that the 'complete' abolition of the slave trade would greatly reduce the state's revenues from the colonies, should Portugal demand of Britain an annual subsidy equivalent to what would be lost?
- Should such guarantees, assistance and subsidies be given in perpetuity, given that Britain was demanding perpetuity in the abolition of the traffic in slaves?
- Should the treaty be signed should Britain refuse to agree to Portuguese claims?[77]

The meeting suggested by Gomes de Oliveira never took place, at least not in the manner prescribed, as there are no records of it in the minutes of the Council of Ministers. In any event, Sá da Bandeira adopted almost all the arguments and suggested line of action from the 1 May official opinion (but had the decency not to request any subsidy whatsoever). And the fact that he did so requires some explanation because, in objective as well as subjective terms, the prospect of the imminent loss of the colonies was not as likely as is generally supposed.

The credibility of the catastrophic scenario outlined by Gomes de Oliveira in connection with Mozambique—and, by extension, all the African colonies—was based in large measure on a positive assessment of the Marquis of Aracaty. But the image of Aracaty as a man above suspicion, solid and wise, which underlies Gomes de Oliveira's arguments, is in marked contrast to the poor opinion Sá da Bandeira himself had of him. In his *Diário* (Diary) Aracaty was described as 'indecisive' and 'a muddler who does nothing'.[78] Having had a career in Brazil, Aracaty had returned to Portugal with the liberals and had been made virtually penniless. Seeing that his financial situation was deteriorating, he was willing to accept 'any proposal', becoming a naturalized Portuguese and setting out, at sixty years of age, for Mozambique, where he would face, as he himself said, 'a thousand certain and irredeemable hardships in the backwoods of Africa'.[79] Given the type of man he was and the situation he faced in 1837–38, it would be difficult to see the governor of Mozambique as a model of firmness on which to base an assessment of how difficult it would be to enforce the law of 1836 and the genuine risks that such enforcement would bring to the colonies—even if, for obvious reasons, Sá da Bandeira gave out that myth to the British ambassador (Howard de Walden, however, was perfectly aware that Aracaty was merely 'a needy member of a great family in Portugal', who had gone to Mozambique to try to restore his fortune).[80]

In addition, the Portuguese Prime Minister was aware of the situation in Mozambique as a result of information that had reached Lisbon in May 1837, and which Aracaty himself had collected and conveyed. According to that information, the latest military revolt had reduced the number of white soldiers in the Mozambique garrison to five, and the few residents at various points on the coast were shut in behind their palisades, in fear of the native population. The dilapidated state of public finances was such that repairs to the vessel employed on the regular run to India had been paid for by some of the passengers. Just before setting sail, Aracaty had asked Sá da Bandeira to reflect on these 'sad circumstances' and to give him the means to do something about them.[81] In this state of affairs, and since those means had not been made available, the decisions the governor took when he arrived in Mozambique could not have been wholly unexpected.

It was also somewhat implausible, despite the troubled times the country was going through in 1838, that Portugal should not be able to supply the military means, in conjunction with the British help that had already been promised, to deal with a possible uprising in Angola or Mozambique. Moreover, several politicians at the time publicly disputed the notion of weakness. The British embassy also regarded the fear of losing the colonies as 'most unreasonable'.[82] And rightly so. To understand the means necessary for such an eventuality, it should be said that in 1822, when it was feared that Angola might rise up in order to join Brazil, the Cortes were asked to send one warship and an army of 300 men: such means were deemed sufficient to uphold national sovereignty.[83] And in 1829, the Lisbon government sent a detachment of 150 men to Angola to suppress possible rebellions that might arise as a result of the Anglo-Brazilian abolition treaty, which it was believed at the time would end the slave trade in the region for good.[84]

Strictly speaking, and contrary to what is generally asserted, it was also not the lack of financial resources or ships that prevented the navy from intervening against the slave trade in 1837–38. Of course, a budget allocation that was already quite low inevitably affected the overall ability of warships to operate effectively. It must, however, be emphasized that the budget question was quite different in relation to ships allocated to fighting the slave trade, since these were the responsibility of the colonies and had to be paid out of the income from their customs duties.[85] Certainly, the Portuguese navy was struggling with several problems, one of which was the small number of suitable ships for a mission that required speed and not much firing power. In 1837–38 the navy had only five or six schooners, seven brigs and seven or eight corvettes. Even if these means were feeble—which they undoubtedly were—such weakness would not prevent them from acting. In actual fact, Portuguese naval resources were no greater in 1839–40—six schooners, seven brigs and six or seven corvettes—when actual suppression began. In this context, we should not forget that Great Britain had started its anti-slave trade patrols in the middle of the Napoleonic wars with only two ships. What is more, suppression was the best way of making good a lack of ships, because captured vessels in good sailing condition could be taken by the navies that apprehended them. Some of the good ships of the Royal Navy were ex-slavers.[86] The first person in Portugal to outline the benefits of the suppression policy in this regard was Marinho: when he arrived in Cape Verde and in Mozambique with no naval resources to start operating to suppress the slave trade, he made a virtue out of necessity, and at the end of a few months already had a small anti-slave trade squadron. This method was naturally followed by the Portuguese navy which significantly enlarged its resources by means of captured ships.[87]

It was a political choice that in fact inhibited naval action in 1837–38: during this time a number of warships that were effectively available remained idle in Lisbon, operating as a backup for the established power:

> Two vessels were fully rigged for 365 days without leaving the port of Lisbon; likewise the corvette *D. João I*; [another] three frigates; etcetera; 27 vessels were in fact rigged out, many of them for the whole year, including many which never left the port of Lisbon: even the steamship *Napier* was in Lisbon for 365 days, fully rigged! [sensation]. And … we had to charter some foreign vessels to go to our colonies [sensation].[88]

Calculations of the time spent in Lisbon by each schooner, brig and corvette generally confirm this charge. Until 1838 the annual average of time spent by each ship (in the Tagus) was high, and it was precisely in that year that it reached its highest: 253 days. It started to go down from 1839 onwards, precisely because warships were sent to Africa to combat the trade in slaves.[89]

It was therefore highly unlikely that enforcement of the 1836 law would bring about a situation that would be beyond the country's military capability to respond to or that might require indefinite British military aid. That this was true was demonstrated six months later when Sá, faced with British intransigence, showed a willingness to modify this obligatory condition, or simply to let it drop.[90] Moreover, despite all the alarmist visions, he kept the 1836 law in force and sought to encourage its enforcement. The fact that he went along with Gomes de Oliveira's official opinion therefore has to be interpreted as a negotiating trick that was substantially motivated by political considerations. Gomes de Oliveira's observations regarding the possible loss of the colonies might have had little credibility, but they were accurate as a warning of Sá's political isolation and as a barometer of internal opposition to the signing of the treaty.

The sector that most clearly opposed suppression was, obviously, the slavers. In 1836 Howard de Walden mentioned the few who were operating out of Lisbon at the time: four Portuguese, three French, one Italian and one Austrian.[91] To these we have to add the big slavers established in Brazil and Cuba, whose operations included Portugal and whose importance could be gauged by the number of people they managed to bribe, at virtually every level of a corrupt administration.[92] Then there were those who associated with slaver undertakings by investing in them. Taipa even thought that the slave trade was the most significant element in the Portuguese financial system at the time, after usury.[93] But that could well be an exaggeration. What is undisputed is the direct influence of the slavers with top figures of Portuguese politics. In fact, Lisbon's slavers were dangerously close to public figures and high officials: they all belonged to the clubs that supported the government. Rio Tinto, the owner of *O Nacional*—the main organ defending the slave trade in Portugal—had funded the *Septembrista* governments.[94] The British ambassador often mentioned the fact that 'wealthy slave traders and the needy political chiefs' had common interests.[95] There are also a number of Portuguese sources, from various political quarters, which confirm these common interests. All the indications are that it was indirectly, by way of intermediaries, that the slavers exercised their influence on the government.

In his letters to the Foreign Office, Howard mentioned countless times the groups and individuals who held back the Portuguese minister's abolitionist intent. In one of these notes he even sought to explain the channels and mechanisms through which this influence was brought to bear on Sá da Bandeira's will:

> In regard to the effectual suppression of the Slave Trade, I conceive him to be labouring under the influence of two Parties. The first represented by leading members of the Clubs and agents of the Government, who are interested in the Slave Trade and whose object is to prolong as long as possible the term previous to its abolition .... With this Party I am inclined to suspect that the Viscount de Sa da Bandeira, during the revolutionary struggles by which he has risen, has deeply involved himself, by some pledge as to delay.
>
> With respect to the stipulations of the Treaty and in opposition to its signature, I have no doubt whatever that the French party, of which one of the most active members is Senhor Manuel de Castro Pereira, have been actively at work .... The failing of the Viscount de Sa's personal character has rendered him susceptible to being worked upon through his passions.[96]

This note by the British ambassador contains two different and contradictory ways of explaining how Sá da Bandeira gave cover to the opponents of abolition: one would have been conscious, a repaying of political favours; the other would have been unconscious, and had to do with the minister's character and psychology. This is not the place to reconcile the contradictions in Howard de Walden's judgements, but one may merely underline the fact there were subscribers to both interpretations at the time, although the prevailing theory was that Sá was collaborating with the slave traders without realizing it. That is how the Marquis of Fronteira, for example, recalled him: 'a capital enemy of slavery who was, without knowing it, surrounded by slave traders, who were his best friends'.[97]

The slave traders may well have influenced the path taken by Sá da Bandeira, but they were not the main factor that led the head of the Portuguese government to delay signing the treaty. More important, apart from his presumable desire to suppress the slave trade gradually, as mentioned above, was his political realism. Sá always denied that his actions had been influenced by the slave trader lobby. But he acknowledged the weight of political pressure and feared the 'unpopularity' which the act of signing the treaty with Great Britain would entail.[98] In connection with the Portuguese refusal to equate the slave trade with piracy, he is said to have confessed to Howard de Walden that he was unable to push such a law through because he faced, on the one hand, 'active opposition to the suppression of the slave trade' and, on the other hand, the 'indifference' of most of those who might help him in his struggle 'against the machinations of those who defended the slave-traders'.[99]

In this confession Sá touched on two key factors: the machinations of the slave traders and the lack of public support for those who opposed them. The only thing he left out was the fact that in the spring of 1838 the slave traders had come upon fertile ground for carrying on their machinations, because they could count on the conjunctural support of those who, while opposing the continuation of the slave trade in principle, feared that its immediate suppression would irreparably harm the national interest.

On arriving at the port of Lisbon on 1 June 1838, and in compliance with the orders he had received to report all he knew about the 'odious commerce', Marques Pereira, the commander of the corvette *Galateia*—the ship which had taken Vidal to Angola—wrote a letter to Sá da Bandeira in which, while describing the slave trade as 'something horrible', he complained about the obstacles placed in his path by the Royal Navy, in particular in São Tomé and Príncipe:

> Happy would those islands be if the importation of slaves or settlers generally were to be increased ...; but the British patrol in the gulf of Guinea, which is made up of many light warships, only lets one or two small schooners pass, which may be hiding half a dozen slaves purchased on the mainland under dye-wood or ebony from Gabon.[100]

Marques Pereira summed up in direct terms the spirit of tolerationism and the main obstacle to signing a treaty with Britain: the certainty that the Royal Navy would tenaciously pursue the slavers and the fear of the repercussions of that pursuit on the economy of the colonies. This type of fear—which was very common among the *Septembrista* elites—had not come out more forcefully into the open at the time of publication of the 1836 law because it was generally held that it would be possible to get around the law or even have it repealed, unlike what would have happened with an Anglo-Portuguese treaty, the provisions of which would be implacably enforced by the British. That is why the hostility emerged in resounding terms as soon as it became clear that London was preparing to suppress the slave trade unilaterally in Angola and Mozambique. We shall analyse below in detail how and to what extent this hostility was manifested in the press and in the Cortes. For now it is sufficient to state that it was considerable in the winter of 1837–38 and grew as the likelihood of signature of the treaty increased and when Aracaty's circular arrived in Lisbon.

One example of the increase in hostility to suppression of the slave trade was precisely Gomes de Oliveira, a man who, two weeks after issuing his official opinion on Aracaty's circular, drafted another one, in which he came out against equating the slave trade with piracy and against the setting up of mixed commissions, which would have placed Portuguese slavers under the jurisdiction of foreigners.[101] Two years later, however, the same man would completely overturn his arguments in another official opinion on the same subject, calling for the withdrawal of all forms of legal protection from those who carried on the slave trade under the Portuguese flag. Gomes de Oliveira would even argue that the thorough suppression of the slave trade should be carried out unflinchingly in order to 'preserve and secure those dominions'.[102]

An about-turn like this, in a relatively short space of time, shows once again the fluctuating nature of tolerationist positions and provides a better understanding of the scale of the objections that sector of opinion would raise to the signing of the Anglo-Portuguese treaty in April-May 1838. The prospect that it would be signed, in the alarmist climate generated by Aracaty's circular, led to an exponential increase in hostility to abolition, weakening Sá da Bandeira's relatively isolated position still further. This was why, in the private letters he wrote to Howard de Walden, Sá stressed the political risk as much as the possible loss of the colonies.[103]

Essentially, it was the build-up of internal hostility to suppression that led the head of the Portuguese government to backtrack from his momentary intention to conclude an agreement that would 'really' prevent the continuation of the Portuguese slave trade. This hostility preceded the arrival of the Mozambique governor's circular. As Sá da Bandeira was to say later in the Chamber of Peers, the circular was just 'one more reason why' it was necessary to 'insist once again' on British military aid.[104] In effect, Sá had already asked for British aid to keep the colonies at the end of 1837, and on 21 April 1838—a week prior to being made aware of Aracaty's circular—he had delivered a memorandum to Howard de Walden asking for guarantees for the African dominions and military aid for the duration of the treaty; three days later he received a promise, confirmed by Palmerston on 5 May, that Britain would guarantee the integrity of the Portuguese colonies against possible interference from Brazil and Spain (the only nations which at the time were still importing slaves) and would grant aid in the form of a naval force, for a period limited to two years.[105]

The requests for aid did not therefore reflect the sudden emergence of a threat to the survival of the colonies, but were the result of objections to abolition in Portuguese society at the time that took that particular form. The circular was just another element that increased the internal difficulties facing the minister in this area, to a point where they became insurmountable. It was these internal difficulties which, in Howard de Walden's view, explained why it had been necessary to move forward with the treaty 'step by step' since May 1837, and why it had been necessary to fight 'the incessant and vexatious delays on the most frivolous pretences which were daily created during the negotiations, and when apparently overcome, were again with pertinacity revived'.[106]

The opposition Sá faced in Portugal was basically the same as that which had affected prior administrations. The major difference was that the margin for conciliation of the various different forces was substantially lower. In order to escape British pressure, the Portuguese minister 'spontaneously' abolished the slave trade in December 1836. This tactic failed because it had been adopted without true political support, and because it exposed him and the country, which did not follow his lead, to even greater British pressure. In practical terms, Sá da Bandeira was now stuck between Palmerston's ultimatum, his desire to suppress the slave trade gradually and opposition from a significant number of his political supporters. It was not, therefore, just the pressure by the slavers that prevented signature of the treaty. It was this pressure coupled with pressure from those who opposed Britain and from tolerationists, a coalition of the unwilling too broad to be faced down by the *Septembrista* leader. But not to sign the treaty, and to admit openly that he would not do so, meant acknowledging to the world that the law of 1836 had been a trick; and it also meant granting Britain legitimacy to intervene on its own account against Portuguese slave ships south of the equator. The only way of trying to reconcile all this was to envisage signing the treaty on highly favourable terms, that is to say, on condition of obtaining, from the British, guarantees for the territorial integrity of the colonies and the promise of indefinite military aid, a bountiful concession that would appease and disarm the tolerationist opposition. And, because Gomes de Oliveira's opinion, in dramatizing the colonial situation, gave him the pretext and arguments to hold on to this last political lifeboat, the Portuguese minister followed it faithfully.

This involved significant risk, not only on account of the British reaction, but also in terms of safeguarding national honour. It was precisely because the *Septembristas* had, from the outset, established a close connection between abolition and national honour that they could not backtrack on their stated abolitionist aims without seriously undermining the honour and decorum of the nation. Sá's last year at the head of the government was a continuous effort to enforce the 1836 law, to put off signing the treaty imposed by Britain and to salvage national honour (thanks to the notion that blame for not having concluded the agreement would fall entirely on the British). In order to succeed at all points along this difficult and wide front, the head of the Portuguese government continued to follow a policy that sought to act and obstruct, reconcile and challenge, all at the same time.

The active side of Sá's political behaviour was seen in his renewed orders to the colonial authorities to enforce the law of 1836 and his attempts to punish some of those involved in breaking it. But these punishments were more or less dilatory according to whose interests were at stake. While those whose main operations were in the slave trade to Cuba were quickly dismissed, the case of Vidal, the governor of Angola, was handled with greater care. Since April 1838 the Foreign Office had insisted on the need to dismiss Vidal, but it was only in the middle of March of the following year that a legal case was brought against the governor.[107] And, while action was slow in this particular case, it was purely and simply non-existent with regard to the Portuguese consul general in Brazil, João Baptista Moreira. At the beginning of 1838, Sá da Bandeira sent out a circular warning Moreira that he would be dismissed if he did not make every effort to prevent the slave trade.[108] But the consul was not dismissed, even though it was confirmed over the following months that he was the person responsible for most of the violations of the 1836 law.[109] At the end of 1838 Sá continued to say that he had a 'very good opinion' of Moreira and to think that the accusations against him were 'mere allegations'.[110] It was only in mid-1839—with Sá already out of government—that the consul would be removed, and then only because the Brazilian government ceased to accept his consular credentials. Even so, and despite the fact that many sources confirmed Moreira's brazen connivance in the slave trade, Lisbon insisted on his being restored to office, as indeed he was.

In a desperate attempt to break the British siege, the *Septembrista* government sought to make alternative abolition agreements with Denmark and France. Denmark, however, operated on the British wavelength: it demanded abolition of the slave trade in perpetuity and a reciprocal right of search, unbounded by geographical limitations.[111] With France the subterfuge failed because Britain was not seeking a monopoly of abolition, and was not opposed to Portugal's signing abolition agreements with other nations, on condition that those agreements contained provisions as strict as those imposed by the British. Given these circumstances, the treaty—which, moreover, in other areas imposed stricter conditions than those of the British—was never signed. The issue lapsed in mid-1840. Significantly, no attempt was made to tie up with the most likely partner. One of the most revealing aspects of Portuguese hesitations on the issue of abolition is the absence of any serious attempts to make an anti-slave trade treaty with Brazil. There were indeed some moves in that direction, but they preceded the September revolution and, surprisingly, came from Brazil itself, which at the time was hard-pressed dealing with the alarm created by the revolt of the Malé.[112] In April 1835 the Brazilian representative in Lisbon asked for Portuguese collaboration in the struggle against the slave trade. At the end of that year, he suggested forming Luso-Brazilian mixed commissions to try slavers that had been apprehended, but the Portuguese government, while not turning the proposal down, adopted a relatively passive approach on this. Once the scare of 1835 was over, the Brazilians lost interest, and the issue was dropped as a result of inertia on both sides.[113]

4.2.3 *From Palmerston's Bill to the Treaty of 1842*

Sá left the government in April 1839, leaving the issue of abolition more than ever mixed up with nationalist feelings. Meanwhile, the elderly Admiral Noronha arrived in Luanda in January 1839 to take up the governorship. Despite opposition from the local Chamber, which wanted anti-slave trade measures to be applied so gradually as to be 'imperceptible', Noronha published the abolition law at the beginning of February, although he did grant a delay of 90 days for the settling of business transactions in hand.[114]

But Noronha did not succeed in Angola. Despairing of the cause, he was to sign an agreement with Lieutenant Tucker at the end of May, giving the Royal Navy the right to seize ships flying the Portuguese flag south of the equator. Agreements between navy men were normal practice, used to circumvent the intricacies of politics and the irritating obstacles of strict legality. Tucker signed a similar agreement in the following year with Lieutenant Paine of the North American navy. In Lisbon, despite various protests, the Tucker agreement was regarded by the government as an honourable way of ending the disagreement with Great Britain, and it was therefore approved by the Council of Ministers on the grounds that, as stated therein, it did not concede anything that Sá was not inclined to concede and it ensured that ships which had been apprehended would be 'tried by our own courts in Angola'.[115] But the British government, which only received news of the agreement after it had adopted a position of strength—the Palmerston bill—refused to ratify it.[116] Noronha came back to Lisbon at the end of the year and was replaced by Colonel Malheiro, who performed the duties of governor until July 1842, initially with relative keenness, but later turning a blind eye to the activities of the slavers or even plotting with them, as the *Correio de Lisboa* accused him of doing.[117]

In Mozambique, the policy of suppression was practically frozen following the death of Aracaty. A government order dated 23 July 1838 set a time limit for complying with the law, so that merchants could withdraw the capital they had invested in the hinterland. The situation would only change when Brigadier Marinho was transferred from Cape Verde to Mozambique (where he arrived in April 1840).

In Lisbon, Ribeira de Sabrosa, the new head of government (and also Minister of Foreign Affairs), strayed not one iota from the policy prescribed by Sá da Bandeira, who continued to watch over the whole business from afar, giving opinions and recommending strategies.[118] For Howard de Walden it was obvious that the new Portuguese minister would never sign the treaty.[119] As we have seen, Palmerston had already decided in 1838, that if Portugal refused to do its part in suppressing the slave trade, Britain would do it forcibly. And, if the Portuguese wanted war, the British government would occupy all its colonies and thereby solve the issue of the Portuguese slave trade.[120] On 10 July 1839, Palmerston introduced a bill in the British Parliament that gave Royal Navy warships the powers to apprehend any ships flying the Portuguese flag (or no flag) which were transporting slaves, or which were equipped to transport them. By the same bill, the ships that might be apprehended were to be adjudicated by the courts of the British Navy, and it was decreed that any legal actions against the captors would be null and void. The bill was approved on 24 August 1839, after some amendments and some opposition (in the Lords).[121]

This drastic measure caused consternation in Brazil and a real upsurge of nationalist fervour in Portugal. In August Ribeira de Sabrosa decided to ask for arbitration from France, which Great Britain refused. At the same time he sent a circular to various governments, in particular to the signatories of the Congress of Vienna, appealing to the text of the declaration approved there.[122] In alluding to the Vienna declaration—under which each state was entitled to determine the most suitable timescale for permanent abolition of the slave trade—the Lisbon government blundered, because it was appealing for a right to abolish gradually when it had already 'of its own accord' published a law by which the slave trade should have been ended for good. While under Sá da Bandeira gradualism had been modestly covered up, it now emerged into the open under Ribeira de Sabrosa. Equally clumsy was the haste to show practical results of suppression. On 31 July the schooner of war *Faial* sailed up the Tagus, having apprehended a slaving ship in the seas of Africa. This was the first arrest on the high seas under the 1836 law, and the *Septembrista* establishment took full propaganda advantage of the fact to publicize Portugal's abolitionist zeal. The schooner's captain even received a decoration. The case was tried at the end of 1839 and the crew were acquitted, to the rejoicing of some of the organs of the *Septembrista* press.[123]

Meanwhile, under cover of Palmerston's bill, British cruisers were arresting or sinking various *tumbeiros* protected by the Portuguese flag.[124] In the process they sometimes interfered with legitimate shipping. Amidst great national agitation, the Ribeira de Sabrosa government fell at the end of November. Bonfim was charged with putting together a new, more moderate executive (with Vila Real as Minister of Foreign Affairs) and, as far as abolition was concerned, its plans were clear: since matters had gone so far, and there was no question of war, it was urgent to sign the treaty with Britain as quickly as possible. In a policy of appeasement, Lisbon sought to respond to all British claims, in order that its good abolitionist intentions should not be put in doubt. Portuguese naval involvement in the fight against the slave trade grew significantly, as most of the navy's schooners, brigs and corvettes were dispatched to Africa, where they were beginning to intervene in the detention of slave ships.[125]

This was the action Sá da Bandeira had sought, albeit happening late. But Palmerston, whose parliamentary bill had given him all the powers he needed, was now in a position of strength and was only prepared to admit signature, with no further negotiation, of the text submitted by Jerningham in the summer of 1838, with a supplementary provision requiring the Portuguese government to pass a law equating the slave trade to piracy (and punishing it as such). The only major objection raised by Lisbon was regarding the duration of the agreement, given that it did not wish to agree to a right of search in perpetuity; Lisbon also requested that, in order to salvage the honour of the Portuguese Crown, the treaty should be signed at the same time as a provision under which the offending bill would be repealed.[126] Palmerston made it clear, however, that he would only accept a time limit on the duration of the treaty after slavery had been completely eradicated from the face of the earth.[127]

The Foreign Office would maintain this position even after Palmerston had left the government at the end of 1841. It was only after the reestablishment of the Constitutional Charter in Portugal—a significant development that made ratification of the treaty possible without prior approval by the Cortes—that the new Portuguese administration resigned itself to the fact that the British would not budge and finally, on 3 July 1842, signed the much anticipated treaty of abolition. The agreement, which was negotiated by Palmela and Howard de Walden, obviously followed the text Jerningham had given Sá da Bandeira, but with small changes that made it even more demanding. It had a new article under which Portugal declared the slave trade to be equivalent to piracy, punishable with the most severe sentence (excluding death), and accepted that a ship might be prosecuted even if it had no slaves on board, or equipment for transporting them, provided that it could be proved that it had had them on board during that particular journey. Portuguese claims regarding a time limit had not been accepted, and the agreement was therefore made in perpetuity. The only small change Portugal succeeded in introducing was an additional article under which some rules might be changed after mutual consultation and joint agreement.[128] A law that regarded the slave trade as piracy was published in Portugal on 25 July 1842, and on 12 August the British Parliament revoked that part of Palmerston's bill relating to ships flying the Portuguese flag.

Thus did the curtain fall on *Septembrista* abolitionism and all its ambiguities. All the indications are that in 1836–39 Sá da Bandeira was a sincere gradualist who had tried out a policy of immediatism in order to shake off British pressure. His strategy might have had relative success if it had been able to achieve something positive against the slave trade in the years 1837–38. But it was founded on too many unrealistic assumptions: it assumed that Britain would allow itself to be quietly distanced from Portugal's efforts at abolition; it assumed that investors and colonists would be open to the opportunities offered by Africa; it assumed finally that there was no longer any opposition to abolition in Portugal and that the slave trade would allow itself to be stifled without opposition. We have already seen that Britain did not accept any avoidance. In Chapter 6 we shall deal extensively with the capitalists and the common people's lack of interest in the African mirage. For the moment, we shall examine how the ideological forces that might have joined together with philanthropy had not yet emerged, and how those which effectively had emerged often went counter to abolition.

4.3 Public Opinion and the Suppression of the Slave Trade

To what extent was the *Septembrista* ambiguity over abolition adopted by Portuguese society? What alternative views were there, what frictions and misunderstandings? Who opposed and who subscribed to the humanitarian cause in Portugal from 1836 to 1842? From the standpoint I have adopted, these are the key questions which I have raised above but which should now be looked at in greater depth. It is certainly important to define what government officials thought and felt on the matter of suppressing the slave trade and of British demands for abolition. But it is equally important to situate and explain the currents of thought in the country at the time and how they affected government action. The ideological ground on which Sá da Bandeira moved has remained in the shadows of History. However, it is possible to identify that ground, mainly by studying journalistic and parliamentary arguments in the years 1838–40, a period that was singularly rich from the point of view of documentation. By reason of the very circumstances in which the country found itself as a result of Palmerston's offensive bill, everyone wanted to express an opinion, either to save face, or to confound the political adversary, or simply to become more popular. There are accordingly a very significant number of opinions in the press, in debates in the Cortes and even in half a dozen more or less specific pamphlets. The study of these opinions shows that Portuguese opposition to the suppression of the slave trade was very strong, and that a sizeable number of figures on the left who made up Sá's political entourage at this time were trying to prolong the slave trade—in some cases, for many years more—rather than trying to put an end to it. The champions of suppression were to be found on the liberal or *Cartista* (Chartist) right. It should be mentioned that they were occasional champions: with few exceptions, their abolitionist position derived more from specific political circumstances than from a deep rooted and lasting choice.

4.3.1 The Issue of Abolition in the Press

The decree of 10 December 1836 was received placidly, even with indifference, by Portuguese public opinion. Some newspapers ignored it; others confined themselves to dashing off hurried philosophical praise for the 'enlightened reason' that had guided the ministers of Portugal to help the oppressed and despised Negroes.[129] Only *O Popular* criticized the law, reminding its readers that 'important interests and fortunes' were tied to the slave business; 'sudden' and 'complete' abolition would therefore be undesirable; instead, action should be taken that would 'gradually diminish' the 'inhuman commerce'.[130] A few days later *O Popular* raised the issue once again, describing the slave trade as a lesser evil, because it made it possible to save the lives of those who had been defeated in inter-African wars. At the same time it let loose a ferocious attack on Sá da Bandeira and his 'anti-patriotic' abolitionism.[131]

The dissonant voice of *O Popular* shows the persistence of a current of opinion opposing abolition, which had been widely seen at the beginning of the century and which remained visible from time to time in the following years. When looked at only in the context of public manifestations at the time, this current of opinion seems actually to be weaker than its opposite. As a rule, the Portuguese newspapers made only fleeting references to the slave trade and to African slavery. The subject generally carried negative connotations and was dealt with in stereotyped form, but was rarely developed. However, since 1835, *O Nacional*, a newspaper for which the deputies Leonel Tavares and Paulo Midosi wrote, had given some space to pro-abolition arguments and to the benefits which such a measure would bring to the African colonies. The newspaper praised Great Britain for its 'noble commitment' to abolition, and regretted that a similar philanthropic zeal was not in evidence in Portugal. It also reminded readers that Portuguese ships continued to be used in the 'odious commerce' and expressed a wish that 'without further ado' the government and the Cortes should put an end to such a shameful practice; there would be 'no excuse for delaying a measure that was so necessary, fair and appropriate'.[132]

This praise for British philanthropy and argument for immediate abolition of the slave trade, coming from a newspaper that was in the *Septembrista* camp and the most important press organ of the time, seemed to grant political and ideological consistency to the decree of 10 December 1836. However, the months that followed publication of the law showed that the cohesiveness and integrity of the anti-slave trade arguments were an illusion. Apparently, many journalists had refrained from coming out against the law in 1836–37 because they anticipated it would not be strictly applied. As we have seen on a number of occasions, silence in the absence of direct threats was entirely compatible with anti-abolitionism—even if it did not necessarily amount to the same thing. So it is not surprising that Portuguese passivity came to an end when it became clear that Britain demanded action, not just words and laws. With British pressure, the doors of controversy were opened wide and *Septembrista* pro-abolition rhetoric dramatically and radically changed.

The change is evident above all in the pages of *O Nacional*, a newspaper that shamelessly reversed its position from 1837 on, largely contributing to laying the ideological foundations for the ambiguous behaviour of *Septembrista* governments. In its new form, the no longer abolitionist but tolerationist or even frankly pro-slavery arguments were expressed in terms of concepts that harked back to ideological frameworks inherited from the past. British philanthropy was immediately portrayed as false and perverse. To prove it, *O Nacional* adopted an idea which at the time hardly required proof, that is, that behind every British political move there was a material interest: 'in a nation of merchants everything taken to heart has a mercantile speculation as its goal'.[133]

At the core of this overall judgement on 'suspect philanthropy' these new arguments reinforced above all the idea that British abolition policy was aimed at Portugal in particular. Britain sought through abolitionism to do away with what remained of the Portuguese empire. If Lisbon were to yield to British demands, it would lose its African possessions for good, and the country would suffer an irreparable financial collapse.[134] The references were to a set of ideas that carried strong defensive connotations, especially the semi-paranoid notion of plunder. There is no point here in analysing whether the projections that had Britain anxious to take possession of the colonies of rival nations were right or wrong.[135] We need only note that *O Nacional* tied its opposition to abolitionism to the more aggressive concept of plunder of the empire, an idea that had strong and ancient roots in Portuguese culture and, through that connection, nourished the fantasies of conspiratorial philanthropy.

To this was added the natural fear of possible insurrection in the colonies. Here too, what was important was not so much reality—in objective terms, the loss of the colonies was an unlikely event, as we have already seen, and as experience would show—as the fact that the anti-abolitionist ideology used that scenario as a way of amplifying the catastrophic implications of abolition. There was, moreover, nothing specific about Portugal. The ghost of secession had traditionally been evoked as a weapon in the fight against abolitionist policies. It had been so evoked in Portugal in the 1810s and 1820s, but also in Cuba, Jamaica, the French colonies and, with greater reason, the United States of America, where there was a white pro-slavery community of sufficient size to be able to do well on its own.[136]

From these ideas and feelings one would necessarily conclude that the abolition treaty Palmerston sought to impose would suit Great Britain but be harmful to Portuguese interests. *O Nacional* consistently spread the message that the treaty implied extremely onerous concessions that were incompatible with national dignity and could not be allowed: 'eternal opprobrium' would attend any national government that 'knuckled under' to Britain.[137] With Palmerston's bill and the first arrests, a wave of defiance and inflammatory discourse swept through Portugal. Some swore eternal hatred to the British, while others were minded to burn clothes of British manufacture in the public square. Echoing these incendiary statements, which it encouraged and highlighted, *O Nacional* even advocated war, inciting all fellow patriots to set about fitting out ships to 'sink' British vessels.[138] There were no half-measures: if the Portuguese were free and independent, they had to retaliate.

In essence this was the re-emergence, with certain adjustments to the events of the day, of the obstructive tolerationism that had prevailed in the early 1810s. The apparent abolitionism of 1835–36 was reversed and gave way to arguments that were ferociously hostile to collaboration with Britain against slavery. It might be thought that this reversal was nothing more than an excessive reaction to foreign interference in Portuguese life. But the opposition generated by Sá da Bandeira's decree, the new views *O Nacional* had on the slave trade, the change in opinion on abolitionism and also the intransigent defence of gradualism all show that the reversal went further back and had deeper roots.

The decree of 10 December 1836, which at one time had been praised as an indispensable step in bringing prosperity to the African possessions, now became 'a death blow' for those same possessions. Naturally, *O Nacional* demanded its immediate repeal.[139] Naturally, too, it declared war on anyone who tried to enforce that law. Vidal, who had refused to enforce it, was praised—or at least excused—while his successor in Angola, the 'demented governor' Noronha, became an object of spite.[140]

The 'horrible' or 'infamous' nature of the slave trade was relativized to such a point that the newspaper adopted in its entirety the theory of the lesser evil, which, as we have seen, was one of the most powerful ideological justifications for slavery:

> If the Negroes had no buyers for their slaves, they would kill their enemies instead of saving their lives, in the light of which abolition of the slave trade is not a good thing for Africa …; abolition would lead to no small ill for that part of the world, that is to say, the cruelty and bloodthirsty nature of the

> Negroes would be encouraged, and even cannibalism, because ... many Negro villages partake of the abominable custom of cutting off and selling in the markets the flesh of their prisoners; *à quelque chose malheur est bon,* the trade in slaves, which has defied the greed of those barbarians, has reduced the frequency of these horrors, and they will surely increase with its extinction.[141]

In its more excitable moments, *O Nacional* even suggested that slavery was an institution of divine origin.[142]

The identification of the European with the Negro slave—one of the strongest devices in the abolitionist psychology—was not only no longer mentioned but, on the contrary, was demolished by means of frequent disassociation (barbarous/civilized, black/white, among others). At the same time, references to the unfortunate Negroes snatched from their homes disappeared completely from the columns of the newspaper, and gave way to the image of the poor slave trader whose funds would find no employment and, above all, of poor Portugal, a weak and trampled nation. In a society that had no abolitionist organizations and where there was no widespread specific condemnation of the slave trade, such arguments went deep, especially if they encountered the political hatred towards Britain among the populace of the cities and if—as in fact happened—these arguments were hammered incessantly. Many of those who said they were against the slave trade also confessed that they were so because they hated oppression and tyranny. For them, the slave trade was ranked alongside other iniquities in the world and, in this bundle of more or less equivalent injustices, the relative order in the hierarchy depended on the circumstances of the moment. If it could be shown that Portugal was in some way being oppressed, that oppression would naturally take pride of place in the line-up of iniquities. Based on a simple rationale that equated freedom for slaves and slavery of whites, many of *O Nacional*'s articles appealed for a switch in roles, at that particular time and in this particular context. The Portuguese were the slaves, and the British were the masters. In the process, they did away with the problem of the slave and Negro slavery.[143]

More important still, from mid-1838 onwards, a year and a half after the export of slaves had been categorically banned by Sá da Bandeira's decree, *O Nacional* started to argue incessantly for gradualism: the slave trade had to end, yes, but 'little by little' and to the extent that Brazil and Cuba developed; the slave trade should be ended through 'enlightened, gradual and compensatory mechanisms', and never by the method the British sought to impose.[144]

As we have already seen, gradualism could be the last barricade for the enemies of abolition. It is therefore not surprising to see gradualist positions defended in circles close to slaver interests. What was surprising was to see them advocated in the pages of *O Nacional,* with the connivance of the *Septembrista* Ministry of Foreign Affairs. The similarity in the arguments of the newspaper, the government and the Luanda town council was, moreover, noticed and emphasized by the British ambassador in Lisbon.[145] In any case, in Portugal the defence of gradualism required a certain amount of legal acrobatics, not only because it was a post-mortem gradualism—the slave trade had effectively been outlawed in December 1836—but above all because there was a commitment, in the Anglo-Portuguese treaty of 1815, to bring about abolition by means of a bilateral agreement with Great Britain. Gradualism's sheet anchor was the separate article in the agreement of 1817. What *O Nacional* advocated, which went counter to the spirit of the treaties but was entirely in accord with *Septembrista* government strategy, was the use of that article to restrict action by British cruisers. Even if the slave trade had been prohibited in the Portuguese dominions, the Royal Navy had nothing to do with that prohibition. Since there was no joint agreement, the convention would remain in force until 1851, and, since it only provided for ships to be apprehended north of the equator and on condition that they had slaves on board, the continuation of the slave trade in the southern hemisphere would be assured. From this point of view, since the summer of 1838 *O Nacional* clung desperately to the letter of the convention, arguing that joint agreement was impossible, for reasons of national dignity.

In sum, the new arguments against abolition contained elements that lead one to believe there was much more to them than a simple exaggeratedly nationalist reaction. It is significant that these arguments should have appeared in the most important newspaper of the time and, what is more, in the newspaper which, in 1835–36, had been the foremost defender of abolitionist theories. More significant still, however, is the fact that *O Nacional*'s message should have found an echo in the vast majority of Portuguese political journals. With minor differences, with more or less vehemence, newspapers on the left and those in sympathy with the Absolutist cause and even some *Cartista* journals endlessly repeated anti-abolition and tolerationist arguments.[146] There was near unanimity in the defence of gradual abolition: Portugal had only promised the British to do away with the slave trade 'gradually'; as to the method of doing so, the nation could only be 'obliged to deal' with Britain on this score 'in 1852, fifteen years after ... the decree of 10 December 1836'.[147] As Palmela acknowledged, the majority of the newspapers showed clearly that 'Portugal did not want the abolition of the slave trade'.[148]

In actual fact, and with the exception of the British papers published in Lisbon, only two or three *Cartista* journals argued in favour of immediate suppression. *O Director* mentioned the subject on occasion, stressing the damage the *Septembrista* attitude caused to national honour and reminding readers that the bill would have no harmful effects on the African colonies.[149] *O Panorama* also touched on the issue, being concerned mainly to provoke feelings of hatred against the slave traders: 'let salt and fire, water and hospitality be denied them; run from them as from a plague. For this we need no slanders. It will suffice to bring to the people's attention selected pages from the history of that detestable commerce. And this should be done in one and a thousand newspapers; one and a thousand times'. And it was precisely this which *O Panorama* tried to do, revisiting the tragic voyage of *Le Rodeur*, the French slave ship whose crew and human cargo had fallen victim to ophthalmia and had drifted for days on the high seas.[150]

The *Correio de Lisboa* insisted on the idea that the slave trade was of no interest to the Portuguese. When it ceased the Negroes would simply be employed locally 'at the right price' and would gradually become civilized.[151] Suppressing it would therefore be beneficial, and the nation should thank the London government, which, in trying to impose suppression, was advocating Portugal's true interests. But, beyond material interest, it was national honour itself that demanded the end of the 'odious commerce'.[152]

The *Correio de Lisboa* became involved in a sharp dispute with the newspapers of the left, particularly *O Nacional*, which it accused of receiving money from the slavers to defend their cause. The newspaper war also involved selective publication of diplomatic notes and official documents, a propaganda exercise in which there was much to gain, with the *Correio* having access to the British embassy and *O Nacional* to the Ministry of Foreign Affairs.[153] The *Septembrista* government itself was an active participant in the propaganda battle, having documents published which gave only a partial version of events.[154] Howard de Walden protested on several occasions at the publication of 'such a selective list' of notes, but it was only in 1840 that equilibrium was restored with the extensive dissemination of documentation of British origin.[155] The propaganda war extended to Britain itself, where, since April 1838, Sá da Bandeira had been trying to get the local press to run translations of Portuguese articles.[156]

But the pro-abolition versions conveyed by two or three *Cartista* journals were in a minority in comparison with the thunderous arguments of the left. Simultaneously dispensed from various sources from the summer of 1838 onwards, and more strongly in 1839–40, obstructive tolerationism reached the reading public in bucketfuls, several articles being published each week for months on end.[157] As *O Athleta* admitted, the clarity of the issue depended on facts which 'the more often repeated, the better'.[158] And even more important than repetition was the strong link the left created between the subject of abolition, which meant little to most Portuguese, and feelings of patriotism and Anglophobia, which struck a much livelier chord. One of the roles of ideology is precisely to merge differing motivations into a whole, so that conflicting interests may converge in a single cause and different sectors may appear to reinforce each other. In the rhetoric of the left, tolerationist arguments were closely connected to extremely powerful core ideological concepts such as 'the British conspiracy' and 'national dignity'. In other words, the tolerationist ideology was clearly anti-British: this big tent provided cover for those who defended the slave trade, the *Septembrista* agitator and the ill-informed patriot, bringing together many people who had nothing to do with the trade in Negroes. It is true that the people rarely read newspapers, but they absorbed propaganda in the taverns and barber's shops, in their courtyards and marketplaces.[159]

Tolerationism at the end of 1830s, interwoven with nationalism, was a very consistent ideology that set out to conquer a legion of sympathizers. By mid-1839 the blending of the issues seemed to be complete and *O Nacional* congratulated itself on the fact that the question was 'fortunately national'.[160] The other side made the same assessment: as the *Correio de Lisboa* acknowledged, the issue had been made into a 'national question' so as to safeguard the slave trade more effectively, as if it embodied the country's interests.[161] Even the *Cartista* press helped in its way to load the debate with nationalist overtones. In its efforts to argue the need for a rapid signing of the treaty with Britain, it appealed above all to national honour, constantly emphasizing the feelings of shame in the eyes of civilized nations at the position Portugal had adopted.

An analysis of the press in the second half of the 1830s shows very strong opposition to the immediate eradication of the slave trade. It also shows that the more obstructive aspects of tolerationism had survived and adapted to the circumstances of the moment. Finally, it shows that the discussion between those in favour of and those against the slave trade was conducted under the cover of national honour. This means that, if we wish to situate and interpret the position of the Portuguese political elites on the problem of the slave trade, we shall have to interpret in that light not only the manoeuvrings of *Septembrista* governments but also the rhetoric of the Cortes.

4.3.2 Parliamentary Manoeuvres

The Cortes discussed the issue of abolition of the slave trade in 1839, 1840 and later in 1842, at the time when the treaty with Britain was signed. For methodological reasons it is best to separate the analysis of these three periods of discussion, because the political contexts in which they occurred were substantially different.

At the beginning of 1839 there was no solid majority in the Cortes, since political dissent had weakened the ranks of the *Septembristas*. In the Chamber of Deputies José Estevão was the rapporteur of the commission responsible for drawing up the reply to the Queen's Speech. His report allocated no more than a small paragraph to the treaty of abolition, viewed the slave trade as 'a scandal' and stated that the Chamber would approve any negotiations with Britain provided they had regard to freedom of trade, the dignity of the flag and the interests of the overseas provinces.[162] The paragraph was discussed in the sessions of 9 and 13 February and was approved as it stood. However, the debate uncovered a range of significant differences. The apparently innocuous recommendation on the need to safeguard freedom of trade and the interests of the colonies was nothing less than an endorsement of the policy followed by Sá, and a brake on British abolitionist ambitions. It was naturally around that recommendation that disagreements arose and that positions became clear.

Moreover, José Estevão had occasion to state more precisely what was meant, in this particular context, by the defence of free trade and colonial interests. From the top of the platform, the deputy requested for Portugal the same treatment that the British had applied to themselves. He reminded the assembly that in Great Britain the abolitionists had flooded the country with articles against the slave trade, but it was only after twenty years of debate that material interests had yielded to those of philanthropy. 'Now', he asked, 'if the abolition of this trade encountered such opposition in England, why should it not face similar opposition in Portugal?' In a word, José Estevão wanted gradualism because 'absolute and immediate extinction' of the slave trade might lead to a revolution in the colonies, which would want to unite with Brazil, a circumstance under which the 'odious commerce' would certainly increase. Portugal should therefore, 'move gradually' in this matter. Immediate abolition was even counter to the interests of the Africans themselves, because it would encourage smuggling and lead to even more horrors.[163] Other deputies, including Paulo Midosi, expressed similar opinions, stressing the risk of losing the colonies if a frontal assault were to be made on the slave trade, and the need to safeguard national dignity from British demands.[164]

From the other side of the benches some of the best *Cartista* parliamentarians argued for the quick conclusion of the Anglo-Portuguese treaty and emphasized the large stain that delay in signing would leave on the national character. Silva Carvalho, for example, warned that if the ministry, by 'neglect or indolence', should let the opportunity slip for making an agreement for which Britain had been waiting for twenty-nine years, this would have serious consequences for the nation.[165] What was at stake, beyond the 'horrors' of the slave trade, was 'a principle of national honour'. Decorum could only be salvaged when promises that had been 'so often made' were fulfilled and treaty negotiations were brought to a conclusion.[166] Likewise, Taipa wanted everything done to speed up the conclusion of the agreement, because the issue had become 'shameful' for Portugal. The question was only being dragged out because there were 'so many people tied to it' and those people resorted to the 'usual fallacies' that the colonies were in danger or that suppression would only bring advantages to the British.[167] Deputies Rodrigo da Fonseca, Tavares de Macedo and Lobo de Moura, who also feared the impact the issue would have on the country's image and were sceptical regarding the potential risks for the colonies, pressed the government to sign the treaty with Britain.[168]

There was a similar confrontation in the Chamber of Senators—which had been created under the Constitution of 1838 to replace the Chamber of Peers. Only Vila Real argued the need for a quick signature of an agreement with Britain. In contrast, Bergara was firmly against 'sudden abolition'. The 'abominable trade' should only be reduced in so far as tropical agriculture progressed; otherwise the fate of the Negroes would be 'more unfortunate'. In Africa—which Bergara knew because he had been exiled there—prisoners of war were usually well treated by their captors because they had market value; if the slave trade were abolished, their destiny would be calamitous: '*the fate of the dead Negro is much worse than that of the slave Negro* [laughter]'.[169] Other senators, including Ribeira de Sabrosa, the future Prime Minister, expressed similar opinions: the government could not be allowed to destroy the colonies in one go by adopting 'rash and premature measures'. Portugal did indeed have an obligation to abolish the slave trade, but only when it was possible to do so.[170]

Ribeira de Sabrosa's speech was printed and disseminated not only in Portugal but also in Britain. In line with earlier practice, Sá da Bandeira gave instructions to the Portuguese embassy to have a translation of this and other speeches published—in particular, his own—in *The Times* or another equally influential newspaper. But he also, understandably, recommended caution in the selection of excerpts to be published, so as not to give occasion for the British to think that the Portuguese parliamentarians wanted the slave trade to continue.[171]

In 1839, therefore, there were two positions in the Chambers. These faithfully reproduced what we have already seen in the press: one sought to speed things up, and the other, which had greater visibility and resonance, sought to prevent or delay the conclusion of the treaty with Britain. Both played on the concept of national honour and the colonial interest, but did so along diametrically opposed lines. From the position of the speakers in the political spectrum, it was clear that the *Septembristas* favoured gradualism while their opponents endorsed immediatism.

What about Sá da Bandeira? As head of the government, Sá spoke in both Chambers, and revealed the strategic contradictions he had set in motion at the end of 1836. At the outset, he was literally halfway between the two opposites. He wanted the slave trade to end and, in theory, he was not in favour of gradualism. He stressed that Portugal had nothing to lose if the *tumbeiros* that used its flag were to be seized and destroyed, because the capital tied up in them belonged 'mostly' to foreign speculators. This meant that, thinking purely in abolitionist terms, the country could only gain as a result of British suppression. Nevertheless, he needed time to launch his colonial plans and, at that stage, he still spoke of ten to twelve years before commodities would be extracted from the African colonies. In addition, as we have seen, he was conscious of his political isolation on the slave trade issue and of the animosity in his own party camp towards suppression (apart from the fact that he had a visceral mistrust of the motives for Palmerston's abolitionism). For all these reasons he kept up a complex array of ambiguities: while on the one hand he would say that it was necessary to sign a treaty so that the slave trade could be pursued south of the equator, on the other hand he tried to include in the treaty clauses that would limit the effectiveness of suppression and, in the last resort, he kept a door open to the complete avoidance of Britain's demands: without a joint agreement, the convention of 1817 would remain in force until 1851 and British cruisers would be confined to the north of the line.[172] This ambivalence explains the fact that he left the Cortes exactly as he entered them. Even though confiding to Howard de Walden that the Chambers had alleviated some of the difficulties he had envisaged, the British ambassador understood 'by his manner of speaking' that he had not altered 'his intention of not signing the treaty'.[173]

As seen from England, the discussion in Parliament and the *Septembristas'* position in particular, took on aspects of the absurd: 'the arguments advanced ..., on this subject, are all very inconsistent. Great credit is taken for the decree of 1836, abolishing the traffic; and yet, the subject is argued as if no such decree existed, and the question of abolition was now for the first time to be discussed on its own merits'.[174]

In 1840 the Cortes allocated a great deal of time to the slave trade issue. In the space of a year much had changed. The new government had requested the reopening of negotiations with the British government and, even though the nature of the conversations was kept secret, it was not difficult to guess that Bonfim was getting ready to grant the Royal Navy the right to suppress the slave trade carried on under cover of the Portuguese flag. This approach was categorically opposed by the left, which was now in a minority in the Chambers.

The first thing that stands out in an analysis of the debates on the reply to the Queen's Speech is the time spent on the subject. In the Chamber of Deputies discussion of the question began in January and took up most of the order of the day from 11 to 25 February. And it did not go on longer only because the Queen, using the powers granted her by the Constitution, decided to dissolve the Cortes and call new elections. It is true that the more than excessive amount of time dedicated to just one paragraph of the Queen's Speech also had to do with the fact that this was a burning topic. The eyes of the country were fixed on the Chamber, and the subject brought great notoriety to anyone who broached it. Understandably, everyone wanted to speak of it so that the whole nation would know what his view was 'on this truly national question'.[175] But, even more than the large number of speakers, the main reason why the controversy dragged on in the Cortes was the tactics used by the *Septembristas* to give the topic maximum exposure and to block any diplomatic advance. There was, moreover, a dual interest in the problem of slavery: it was a topic in its own right and, in a broader sense, an instrument of opposition to the government.[176] In order to achieve their objectives, the

Septembrista deputies endlessly repeated the arguments that appeared in the columns of the newspapers, went over the history of the treaties and of the diplomatic notes, discussed each point at length and forced the Minister of Foreign Affairs to 'go over the topic again at any and every moment, arguing over each individual word', as he himself said in exasperation.[177]

The left put forward a draft response to the Queen's Speech different from that of the majority, the author once again being José Estevão. As had occurred in 1839, the *Septembrista* deputies wanted the conclusion of the Anglo-Portuguese abolition treaty made conditional on a defence of Portuguese independence, the interests of the slave trade and the safety and prosperity of the overseas provinces. But now they added—as a result of recent developments—a demand for 'solemn satisfaction' for Palmerston's bill; they also stressed the 'spontaneity' with which the Portuguese government had published the decree of 10 December 1836, the 'lively solicitude' with which it had carried it out and the 'fiery zeal' with which it had collaborated with governments of other nations to 'improve' conditions for the Negroes. They considered that it had been the 'extraordinary and unfounded British demands' that had delayed the negotiation of the agreement. They also sought to insist that any agreement that might eventually be concluded should remain in force for a minimum period of time.[178] There was none of this in the majority's draft, which was much more succinct: the interests of the colonies were not mentioned, no reference was made to the decree of 1836—let alone to its allegedly 'spontaneous' nature—nor were any remarks made on the way previous administrations had behaved in carrying out the law and in negotiations with Britain.[179]

The debate dragged on around these different drafts. On 19 February, the *Cartistas* became exasperated: 'eight days had passed and the assembly had not yet finished discussing article one'. But the *Septembrista* Leonel Tavares thought it necessary that the debate should be a long one, 'so that the feelings of the Chamber and of the government shall be made known'.[180] Thus did the controversy proceed, in an uninterrupted vicious circle. On 24 February, the eve of the dissolution of the Cortes, Rodrigo da Fonseca summed up what was going on, with characteristic irony:

> Every day we repeat the same story, from 1815 to the present day, bringing to bear on it lengthy considerations which may be all very correct but [which], for the most part, have nothing to do with the matter. We have had the patience to use up … nearly two weeks on the suitability of the verb *to cooperate*. We finally reached a decision on this vital matter. But this is nothing compared to the difficulty surrounding the style of a particular sentence in the majority's or the minority's draft …. And what can I do, except enter the fray? I know I won't say anything new, but I have to say something.[181]

While at first sight, the hours seem to have been wasted in resounding rhetoric and verbatim reproductions of the diplomatic notes and provisions of the treaties, a more careful analysis shows us that the way time was managed involved a deliberate strategy of blocking any abolition agreement with Britain. Military confrontation would of course have been the radical solution, but even though several deputies on the left had allowed that threat to float over the assembly, they did not in fact seem prepared to follow it through. So what did they want? Quite simply they wanted to bind the new government to the policies that had been followed by the *Septembrista* governments.

To achieve this aim they systematically brought to the forefront of debate not the issue of the slave trade but that of national honour. The press had sprung such a trap that no right-wing deputy dared to raise the issue without making sure that his nationalist credentials were incontestably established. But the left-wing deputies themselves had, in a meeting four months earlier, drawn up a strategy that exploited those nationalist feelings.[182] More recently, the strategy had acquired significant theoretical backing with the publication of Sá da Bandeira's pamphlet (which will be analysed below). The *Correio de Lisboa* looked on it with great reservations, but the work was praised by *O Nacional*, which published it. In the Chamber of Deputies, the *Septembrista*s wanted to have it approved in binding form for the whole nation.[183] The trap was clear, and the *Cartistas* immediately objected to the hasty approval of the pamphlet, fearing that this would imply the Chamber's acquiescence 'in all the doctrines' found in it.[184]

Taking advantage of Sá's pamphlet was just the first stage of a pincer movement aimed at committing the Bonfim administration to gradualism. After 10 February, and through the constant speeches by José Estevão, Paulo Midosi, Leonel Tavares and many others, the left set up its target and tried to hit it in every way possible. The most devious way of doing this was a diversion of purpose, to take advantage of the nationalist fervour that was convulsing the country. Portugal was accused in the British Parliament and in the British press of reneging on its treaties and of not wishing to abolish the slave trade. It was therefore necessary to examine the behaviour of *Septembrista* governments in this context, to decide whether or not they were guilty. This was, of course, not an investigation at all, but a rubber stamp of approval. Moreover, a few days later, Midosi set it all down in black and white: 'on the one side, the minority wishes that the policy of the previous executive be hereby explicitly approved; on the other side, there is a desire explicitly not to approve the dealings of that executive'.[185]

The majority was therefore faced with a political labyrinth. Many deputies and *Cartista* members of the government were critical of the way the negotiations had taken place and had serious reservations about the *Septembristas'* keenness on abolition. But preserving national honour and the need to save face were as pressing for the *Cartistas* as for the *Septembristas*, albeit for different reasons. If they were to make their criticisms and comments too openly, they would inevitably strengthen Britain's arguments. They were therefore obliged not to attack their opponents except between the lines. They even made some concessions, accepting the 'spontaneity' of the 1836 decree and being willing to agree that the failure to conclude the anti-slave trade treaty was due to 'some' British demands.[186] They also allowed Sá's pamphlet to pass. However, commending the *Septembristas* meant approving what they had done and implicitly acknowledging that theirs was the only possible way of conducting the matter.

The dilemma was obvious, and there seemed to be no way out of it. It was Vila Real who would find a solution by running ahead, demanding that his conduct while at the Ministry of Foreign Affairs and, more generally, that of all his predecessors should also be examined.[187] The *Cartista* deputies willingly seized the opportunity offered them: governments prior to September 1836 had also been accused by the British, and for that reason any commendation would not be restricted to the *Septembristas*. A commendation would have to be given to all the prior administrations, because all of them had zealously sought to find a means to put an end to the 'odious commerce'. There should therefore be 'justice for all', said Taipa.[188] The leftists saw the trap immediately. That day's session ended in uproar, with deputies rising to speak, while others left the chamber.[189] On the following day the galleries were full of silent and attentive spectators, but the *Cartista* majority won the vote by 60 to 51.[190]

Having broken this insidious siege, the government still had to face all sorts of blocking tactics on a daily basis. The most serious of these was the demand that it should not negotiate any treaty without obtaining prior satisfaction for insults proffered, or while Palmerston's bill was not repealed. Another front was opened up in the attempt to bind the Bonfim government explicitly, point by point, to the negotiating philosophy of Sá da Bandeira. Despite being worn down, and often violently opposed, the government held out, without ever stating precisely on which points it intended to diverge from Sá's principles. Its position became increasingly clear: it would not accept any clauses restricting its powers to negotiate with Britain on the suppression of the slave trade.

Once again, as the newspapers and the Cortes of 1839 had shown, the conflict between two opposing positions was not crystal-clear, only because they were both wrapped up in nationalist language. The *Cartista* side believed that the slave trade must cease; Portuguese decorum demanded it, the philosophical opinion of the century demanded it, the clamour of Christianity demanded it and so did the true, though remote, interests of the overseas provinces. It was therefore urgent that the treaty with Britain be concluded. There was no question of 'placing obstacles' in the way of the total extinction of the slave trade; on the contrary, it was necessary to make punishments more severe and to hang the offenders.[191] For their part, the *Septembristas* argued for gradual abolition in the name of Portuguese honour and preservation of the colonies. In order to ensure that the slave trade did not end in an abrupt manner, it was essential to keep Britain out of the process of suppressing it. To this end, they were willing to accept various forms of legal interpretation. The left had started out arguing for a position of intransigence, which would prevent the British cruisers from intervening south of the equator before 1852. But, as the debate went on and it lost ground, it began to be satisfied with less drastic solutions, which would in any event safeguard essentials. Thus, on 22 February, it was willing to accept that the Royal Navy should intervene in the southern hemisphere, but only under the terms of the convention of 1817—that is, only to seize ships that had slaves on board at the time of the search.[192]

The Cortes reopened on 25 May, after the elections, and the issue returned to the debating table at the beginning of July.[193] But now there was less venom in the air. Despite strong appeals in the press—'to the ballot-box, fellow-countrymen, and you will see Lord Palmerston's minions defeated'[194]—the *Septembristas* had lost ground, and some of its more disorderly representatives had lost their seats. Agitation was now carried on mainly from the columns of the press, but even here there was some fall-off. At the beginning of 1840 *O Nacional* carried a true barrage of articles against abolition, which advocated a Luso-Brazilian alliance to challenge Britain; or which asked that the British should allow the slave trade to continue 'even if only for ten years'; or which transcribed articles from the most inflammatory elements of the pro-slavery press of Rio de Janeiro.[195] In mid-year, after the failure of the blocking strategy in the Chamber of Deputies, Rio Tinto's paper sought above all to keep the flame of disagreement alive, protesting at the lethargy that seemed to be taking hold of the nation, fretting at the 'government's apathy' and the 'fakir-like impassiveness' with which it carefully tallied acts of piracy by Royal Navy cruisers. It was indispensable that 'true Portuguese' should abandon their indifference and give some 'sign of life'.[196]

The journal's invective was a prelude to the start of discussions in the Chamber of Senators. The matter had been raised at the beginning of the year, but the dissolution of the Cortes had prevented it from coming to debate, and now the left was in a minority. Accordingly, the draft reply to the Queen's Speech was a common draft—signed by Palmela, Miranda (a former Navy minister) and Sá da Bandeira—which, while reiterating the protests at the bill and its consequences, placed no specific conditions on the signature of the treaty. Nor did it mention trade or the security of the colonies.[197] Accordingly, too, the debate was shorter and less turbulent: two sessions (14 and 16 July) sufficed for discussion of the issue.

Ribeira de Sabrosa still attacked the treaty with passion, using the whole panoply of tolerationist arguments, including Brazilian interests and the sentimental appeal on behalf of Portuguese who might end up caught in the mesh of British suppression. Sabrosa reminded the assembly that Portugal was master of most of the territory where the 'ill-fated black fruit' was produced; that its relations with Brazil, the country which needed that fruit the most, were 'intimate and long-standing'; and it was certain that, with the suppression of the slave trade, Brazilian production would fall by half. Portugal still had a guaranteed 'reserve of 15 years' under the 1817 convention, and should not yield to British demands. If only to safeguard its own people:

> The idea that a poor Portuguese might be imprisoned south of the Cape of Good Hope appals me. Thrown in chains on the deck of a ship and dragged by greedy people with vested interests in seeing him punished before a court whose judges he does not know, whose laws he does not know and whose language he has maybe never heard ...; if there is a minister who allows such an insult, let Heaven's curse fall upon him [sensation].[198]

Speeches such as this were desperate tirades—and all the more revealing for that—but they could no longer halt the onward march of events. Little by little, the *Cartistas* had succeeded in divesting the subject of its ultra-nationalist associations and revealing it in its true light. Even Sá no longer insisted that the risk of losing the colonies was an insurmountable obstacle to concluding the treaty with Britain.[199] In the Chamber of Senators there were half a dozen major speeches along the lines that it was essential to reach agreement on abolition and to counter the diplomatic activity of the *Septembristas*.

It was above all Palmela's speech which, with his diplomatic stature, undermined the left's position for good, pointing out its mistakes and deconstructing its mystifications. Sá had made many diplomatic errors. He had been wrong in promulgating the decree, because it strengthened British demands. He had been wrong in allowing the disagreement with London to get worse. He had also been wrong in dragging the country into a position that was untenable in the civilized world, because there was no avoiding the fact that the British had used every means available to curb the slave trade, while the Portuguese had held out, 'arguing the need for certain changes in the articles of the treaty, some reasonable, others less so, and some not reasonable at all'. In effect—and this was his fourth mistake—the *Septembrista* Minister had shrouded the issue in mystification. Of all the reasons he had drawn on to oppose British demands, only one was valid: the issue of the perpetuity of the treaty. British intervention against the slave trade did not harm Portuguese capitalists, and the risk of loss of the colonies was tiny. But, even had it not been so, there was no option but to end the traffic in slaves, because national honour was at stake. The treaty was therefore inevitable, because Portugal had contracted an obligation to sign it and because it was the only way to protect legitimate maritime trade. As a result, the Chamber should grant the government some power, so that it could extract the country from the sad diplomatic pass to which it had come, and ministers, even if they had to accept 'harsh stipulations', should take upon themselves the weight 'of any momentary reluctance' there might be. It would disappear soon enough, just as soon as it was seen that it was without foundation.[200]

Palmela's speeches marked the fall-off of parliamentary opposition to suppression of the slave trade. Even the *Septembrista* press resigned itself bitterly to the new times and to the new party representation in the Chambers: 'let the treaty be signed as they the [British] may determine, and everything will be approved afterwards'.[201]

Opposition still arose in the Cortes of 1842 regarding the recently concluded treaty with Britain. In the Chamber of Peers—which had been restored by the Constitutional Charter—Lavradio and Sá da Bandeira brandished some of the usual arguments, such as the fact that the treaty had been ratified without prior reparation for the insult represented by the bill, that the treaty had been made in perpetuity and that the slave trade had been classified as piracy.[202] However, it was an easy matter for Palmela to evoke 'sad memories', recalling that it had been Sá da Bandeira and Ribeira de Sabrosa who, with their obstinate refusal to sign any agreement, had produced the greatest insult the Portuguese monarchy had ever suffered.[203] Of course, Palmela regretted the perpetuity clause, but he was resigned to it, because the great powers had agreed on it. The same was true of equating the slave trade with piracy.

Lavradio and Sá da Bandeira attacked again at the end of August, but all in all this was a mild attack, dictated by the game of party politics.[204] Most of the politicians in the Cortes ended up recognizing how inappropriate the crisis generated by the *Septembristas*, the slavers and their agents had been. Sá da Bandeira would publicly repent when he accepted that the 10 December decree was nothing more than a 'rehearsal' and, above all, that the policies he had pursued in 1836–39 were wrong.[205] But his example was not generally followed: most of the *Septembristas* simply remained silent. Only much later did a few of them, like José Estevão, for example, make eloquent acts of contrition:

> I have vented great gusts of patriotism and national honour here, and I almost declared war on Britain, together with many of my friends on this side of the Chamber, on account of the question of the slave trade .... And this was all for nought, because in the end the British were absolutely right, and we showed great feeling but did not cut a very good figure. They were right, and everything they did to end slavery [*sic*] was well done; I don't know if it was in their interest, but I do know it was in the interest of humanity.[206]

4.3.3 *Six Pamphlets*

In 1839–40 the struggle over abolition of the slave trade took place mainly in the press and in the Cortes. Outside these forums only half a dozen publications illustrated and reinforced either of the two sides of the question.

Arguments in favour of immediate suppression of the slave trade are to be found clearly expressed in a work by Xavier Botelho published in 1840, which can be seen as a resumption of the British approach to abolition in Portugal. At the beginning of the 1820s three or four journals had drawn directly on British influences. Botelho reopened that channel and, going further still, used his own experience in Africa, as governor of Mozambique, to adapt the apostles of anti-slavery to the specifically Portuguese situation.

In that it was a summary of Benezet, Ramsay and Clarkson, his argument followed the structure of these classic anti-slavery thinkers closely and had much the same content. He began by explaining the origins of the transatlantic slave trade and of slavery, not on account of the need to cultivate the land in America, but rather as the result of human greed and ambition. As he went on, he described an Africa that was fertile and settled by peaceful people. If those people preferred to sell men, it was only because the Europeans demanded it. Europe had taken to Africa its lust for gold and its violence: 'if the trade in Negroes were to end, so too would the wars between these unfortunates end'.[207] Part of the pamphlet was devoted to material interests, outlining the riches of Africa and promoting the establishment of a company that might exploit them. But he did not pass over the slave trade itself. As with Clarkson, the slave trade was seen as the sailor's grave. Again, as with the British abolitionists, Botelho sought to make a clear distinction between the problems of the slave trade and the problems of slavery, because he saw clearly that those who confused the two did not always do so innocently. Then he went on to describe how that trade operated, which gave him the chance to introduce the emotional aspect, through poignant descriptions of the conditions under which Africans were transported.[208] Those who survived the crossing would later undergo enough suffering in America to justify a state of permanent revolt.[209]

Another attempt at applying the British approach to Portuguese abolitionism is to be found in an anonymous pamphlet, the main concern of whose author was to glorify and extol the 'disinterested act of philanthropy' and the great sacrifices Britain had made in abolishing the slave trade. The pamphlet in question was written by Sebastian Charles Rosas, the editor of *The Lisbon Mail*, which accounts for its strong pro-British bias.[210] Rosas explained to his readers that London in no way coveted the Portuguese colonies and argued that, if Portugal truly wished to put an end to the traffic in slaves, it could only gain by cooperating with British forces, which were much more numerous and more powerful.

On occasion, *Septembristas* who knew the ground, and understood how Portuguese abolitionism had got stuck in a dead end, might back the pro-British approach, which, as we have seen, was in line with the typical *Cartista* position. Thus, for example, Brigadier Marinho, the ex-governor of Cape Verde and Mozambique, thought that the struggle against the slave trade was lost in Lisbon, and not in the colonies. Although the slavers were strong in Mozambique, they were by no means unbeatable. The ex-governor boasted that he could put a stop to the slave trade in less than a year, even with the very meagre means at his disposal (and which he himself had mostly raised). Unfortunately, the slavers enjoyed protection in the capital of the empire from 'obscure sources' who handled large amounts of money and had 'enormous power'.[211] Throughout his memoir, Marinho never ceased to point a finger at Bonfim, who, by discharging him, had sabotaged all the abolitionist work done until then. In some passages the ex-governor suggested that Bonfim had been bought; in others, that he had been progressively worked on by the Navy Ministry, which directly protected the slave traders.[212] In effect, few in Portugal could resist the 'seductive charms' of the slavers.[213] Corruption worked its way even into officers of the navy, which made him long to have under his orders a simple 'British 5-piece war brig', instead of the ships of the Portuguese navy.[214] On the question of slavery the whole of Portugal was corrupt or was acting in bad faith. The general conviction of the Portuguese was that the abolition law of 1836 was just a pretext with which to deceive London. In this state of affairs laws would not be enough, nor would good-quality military means, even if they had been available. If the British government really wanted to wipe out the slave trade, it could not trust the Portuguese ministries; 'it needed the vigour of its bill'.[215]

At the time, Marinho was exceptional. As a general rule the *Septembristas* and the Absolutists, who were not represented in the Cortes, were opposed to British abolitionist methods, and supported all sorts of schemes and stratagems to delay suppression. Some of them did not trouble to hide their opposition to abolition itself. This is what emerges from the memoir written by Saldanha da Gama in 1814, which we have already mentioned, and which was published in Paris in 1839. The writer added a preface and some notes to the original. In one of them he explained at some length his ideas on the abolition of the slave trade. The note began by promoting the theory that British philanthropy was suspect, and by belittling abolitionism. Moving on to the heart of the matter, Saldanha da Gama argued that the abolition of the traffic in slaves would quite simply be inhuman. Any man who had seen African peoples close up, and knew the ferocity of their laws and customs, could not but admit that the slave trade was good for humanity, above all for the Africans themselves, because slavery in the land of Christians, however hard it might be, would always be preferable to what they experienced in their own lands. And this was all the more true in that, even though there were many free Negroes in Brazil, not one of them had wanted to return home. Therefore, and from a purely philanthropic point of view, the end of the slave trade would be 'an evil for humanity'.[216]

A similar but more elaborate and disguised approach appeared in a pamphlet by José Joaquim Freire, the formal purpose of which was to argue in favour of abolition but which was nothing more than a plan for the continuation of the slave trade under cover of the employment of Negroes and free of British police action. Freire sought to establish what he called the 'system of civilization and Christian teaching' or, as he also said, the system of 'the embrace', something that would reconcile the dignity of the Portuguese Crown with the common interests of Britain, Brazil and the Portuguese overseas provinces. The system would be based on the hiring of supposedly free Africans. On the African coast, Portugal would civilize and baptize its 'Negro colonists'—the integrationist and mild form used in the pamphlet to refer to slaves—and then it would allow as many as it could to emigrate to Brazil, 'to be employed there'. The recommended wage was 20 *réis* per day, and employment would be for a period of six years, at the end of which the Negro would be free of his contractual obligation (only then would he receive the 43,200 *réis* of wages accumulated over a period of six years of work).[217]

To implement this whole plan in practice, Freire proposed setting up a company that would obtain the Negroes in the interior, until they came to offer themselves 'voluntarily' at the Portuguese establishments on the coast. Transportation to Brazil would never be by violent means, and the Africans would be extremely happy when they saw that they had exchanged an apocalyptic land for paradise: 'they are leaving a thankless country where plague, hunger and war have always pursued them; and they will enjoy a pleasant and healthy country …; and they are going to live with white people, under the law, among their fellow-countrymen and maybe relatives, earning a daily wage for their work'. This would put an end to the slave trade, not 'in the British way', not 'with brute force', but with 'an embrace'. Naturally the system would have to be recognized and approved by a triple alliance between Britain, Portugal and Brazil, from which all three nations would profit: it would become possible for Portugal to pursue its plans for the development of its overseas possessions, Britain would not need to use even one warship to put an end to the 'odious commerce' and Brazil would have the hands it required.[218]

Seeking to bring his influence to bear in the highest places, Freire offered his article, prior to publication, to the Queen and to Sá da Bandeira. The manuscript had on its frontispiece a print 'with the appropriate allegories' to give life and strength to the plan. Unfortunately the print was not used for the printed edition, and my efforts to find it came to nothing. Nevertheless, the author has left us with a detailed description of the drawing in question, which gives us an idea of the way he used images to emphasize his tolerationist message: in the centre, on a pedestal, was the figure of the Queen; on the right a strong arm holding the sword of Alexander, 'who, with a single blow, had cut the chains of slavery'; on the left of the pedestal, a Negro lying 'prostrate on the ground', with his small son, holding a ribbon which hung from the royal crown and which read: 'decrees the abolition of the slave trade'; to the right of the pedestal, a Negress and her daughter, holding another ribbon which said: 'decrees employment for six years, and a daily wage'.[219]

Involuntarily, Sá da Bandeira himself was to reinforce these tolerationist or even pro-slavery positions. When the ships of the Royal Navy began to intervene under Palmerston's law, the ex-minister published a pamphlet specifically on the process of abolition in Portugal. Even though it provided a summary outline of the history of the abolition of the slave trade, the pamphlet was mainly an attempt to justify the positions adopted by the *Septembrista* governments. It sought to mark out territory in a political controversy. For the most part it reproduced what had already been seen in diplomatic notes, reorganizing the ideas they contained in a more methodical manner so as to enable a more effective political counter-attack to be made. Basing himself on a central idea—that Great Britain had been responsible for the failure to conclude the treaty—Sá da Bandeira played on two registers simultaneously, one negative, the other positive, and developed a chain of arguments that would have a long future in Portugal.

The objective of the positive line of argument was to state Portugal's complete willingness to abolish the 'iniquitous commerce'. Three factors converged to create that willingness: first, the idea of having been the first to abolish, because, if one took into account the Marquis of Pombal's anti-slavery laws, which applied to Madeira and the Azores, Portugal had been the first Christian power to abolish the slave trade in its own colonies;[220] secondly, the idea of an early connection with British abolitionist plans, because Portugal was the first nation that allied itself with Britain 'to promote the suppression of the trade in Negro slaves';[221] and, thirdly, the idea of an effective and spontaneous internal abolition, given that, as a result of the writer's own initiative, the slave trade had been abolished in all territories under Portuguese administration on 10 December 1836.[222] These three reasons were, in theory, an assurance of the genuine nature of Portuguese abolitionist feelings, and would therefore prove that Britain's accusations against Portugal were unjust.

Alongside this positive line of argument, Sá also developed a negative one, with which he sought to show that British demands for abolition were completely unnecessary. What did Britain really want? That Portugal should grant it an extended right of search and that it should equate the slave trade with piracy. But such concessions would be to no avail, because the system adopted by Britain was 'entirely wrong'. The 'only way' of putting an end to the slave trade was to end slavery in the countries that imported slaves. The bill was therefore insulting to Portugal, and did nothing to deter the slavers, who could always use the American flag, or any other.[223]

To justify his negativist thesis, Sá based himself on the most recent currents in the British abolitionist movement. The idea that the effort to suppress was relatively useless was not new, either in Portugal or in the world at large, but in Britain it had come into fashion: organizations such as the recently established British and Foreign Anti-Slavery Society had started to question the methods of suppression recommended by the government and to advocate anti-coercionism: a total refusal to use force, and the destruction of slavery as a way of strangling the slave trade. Buxton, who had been the leader of the campaign for emancipation in the

British Parliament, had also recently addressed the issue of the Western countries' slave trade. In two books on the subject Buxton took stock of thirty years of suppression, identified the position of each of Britain's abolitionist partners and recommended new solutions. The data he compiled led him to believe that annual exports from Africa amounted to some 150,000 slaves—double the numbers in Wilberforce's time—and to conclude that nothing positive had been achieved under that heading as a result of the onerous anti-slave trade campaign: quite the contrary.[224] Sá made use of the British arguments themselves to uphold the idea that Britain had chosen the wrong abolitionist method. In his hands this was, of course, an opportunist theory, because he himself had argued months before that the method 'of terror'—that is, the harassment of slave traders by war navies—would be the great means for effectively combating the slave trade.[225] Nonetheless, this opportunist theory allowed him to state that Palmerston wanted to turn Portugal into 'the scapegoat for the errors committed', not only to justify the failure of the line of action he had followed, but also to disguise British involvement in this scandalous business.[226] The slave trade was a diversified activity that attracted people of various nations, each contributing in their own way: some supplied capital; others, the ships; others fitted them out; some procured false flags and papers; while others contributed their labour as captains and sailors. Based on this functional and national diversity of slaving, Sá drew up a hierarchy of blame: the most criminal—because they made large profits from the slave trade—were the capitalists who supplied the goods used in Africa to buy slaves. Ultimate blame for this trade was therefore attributable to Britain, which exported to Brazil and Havana products that it knew were destined exclusively for the slave trade. Portuguese responsibility was correspondingly diminished, not only because the Portuguese government could not be made responsible for acts committed in violation of the country's laws, but also because most of the Portuguese involved in the slave trade were mere captains and sailors (and these, in Sá's hierarchy of guilt, were the least guilty). This negative line of argument, which shifted blame to Britain and underrated British anti-trafficking methods, was a perfect match for the views of all those who opposed suppression. Ironically, both diplomatic activity and the arguments of the man who was the main proponent of abolitionism in Portugal helped to strengthen the ideas of those who opposed that very abolitionism.

Traditionally, historians have attributed the failure of the abolitionist measures of 1836–39 to opposition in the colonies, to the lack of means and to the non-existence of abolitionist opinion in Portugal. Like all partial truths, this view is deceptive in respect of the last of these reasons, because it conveys the idea that there was an ideological vacuum, a blank space in terms of public opinion. In actual fact, Portuguese society from 1830 to 1840 admitted a very strong degree of tolerance for the trade in slaves and embodied clear opposition to its immediate suppression. These trends are only not immediately identifiable because they are wrapped up in nationalist pronouncements. But the tolerance was there, along with a rhetoric pattern that conveyed the notion that suppression was a British strategy that would severely harm the country's interests. The fact that this rhetoric was embedded in the thinking of most journalists and *Septembrista* politicians and, particularly, of the men who were in charge at the Ministry of Foreign Affairs—like Gomes de Oliveira, Midosi, Ribeira de Sabrosa and, to a certain extent, Sá da Bandeira—helps to explain the setbacks and hesitations in the 'spontaneous' abolitionism of 1836. It is true that the issue of suppressing the slave trade was also a channel for political intervention, and that the differences between the *Cartistas* and the *Septembristas* were often artificially exaggerated for party political reasons. It is equally true, however, that many of those who provided Sá da Bandeira's political base saw the decree of 1836 as a sham that was aimed at avoiding British diplomatic pressure, but they did not accept the contents of the law: quite the contrary. It should not be forgotten that deputies such as Midosi and Alberto Carlos went so far as to argue that Portugal was merely obliged to 'decree abolition and nothing more'; as it had already done so of its own accord on 10 December 1836, it was only 'obliged' to implement the measure fifteen years later, that is to say, in December 1851.[227]

While not doubting the significance of opposition in the colonies and the weakness of naval and financial means—all of which are obvious—we should emphasize that the major obstacle to the suppression of the slave trade at this time was in Portugal itself. Moreover, few had revealed this better than Brigadier Marinho in his actions and in his writing.

It has been said that the hesitant policies of the *Septembrista* governments (and of those which preceded them) cannot be seen as the result of mere yielding to the interests of the slavers. In order to prove this point, it is argued that there were few Portuguese politicians directly involved in the slave trade. But national opposition to a specific policy cannot be deduced in this manner alone, because it does not derive solely from the material interests that are directly affected. As Davis showed in connection with British opposition to abolition at the end of the eighteenth century, British parliamentarians who had direct interests in the slave trade or in the American plantations were few in number. However, they had the support of the king and the royal family, trading interests in London, Liverpool and Bristol, Royal Navy admirals and, above all, the British landowning class, which feared that abolitionist innovations might weaken the empire, lead to increased taxation or establish a precedent for more dangerous social reforms.[228] In Portugal something similar took place as Anglophobic *Septembristas* merged with false and with sincere tolerationists—who were petrified at the prospect of losing the colonies.

Of course, this study has also shown that there was a pro-abolition position as well, generally articulated by *Cartista* journalists and politicians. Here, too, the position on abolition—in this case, support for it—was the result of a meeting of different motivations and biased trajectories, which had little to do with the defence of any material interests resulting from abolition. In 1838–40 *Cartista* journalists and deputies argued in favour of abolition for humanitarian reasons, for political expediency or to salvage national honour. It was a position with no underlying anti-slavery militancy in it, which basically arose out of British political pressure. The outcome of this pressure was a manner of thinking and a new attitude, in which the idea of shame played a significant part. The slave trade had to end because, if it persisted, this would create an indelible stain on the country's prestige. The parliamentarians' speeches and the *Cartista* press are the first demonstrations of what would become the main engine of Portuguese action to suppress the slave trade: the need to safeguard national honour. It was neither the colonial plan of a Sá da Bandeira nor the pressure of business sectors with an interest in exploiting African resources that would drive the anti-slave trade struggle of Portuguese governments from 1839 onwards, but the urgent need to show the world—and especially Great Britain—that Portugal was not protecting the slavers.

Notes

1. Serge Daget, 'A Model of the French Abolitionist Movement and its Variations', in Christine Bolt and Seymour Drescher (eds), *Anti-Slavery, Religion and Reform: Essays in Memory of Roger Anstey*, Dawson, Folkestone, 1980, pp. 70–72.
2. Serge Daget, 'Armateurs Nantais et traffic illegal: une histoire sans petite boîte verte', *Enquêtes et Documents*, XIII, 1987, p. 89 ff.; idem, 'The Abolition of the Slave Trade by France: the Decisive Years, 1826–1831', in David Richardson (ed.), *Abolition and its Aftermath. The Historical Context, 1790–1916*, Frank Cass, London, 1985, pp. 144–51; idem, 'Les croisières françaises de repression de la traite des noirs sur les côtes occidentals de l'Afrique (1817–1850)', *Enquêtes et Documents*, XIV, 1988, pp. 31–32; David Eltis, 'The Nineteenth-Century Transatlantic Slave Trade: An Annual Time Series of Imports into the Americas, Broken Down by Region', *Hispanic American Historical Review*, 67, 1987, p. 132.
3. Eltis, 'The Nineteenth-Century', pp. 122–23.
4. David R. Murray, *Odious Commerce: Britain, Spain and the Abolition of the Cuban Slave Trade*, Cambridge University Press, Cambridge, 1980, p. 82.
5. Ibid., chaps. 5 and 6.
6. Pierre Verger, *Flux et reflux de la traite des nègres entre le golfe de Bénin et Bahia de Todos os Santos du XVIIe au XIXe siècles*, Mouton, Paris and The Hague, 1968, pp. 315–19.
7. Eltis, 'The Nineteenth-Century', p. 115.
8. David Eltis, *Economic Growth and the Ending of the Transatlantic Slave Trade*, Oxford University Press, New York, 1987, p. 150.
9. Hoppner to Santarém, 12 March 1832, ANTT, MNE, *cx.* 930; Hoppner to Santarém and to Palmerston, 5 and 7 January 1833, respectively, PRO FO 84/140; Xavier to Russell, 20 September 1833, ANTT, MNE, *liv.* 181.
10. Palmerston to Howard de Walden, 8 September 1834 in *Documentos àcerca do tráfico da escravatura extrahidos dos papéis relativos a Portugal apresentados ao Parlamento Britannico*, Lisbon, 1840, p. 1.

11. See, for example, the minute of an inspection aboard the schooner *Esperança* and accompanying dispatches, 10 and 11 February 1835, AGM, *cx.* 311.
12. In addition to the charter of 1818 there was in fact legislation that could be used to prosecute the traders, namely a principle of Public Maritime Law that stipulated that no Portuguese ship could sail unless at least two-thirds of the crew was of Portuguese nationality (opinion of the Supreme Council of Military Justice, 25 April 1837, attached to dispatch of Vieira de Castro to Sá da Bandeira, 3 May 1837, ANTT, MNE, *cx.* 382).
13. Vila Real to Howard de Walden, 12 February and 19 May 1835; Palmela to Howard de Walden, 23 September 1835, ANTT, MNE, *liv.* 181; Vila Real to Miranda, 21 June and 3 July 1836, ANTT, MNE, *liv.* 315.
14. Howard de Walden to Vila Real, 20 October 1834, ANTT, MNE, *cx.* 930; see also Leslie Bethell, *The Abolition of the Brazilian Slave Trade. Britain, Brazil and the Slave Trade Question (1807–1869)*, Cambridge University Press, Cambridge, 1970, p. 135 ff.
15. On the British desire to keep up the appearance of not meddling with the abolitionist decisions of other countries, see Bethell, *The Abolition of the Brazilian*, pp. 43–44; Murray, *Odious Commerce*, p. 32; and Daget, 'A Model', p. 73.
16. Minutes of Cabinet Meeting, 20 February, 2 and 26 March 1835, ANTT, Ministério do Reino, Conselho de Ministros, *liv.* 1, pp. 53 (verso), 54, 56 and 60 (verso).
17. Palmela to Howard de Walden, 10 July 1835, in *Documentos àcerca*, p. 14.
18. For the turbulent months of 1834–35, see Vasco Pulido Valente, *Os Devoristas. A Revolução Liberal, 1834–1836*, Quetzal Editores, Lisbon, 1993.
19. Palmela to Howard de Walden, 10 July 1835, in *Documentos àcerca*, pp. 14–15.
20. Circular of 22 October sent by Palmela to Portuguese consuls abroad, in ibid., p. 16.
21. Bethell, *The Abolition of the Brazilian*, pp. 97–100.
22. Mentioned in Howard de Walden to Palmerston, 26 March 1836, in *Documentos àcerca*, pp. 16–17.
23. *DG*, 2 April 1836.
24. Visconde de Sá da Bandeira, *Diário da Guerra Civil (1826–1832)*, vol. 1, Seara Nova, Lisbon, 1975–76, p. 153.
25. For a eulogy of British abolitionism, see the anonymous tale, *Russell de Albuquerque. Conto moral por um portuguez*, Cintra, 1833, pp. 206–07. In actual fact this was written by Alexandre de Morais Sarmento.
26. Chamber of Peers, session of 26 March 1836, in *DG*, 29 April 1836.
27. Palmerston to Moncorvo, 30 April 1836, PRO FO 84/202.
28. See *Documentos Officiais sobre a negociação do Tractado para a Supressão do Tráfico da Escravatura, mandados publicar por ordem da Câmara dos Senadores*, Lisbon, 1839, pp. 1–13.
29. See memorandum of meeting between Vila Real and Howard de Walden, 20 May 1836, ANTT, MNE, *cx.* 930; and also Vila Real to Howard de Walden, 28 July 1836 ANTT, MNE, *liv.* 182, and Vila Real to Moncorvo, 23 July 1836, ANTT, MNE, *liv.* 575.
30. Vila Real to Moncorvo, 17 August and 3 September 1836, ANTT, MNE, *liv.* 575.
31. Howard de Walden to Palmerston, 14 January 1837, PRO FO 84/215; Palmerston to Howard de Walden, 17 January 1837, in *Documentos àcerca*, p. 7.
32. Howard de Walden to Palmerston, 5 May 1837, in *Documentos àcerca*, p. 18.
33. Observations dated 4 May 1837, ANTT, MNE, *cx.* 930.
34. Bethell, *The Abolition of the Brazilian*, pp. 94–95.
35. Howard de Walden to Sá da Bandeira, 13 May 1837 (private), PRO FO 84/215 and Howard de Walden to Palmerston, 12 March 1837, PRO FO 84/215.

36. Howard de Walden to Ribeira de Sabrosa, 11 October 1839, ANTT, MNE, *cx.* 930.
37. Palmerston to Howard de Walden, 27 October 1837, in *Documentos àcerca*, p. 18.
38. José Capela, *A burguesia mercantil do Porto e as colónias (1834–1900)*, Afrontamento, Porto, 1975, pp. 11–12; idem, *As burguesias portuguesas e a abolição do tráfico da escravatura*, Afrontamento, Porto, 1979, pp. 45–46; Valentim Alexandre, *Origens do colonialismo português moderno (1822–1891)*, 1979, p. 46; idem, 'O liberalismo português e as colónias de África, 1820–1839', *Análise Social*, 16, 61–62, 1980, p. 338.
39. Sá da Bandeira, *Diário*, p. 141. For the absence of any moral strictures or even of critical opinions on the day-to-day aspects of the world of slavery, see also pp. 99, 135, 153 and 186.
40. *Memorial Ultramarino e Marítimo*, no. 1, March 1836, pp. 13–14 (report dated 19 February 1836).
41. Note by Sá da Bandeira (undated), AHU, Sá da Bandeira Papers, *ma.* 824.
42. Decree law of 10 December 1836, in José F. Borges de Castro, *Collecção dos tratados, convenções, contratos e actos públicos celebrados entre a Coroa de Portugal e as mais Potências desde 1640 até ao presente*, vols. IV and V, Imprensa Nacional, Lisbon, 1857–58.
43. Sá da Bandeira to Rebelo de Carvalho, 15 December 1838, ANTT, MNE, *liv.* 576.
44. By way of example, see Sá da Bandeira to Vieira de Castro, 20 December 1836, AGM, *liv.* 135, and instructions to the schooner Amélia, 16 January 1837, AGM, *liv.* 32, pp. 47 (verso) and 48.
45. Sá da Bandeira to Vieira de Castro, 14 April 1837, ANTT, MNE, *liv.* 315.
46. Howard de Walden to Palmerston, 12 and 18 March and 2 April 1837, in *Documentos àcerca*, pp. 17–18; Howard de Walden to Sá da Bandeira, 13, 16, 21 and 25 April 1837, ANTT, MNE, *cx.* 492.
47. Sá da Bandeira to Vieira de Castro, 14 April 1837, ANTT, MNE, *liv.* 315.
48. *DCP*, session of 5 August 1842, p. 123.
49. See Maria de Fátima Bonifácio, '1834–42: a Inglaterra perante a evolução política portuguesa (hipóteses para a revisão de versões correntes) ', *Análise Social*, 20, 83, 1984, pp. 467–88.
50. Sá da Bandeira to Bonfim, 13 November and 16 December 1837, ANTT, MNE, *liv.* 316.
51. Bonfim to Sá da Bandeira, 19 December 1837, ANTT, MNE, *cx.* 382.
52. Howard de Walden to Sá da Bandeira, 7 December 1837 ANTT, MNE, *cx.* 492.
53. Official opinion dated 15 January 1838, attachment to memo from Bonfim to Sá da Bandeira, 27 January 1838, ANTT, MNE, *cx.* 382. On the increasing use of the Portuguese flag in the slave trade, see Palmerston to Howard de Walden, 24 March 1838, PRO FO 84/248.
54. Murray, *Odious Commerce*, p. 101.
55. Ibid., p. 104. For reports on Portuguese consuls, see Commissioners of Sierra Leone to Palmerston, 30 May 1838, in *Documentos àcerca*, pp. 7–8; and Jerningham to Sá da Bandeira (attachments), 16 November 1838, ANTT, MNE, *cx.* 492.
56. Marques Pereira to Sá da Bandeira, 18 June 1838, AHU, Sá da Bandeira papers, *ma.* 824. For Vidal's intervention see draft of 30 April 1838, PRO FO 84/248.
57. Circular by Marquis d'Aracaty, 11 November 1837, in *Documentos Officiais*, pp. 31–32.
58. *Memória àcerca da extinção da escravidão e do tráfico de escravos no território portuguez*, Ministério da Marinha, Lisbon, 1889, p. 85.

59. Joaquim Pereira Marinho, *Memória Official em resposta às accusações dirigidas a Sua Magestade contra o Governador Geral da Província de Cabo Verde,* Lisbon, 1839, pp. 93–94; Kendall (British consul in Cabo Verde) to the mixed commission of Sierra Leone, 14 November 1839, PRO FO 84/284; and Rodrigo da Fonseca to Howard de Walden, 4 September 1840, ANTT, MNE, *liv.* 183.
60. Palmerston to Howard de Walden, 24 March, 28 April and 12 May 1838, in *Documentos àcerca,* pp. 20–22. For the hardening of the British position during March–April 1838, see Bethell, *The Abolition of the Brazilian,* p. 105.
61. Sá da Bandeira to Howard de Walden, 10 April 1838, ANTT, MNE, *liv.* 182.
62. Official opinion of António Joaquim Gomes de Oliveira, 13 April 1838, ANTT, MNE, *cx.* 930.
63. Howard de Walden to Palmerston, 7 May 1838, in *Documentos àcerca,* p. 23.
64. Sá da Bandeira to Howard de Walden, 8 May 1838, in *Documentos Officiais,* pp. 29–30.
65. Howard de Walden to Palmerston, 10 May 1838, in *Documentos àcerca,* p. 24.
66. Howard de Walden to Sá da Bandeira, 10 May 1838, in *Documentos Officiais,* pp. 33–38. For the British ambassador's prior familiarity with Aracaty's circular, see Howard de Walden to Palmerston, 7 May 1838 (confidential), PRO FO 84/249.
67. Howard de Walden to Sá da Bandeira, 12 and 19 May 1838, AHM, Division 3, Section 18, Sá da Bandeira archive, *cx.* 5.
68. Additional article suggested by Sá da Bandeira, in *Documentos Officiais,* p. 76.
69. Sá da Bandeira to Howard de Walden, 23 May 1838, AHM, Division 3, Section 18, Sá da Bandeira archive, *cx.* 5.
70. Bethell, *The Abolition of the Brazilian,* pp. 90–95; and Eltis, *Economic Growth,* pp. 85–90 and 210.
71. Palmerston to Howard de Walden, 12 May 1838, in *Documentos àcerca,* pp. 21–22, and memorandum from Bandinel to Palmerston, 4 January 1839, PRO FO 84/251.
72. Christopher Lloyd, *The Navy and the Slave Trade. The Suppression of the African Slave Trade in the Nineteenth Century,* Frank Cass, London, 1968 (1st edition 1949), p. 42.
73. Sá da Bandeira to Jerningham, 29 May 1838, in *Documentos Officiais,* p. 87, and Jerningham to Palmerston, 4 June 1838, PRO FO 84/249; for the *Septembrista* minister's political bluff, see Sá da Bandeira to his brother A.C. de Sá Nogueira (in London at the time), 18 June 1838, AHM, Division 3, Section 18, Sá da Bandeira archive, *cx.* 14.
74. Jerningham to Sá da Bandeira, 1 August 1838, in *Documentos Officiais,* pp. 90–92.
75. Valentim Alexandre, 'Portugal e a abolição do tráfico de escravos, 1834–1851', *Análise Social,* 26, 111, 1991, pp. 313–15.
76. Official opinion of Gomes de Oliveira, 1 May 1838, ANTT, MNE, *cx.* 930.
77. Ibid. (the issues summarized here are contained in points 5 to 9 of the opinion).
78. Sá da Bandeira, *Diário,* pp. 111 and 130. Aracaty was at the time Foreign Minister of Brazil.
79. Aracaty to Sá da Bandeira, 8 January 1837, AHM, Sá da Bandeira archive, Division 3, Section 18, *cx.* 7 (*proc.* 59); for Aracaty's financial circumstances, see the Marquis of Fronteira, *Memórias do Marquês de Fronteira, D. José Trazimundo Mascarenhas Barreto,* vol. 3, Imprensa da Universidade, Coimbra, 1929, p. 208.
80. Howard de Walden to Palmerston, 7 May 1838 (confidential), PRO FO 84/249.
81. Aracaty to Sá da Bandeira, 29 May 1837, AHM, Division 3, Section, Sá da Bandeira archive, *cx.* 7.

82. Jerningham to Palmerston, 13 August 1838, PRO FO 84/250.
83. *Diário das Cortes*, 14 September 1822, p. 437 (speech by Correia de Castro). In actual fact the battalion sent to Angola in 1823 to suppress a possible uprising (or Brazilian attack) numbered 280 men. Around the same time, and for the same purpose, around 100 soldiers were sent to Mozambique.
84. Joseph C. Miller, *Way of Death. Merchant Capitalism and the Angolan Slave Trade, 1730–1830*, University of Wisconsin Press, Madison, 1988, p. 643.
85. It was only after 1852 that Lisbon would begin to send funds to pay for the vessels stationed in the colonies (see *DCD*, session of 7 May 1856, p. 75).
86. Lloyd, *The Navy*; and Bethell, *The Abolition of the Brazilian*, p. 123.
87. Five of the eight schooners in the navy between 1838 and 1843 were ships that had been seized as slavers; five of the ten brigs that entered service between 1840 and 1848 were ex-slavers; between 1837 and 1842 the State took delivery of only two new corvettes, and both were the result of arrests of slavers. For data on the ships discussed here see António Esparteiro, *Três séculos no mar (1640–1910)*, 32 vols., Ministério da Marinha, Lisbon, 1974–86.
88. *DCD*, session of 7 May 1839, p. 403 (speech by Morato Roma).
89. This was recognized at the time by Sá da Bandeira himself (*DCD*, session of 5 March 1839, p. 470). For a table showing idle times in Lisbon and activity in Africa, for each ship, see Annexes A and B.
90. Jerningham to Palmerston, 8 October 1838, PRO FO 84/251, and Howard de Walden to Palmerston, 26 November 1838, in *Documentos àcerca*, p. 52.
91. Howard de Walden to Palmerston, 22 April 1836, PRO FO 84/202.
92. Howard de Walden to Palmerston, 7 May 1838 (confidential), PRO FO 84/249.
93. *DCD*, session of 9 February 1839, p. 241.
94. *DCD*, 22 April 1836 and 20 May 1839, PRO FO 84/202 and 84/282, respectively.
95. Howard de Walden to Palmerston, 2 September 1839, PRO FO 84/282.
96. Howard de Walden to Palmerston (confidential), 23 February 1839, PRO, FO 84/281; for additional references to the involvement of the leaders of political clubs in the slave trade, see idem, 22 April 1836, PRO FO 84/202; idem, 14 February 1838, FO 84/248; and 8 July 1839, PRO FO 84/282.
97. Fronteira, *Memórias*, p. 161.
98. Howard de Walden to Palmerston, 14 February 1838, PRO FO 84/248; idem, 10 May 1838, in *Documentos àcerca*, p. 24.
99. Howard de Walden to Palmerston, 20 May 1838, in *Documentos àcerca*, p. 29.
100. Marques Pereira to Sá da Bandeira, 18 June 1838, AHU, Sá da Bandeira papers, *ma.* 824.
101. Observations, 15 May 1838, ANTT, MNE, *cx.* 930.
102. Gomes de Oliveira to Rodrigo da Fonseca, 30 September 1840, ANTT, MNE, *cx.* 930.
103. Sá da Bandeira to Howard de Walden, 23 May 1838, AHM, Division 3, Section 18, Sá da Bandeira archive, *cx.* 5.
104. Chamber of Senators, session of 16 July 1840, *DG*, 1 August 1840.
105. Howard de Walden to Palmerston, 14 November 1837 (confidential) and Palmerston to de Walden, 9 December 1837, PRO FO 84/215; Howard de Walden to Palmerston, 24 April 1838, PRO FO 84/248 and Palmerston to Howard de Walden, 5 May 1838, in *Documentos àcerca*, p. 21. For the text of the British promise to provide aid, see *Documentos Officiais*, pp. 39–40.
106. Howard de Walden to Ribeira de Sabrosa, 7 October 1839, ANTT, MNE, *cx.* 930.
107. Government order of 16 March 1839, *DG*, 2 April 1839.
108. *DG*, 5 March 1838.
109. Figanière e Morão to Sá da Bandeira, 1 August and 28 December 1839, AHM, Division 3, Section 18, Sá da Bandeira archive, *cx.* 6, *proc.* 79. The con-

sul general had the open support of various Brazilian ministers and of the Luso-Brazilian merchant community in Rio. Among 96 signatures to a certificate of his honourable character were of course the major Portuguese slavers like Manuel Pinto da Fonseca and José Bernardino de Sá (affidavit of 14 March 1839, *DL*, 12 October 1861). In addition, the important services Moreira provided for the liberal cause, such as the warships he supplied for the conquest of the Azores and the help and welcome he gave to many refugees in Brazil, ensured that he had significant and lasting recognition in Portugal (see, by way of example, Chamber of Deputies, sessions of 15 July 1861 and 3 May 1862, *DL*, 17 July 1861 and 6 May 1862, speeches by Afonseca).

110. Howard de Walden to Palmerston, 30 November 1838, in *Documentos àcerca*, p. 55; Sá knew Moreira personally, having stayed with him when visiting Brazil.
111. Rowenttou (Danish chargé d'affaires) to Sá da Bandeira, 13 April 1839, *Documentos àcerca*, p. 97.
112. The so-called revolt of the Malé was an insurrection movement by Negroes in Bahia, which was defused while still being hatched. Nevertheless, several deaths did occur, and Brazil was terrified. This led to a growing current of opinion opposing the importation of more slaves (see Verger, *Flux et reflux*, pp. 335–50 and 355 ff.).
113. Palmela to Sérgio Teixeira de Macedo, 7 July and 12 November 1835, ANTT, MNE, *liv*. 592.
114. Noronha to Sá da Bandeira, 22 February 1839, ANTT, MNE, *cx*. 382.
115. Minutes of Council of Ministers' meeting, 29 September 1839, ANTT, Ministry of the Realm, Council of Ministers, *liv*. 1, pp. 132 (verso) and 133.
116. Bethell, *The Abolition of the Brazilian*, p. 191. Neither was the Tucker–Paine agreement ratified by their respective governments (see A.R. Booth, 'The United States African Squadron, 1843–1861', in *Boston University Papers on Africa*, vol. 1, Boston, 1964, pp. 86–87).
117. *Correio de Lisboa*, 4 May 1841.
118. Sá da Bandeira to Ribeira de Sabrosa, 25 May 1839, AHM, Division 3, Section 18, Sá da Bandeira archive, *cx*. 2 (*proc*. 14).
119. Howard de Walden to Palmerston, 20 May 1839, PRO FO 84/282.
120. Bethell, *The Abolition of the Brazilian*, pp. 105 and 155–56; and Howard W. Temperley, *White Dreams, Black Africa: The Antislavery Expedition to the River Niger, 1841–1842*, Yale University Press, New Haven, 1991, p. 27.
121. Transcription of Palmerston's bill, *DG*, 9 August 1839.
122. Julio Firmino Júdice Biker, *Suplemento à colecção de Tratados, Convenções, Contratos e Actos Públicos celebrados entre a Coroa de Portugal e as mais Potências desde 1640 até ao presente*, vol. XXVIII, Lisbon, 1879, p. 387.
123. *Paquete do Ultramar*, 21 November 1839.
124. In the space of one year, 65 ships were prosecuted under Palmerston's bill (see Lloyd, *The Navy*, p. 48).
125. *Memória àcerca da extinção da escravidão*, pp. 85–90; Joaquim Pereira Marinho, *Memória contra a facção dos negreiros*, Lisbon, 1842. For seizures of slave ships, see Annexes C, D and E.
126. Vila Real to Howard de Walden, 23 April 1840, ANTT, MNE, *cx*. 930.
127. Palmerston to Howard de Walden, 29 February 1840, PRO FO 84/320.
128. Text of the treaty in Castro, *Collecção*.
129. *A Vedeta da Liberdade*, 4 January 1837; see also *O Nacional*, 23 December 1836, and *DG* of the same date.
130. *O Popular*, 5 January 1837.
131. Ibid., 19 January 1837.
132. *O Nacional*, 24 July 1835 and 13 April 1836.

133. Ibid., 28 July 1838.
134. Ibid., 30 March 1839.
135. All indications are that this is a very fuzzy image, which had some elements of reality but did not truly reflect it (David B. Davis, *Slavery and Human Progress*, Oxford University Press, Oxford, 1984, p. 300; and Temperley, *White Dreams*, pp. 23–31, 53–59, 135–36 and 176).
136. David B. Davis, *The Problem of Slavery in the Age of Revolution,1770–1823*, Cornell University Press, Ithaca, NY, and London, 1975, p. 190 ff.
137. *O Nacional*, 6 February 1839.
138. Ibid., 13 December 1839.
139. Ibid., 22 July and 17 August 1839, and 17 March 1840.
140. Ibid., 4 July and 13 December 1839.
141. Ibid., 25 September 1838.
142. Ibid., 22 June 1840.
143. Ibid., 4 June and 31 August 1839.
144. Ibid., 1 and 28 July 1839.
145. Howard de Walden to Palmerston, 20 May 1839, in *Documentos àcerca*, pp. 97–98. The ambassador took care regularly to send to London various examples of the Portuguese press (with translations) so that London could assess the prevailing currents of opinion in Portugal on the slave trade (PRO FO 84/281 and 282).
146. By way of illustration only, see *Miscellanea Politica*, 18 August 1838; *O Athleta*, 26 September 1838; *O Constitucional*, 30 March 1839; *O Tempo*, 13 August 1839; *O Democrata*, 31 August 1839; *O Ecco*, 3 September 1839; *Paquete do Ultramar*, 13 October 1839; *A Lança*, no. 5, 1840.
147. *DG*, 9 August 1839.
148. Chamber of Senators, session of 16 July, *DG*, 1 August 1840.
149. *O Director*, 28 August 1839; see also the 25 September 1839 edition. For examples of the abolitionist approach in the Lisbon British press, see *The Lisbon English Journal*, 13 August 1836; *The Lisbon Mail*, 14 January 1837; *The Lisbon Chronicle*, 23 March 1839.
150. *O Panorama*, 14 July 1838, p. 221.
151. *Correio de Lisboa*, 13 October 1838.
152. Ibid., 30 May 1838.
153. *O Nacional* received information through Gomes de Oliveira or Paulo Midosi, a man who was at the same time editor of the newspaper and Under-Secretary of State for Foreign Affairs. For the connection between Gomes de Oliveira and *O Nacional*, see Howard de Walden to Palmerston, 2 September 1840 (confidential), PRO FO 84/321.
154. *Documentos officiais*; and *Documentos relativos à negociação do Tratado entre Portugal e a Gram-Bretanha para a abolição do Tráfico da Escravatura, mandados publicar por ordem do Governo de Sua Magestade em aditamento aos que a Câmara dos Senadores mandou imprimir*, Lisbon, 1839.
155. Howard de Walden to Palmerston, 28 April 1839, in *Documentos àcerca*, p. 96.
156. Sá da Bandeira to Rebelo de Carvalho (Portuguese representative in London), 9 April 1838, ANTT, MNE, *liv.* 576.
157. Taking the month of August 1839 by way of example, we find it in *O Athleta* (5, 9, 16 and 28); in *O Nacional* (2, 3, 8, 10, 12, 17, 20, 24, 26, 28, 30, 31); in *O Tempo* (1, 7, 22); and in *DG* (1, 2, 9, 26, 31); etc.
158. *O Athleta*, 9 August 1839.
159. Maria de Fátima Bonifácio, 'Os arsenalistas da Marinha na Revolução de Setembro (1836)', *Análise Social*, 17, 65, 1981, p. 55.
160. *O Nacional*, 20 July 1839.
161. *Correio de Lisboa*, 28 June 1839; for an identical opinion see *O Director*, 28 August 1839.

162. *DCD*, session of 29 January 1839, p. 121.
163. *DCD*, session of 9 February, pp. 238–39.
164. For the speech by Midosi, see *DCD*, session of 13 February 1839, pp. 249–50.
165. *DCD*, session of 9 February 1839, pp. 234–35 and 241–42.
166. *DCD*, session of 13 February 1839, p. 250.
167. *DCD*, session of 9 February 1839, pp. 237 and 242.
168. Ibid., pp. 233–35, and session of 13 February 1839, pp. 248–49.
169. Chamber of Senators, session of 26 February, *DG*, 4 March 1839 (italics in original).
170. Ibid.
171. Sá da Bandeira to Rebelo de Carvalho, 5, 11 and 18 March 1839, ANTT, MNE, *liv.* 576.
172. *DCD*, session of 13 February 1839, pp. 245–48.
173. Howard de Walden to Palmerston, 15 February 1839, in *Documentos àcerca*, p. 64.
174. *The Globe*, 9 March 1839 (transcribed in *The Lisbon Chronicle*, no. 4, 23 March 1839).
175. *DCD*, session of 14 February 1840, p. 158 (speech by José Maria Grande).
176. Minute of the session of the Council of Ministers, 24 February 1840, ANTT, Ministério do Reino, Conselho de Ministros, *liv.* 1, p. 137 (verso).
177. *DCD*, session of 22 February 1840, p. 274.
178. *DCD*, session of 25 January 1840, p. 163.
179. Ibid., p. 164.
180. *DCD*, session of 19 February 1840, speeches by Seabra and Leonel Tavares, pp. 227 and 238, respectively.
181. *DCD*, session of 24 February 1840, p. 291 (italics in original).
182. *O Nacional*, 23 October 1839.
183. *DCD*, session of 1 February 1840, p. 3.
184. Ibid., p. 4 (speech by Seabra).
185. *DCD*, session of 18 February 1840, p. 211.
186. *DCD*, session of 11 February 1840, p. 131.
187. Ibid., pp. 209–10.
188. Ibid., p. 218.
189. Ibid., pp. 215–19. For a description and analysis of this parliamentary session, from the point of view of the left, see *O Democrata*, 19 February 1840.
190. *DCD*, session of 19 February 1840, pp. 223–24.
191. Chamber of Deputies, session of 17 February 1840, *DG*, 18 February 1840 (speech by Taipa).
192. Always watchful, the British ambassador sent copies and summaries of the speeches to London, so that an assessment could be made there of the positions of the Portuguese parliamentarians (Howard de Walden to Palmerston, 28 February and 1 August 1840, PRO FO 84/320 and 321, respectively).
193. *DCD*, sessions of 2 and 3 July 1840.
194. *Paquete do Ultramar*, 18 March 1840.
195. See, for example, *O Nacional*, 11 and 13 February 1840.
196. Ibid., 12 May and 6 June 1840.
197. Chamber of Senators, session of 6 July 1840, *DG*, 17 July 1840.
198. Chamber of Senators, session of 14 July, *DG*, 29 July 1840; see also session of 23 June 1840, *DG*, 7 July 1840.
199. Chamber of Senators, session of 16 July 1840, *DG*, 1 August 1840.
200. Chamber of Senators, sessions of 14 and 16 July 1840, *DG*, 29 July and 1 August 1840, respectively.
201. *A Revolução de Septembro*, 15 July 1840.
202. *DCP*, session of 5 August 1842.
203. *DCP*, sessions of 5 and 27 August 1842, pp. 119–24 and 214–15, respectively.

204. *DCP*, sessions of 27 and 29 August 1842.
205. *DCP*, session of 5 August 1842, pp. 122–23.
206. *DCD*, session of 26 January 1858, p. 216.
207. Sebastião Xavier Botelho, *Escravatura: benefícios que podem provir às nossas Possessões d'Africa da prohibição daquelle tráfico*, Lisbon, 1840, pp. 7–8.
208. Ibid., pp. 1, 17 and 21–27.
209. Ibid., p. 3.
210. (Sebastian Charles Rosas), *Breves Reflexões àcerca do estado actual do Trafico da Escravatura, em relação ao Progresso da Civilização Europea*, Lisbon, 1839, pp. 7–15. For authorship of the anonymous pamphlet, see Howard de Walden to Palmerston, 22 December 1839, PRO FO 84/283.
211. Marinho, *Memória contra*, pp. 13–14 and 41.
212. Ibid., pp. 89 and 96; see also pp. 13, 15, 17, 18, 25, 29.
213. Ibid., pp. 26–27. Marinho's charges were not idle speculation, as was demonstrated in the case of the barque *Glória*, which was apprehended and prosecuted in Mozambique in 1840, and subsequently delivered to its owner in Lisbon and almost released, had it not been for very strong opposition from the British embassy and some members of the Portuguese Parliament.
214. Ibid., pp. 20–21 and 101–02.
215. Ibid., pp. 96 and 39.
216. António Saldanha da Gama, *Memória sobre as colónias de Portugal situadas na costa Ocidental d'Africa, mandada ao Governo pelo antigo Governador e Capitão-Geral do Reino de Angola... em 1814, precedida de um discurso preliminar, augmentada de alguns additamentos e notas,...*, Paris, 1839., pp. 110–12.
217. José Joaquim Freire, *Projecto para a abolição do tráfico da escravatura*, Lisbon, 1840, pp. 2, 11, 13 and 17. To justify his choice of a six-year period—which, significantly, was roughly the average lifespan of a slave on a plantation—Freire found a biblical pretext: 'if you buy a Hebrew slave, he shall serve you six years' (ibid., p. 18).
218. Ibid., pp. 14–15.
219. Ibid., p. 1.
220. Visconde de Sá da Bandeira, *O tráfico da escravatura e o bill de Lord Palmerston*, Lisbon, 1840, pp. 3–4. Sá was referring to the charters of 19 September 1761 and 16 January 1773, which applied only to Portugal and adjacent islands.
221. Ibid., p. 9.
222. Ibid., p. 10.
223. Ibid., pp. 4–5 and 45.
224. Thomas F. Buxton, *The African Slave Trade, London, 1839*, pp. 195–220; and idem, *The Remedy: Being a Sequel to The African Slave Trade*, London, 1840.
225. Chamber of Senators, session of 26 February 1839, *DG*, 4 March 1839.
226. Sá da Bandeira, *O tráfico*, pp. 5–8.
227. *DCD*, sessions of 14 and 15 February 1840, pp. 199 and 172 (speeches by Paulo Midosi and Alberto Carlos, respectively).
228. Davis, *Age of Revolution*, pp. 102–03.

– *Chapter 5* –

NATIONAL HONOUR: PORTUGAL AND THE STRUGGLE AGAINST THE SLAVE TRADERS IN THE MID NINETEENTH CENTURY

One of the major difficulties in the struggle against the slave trade was achieving synchronous successes. As Buxton pointed out, the slave trade operated almost randomly through numerous 'doors'—the French, the Spanish, the Portuguese, etc.—so that the legal closure of any one of them meant merely that the slavers would use one of the others that was still open.[1] This constant escaping from one place to another meant that there would be no success until the last 'door' had been shut off, and this feeling of a permanently unfinished task reinforced the arguments of those who disapproved of the British method. Despite this, the more persistent politicians and abolitionists believed that the final victory over the 'iniquitous commerce' could be obtained bit by bit, and for them the 1830s ended on an auspicious note with Palmerston's bill, subsequently complemented by the Anglo-Portuguese treaty of 1842. The closing of the Portuguese 'door' coincided, moreover, with the reinforcement of the maritime police. In 1831 commodore Hayes of the Royal Navy gave assurances that if he had a free hand he would need no more than three years to put an end to the 'odious commerce'. This was a commonly held view amongst navy commanders of all nations, who generally favoured using all the means at their disposal, and had little inclination to put up with irritating political and diplomatic obstacles.[2] Obviously the British navy could not treat foreign nationals and property in this unrestricted manner without the backing of laws and agreements that would allow it to do so, and these fundamental conditions had not changed between 1839 and 1842. But from then on, and for the first time, African waters would be patrolled simultaneously by British, French, North American and Portuguese warships. This joint effort heralded much greater effectiveness in suppressing the slave trade. The results, however, were far below the more promising expectations, and the 1840s would end up being one of the most unrewarding periods in the struggle against the slave trade.

5.1 The End of the Transatlantic Slave Trade: a Victory for Persistence

The period from 1835 to 1839 saw total exports of slaves reach very high levels—above 90,000 per annum. When Palmerston's bill came into force, exports fell, and by the mid-1840s they were running at around 33,000 per annum.[3] This was a significant drop, but it was incidental. On the ground, the situation was mixed, with some victories for suppression alongside persistent frustration, and it became clear that a number of difficult problems would persist.

While some export markets in Africa were closing or fading away, others remained open, sometimes wide open. The Portuguese settlements at Bissau and Cacheu, which were still very active at the end of the 1830s, closed down completely in 1843.[4] The Ivory and Gold Coasts were also almost entirely free of slavers. Further east, in the bight of Biafra, suppression had been successful as a result of a policy of understanding with the African authorities and the development of the palm oil trade. The slave trade from Angola (Map 5.1) also fell, although it did not disappear. In order to avoid pressure from the authorities and from cruisers, and adopting once more a strategy of evasion that had often been used in the past, much of the Luanda slave trade was transferred to the north, in particular to Ambriz and adjacent areas, at the time still outside Portuguese territory (which only went up to the 8° south parallel). This immediately gave rise to a string of British complaints.[5] Benguela also kept up a significant flow of exports, despite suppression. Even so, when compared with the volume of the slave trade in the immediately preceding period, the total volume of exports of slaves in the Angola area—defined here as the whole western coast south of the mouth of the River Zaïre—had clearly declined and reached its lowest level in 1845; the drop in transatlantic exports from the east coast of Africa was similar.[6]

But alongside these clear or moderate successes, there were other areas where there had been clear failures. In Upper Guinea the slave trade still flourished in the estuaries of the Sherbro, the Pongo and especially the Gallinas Rivers. In the bight of Benin, as in the northern Congo, from the mouth of the Zaïre (inclusive) up to Cape Lopes, there was just a slight drop in exports.[7] Of greater concern, however, was that this overall poor result worsened substantially in the second half of the 1840s, with total exports of slaves reaching very high levels again, close to 80,000 per annum. This increase in exports came from the Gallinas River area and from the bight of Benin (which maintained their normal levels), from Angola and Mozambique (where exports rose again, even though levels remained much lower than those reached between 1836 and 1839)

MAP 5.1. The coasts of the Congo and Angola.

and above all, from the Zaïre River and ports to the north, where exports more than doubled in comparison with the previous ten years.

The failure to suppress the slave trade in these areas can be explained in part by their peculiar geography. In the bight of Benin, for example, the export centres were located in a network of lagoons and rivers parallel to the sea and separated from it by a spit of sand. When necessary, slaves to be embarked on the *tumbeiros* could be quickly transported along that network of rivers and be dispatched somewhere else along the strip of sand, so as to avoid the cruisers. The geography of northern Angola and of the Congo also made suppression difficult, not only because there were countless small harbours and anchorages north and south of the Zaïre River, but because the river itself, which was broad and full-flowing, allowed the slave ships to escape at night, by floating on the current with sails furled.[8] There were similar difficulties at several points on the Mozambican coast, which is generally low-lying and where the range of the tide was extremely helpful to the slave traders. In Mocambo bay, for example, the difference between high and low tides at the time of the equinox was so great that, when the water covered the land, it was possible for the slave ships to hide in the undergrowth.[9]

Nonetheless, however unfavourable the geography of the African coast may have been, the main reasons for the relative failure of suppression had to do with human decision-making and the fact that many of the optimistic expectations of 1839–42 had not materialized. A more detailed analysis will follow of the difficulties of anti-slave trade actions in areas administered by Portugal. For now it will be sufficient to mention that, contrary to what the optimists thought, the Portuguese 'door' did not close: it merely shut halfway.

In addition, cooperation between the great powers in pursuing abolition remained a fiction. The United States maintained its policy of refusing the right of search and of not coordinating efforts to suppress the slave trade with the British. In the Webster–Ashburton treaty of 1842, they agreed to reactivate an anti-slave trade patrol. But the American war navy—which would eventually put half a dozen warships into operation on the coast of Africa—was interested above all in protecting the trade and property of its citizens, and made few arrests.[10] Anglo-French abolitionist cooperation lessened as British naval policing hardened towards the end of the 1830s. The fact that some French ships had been apprehended by the Royal Navy caused indignation in France, and the press demanded an end to the right of search. Initially Guizot, the Minister of Foreign Affairs, sought to maintain cooperation with Britain on anti-slave trade issues and, in 1841, he even negotiated a new treaty involving France, Britain, Austria, Russia and Prussia, which established the right of search, regarded the slave trade as piracy and provided that any citizen of the contracting countries involved in this trade would, *ipso facto*, forfeit the right to the protection of his flag. But Guizot was forced to withdraw when the legislative assemblies refused to ratify the agreement.[11] This setback was to lead to the signature of another agreement on 29 May 1845, one that reserved to the French navy alone the right to arrest ships of its own flag. The British were limited to checking irregularities regarding the nationality of the ship. It is true that, in this new agreement, France did undertake—as did Britain—to place a twenty-six-vessel patrol in African waters. This was a significant naval force but, in the French case, it seemed somewhat redundant, as its slave traffic had ceased, and there were no agreements with Portugal, Spain or Brazil that would have allowed it to intervene against ships of those nations.[12]

Another cause of the relative failure of the policy of suppression was the difficulty at the heart of British politics of reconciling abolitionism and free trade, an old dilemma, which has been touched upon in chapter 3 and which became more prominent with the passing of the Sugar Bill, a measure approved in 1846, which provided for the progressive reduction of taxes on foreign sugar until they aligned with those paid by British producers. The end of the system of protection that had until that time shielded West Indies production meant that Brazil and Cuba could penetrate the British sugar market, and it was reasonable to expect that this opening would encourage their production and, in consequence, the importation of slave labour. For many abolitionists, the contradiction was clear: Britain had crusaded for decades against the slave trade and was now preparing to take measures that, indirectly, would encourage it.[13]

The Sugar Bill was merely the most glaring example of how economic liberalism was incompatible with abolition. There were others of a more practical and immediate nature that militated directly against the practice of suppression. In effect, Royal Navy seamen had been trying since the 1830s to suppress the slave trade on land. In 1838 they made an incursion at Bulama. Two years later, Commander Denman blockaded the Gallinas estuary and, at the beginning of 1841, he destroyed the barracoons where slaves were deposited, forcing the local chieftain into making a treaty for abolition of the slave trade. Similar actions were taken in other areas of Guinea, Cabinda and the Ambriz.[14] However, governments in London were unable to keep up the blockades and attacks on slavery facilities because they upset the trade of various nations (including that of Britain itself). Inasmuch as legal and illegal trade coexisted on the African coast and naval actions could not tell the difference between them and so might destroy them both, these actions attracted a great deal of protest. When Palmerston left the government in the autumn of 1841, London relented with regard to the strong-arm tactics it had pursued until then. In a despatch to the Admiralty in mid-1842, Aberdeen made it known that the actions of Denman and other naval commanders were not entirely legal:

> Blockading the rivers, landing and destroying buildings and carrying off persons held in slavery, in countries with which Great Britain is not at war, cannot be considered as sanctioned by the law of nations or by the provisions of any existing treaties …; a good, however eminent, should not be attained otherwise than by lawful means.[15]

As an alternative, London advocated the establishment of further agreements with African authorities with the objective of restricting the slave trade at source.[16] This easing of British repressive policy allowed some slaving facilities to be rebuilt. At the same time, those who had suffered as a result of the Royal Navy attacks took action in the British courts against Denman and other officers, asking for compensation for losses and damages totalling 370,000 pounds sterling. The large amount and the liability involved helped to cool the naval commanders' ardour. Only after Palmerston had come back into government, and in particular after Denman had been tried and acquitted in 1848, did cruiser crews feel at ease to intervene on land once more.[17]

As always, however, the most important reasons for the failure to suppress effectively lay on the other side of the Atlantic, where the Cuban and Brazilian 'doors' remained open, in spite of laws and treaties. Cuban imports had fallen to generally low levels, but the Brazilians kept up their voracious appetite for African labour. Between 1846 and 1849, the Brazilian trade went through a period of significant growth: in those four years its trading volumes were close to their all-time highs.[18]

It should be added that these more or less serious difficulties were taking place against a backdrop of disputes in which the London government faced strong internal opposition to continuing with its anti-slave trade crusade. Popular abolitionism in Britain had taken a knock with the failure of the Niger expedition (1841–42), and part of the 'public zeal' for Africa evaporated during 1842, when public opinion shifted from enthusiasm to disenchantment.[19] The results of emancipation, decreed in 1833 and brought into full effect five years later, were a further blow. Contrary to the fears of many, the liberation of the slaves did not bring about any revolts. However, the main criteria for the success of emancipation were cultural and, above all, economic: it depended on the willingness of Negroes to adopt the Western way of life and their ability to produce more goods more cheaply than the slave plantations in Brazil, Cuba or the United States. What happened in part of the West Indies after emancipation was that the cost of labour rose, land values fell and production of sugar and other tropical products declined.[20] Thanks to the combined effect of the disasters in the Niger and the experience of emancipation, some parts of British public opinion began to see the Negro as a lazy human being who was undeserving of the sacrifices the European was making to bring him into civilization's enclosure.[21] Moreover, what good was so much effort to civilize Africa if Europeans were unable to breathe the African air without succumbing?

It was in this context of discouragement that many of the most well-known defenders of the free trade ideology let loose a prolonged attack on the costs of the British anti-slave trade policy. A trade that was so profitable, they argued, could not be stopped by force, and naval intervention, which was very costly, would achieve nothing more than to exacerbate the horrors of the middle passage. This movement against the government's suppression policies had strong representation in Parliament, in a group led by William Hutt, and was supported by British merchants and manufacturers whose financial interests would certainly not suffer if the Brazilian and Cuban trade were to increase. The attacks by those opposed to naval coercion began with a motion in the House of Commons submitted on 24 June 1845 and continued in the years that followed, reaching their high point at the end of the decade. At this time, there were even proposals to restart the British slave trade, and a motion in favour of ending anti-slave trade naval patrols was almost carried in Parliament.[22]

Despite strong internal opposition, the British government persisted in its crusade for 'the cause of humanity', and even increased its efforts. Palmerston returned to the Foreign Office in July 1846, but it was only at the end of the decade that the political circumstances were right for unleashing a full attack against the slavers.[23] Their settlements on the River Gallinas were destroyed in 1849–50, putting an end to their activities for good. Lagos was bombarded in 1851, as part of the blockade of the bight of Benin—but this would fail, as did that of the Zaïre. Yet, the most significant aspect of Palmerston's tough policy was the frontal attack on the Brazilian slave trade. On 8 August 1845, the British Parliament approved a law—the Aberdeen Act—which was rather like a second edition of the Palmerston bill, but this time applied to Brazil. The purpose of the law was above all to ensure that there would be British intervention against the Brazilian slave trade. At the time of independence, in 1822, the Rio government had adopted the agreements on abolition that had already been ratified by the Portuguese government, in particular the convention of 1817. But, when the Anglo-Brazilian abolition treaty came into force in 1830, Brazil took it as putting an end to earlier agreements and consequently claimed the right to try in the Brazilian courts those who might eventually be captured. To prevent this from happening, London resorted to the supplemental article of the convention of 1817, which, as we have already seen, extended it for a further fifteen years—that is, until 1845—unless the contracting parties agreed otherwise. The Aberdeen Act therefore sought to fill the vacuum that had emerged after the end of this extension of time, but it was not immediately used to its full extent. Palmerston actually used it more aggressively, encouraging the Royal Navy to intervene even in Brazil's own territorial waters. From mid-1849 onwards, the navy began to arrest slave ships in the rivers and ports, sometimes under the guns of the Brazilian fortresses, even though such action was a clear violation of the sovereignty of an independent nation.[24] On 4 September 1850, the Brazilian government published 'of its own accord' a law that put an end to the Brazilian slave trade, and the importation of slaves into Brazil fell dramatically: in 1851 only 5,000 slaves were imported, and in the following year a little over 1,000; from then on, with the exception of one cargo of 300 slaves imported in 1856, the Brazilian slave trade ceased to exist.[25]

The closing of the Brazilian market was a severe blow to the trans-atlantic slave trade, but it was not its end. In the years following, exports of Negroes continued in small numbers from Portuguese southern Africa, from the bight of Benin and, on a much larger scale, from the Zaïre River and ports to the north.[26] These exports went exclusively to Cuba, the last 'door' that remained open. After a period of relative tranquillity, Cuba had again taken up the slave trade, to the extent that in 1858 the island imported 25,000 slaves, an annual number only surpassed three times in the whole of the nineteenth century.[27] Even though the traffic in slaves was now limited to only one import centre, it was difficult to cut back, for technical and political reasons. As we saw earlier, the naval blockade was useless (for geographical reasons), and the British government, even when pressed, refused to contemplate this line of action on principle.[28]

But, in addition to this, there were strong political factors inhibiting British intervention against the Cuban trade.

The major obstacles were no longer internal. It is true that the opponents of coercive intervention remained active and that, in 1857, Hutt was still fighting for the withdrawal of the Royal Navy African coast patrol, but his motion was easily defeated in Parliament. At that time, Britain's commitment to the continuation of the struggle against the slave trade was so clear that even the pacifists in the British and Foreign Anti-Slavery Society did not rule out the use of force.[29] Nevertheless, there was a fundamental problem in enforcing a drastic policy against Cuba. In the final fifteen years of the Transatlantic slave trade, and in line with the trends that became apparent in the 1840s, slavers preferred to trade under the flag of the United States. Since the United States had not granted the right of search, this trade was almost entirely outside the control of the British cruisers. The North Americans had a small patrol on the African coast, but it was ineffective and had no rearguard support. Those who were charged spent a short time in prison, only until required to pay a small amount of bail or being released on technical grounds. Thirteen slave ships were captured by the cruisers between 1843 and 1859; however, no one was ever convicted by the North American courts.[30]

It was only with the approaching onset of the American civil war that the situation changed. The British captured some slave ships flying the United States flag. When the American ambassador protested, the Foreign Office replied, as it had done to the Portuguese, that if the Americans failed to comply with their obligations the British government would be forced to do so on their behalf.[31] Britain's challenge took place at a time when the United States government itself was showing signs of wanting to act decisively. For several years voices had been heard arguing for the re-opening of the 'odious commerce', and the fear that it might be restored to North American ports forced the government to face up to the issue.[32] In 1859 Commander Inman solved the problem of refuelling his ships—which had to intervene in the Zaïre, a long way from his naval base at Cape Verde—by placing refuelling vessels in Congolese waters and, from December 1859 to June 1861, the small North American squadron captured fourteen slavers, freeing some 4,000 slaves. In eighteen months Inman did more than his predecessors had done in 18 years.[33]

Action against the Spanish-American slave trade continued thereafter, but it was entrusted to the British and the Spanish. Since Lincoln had to withdraw his warships from the African coast on account of the civil war, he was forced to yield to British demands and, in 1862, the United States granted the right of search on an exceptional and transitory basis, accepting the establishment of mixed commissions for the summary trial of the slave ships, which would be dismantled. In the same year North American courts hanged the first (and only) slave trader. This was the beginning of the end of the Cuban slave trade, which could no longer count on ships flying the United States flag. Moreover, at around the same time, the Spanish authorities were also taking on the responsibility of attacking the 'infamous commerce': they expelled eight Portuguese slave traders from Cuba. In 1866 the Madrid government promulgated a decree that established harsh measures, and imports of slaves into Cuba thereupon ceased immediately.[34] Thus did the transatlantic slave trade come to an end. All that remained was the short-distance traffic, on the East coast of Africa and in the islands of São Tomé and Príncipe (a traffic which was protected by the Portuguese authorities, as we shall see below).

5.2 Portugal and the Slave Traders

If, in overall terms, Palmerston's bill did not achieve the outcomes its promoters had in mind, it was a measure that proved decisive in Portugal. It brought about significant changes in the Portuguese attitude to the slave trade. As Bandinel, the secretary of the Slave Trade Department, noted, the Portuguese government, 'shamed into something like a co-operation for this object', was now prepared to act against the slavers.[35] Faced with the accusations that saturated travel literature, diplomatic notes and the pages of foreign newspapers, Portugal had a political need to enforce suppression both in the colonies, which depended almost exclusively on the slave trade, and in Portugal itself, where the traffic not only was not morally condemned but very often was actually protected. This need brought about a minimally consistent action against the slave trade and was at the root of a new way of thinking on the issue.

5.2.1 Between Connivance and Commitment to Abolition

The major concern of all Portuguese governments throughout the 1840s was to line up unequivocally behind British abolition policy, while at the same time securing Portuguese sovereignty in Africa. This is why every communication from London was taken seriously and, as a general rule, dealt with quickly. And the British, who continued to inundate the Ministry of Foreign Affairs with accusations of Portuguese involvement in the 'odious commerce', pried into everything, from the guilty or merely suspect behaviour of the Portuguese authorities to the most recondite details of day-to-day life in Portugal.[36]

In their efforts to cooperate with Britain, the Portuguese ministries often went beyond what had been stipulated in 1842. In May 1845, the governor of Mozambique, Abreu de Lima, authorized British cruisers to enter the ports and bays that were not guarded by the Portuguese authorities. Lisbon initially refused to allow this concession but, with London insisting, it eventually did so, on 12 August 1847, in an Anglo-Portuguese agreement that gave British cruisers the power to carry out their anti-slave trade operations at any point on the Mozambican coast except for Inhambane, Sofala, Quelimane, the bay of Lourenço Marques, Mozambique and Ibo. The agreement, initially valid for three years, would end up being extended for a further three years.[37] In Angola, where Portugal had most of its colonial forces, Luso-British cooperation was more limited. At the beginning of the 1840s, the Royal Navy made some landings in Portuguese—or Portuguese-claimed—territory, with a view to combating the slave trade ashore. Although this aggressive and abusive behaviour continued sporadically, from 1842 onwards the British authorities started asking for permission to land small detachments in specific areas, particularly in the Ambriz, where there were barracoons housing slaves destined for export.[38] The Portuguese government, jealous of its sovereignty, avoided granting such permissions, deciding to destroy the barracoons itself as soon as it had been notified of their existence by the British authorities.[39]

The matter of the barracoons took on greater significance from 1845, as a result of the Anglo-French treaty we have already mentioned, because, in order to end the slave trade at its source, the two contracting powers authorized each other to make agreements with African potentates and, in some cases, to use force and territorial occupation. The treaty naturally caused concern to the Lisbon government and, in consequence, the Navy Minister, Joaquim José Falcão, reinforced the Portuguese patrol as well, and gave orders to the colonial governors and ships' commanders that they should redouble their efforts to combat the slave trade, cooperating closely with the British. They were also encouraged to make treaties of abolition with African rulers, and to combat the 'barbarous commerce' on land by destroying the suspect barracoons.[40] But, while trying to prevent future complications, the Portuguese minister also made sure that advantage was taken of accumulated credit. Since London was the first to acknowledge 'the good faith and scrupulous punctuality' with which Portugal was fulfilling its commitments to abolition, Falcão requested the British government not to regard as applicable to Portuguese territory the articles it had just negotiated with France—a request that was granted.[41]

In actual fact, since 1840 Portugal had placed most of its warships in African naval stations, and their primary mission had been the suppression of the slave trade. In mid-1842 and with a view to making suppression more effective, the government chose to give warship commanders autonomy, releasing them from blind obedience to the directives of the colonial governors and allowing them to carry out their 'principal mission' as they saw fit.[42] Freed from the often constricting oversight of the governor's palace, the Portuguese cruisers carried out numerous successful operations on the east and west coasts of Africa: between 1839 and 1842 the *Armada* had captured or destroyed seventeen ships; but from 1843 to 1850 its effectiveness almost doubled. It captured or destroyed fifteen barges and forty-six ships; later on, with the slave trade declining as a result of the end of exports to Brazil, the Portuguese navy would still manage to arrest eleven barges and twenty-two ships.[43] Commanders such as Pedro Alexandrino da Cunha, Francisco Gonçalves Cardoso, João Máximo Rodovalho and several others distinguished themselves in these operations against the slave trade: these were men who, while defending national sovereignty, also actually inhibited the slave trade, gaining merit with their British peers and frequent praise from the governments in Lisbon and London.[44]

It has been said that during the 1840s the Portuguese squadron was used selectively, according to the opposing interests of the two largest groups of slave traders in Luanda: the one that found favour with the governor would seek to use the squadron to cut out the competition of the rival group.[45] But this assessment seems to derive above all from the campaign against naval intervention conducted by the slavers themselves. In general, the intervention had sufficient merit and was sufficiently reliable to enable a formal agreement between the government of Angola and the British commodore to be made, under which the coast from Ambriz to Cafe Ledo was entrusted to the Portuguese *Armada*, thus freeing up British ships for other areas to the north and south of that strip of coastline.[46]

Recognition of the merit of Portuguese anti-slave trade operations did not mean that the warships went straight at it in the hunt for slavers. In actual fact there were a number of dilemmas that limited or might limit their operations. In a way, the Portuguese navy became the victim of its own effectiveness. One of the aspects of the problem was diplomatic in nature and put the *Armada* in the situation the Royal Navy had known for decades. Most of the ships apprehended and tried in the Luanda prize court—established in 1844 to try ships that did not fall under the jurisdiction of the mixed commission—were Brazilian. This produced a series of complaints by the Rio government. Endeavouring to cater to those complaints, at the end of 1844 Lisbon gave orders for the squadron to confine its anti-traffic operations: 'commanders of Portuguese warships may not register Brazilian ships for reasons of trading in slaves, except in our ports'.[47] The navy commanders were astonished at these instructions, and resisted them to some degree: they could not reconcile themselves to the prohibition of registering the Brazilian flag on the high seas. Men like Alexandrino da Cunha and Rodovalho called the government's attention to the difference between 'engaging in search operations'—something the cruisers could only do under cover of treaties, since it involved opening hatches, unpacking the cargo and checking the content of packages—and 'registering' a ship, that is to say, checking that its papers were in order. They insisted that this latter act was entirely lawful.[48]

Despite these restrictions, the seizures did not stop, so the Brazilians claimed that they were illegal, on the grounds that they were allegedly carried out outside territorial waters. In fact, the coast to the north of the

8° south parallel was not yet unanimously recognized as belonging to the Portuguese Crown and, moreover, some of the Portuguese arresting officers had the bad habit of forgetting to take note of the exact distance from the coast at which they had made their capture (or started the pursuit that led to the capture).[49] Accordingly, and in order to avoid any further misunderstanding with Brazil, the Portuguese commanders were ordered not to intercept foreign ships unless they were unquestionably slavers and were in Portuguese waters.[50]

But it was not just diplomatic issues that placed constraints on naval action. Colonial finances depended in large measure on the taxation of foreign trade, most of which was Brazilian. When pursued, the Brazilian slavers tended to move away from the area administered by the Portuguese, sailing to Ambriz and other ports to the north, with inevitable losses to Portuguese customs. The governor of Angola, Silveira Pinto, set out the situation clearly:

> Imports into this province amount to approximately 1292 *contos de réis*, exports of legally traded goods do not amount to more than 651 *contos*; how will the difference be made up? In slaves, unfortunately, and though they are not loaded at points where there are Portuguese authorities … the further those embarkation points are from the provincial capital, the fewer exchange goods will come in, and, in consequence, income will decline.[51]

In other words, the more effective the suppression, the worse the situation became for the colonial finances. This dilemma was nothing new: all Silveira Pinto's predecessors had faced it as soon as the slave trade became illegal. As a rule, and in order to maintain the economic stability of the colonies, governors tended to operate as a kind of counterweight to the action of the naval commanders. Sometimes they did it with excessive commitment, as occurred, for example, with Possolo, who was sued for 'conniving' in the slave trade.[52] Portuguese duality regarding suppression was only broken when the colonial governorship fell to a navy commander who was in total sympathy with the political need to suppress the slave trade. This is what happened in Mozambique with Fortunato do Vale, and above all in Angola when, from 1845 to 1848, the government was in the hands of Pedro Alexandrino da Cunha and the Naval Station was under Gonçalves Cardoso. As was to be foreseen, Cunha and Cardoso were subjected to virulent attacks, both in Angola, where their intervention brought out once again all the doom-laden arguments whereby the colonies would collapse and be lost, and in Lisbon, where the *Septembrista* press got together in a campaign against 'naval oppression'. The invective hurled at them and at other 'stupid, brutal and wild sailors', who were viewed as 'the main obstacle' to colonial prosperity, continued subsequently, up to the beginning of the 1850s.[53]

The Lisbon government's anti-slave trade actions had to be managed within very narrow limits, defined by the opposing pressures of Britain and Brazil, by the overarching need to salvage national honour and by the parlous state of the colonial finances. In addition to all this, the cruisers were materially dependent on the colonies they served. The financial straits were such that the Navy Ministry pressed for the withdrawal of a number of ships from the Luanda Naval Station.[54] Within these constraints, and in most cases, the squadron accomplished its mission, driving the trade in slaves away from the Portuguese area. In the mid-1840s, Demony, the Portuguese judge on the Luanda mixed commission, advised that there were no longer any slavers flying the Portuguese flag and that the slave trade had practically ceased in Angola since the time the government had had the barracoons burned.[55] Some months later, Duprat, the Portuguese commissioner at the Cape, passed on information from the governor of Mozambique that 'this coast is entirely cleansed of slavers'.[56] As we know, these celebratory reports were premature. In April 1847 despatches from the Portuguese consul in Rio mentioned that the slave trade was 'extremely lively'—information that was moreover confirmed by British sources. But, at the same time as he warned of the increase in trade with Brazil, the consul also emphasized that Portugal was no longer involved in the 'odious commerce'.[57]

In actual fact the joint action of the British and Portuguese navies led to much lower involvement of the Portuguese flag in the slave trade. After the signature of the treaty of 1842 the vast majority of ships involved in the traffic in slaves on the African coast flew the Spanish, North American or Brazilian flag, or no flag at all, for the simple reason that many of the slavers preferred, if they were apprehended, to be tried in the British Admiralty courts under the Palmerston bill—which was still valid for ships with no flag and which envisaged no penalties for the crews involved. For this reason, and although there were large number of captures in the 1840s, the Anglo-Portuguese mixed commissions ended up trying very few of these cases, in clear contrast to the courts of the British Admiralty. Even the Luanda mixed commission, which in 1844 and 1845 was called upon to try fifteen cases (of which only six involved the Portuguese flag), had few cases thereafter.[58] The same is true for the prize court established in Luanda in 1844 to consider captures made by the Portuguese authorities under cover of territorial rights, and which fell outside the mixed commission's jurisdiction: between 1840 and 1850 Portuguese cruisers, which were active mainly in the mouth of the River Dande and in the areas of Ambriz, Benguela and Quicombo, captured some barges and forty-one ships suspected of being involved in the slave trade, but only five of them were flying the Portuguese flag.

Based on the fact that the transatlantic trade grew to very high levels in the five years from 1846 to 1850, it is often stated that the suppression carried out in Angola and Mozambique did not do much good. This is the view held by those who look at the issue from the destination points, where in fact a very high number of slaves continued to arrive. However, at the points of origin on the African coast, and from a Portuguese point of view, much had changed. Formally, the Portuguese share of the trade diminished, as we have seen. But the quantity of slaves exported from Portuguese Africa in ships of any nationality also fell, and this represented a positive outcome for efforts at suppression—not so much for the British efforts, which were aimed at the end of all trade in slaves, but the Portuguese perspective was substantially different from that of the British. The political objective of the Lisbon government, apart from safeguarding national honour, was to restrict and suppress the slave trade in the Portuguese possessions. Sá da Bandeira had announced this himself in 1839, and António José de Ávila would recall it a few years later: 'we did not undertake to end the slave trade in possessions other than ours'.[59] This means that suppression, without being a triumph, was nonetheless reasonably successful.

According to Eltis's estimates, the slave trade in Angola—defined as the whole coast south of the Zaïre, including therefore ports that were still outside Portuguese control, like Ambriz and Ambrizete—effectively fell from 1839 onwards (the date when naval suppression began) and, although it rose again from 1846 to 1849, it never attained the old levels. The same can be said for the east coast of Africa. Later on, with the end of the Brazilian slave trade, the drop in both areas was very sharp and, after 1864, transatlantic exports from those areas ceased altogether (Fig. 5.1).

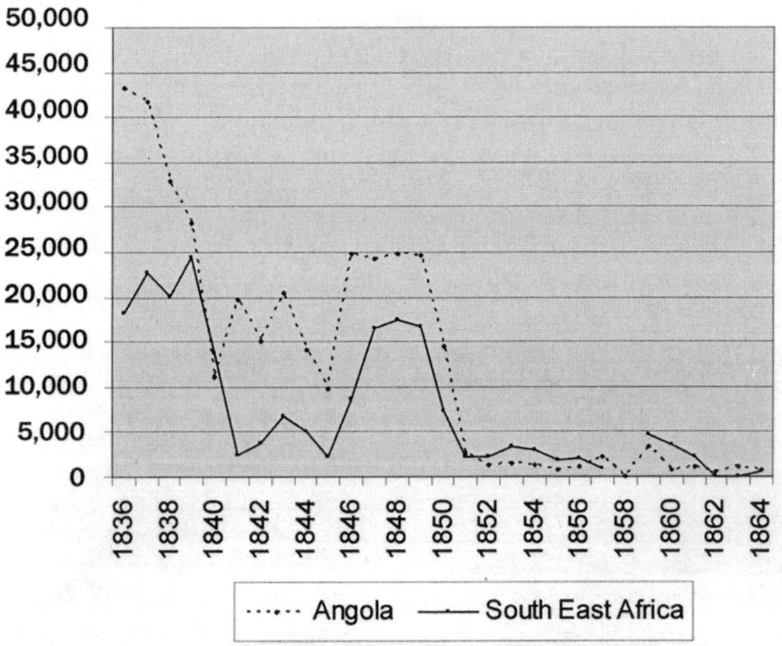

FIGURE 5.1. Transatlantic exports of slaves from Angola and South-East Africa (1836–64).

There is no reason to question the zeal of the war navy, but the same cannot be said of the land-based authorities, particularly in the lower ranks. At the end of 1846, the Portuguese representative on the Cape mixed commission reported to Lisbon on one more episode of that lack of zeal: 'Major Teixeira, the governor of Quelimane, and the mayor of that town, have fled in a ship charted by them, in the direction of Rio de Janeiro, together with 500 slaves. I was very saddened to receive this news, which is undoubtedly a dishonour for us Portuguese'.[60] Colonel Resende, who succeeded Major Teixeira, managed to save up enough to buy a large property on the south bank of the Tagus during the short time he was governor of Quelimane.[61] This was nothing unusual. Many of the lower ranks, who were paid little and late, were unable to resist the lure of the slave trade. Corruption and connivance with the slavers extended like a large network throughout the whole resident European or mixed population, and even affected the Anglo-Portuguese mixed commission in Luanda.[62]

The involvement of official representatives with the slavers was almost inevitable, not only because trading slaves was, directly or indirectly, the main way of life and means of subsistence in the African colonies, but also because the slavers were prestigious members of their communities, major benefactors who gave support to institutions: Ana Joaquina dos Santos offered to send two of her ships to Montevideo to fetch horses and mules for the Angola government;[63] Arsénio de Carpo offered the city of Luanda a house to serve as a hospital for the personnel of the Naval Station, and a printing works;[64] Augusto Garrido promoted a collection on behalf of the destitute colonists of Moçâmedes (to which other slavers contributed);[65] examples of the civic generosity of the slavers are legion.

The most serious aspect of connivance with the slave traders, however, was the complacency of the judicial authorities. This complacency was so obvious that in 1847 the then commander of the Naval Station, Gonçalves Cardoso, threatened to resign if José Maria Mattoso and Augusto Garrido, who had personally supervised the embarkation of 150 slaves on a ship fitted out in Luanda, were not punished.[66] The Angola judges would often acquit slaver crews, even when the mixed commission or the prize court had condemned the vessels. This naturally caused indignation among the British authorities.[67] And the problem was not exclusive to Angola. In Cape Verde someone like Francisco Cardoso de Melo, who appeared as the owner of several *tumbeiros* condemned in Sierra Leone in the 1830s, was acquitted by the court.[68] To deal with the exemptions from punishment that resulted from this placid jurisprudence, colonial governors were authorized to appeal to Lisbon in all cases where the judges had not compulsorily punished those accused of the crime of trafficking in slaves.[69] But, as Demony acknowledged in 1851, this did little good: 'I am informed of the conclusion of the case of the Portuguese brigantine Veiga which in November of last year sailed from this city's port, and on the next day was … apprehended by British cruisers while laden with slaves …; and it seems the judge has found no cause to prosecute anyone at all'.[70]

In Lisbon things were not necessarily very different. Sometimes the courts in Portugal did indeed reverse the acquittals of the slavers.[71] It is also true that on other occasions this was not technically possible, on account of procedural errors (which were possibly deliberate). But apart from these cases, the judicial authorities still showed some tolerance towards the slave traders. The most glaring example was that of Arsénio Pompílio Pompeu de Carpo, one of the most important slavers operating in Angola. The first act of the government of Alexandrino da Cunha in 1845 was to imprison and deport Arsénio, first to Cape Verde and then to Lisbon. But in the capital of the empire his imprisonment and deportation were strongly condemned. Howard de Walden reported that people of the *Septembrista* party, including men of high social standing, were making great efforts to influence the judges in favour of Carpo.[72] Indeed, Arsénio boasted that he had many and powerful friends in Lisbon to protect him. And the fact is that he survived not just that case but other legal actions against him. In 1849 he returned to Angola after travelling around Europe displaying 'Asiatic opulence, as if he were a prince with a huge income'.[73]

In the Cortes, Sá da Bandeira publicly criticized the discrepancy between the sentences handed down by the prize courts and the ordinary courts of the colonies.[74] But in a document from the same period the ex-minister acknowledged that the whole system of punishment was not working, including that of metropolitan Portugal.[75] His disenchanted view of the whole situation was quite accurate, and perhaps only erred by being somewhat excessive. In the second half of the 1840s there were one or two cases in which humble people were punished—sailors and others—but these sentencings were never taken to their full consequences. The most common sentence was compulsory unpaid service for two or three years on the ships of the *Armada*, but it was rarely carried out in full, either because the sentences were annulled or by virtue of general pardons.[76]

The complacency of the courts in Portugal and in the colonies in relation to the slavers persisted, with variations, during the whole period under study, that is, right up to the 1860s.[77] This complacency does not, however, nullify the efforts of administrations after 1839 to suppress the slave trade. Palmerston himself praised this effort, which was considerable for a country with resources as limited as those of Portugal: 'the Portuguese government has co-operated actively, cordially and sincerely in the suppression of the slave trade, and if by chance there has been any exception to this honourable conduct, it is only to be found among lower-order civil servants who, unfortunately, may have yielded to the temptations of the slavers'.[78] Up to the middle of the 1850s collaboration had meant following British anti-slave trade policy, giving up independent action. It is true that already in 1842 Sá da Bandeira, who was freer of party politics and of the network of concessions he had been forced to make years before, when he was a minister, emerged, giving free rein to his abolitionism and suggesting measures to improve the decree of 1836.[79] But there was no follow-up to these proposals, and it was only later, in the mid-1850s, that the Portuguese dared to mark out their own independent abolitionist path which might diverge from British interests.

In actual fact, once Portugal had been able to restrict the slave trade or even prevent it from being carried on from those areas it controlled, one possible way of improving the results of suppression in Africa involved extending Portuguese administration to areas the Crown had claimed but did not yet occupy. The occupation of territories like Cabinda and Ambriz was an old political objective of the Lisbon government, which had never made headway on account of weaknesses and internal ambiguities, and also on account of opposition from the British government. In order to give legitimacy to their demands and force London's consent, the Portuguese government invoked not only historical reasons but also the expansion of territorial occupation under cover of philanthropy and the moral right to intervene in the struggles against the trade in slaves. During the 1840s Sá da Bandeira was among those who insisted that Ambriz, Cabinda and the mouth of the Zaïre should be occupied 'for greater effectiveness in repressing the slave trade'.[80] But this was an objective that had been adopted by all Portuguese governments. In 1848, for example, Gomes de Castro wrote to the British ambassador informing him of recent huge consignments of slaves at Ambriz, and emphasizing that these lamentable events might have been avoided if the region had already been under Portuguese control.[81]

Gomes de Castro's observations and, more generally, Lisbon's and London's positions on the extension of Portuguese sovereignty on the African coast were full of ironies. The first was that Portugal was seeking to take advantage of the problem of suppression to expand its dominion in Africa—that is, it was trying to put into practice what in the past it had so much feared Britain would do. A second irony was that its ambitions were backed by the British commissioners in Luanda, who were profoundly concerned with humanitarian questions, and who saw in the expansion of Portuguese sovereignty to Cabinda and Molembo 'additional hopes of success in this noble cause of humanity'.[82] Another irony was that Palmerston, the champion of suppression, did not share the views of his commissioners—or, of course, those of the Portuguese. In this particular case, suppression came second in the list of priorities. And the final irony was that London's policy had been strengthened by several Angola judges, who, in order to absolve the Brazilian slavers, invoked, among other justifications, the fact that arrests made to the north of the 8° south parallel were illegal, because they had not occurred in Portuguese waters.[83] Ambriz would effectively be occupied by the Portuguese at a time when the Crimean war had substantially reduced

British naval power on the west coast of Africa.[84] But Britain's opposition to any occupation of the area of the Zaïre River could not be overcome.

Another aspect in which Portugal strayed from British directives—and this time not to promote abolition, but to get around it—was in connection with the transfer of labour to São Tomé and Príncipe, an old problem that was exacerbated as the plantation economy developed on the islands during the 1850s. In accordance with the provisions of the Anglo-Portuguese treaty of 1842, colonists who wanted to move from one colony to another were allowed to take with them ten domestic slaves. This was clearly an insufficient number for the labour needs of the *roças* (plantations) and quite early on ways were sought to get round the legal provisions.

Initially, it was ships of the *Armada* itself—which were not subject to inspection by the British cruisers—which were used to transfer Negroes from one colony to another. In 1852 the corvette *8 de Julho* took to São Tomé recaptured slaves from the areas of Angola and Costa da Mina.[85] Sometime later, the colonial government, presided over by the bishop of Luanda, ordered the commander of the sumacca *Trindade* to transport forty-two slaves to São Tomé.[86] A practice of this sort carried enormous political risks, since a British officer exceeding his instructions might well arrest the ship (an outcome that was feared both in Luanda and in Lisbon). Even if this did not happen, the very fact that the transport had taken place was enough significantly to undermine Portuguese abolitionist credentials. As was exclaimed in the Chamber of Peers, 'what shame for us! Do we now export slaves from Luanda to São Tomé by labelling them passengers of the State travelling in ships of the State? (sensation all over the Chamber)'.[87]

Lisbon condemned the behaviour of the governor of Angola and forbade the transport of slaves to São Tomé on board ships of the *Armada*.[88] False colonists then emerged to act as figureheads for the island landowners. They made two or three trips a year between Luanda and São Tomé, taking ten slaves with them each time; sometimes they would nominally distribute the slaves among the passengers on the ship, so as not to violate the letter of the treaty of 1842. Later on, the whole process became more sophisticated as the governors themselves became involved. Since the export of slaves was prohibited by law, the Portuguese authorities adopted a new terminology, granting the slaves 'passports' and calling then *libertos* (freedmen). In 1853 the government gave special permission for the ex-slaver and new plantation owner João Maria de Sousa e Almeida to transport 100 of those *libertos* to the islands.[89] This practice would continue in subsequent years, especially from the late 1850s onwards, despite British protests.

A commitment to abolition and, at the same time, connivance with slavers were two contradictory aspects of Portuguese action. But, something positive did come out of this contradiction in Portuguese Africa, where the slave trade declined, as in Portugal itself, where a new way of looking at the 'iniquitous commerce' had emerged.

5.2.2 *National Honour*

In the summer of 1848, to fulfil a pledge he had made earlier, a conspicuous citizen who had risked his money in the slave trade donated part of the profit obtained to the traditional festival of Colares (Sintra) in honour of the Virgin Mary. Writing about this minor episode of local and religious life, Seymour, the British ambassador in Lisbon, mentioned that large sums of money were still being made in speculative slave trading, and expressed the opinion that the extent of those interests made the Portuguese government's efforts at abolition all the more noteworthy, if only because the moral climate was adverse. In Portugal there was not the 'public feeling by which the trade in human flesh is stigmatised in England', or even the conviction that the trade went counter to the principles of religion.[90]

There was a great deal of truth to the British ambassador's assessment, but it was not the whole truth. Following the major upheaval caused by the bill, the subject of the slave trade had once again fallen into relative obscurity and quiet. In the Cortes, the issue was raised two or three times a year, in the Navy Minister's report or when a member of Parliament—generally Sá da Bandeira—enquired of the government what had been the results of the action to suppress the slave trade. The newspapers gave little space to the subject, only covering it when there was one or other controversial arrest or when they transcribed debates of the British Parliament and Cuban or Brazilian complaints.

It is true that for a time at the start of the 1850s some newspapers played an active role in favour of abolition. The cases of the *Guerra* and the *Trajano*, two slaver brigs that were fitted out in Oporto, were denounced by *O Portuguez*, and other newspapers followed suit.[91] However, this abolitionist zeal was episodic. The only newspaper that was consistent in its efforts in this direction was the *Boletim Oficial do Governo-Geral da Provincia de Angola* (Official Bulletin of the Office of the Governor-General of Angola), mainly at the time Pedro Alexandrino da Cunha was governor of the colony. The *Boletim* often made references to the inhumanity of the slave trade, lengthy descriptions of the capture of slavers and exposed perpetrators—whom it labelled criminals. In addition, it did not hesitate to support British action to suppress the slave trade, publicizing arrests by the Royal Navy and summaries of the sentences handed down by the St Helena vice-admiralty court.

Fewer still were the Portuguese anti-slavery arguments that followed the British pattern. At the end of 1844, *A Revolução de Septembro* (The September Revolution) published an article by António Lopes de Mendonça, a young officer in the *Armada* (and future deputy), who, in describing an episode in the battle against the slave trade that he himself had experienced—the arrest of the Brazilian brig *Caçador* at the mouth of the Dande—sought to emphasize the horror and inhumanity of the 'infamous commerce':

> There were eight hundred and forty-four blacks lumped together in confusion in the narrow confines of the brig … For two long days they had not given them any food, their entrails were wasted from hunger and their throats were parched. The weather was very hot, and the heat coming out of that slow slaughterhouse burned our faces; and they, pressed together body to body, hardly able to breathe, I don't know how they did not die of suffocation. … we emptied buckets of water over them and made generous distribution of victuals …. In the three days it took us to take that captured ship to the port of Luanda, we went through a lifetime of anguish … At night we heard for hours the sounds of groans, shouts and weeping: air, air—they begged for in their language … Twenty-two Negroes died on this short journey.

On the basis of this account, which derived from personal contact with the facts, Lopes de Mendonça built an argument for guilt and remorse, the ultimate purpose of which was to encourage proactive behaviour: 'the people have the instinct for generous feelings, they will listen to our clamour and will wax indignant, as we have, at this atrocity against humanity and against God'. This was, in sum, the abolitionist argument following the British pattern, which made the evil explicit and stigmatized the slaver, who was seen as a man who sold his soul to the devil, a 'solitary man in the moral universe'.[92]

This line of argument also emerged in translations of writings from abroad. In the 1850s, for example, the *Diário do Governo* (Official Gazette) transcribed the Quakers' message to Christian sovereigns, a text that attacked the slave trade in terms of sin and remorse, as being something totally incompatible with the Christian message.[93] A little later, and in the wider struggle against slavery, *A Revolução de Septembro* published, in serial form, a translation of Harriet Stowe's book, *Uncle Tom's Cabin*, a work that had been a huge publishing success and at which, as the newspaper itself stated, 'the whole world shudders in horror'.[94] But pro-abolition rhetoric in the Anglo-Saxon mould, based on making the crime explicit and moral condemnation of the slaver, aimed at encouraging action to deal with the problem, was and continued to be infrequent in the press, in literature and, as far as one can see, in the concerns of the time. And, apart from being infrequent, it was also ineffective. In 1854, at the time Sá da Bandeira submitted a draft law for the abolition of slavery, Gomes de Amorim wrote the play called *Ódio de Raça* (Race Hatred) in order, as he himself admitted, to help the public 'make a judgement with which to bolster the legislators' purpose'.[95] But in 1869, in the preface to the book edition of his play, the writer made a dispirited assessment of those proselytizing efforts:

> Fifteen years have gone by. *Ódio de Raça* has been put on almost the whole time over that period …; but I have to confess … its only success was the odd fainting fit and the tears of sensitive and highly strung people, and the applause of sincere men who are not legislators. Certainly I did not expect to regenerate the blacks and make moral men out of whites with my humble

> work; but I supposed that it merited discussion in a nation which owns slaves, a matter which has been of concern to the great statesmen, philosophers and poets in other civilized nations. I was wrong.[96]

Despite some criticism, there was in Portugal still no widespread consistent condemnation of the slaver. Sá da Bandeira even suggested that voting rights should be taken away from all persons who had trafficked in slaves, arguing that those people would be permanently stigmatized and that their 'crime' was not time barred.[97] Moreover, this was not an original suggestion: Lavradio had put forward something similar in a speech strongly condemning the activities of the slavers.[98] But neither one of them found an echo in the Portuguese Cortes, even though the Cortes had on several occasions condemned the activities of the slavers. The discrepancy between word and deed was also to be found in the newspapers, which always described the slave trade as 'shameful', 'criminal', 'infamous', but never pointed the finger at actual cases. From the 1840s onwards some left-wing newspapers ceased to make the arguments in abstract terms, without naming names, and started to accuse two or three slavers in the colonies directly, describing their influence on the local political scene. But this was more than anything a way of attacking the presumed incompetence of a right-wing government that was allowing the slave trade to continue. In this context, slavers were just pawns in a party political game, but were not outlawed or criticized on account of what they actually did. In fact quite the contrary: in a different context they might well be defended and praised. In 1855 a newspaper that undertook to be severe in its treatment of 'the smugglers of human flesh' remembered the recently deceased Manuel Pinto da Fonseca—one of the most prominent slavers of the 1840s—as a benefactor who had 'applied his capital in useful works for the nation'.[99]

In addition to these occasional condemnations of the slavers, there was, of course, also a genuine non-condemnation, which in a way represented the traces of pro-slavery thinking. This non-condemnation is reflected in *Mario*, a historical novel by Silva Gaio, first published in 1868. Its value as a historical source lies in the inescapable fact that every writer writes for an audience, and cannot do so without making assumptions about his readers' mental world. This is the sense in which Silva Gaio's fleeting and unremarked allusions to the behaviour of the slave trader are eloquent testimonials to the images and values a particular audience at that time tacitly accepted. Mario was a young liberal who had been deported to Angola. There, in the harshest of exiles, he struck up a firm friendship with a Herculean Negro slave, and both ended up escaping, wandering through the bush until they reached the coast, where they met up with a ship that was loading slaves in the vicinity of Moçâmedes. What is significant in *Mario* is that there is no pejorative reference to the *tumbeiro* and to the activities of its crew. On the contrary, the captain of the slave ship whom Silva Gaio offers the reader is a profoundly human character who feels sorry for the fugitives, gives them food and clothing, and takes them to Brazil for free, making their journey 'comfortable and salubrious'.[100]

It was, moreover, difficult for condemnation of the slaver to become widespread in a society that showered him with distinctions and rewards of various sorts, in particular by way of ennoblement. During the 1840s various men connected to the slave trade were rewarded by the central government. Caetano José Nosolini, the slaver from Bissau who was caught in the act of engaging in illegal trade in slaves, was promoted to lieutenant-colonel in 1843, to the indignation of the British.[101] Arsénio de Carpo was made *comendador* (knight-commander). Others became nobles or peers, such as Joaquim Ferreira dos Santos (Baron and later Count of Ferreira, and peer in 1842). In mid-century, with the ending of the Brazilian trade, even more honours were seen to be bestowed as hundreds of slavers came home or invested their money in Portugal. In 1850 José Bernardino de Sá, one of the major slavers in Rio, a man who had very recently had a ship arrested and had been condemned by the Luanda mixed commission, was made Baron (and later Viscount) of Vila Nova do Minho; João Maria Sousa e Almeida was made Baron of Água-Izé; Vicente Rio Tinto, former owner of *O Nacional*, was made Baron of Rio Tinto in 1853; the renowned João Baptista Moreira became a Baron in 1855.

It was also difficult to condemn the slaver in a society where, alongside some critical views, forms of tolerationism persisted that strongly relativized the malignity of the slave trade and those involved in it. There was, moreover, a parallel issue the press was much more interested in, and which helped to stifle the subject once more: Portuguese emigration to Brazil and Guyana, in circumstances that were regarded as equivalent to those of the trade in Negroes (and were much more objectionable because they involved Portuguese).[102]

In mid-nineteenth-century Portugal much more was written about white slavery than about the trade in African slaves. This in a way testifies to the relative significance of the two topics in the Portuguese imagination. Lopes de Mendonça himself—who, as we have seen, had written a pro-abolition article in connection with the capture of the brig *Caçador*—gained some celebrity for his newspaper articles on emigration to Brazil. And there is other evidence that even those whose job it was to fight the battle against the slave trade in African waters tended to downgrade the issue of the trade. Navy officer Francisco Maria Bordalo wrote the novel *Eugénio*, which was first published in Rio de Janeiro in 1846 (and republished in Lisbon in 1854). This is a work that portrays the sailor's life on Portuguese warships, his vision of Africa and also the problem of the slaves. Part of the action takes place on board a navy corvette that sailed to Angola in 1842 to suppress the 'odious commerce'. But what comes across in Bordalo's view is a critique of telescopic philanthropy:

> The philanthropist employs money, life and talent in the great work of repressing the slave trade ... he forgets that beside him, almost in front of his very eyes, many of his fellow-countrymen, of the same colour, groan like the Negroes, because they are slaves, because against their will they were forced to be soldiers or cabin-boys ... Do not white men have their Brougham, or their Palmerston?[103]

In sum, the old ideological frameworks did not suddenly disappear. When we look at the arguments for and against abolition in Portugal from 1840 to 1865, we still find the backdrop of an apparently dominant tolerationism, and a British-influenced abolitionism that only appeared now and again. But, against that backdrop, which had its origins in the past, a conviction gathered strength that the slave trade had to cease because national honour was at stake. This was something that Seymour's assessment missed. The big difference in relation to earlier periods was the convergence of national honour and abolitionism: instead of a conception of national honour that was mainly hostile to British humanitarian pressure (as had occurred up to the *Septembrista* period), now national honour was almost unanimously seen as being compatible with suppression imposed by international action. The political elites in government and in the Cortes came to see abolition as an unavoidable necessity, not only for humanitarian reasons or future economic interests, but mainly because Portuguese respectability was at stake. Members of the government and parliamentary speakers began to manifest this concern from 1839 onwards. From there it trickled down into civil society.

It was in order to safeguard 'national dignity' that in 1845 the governor of Mozambique, for example, authorized British cruisers to enter ports and bays that were not guarded by the Portuguese authorities.[104] The many pencilled comments in the margin of notes received from the British embassy show that ministers' main concern was not to give anyone cause to think that Portugal was not applying itself in the fulfilment of a duty to which it had committed itself. The Anglo-French treaty of 1845 worried the Lisbon government not so much because it represented a direct threat to the integrity of the Portuguese colonial territory, but rather because it might put national pride and dignity in jeopardy if the British and French were to do what it behoved the Portuguese to accomplish. Accordingly Portugal reinforced its fleet in African waters and speeded up its efforts to suppress the slave trade, so as not to fall behind its partners. It did so without ostentation, precisely in order to preserve the national honour, so that people would not erroneously judge that 'only now, when those two powerful nations put into practice such effective means of repressing the slave trade, do we remember to do the same'.[105]

Concerns that were expressed privately in correspondence between ministers became public knowledge by way of government reports, ministers' speeches or the Queen's speech. Year after year members of the government stressed that it was not only 'on moral grounds of respect for the dignity of the human species', but also 'by reason of international obligations' that Portugal had to make an effort to end the slave trade.[106] Virtually unanimous parliamentary oratory echoed this line. Even though the Cortes did not allocate much time to the problem of the slave trade, any action or omission by government that might be interpreted as an administrative concession to the slavers began to be scrutinized and censured because, as deputy Otolini said, 'it affects our national honour vis-à-vis Great Britain'.[107]

And, because what was at stake was, above all, national honour, no serious consideration was ever given to withdrawing the cruisers, despite the fact that there were many Parliamentarians who questioned the effectiveness of suppression, in line with the British anti-coercion movement. For nearly everyone who spoke on the matter, the squadron was a burdensome and inefficient institution. When the matter came up in the Cortes, only Minister Gomes de Castro argued for its practical use.[108] But, even if it was common for people to regard the presence of the cruisers as 'a mere formality, to comply with the treaty', they all recognized that the effort should continue for reasons of political sensitivity: 'for sure, our flag is no longer used in such trade; but the patrol should continue, because that's how things should be'.[109] Even after the Brazilian slave trade had ended, Portuguese Members of Parliament continued to be extremely cautious regarding changes to the abolitionist status quo. The parlous state of the public treasury also led some to think of doing away with the mixed commissions, which were expensive and redundant. But all recognized the sensitive nature of the situation. The deputy Santos Monteiro trembled merely from contemplating the possibility that 'any change' to the treaty of 1842 might put the country in an awkward position.[110]

Precisely because the struggle against the slave trade served no immediate material purpose—as we shall see in the next chapter—and because it was expensive in lives and resources, very early on suppression became associated with the idea of sacrifice. In 1840 Bonfim, who was Navy Minister at the time, diagnosed the problem: the government could not tolerate the slave trade, but it was necessary for the Portuguese to understand that they would have to make sacrifices.[111] In subsequent years, teaching people the need for sacrifice went hand in hand with efforts to defend national honour: the nation was 'deeply committed' to abolition because it was obliged to be so by treaties and because it wished to prepare for the future prosperity of the colonies. But, in order to achieve this, enormous financial and human sacrifices would be required.[112] These pedagogical arguments, which, unlike the mirage of profits, raised the spectre of sacrifice in the name of future redemption and reward, gradually gained ground at the expense of the old conviction that only selfish mercantile instincts lay behind British anti-slavery. 'Suspect philanthropy', that old idea of obstructive tolerationism, became rare among the Portuguese elites. On the contrary, the elites increasingly appealed to an image of a Britain that had made material sacrifices in the name of humanity, as an example to be followed: 'Britain, in economic terms, actually lost out in 1807 when it abolished the slave trade .... The issue of slavery has been seen by the more civilized nations as an issue of necessary sacrifice in the name of a humanitarian idea and not as an economic issue'.[113] The sacrifice involved in the struggle against the 'iniquitous commerce' would allow moral purification of the country and, at the same time, preserved its honour. This concept of double utility—or triple utility, if we take into account the potential long-term economic benefits for the colonies—was frequently emphasized by opinion-makers, sometimes in an abstract way and at other times by way of concrete examples (which reinforced that utility).

One of the key moments in such reinforcement—perhaps its high point—took place in 1858–59, in connection with an international incident that brought the Portuguese and French governments into disagreement. Since the mid-1850s, France, facing a shortage of labour in its colonies, had sought to obtain permission from the Portuguese government to hire slave workers (the so-called *engagés*) on the Zaïre and on the coast of Mozambique. They promised formally to free these people when they were hired and to return them to their places of origin once their compulsory work period in the French colonies came to an end. The French government was even prepared to pay a per capita export duty to the Portuguese state.[114] But this was effectively a way of restarting the slave trade: Portuguese ministers turned down the French requests.

This did not prevent French ships from coming to the coast of Africa to transport Negroes. It was as part of this activity that, on 29 November 1857, the barque *Charles et George* was arrested by a ship of the *Armada* on Quitangonha Island, a part of the Mozambican coast that was completely off-limits to foreign trade. The barque had 110 Negroes on board—some of them bound—in addition to a number of objects that were expressly forbidden by anti-slave trade laws. The ship was condemned in Mozambique on 8 March 1858, the captain being punished with two years of community service. The case took on an international dimension when the French government demanded the return of the ship and the release of its captain. Following a verbal ultimatum backed up by the arrival of French warships in the Tagus, Portugal finally released the ship and its captain.

The *Charles et George* case was not the first. Similar episodes had occurred before, in particular the giving up to the Spanish government of the slaver ship *Glória*, captured and condemned in Mozambique in Governor Marinho's time. But the *Charles et George* took on enormous significance in building Portugal's good abolitionist conscience, because it had international repercussions. It established a direct connection between abolitionism and national honour, creating an image of Portugal as being at the forefront of humanitarianism. In fact, in the case of the French barque, the traditional situation had been reversed: instead of Portugal conniving in the 'odious commerce', the world was able to see a small country that was complying faithfully with its abolitionist agreements and undertakings and, for its pains, was incurring the wrath of all-powerful France—something even Britain would not dare to do. It is true that in the aftermath of this defiant action Portugal ended up bending to the French ultimatum. But, in the context of the time, this surrender was not truly humiliating, because it represented a sacrifice on behalf of a noble idea, which the whole political nation should praise. As Mendes Leal said, 'it is fine and noble to suffer for such a cause (hear! hear!)'.[115] With the *Charles et George*, the country had had a moral victory that made its defiance a noble thing: 'the strong only appeared to win, it was the weaker one that was honoured (hear! hear!)'.[116] And all the more honoured in that the Portuguese commitment to abolition, in this case, went counter to immediate material interests. Portugal, which had much to gain from a revival of the slave trade because of the size of its colonies, had sacrificed immediate gain and was suffering as defender 'of rights and the dignity of the human species, in a painful but noble sacrifice' in which it had offered itself up as the victim.[117] The reward for this sacrifice could be measured in terms of the prestige the country had gained, because the *Charles et George* affair had had wide international coverage, and the civilized world was unanimously supportive of the way the Portuguese had behaved:

> With this conduct Portugal drew Europe's attention … An insult is always painful but, as far as we are concerned, we give thanks that these [events] have shown up this violence. Instead of humiliating us they have exalted us … There was no shortage of publicity: it was the longest and the most honourable which Portugal has enjoyed for many years.[118]

Some thought that, in addition to giving the country international prestige, the sacrifice in the face of French violence had direct merits for the abolitionist cause. Even though Lisbon had been forced to release the slave ship, the episode had served 'the cause of humanity' because, since it involved universal European censure of French behaviour, it would oblige the government of that country to rethink its engagement system and outlaw it.[119] In other words, on account of the *Charles et George* Portugal was at the forefront of the anti-slavery battle and, what is more, in a context where Britain had been complacent and weak: 'the banner of philanthropy wavered in the hands of mighty Britain and Portugal, little Portugal, raised it up from the dust where it lay and raised it sufficiently high for a speechless Europe to see, in an instant, Portugal playing Britain's part! Portugal at the head of the crusade to abolish the slave trade!'.[120]

In a country that was at once hostile to the slave trade and complacent in its attitude to the slavers, the ideological function of the *Charles et*

Georges episode went beyond the humanitarian catharsis. Portugal also had islands that were short of labour. While on the one hand the *Charles et George* episode gave it the moral legitimacy to claim its place in the vanguard of abolitionism, thereby strengthening an option for abolition based on defence of national honour, it also served, paradoxically, as grounds for claiming that the restrictions on the transfer of labour from Angola to São Tomé and Príncipe should be eased. In the Cortes, Abranches (the deputy for São Tomé) was the staunchest defender of this tolerationist policy. He asked that the Cortes authorize, 'for the benefit of humanity and liberty', slaves to be bought in Angola, freed and, already as freedmen, transported to the islands, where they would work for a few years for those who had redeemed them. He would return to the subject insistently, quoting the example of the French and asking that an agreement should be made with the British to take Negroes to São Tomé—he spoke of around 20,000.[121] He had the express support of some deputies, but not of a majority in the Cortes—hence his insistence. In contrast, he found support among government ministers and in the Conselho Ultramarino (Overseas Council). Since São Tomé's prosperity was at stake, it was necessary to take advantage of Portuguese abolitionist prestige, with a view to obtaining a favour from Britain. As the Navy Minister at the time, Mendes Leal, said to his Foreign Affairs counterpart: 'we have made the most costly sacrifices ... for our observance and loyalty to the treaty of 1842. It is necessary, it is indispensable, that that treaty shall not become an instrument of intolerable pressure on all our efforts at development'.[122]

The case of the *Charles et George* and the freedmen transferred to São Tomé and Príncipe are examples of Portuguese duality in relation to suppression. The way the nation dealt with that duality was not consistent. As a rule, silence was the method chosen to attempt to reconcile the newly gained anti-slavery reputation with tolerance of a new kind of traffic to São Tomé and Príncipe. This was a compromised and shy silence that was only broken now and again for recommendations to be made on the overarching need to safeguard national honour. As Sá Nogueira warned, 'I have no wish that suspicion should fall on the Portuguese government that it shuts its eyes to this traffic'.[123] However, behind this more or less compromised silence, there were also the obstructive arguments of those who opposed abolition and had learned to blend the recent claims to philanthropic vanguardism with the pro-slavery arguments of old. One of the most eloquent examples of this type of argument is to be found in the *Revista das Colónias* (Colonial Review): 'When Britain set out to end the detestable traffic of African slaves, Portugal welcomed that idea with enthusiasm ... When posterity remembers the names of the most distinguished Negrophiles ... it will place on the same page the men from Britain and Portugal, Wilberforce and Sá da Bandeira.' However, at the same time as it placed Portugal in the vanguard of abolitionism, and a Portuguese in the humanitarian pantheon, the newspaper also argued in favour of transporting freedmen to São Tomé, on lines very close to those of the pro-slavery discourse at the beginning of the century. It asserted, in particular, that such transport would be to the advantage of all involved, including the slaves. If 'savage hordes' could sell the prisoners taken in their constant wars, this would certainly save their lives. It would therefore be a humanitarian act to buy these prisoners, baptize them and compel them to work for five years as freedmen. This would make it possible:

> To save as many lives as slaves were redeemed; bring into the Christian fold an equivalent number of souls, who in the bush were devoted to the evil ways of fetishism …; turn into free and useful members of society an equal number of men who were currently enemies of civilization and of work, who were today deprived of membership in the great human family on account of ignorance, laziness and barbarity; supply the Portuguese colonies, where hands are short, these much-needed and much-appreciated agents of wealth and prosperity, who would be received there as brothers and treated as natives of the islands.[124]

The United States, France and Britain were already engaged in transporting freedmen to the colonies, so Portugal should have the right to do the same.

The article in the *Revista das Colónias* is quite clearly nothing more than an updating of the pro-slavery argument, which had made its last open appearance at the beginning of the nineteenth century by the pen of Azeredo Coutinho and then disappeared, emerging only when the tensions of controversy caused it to come out of its gradualist, false-abolitionist disguise. It combined very old elements (ransoming slaves, salvation of souls, the civilizing mission of compulsory labour) with more recent ones (the employment of freedmen), and even entirely new ones (such as taking advantage of the *Charles et Georges* episode). At its heart, however, were the old notions of the intrinsic barbarity of the African and the theory of the lesser evil. This is testimony to the perennial nature of the major strains of pro-slavery thought throughout the period under study.

In the 1860s, the arguments put forward by some deputies, members of the government and journalists highlight the fact that obstructive tolerationism had survived in Portugal and was constantly updated, even to the point of creating a godlike figure out of Sá da Bandeira to cover up slavist proposals behind his prestigious image. In any event, this survival no longer reflected the feelings of the country, and its extent was not as widespread as it had been at the end of the 1830s. In the approximately 20 years between Palmerston's bill and the *Charles et George* episode, the Portuguese ruling classes changed sides, not so much because the country had been taken up in a wave of anti-slavery, but because the defence of sovereignty and national honour had forced them to match the pace set by Britain. In this sense, the struggle against the slave trade in Portugal can be explained, first and foremost, on political grounds and by the need to restore a national prestige that had suffered greatly on account of the build-up of charges, which had reached their high point in the major crisis of 1838–39 but persisted in the years that followed.

Of course, alongside the defence of national honour, there was also talk of doing away with the slave trade for economic reasons, in order to allow the rich African colonies to be exploited and developed. One of the characteristics of pioneering abolitionism was the conviction that change in Africa would be swift. All sorts of evils were assigned to the slave trade, and it was supposed that its suppression would almost immediately bring beneficial changes. In Portugal, however, and for reasons that we shall see below, these arguments were uninspiring, and few believed that the African Eldorado was just around the corner. In fact, there were not even enough people interested in investing capital or lives in the economic exploitation of Africa. And among the political elites there was also no sign of consensus on plans for expansion that would make Africa one of the priorities of national life.

Notes

1. Thomas F. Buxton, *The African Slave Trade*, London, 1839.
2. See David Eltis, *Economic Growth and the Ending of the Transatlantic Slave Trade*, Oxford University Press, New York, 1987, p. 84. For a similar opinion from a Portuguese commander, see report of frigate captain João Máximo Rodovalho, in *BOGGPA*, 20 June 1857, p. 7.
3. David Eltis, 'Slave Departures from Africa, 1811–1867. An Annual Time Series', *African Economic History*, 15, 1986, p. 171.
4. Eltis, *Economic Growth*, p. 166.
5. See, for example, the report by Captain John Foote to the Governing Council of Luanda, 23 August 1843, ANTT, MNE, *cx.* 496 (*ma.* 1844) and report by Gabriel to Palmerston, 5 August 1850, PRO FO 84/792.
6. In 1845 exports of slaves from Angola numbered around 9,700, in comparison with the 43,200 exported in 1836; a little over 2,000 slaves were exported from Mozambique, as against the approximately 24,000 exported in 1839 (Eltis, 'Slave Departures', pp. 169–70).
7. The Benin region, which exported some 50,000 slaves between 1836 and 1840, still exported close to 45,000 from 1841 to 1845; and, in the region comprising the Zaïre River and ports to the north, there was a similar setback: exports of 36,000 slaves from 1836 to 1840 fell to *circa* 34,000 in the five years that followed (ibid., pp. 166 and 168).
8. Eltis, *Economic Growth*, p. 176; Jackson and Gabriel to Palmerston, 5 February 1850, PRO FO 84/793; Gabriel to Palmerston, 5 August 1850, PRO FO 84/792.
9. *Repressão do Trafico da Escravatura. Extracto de Documentos Officiaes*, Imprensa Nacional, Lisbon, 1888, p. 5.
10. A.R. Booth, 'The United States African Squadron, 1843–1861', in *Boston University Papers on Africa*, vol. 1, Boston, 1964, p. 89; Leslie Bethell, *The Abolition of the Brazilian Slave Trade. Britain, Brazil and the Slave Trade Question (1807–1869)*, Cambridge University Press, Cambridge, 1970, pp. 191–92.

11. Lawrence C. Jennings, 'The French Press and Great Britain's Campaign Against the Slave Trade, 1830–1848', *Revue Française d'Histoire d'Outre-Mer*, 67, 246–47, 1980, p. 9 ff.; and Serge Daget, 'France, Suppression of the Illegal Slave Trade, and England, 1817–1850', in David Eltis and James Walvin (eds), *The Abolition of the Atlantic Slave Trade. Origins and Effects in Europe, Africa, and the Americas*, University of Wisconsin Press, Madison, 1981, pp. 204–05.
12. For the relative uselessness of the French patrol, see *DG*, 29 January 1848.
13. Bethell, *The Abolition of the Brazilian*, pp. 224 ff. and 273–74; W.A. Green, *British Slave Emancipation: The Sugar Colonies and the Great Experiment, 1830–1865*, Clarendon Press, Oxford, 1976, pp. 231–32; Howard H. Temperley, *White Dreams, Black Africa: The Antislavery Expedition to the River Niger, 1841–1842*, Yale University Press, New Haven, 1991, p. 134. For a critique of the measure, see report by Gabriel to Palmerston, 5 August 1850, PRO FO 84/792. It should be remembered that between 1845 and 1854, the year when full tax equalization occurred, the London sugar price fell by 44 per cent, while per capita consumption doubled (Philip D. Curtin, *The Image of Africa. British Ideas and Action, 1780–1850*, University of Wisconsin Press, Madison, 1964, p. 443).
14. Christopher Lloyd, *The Navy and the Slave Trade. The Suppression of the African Slave Trade in the Nineteenth Century*, Frank Cass, London, 1968 (First edition 1949), p. 94 and ff.; Pierre Verger, *Flux et reflux de la traite des nègres entre le golfe de Bénin et Bahia de Todos os Santos du XVIIe au XIXe siècles*, Mouton, Paris and The Hague, 1968, p. 548; Bethell, *The Abolition of the Brazilian*, p. 183; Mary Karasch, 'The Brazilian Slavers and the Illegal Slave Trade, 1836–1851', University of Wisconsin, Madison, 1967 (unpublished Master's degree thesis), p. 4.
15. Aberdeen to the Admiralty, 20 May 1842, PRO FO 84/436.
16. Lloyd, *The Navy*, pp. 97 and 150; Bethell, *The Abolition of the Brazilian*, pp. 185–86. Between 1842 and 1850 the British made fourty-two such treaties.
17. Lloyd, *The Navy*, pp. 98–99.
18. In Cuba in the 1840s, imports ran at an average of just over 5,000 slaves per annum, as against the over 20,000 p.a. of the previous five years (see David Eltis, 'The Nineteenth-Century Transatlantic Slave Trade: An Annual Time Series of Imports into the Americas, Broken Down by Region', *Hispanic American Historical Review*, 67, 1987, pp. 115 and 122–23). Growth in Brazilian imports took place despite the fact that large numbers of slave ships were captured during this time by naval war fleets (see Bethell, *The Abolition of the Brazilian*, p. 283 and, for the seizures by the Portuguese navy, Appendexes C, D and E at the end of this book). This suggests that, without repressive action, imports would have been even higher (for a defence of this viewpoint, see E. Philip LeVeen, *British Slave Trade Suppression Policies, 1821–1865*, Arno Press, New York, 1977).
19. Curtin, *Image of Africa*, p. 304.
20. David B. Davis, *Slavery and Human Progress*, Oxford University Press, Oxford, 1984, p. 219 ff.; W.A. Green, 'Was British Emancipation a Success? The Abolitionist Perspective', in David Richardson (ed.), *Abolition and its Aftermath. The Historical Context, 1790–1916*, Frank Cass, London, 1985, pp. 183–202; for the drop in production in the post-emancipation period, see David Eltis, 'Abolitionist Perceptions of Society after Slavery', in James Walvin (ed.), *Slavery and British Society, 1776–1846*, London, 1982, pp. 204–05; Seymour Drescher, *The Mighty Experiment. Free Labor versus Slavery in British Emancipation*, Oxford University Press, Oxford and New York, 2002, p. 158 ff.
21. Catherine Hall, *Civilising Subjects. Metropole and Colony in the English Imagination, 1830–1867*, Polity Press, Cambridge, 2002.

22. Lloyd, *The Navy*, pp. 107–08 and 147; Curtin, *Image of Africa*, pp. 316, 341 and 444 ff.; Bethell, *The Abolition of the Brazilian*, pp. 260 ff., 297 ff. and 321 ff.; Eltis, *Economic Growth*, pp. 26–28 and 83.
23. Bethell, *The Abolition of the Brazilian*, p. 322; and Roger Anstey, 'The Pattern of British Abolitionism in the Eighteenth and Nineteenth Centuries', in Christine Bolt and Seymour Drescher (eds), *Anti-Slavery, Religion and Reform: Essays in the Memory of Roger Anstey*, Dawson, Folkestone, 1980, p. 34.
24. Lloyd, *The Navy*, pp. 143–45; Verger, *Flux et reflux*, pp. 381 ff.; Bethell, *The Abolition of the Brazilian*, p. 309 ff.
25. Verger, *Flux et reflux*, pp. 390–91; Bethell, *The Abolition of the Brazilian*, p. 327 ff.; for the importation of slaves into Brazil, see Eltis, 'The Nineteenth-Century', p. 115.
26. If we take into account the forced emigration of Negro contract labourers, exports from the Zaïre River and ports to the north of its mouth came close to their all-time high in the five-year period from 1858 to 1862 (Eltis, 'Slave Departures', p. 168).
27. Eltis, 'The Nineteenth-Century', pp. 122–23.
28. Lloyd, *The Navy*, p. 171.
29. David R. Murray, *Odious Commerce: Britain, Spain and the Abolition of the Cuban Slave Trade*, Cambridge University Press, Cambridge, 1980, pp. 261–66 and 301–02.
30. Booth, 'The United States', pp. 88 and 116; Murray, *Odious Commerce*, p. 247.
31. Booth, 'The United States', p. 109.
32. Davis, *Slavery and Human*, pp. 233–43.
33. Booth, 'The United States', pp. 109–10.
34. Ibid., pp. 107 and 110; Murray, *Odious Commerce*, pp. 305 and 312.
35. James Bandinel, *Some Account of the Trade in Slaves from Africa, as Connected with Europe and America. From the Introduction of the Trade into Modern Europe, down to Present Time, especially with Reference to the Efforts made by the British Government for its Extinction*, Frank Cass, London, 1968 (1st edition 1842), p. 299.
36. In 1847 the British ambassador in Lisbon even denounced a small advertisement placed in the *Periódico dos Pobres* in which a 'shameful' reward was offered to whomsoever would restore to his owner a slave belonging to the crew of a Brazilian ship at anchor in the River Douro (Luz to Seymour, 5 October 1847, ANTT, MNE, *liv.* 184).
37. Gomes de Castro to Howard de Walden, 30 December 1845, ANTT, MNE, *liv.* 185; Bayard to Seymour, 27 May and 16 July 1847, ANTT, MNE, *liv.* 184; and Tojal to Bayard (documents attached), 17 July 1847, ANTT, MNE, *cx.* 387.
38. Howard de Walden to Gomes de Castro (documents attached), 8 March and 12 December 1844, ANTT, MNE, *cx.* 496.
39. Gomes de Castro to Howard de Walden, 15 April and 17 May 1844, ANTT, MNE, *liv.* 185.
40. Government Order of 8 July 1845, AGM, *cx.* 311.
41. Falcão to Gomes de Castro, 8 July 1845, ANTT, MNE, *cx.* 386.
42. António M. Campelo to the major-general of the *Armada*, 18 June 1842, AGM, *cx.* 311.
43. For the list of arrests and sinkings of slave ships, see Appendixes C, D and E.
44. The capture of the brig *Caçador* in the mouth of the Dande, with almost 850 slaves on board, was seen by the British authorities as decisive proof that Portugal was effectively cooperating in the fight against the traffic (Howard de Walden to Aberdeen, 28 July 1844, PRO FO 84/521). For the operations of the Portuguese navy, see João Pedro Marques, 'A Armada portuguesa no combate ao tráfico de escravos em Angola (1839–1867)', *Anais de História de Além-Mar*, 1, 2000, pp. 161–93.

45. Eltis, *Economic Growth*, p. 95. On the existence of two trafficking groups in Luanda and on the way in which the Portuguese squadron favoured one of the groups in question, see Gabriel to Canning, 12 and 13 September 1845 (private), PRO FO 84/569.
46. Lloyd, *The Navy*, pp. 101 and 119; Eltis, *Economic Growth*, p. 175 (note 49).
47. Circular of 12 December 1844, AMNE, *cx.* 1153.
48. Falcão to Gomes de Castro (attached documents), 12 July 1845, ANTT, MNE, *cx.* 386.
49. Catela to Minister of Foreign Affairs, 31 May 1848, ANTT, MNE, *cx.* 223.
50. Tojal to the Major-General of the *Armada*, 30 July 1847, AGM, *cx.* 311; and Gomes de Castro to the Minister of Foreign Affairs, 15 February 1849, ANTT, MNE, *cx.* 387; for the British government's consent to this restrictive policy, see Palmerston to Seymour, 25 January 1849, PRO FO 84/762; it should be noted that, even if the slave ship were sighted and pursued while still within Portuguese waters, it would suffice for it to leave those waters (three miles) to become untouchable.
51. Vila Nova de Ourém to Minister of Foreign Affairs (attached documents), 30 May 1849, ANTT, MNE, *cx.* 387 (my italics).
52. Falcão to the Major-General of the *Armada*, 20 November 1845, AGM, *cx.* 311. In his efforts to protect the slavers Possolo even tried to interfere with the decisions of the mixed commission (see commissioners' report, 31 December 1844, ANTT, MNE, *cx.* 223).
53. *A Revolução de Septembro*, 27 February 1846, 4 September 1847, 23 May 1849, 31 January 1850 and 29 October 1851; Alexandrino da Cunha was also attacked by the slavers in Brazil, and his personal safety was threatened when he travelled there at the end of the 1840s.
54. Tojal and Gomes de Castro to Minister of Foreign Affairs, 17 May 1847 and 30 December 1848, respectively, ANTT, MNE, *cx.* 387.
55. Demony to the Minister of Foreign Affairs, 30 December 1845, ANTT, MNE, *cx.* 223.
56. Duprat to the Minister of Foreign Affairs, 3 February 1847, AMNE, *cx.* 1150.
57. Bayard to Seymour, 11 August 1847 (attached documents), PRO FO 84/676; see also Saldanha to Seymour, 22 March 1848, ANTT, MNE, *liv.* 184.
58. Bethell, 'The Mixed Commissions for the Suppression of the Transatlantic Slave Trade in the Nineteenth Century', *Journal of African History*, p. 91; idem, *The Abolition of the Brazilian*, pp. 188–89.
59. *DCD*, session of 24 December 1858, p. 257; see also the missive of the commander of the Luanda Naval Station, Manuel Tomás Cordeiro, to the Queen, 21 November 1849, PRO FO 84/793.
60. Duprat to the Minister of Foreign Affairs, 20 May 1848, AMNE, *cx.* 1150; see also Palmerston to Seymour, 16 January 1849, PRO FO 84/762.
61. Howard to Palmerston, 28 August 1850, PRO FO 84/799.
62. Duprat and Catela to the Minister of Foreign Affairs, 12 December 1846 and 15 February 1847, respectively, ANTT, MNE, *cx.* 223.
63. *Annaes Maritimos e Coloniaes*, no. 4, 1841, p. 159.
64. Ibid., no. 1, 1844, p. 10, and *BOGGPA*, 12 March 1849, p. 2.
65. *BOGGPA*, 2 February 1850, p. 2.
66. Cardoso to Cunha, 2 April 1847, *BOGGPA*, 24 April 1847, p. 3.
67. See, for example, the cases of the *Lealdade* and the *Espírito Santo*, *BOGGPA*, 2 and 9 May and 21 and 24 October 1846; for British indignation, see, for example, Jackson and Gabriel to Palmerston, 14 February 1848, PRO FO 84/719.
68. Falcão to the Minister of Foreign Affairs (attached documents), 3 October 1842, ANTT, MNE, *cx.* 384.
69. Government order of 12 February 1848, *BOGGPA*, 15 April 1848, p. 2.

70. Demony to Atouguia, 4 November 1851, AMNE, *cx.* 1153; on the case of the brigantine *Veiga*, see also Jackson to Palmerston (private), 12 December 1850, PRO FO 84/792.
71. These reversals of sentences were favourably viewed by the British commissioners in Luanda, not so much because there was any punishment for the criminals—who had meanwhile escaped—but because they were proof of the sincerity of the Portuguese authorities (Jackson and Gabriel to Palmerston, 30 April 1847, PRO FO 84/671).
72. Howard de Walden to Aberdeen, 28 December 1845, PRO FO 84/579.
73. Sentence handed down to Arsénio for criminal bankruptcy, *BOGGPA*, 3 July 1852, p. 7. It should be noted that this sentence was also rescinded in Lisbon. For a biography of Arsénio see João Pedro Marques, 'Arsénio Pompílio Pompeu de Carpo: um percurso negreiro no século XIX', *Análise Social*, 160, 2001, pp. 609–38.
74. Chamber of Peers, session of 24 May 1848, *DG*, 25 May 1848; see also session of 7 April 1851, *DG*, 21 April 1851 (speeches by Sá and also by Lavradio).
75. Sá da Bandeira to Palmela, draft, July 1849, AHU, Sá da Bandeira papers, *ma.* 824.
76. See dispatches of the Royal Procurator to Lazarim, 21 January and 8 July 1848; and José Maria de Araújo to the Major-General of the *Armada*, 6 July 1849, AGM, *cx.* 311.
77. *BOGGPA*, 31 March 1860, pp. 4–5; Rodrigues to the Minister of Foreign Affairs, 6 March 1863, AMNE, *cx.* 1153.
78. *BOGGPA*, 24 January 1852, p. 3 (summary of speech by Palmerston in the parliamentary sessions of 14 July 1841).
79. *DCP*, session of 16 August 1842, p. 175.
80. Chamber of Peers, session of 5 February 1846, *DG*, 13 February 1846.
81. Gomes de Castro to Seymour, 12 December 1848, ANTT, MNE, *liv.* 184; see also Tojal to Howard, 6 November 1850, PRO FO 84/799.
82. Gabriel and Brand to Aberdeen, 25 March 1846, PRO FO 84/626.
83. See, for example, the court judgment regarding the crew of the *Lealdade* and the remarks this decision elicited from the British ambassador in Lisbon (Seymour to Saldanha, 30 December 1847, PRO FO 84/676).
84. Eltis, *Economic Growth*, pp. 92–94.
85. Demony to the Minister of Foreign Affairs, 8 August 1852, AMNE, *cx.* 1153.
86. Demony to Atouguia, 16 April and 25 August 1854 (and attached documents), AMNE, *cx.* 1153.
87. Chamber of Peers, session of 28 February 1855, *DG*, 12 March 1855 (speech by Tomar).
88. Chamber of Peers, session of 28 February 1855, *DG*, 13 March 1855 (speech by the Minister of the Navy).
89. *O Portuguez*, 22 November 1853. For the usage of the term *liberto*, see João Pedro Marques, 'Uma cosmética demorada: as Cortes portuguesas face ao problema da escravidão (1836–1875)', *Análise Social*, 158/159, 2001, p. 227 ff.
90. Seymour to Palmerston, 27 September 1848, PRO FO 84/724.
91. *O Portuguez*, 26 and 31 December 1853, 12 and 14 January 1854.
92. *A Revolução de Septembro*, 7 December 1844, pp. 1–2.
93. *DG*, 21 April 1852.
94. *A Revolução de Septembro*, 22 December 1853. *Uncle Tom's Cabin, or Life Among the Lowly*, was first published in 1852 and was a huge success; the author, Harriet Beecher Stowe, obtained an enthusiastic reception on visiting England in 1853. Her second anti-slavery novel, *Dred*, came out in 1856 and was another smashing success in England, with 100,000 copies sold in under a month (see David Turley, *The Culture of English Antislavery, 1780–1860*, Routledge. London, 1991, pp. 103–04).

95. Francisco Gomes de Amorim, *Ódio de Raça*, Lisboa, 1869, p. 10.
96. Ibid., pp. 11–12.
97. Chamber of Peers, session of 1 July 1852, *DG*, 7 July 1852.
98. *DCP*, session of 5 August 1842, p. 118.
99. *A Revolução de Septembro*, 20 January 1854 and 30 August 1855.
100. António da Silva Gaio, *Mario. Episódios das luctas civis portuguezas de 1820–1834*, Guimarães eds, Lisbon, 1924 (1st edition 1868), p. 247.
101. Howard de Walden to Aberdeen, 20 May 1843, PRO FO 84/464.
102. *O Correio Portuguez*, 30 March 1843.
103. Francisco Maria Bordalo, *Eugénio. Romance Marítimo*, Lisbon, 1854 (2nd edition), p. 110.
104. Document attached to despatch from Tojal to Bayard, 17 July 1847, ANTT, MNE, *cx.* 387.
105. Falcão to Gomes de Castro, 8 July 1845 (and attached documents), ANTT, MNE, *cx.* 386.
106. *DCD*, session of 19 June 1852, pp. 4–5 (report by the Minister for the Navy).
107. *DCD*, session of 7 September 1842, p. 115; for subsequent examples see *DCD*, sessions of 18 July 1854 and 5 June 1855, pp. 330 and 62, respectively (speeches by Correia Caldeira).
108. Chamber of Peers, session of 4 May 1849, *DG*, 29 May 1849.
109. Chamber of Peers, session of 12 August 1848, *DG*, 14 August 1848 (speech by Tojal); on the same issue see also *DCD*, session of 18 June 1850, p. 275 (speech by Fontes Pereira de Melo).
110. *DCD*, session of 6 June 1855, p. 78.
111. *Annaes Maritimos e Coloniaes*, no. 8, 1841, p. 350.
112. DCD, session of 13 February 1846, p. 8 (speech by Falcão).
113. *DCD*, session of 7 March 1856, p. 74 (speech by Martens Ferrão); see also, *DCD*, session of 18 December 1858, p. 198 (speech by Pequito).
114. Duprat to Loulé, 25 November 1858 (confidential), AMNE, *cx.* 1151.
115. *DCD*, session of 21 December 1858, p. 221.
116. *DCD*, session of 18 December 1858, p. 194 (speech by Bartolomeu dos Mártires); see also Chamber of Peers, session of 5 January 1859, DG, 24 January 1859 (speech by Algés).
117. *DCD*, session of 18 December 1858, p. 198 (speech by Pequito).
118. *DCD*, session of 21 December 1858, pp. 221–22 (speech by Mendes Leal); see also *DCD*, sessions of 15 November and 24 December 1858, pp. 47 and 257 (speeches by S. Vasconcelos and Casal Ribeiro, respectively).
119. *DCD*, session of 20 December 1858, p. 207 (speech by Sá da Bandeira); see also Chamber of Peers, session of 4 January 1859, *DG*, 19 January 1859 (speech by Porto de Mós).
120. Chamber of Peers, session of 5 January 1859, *DG*, 24 January 1859 (speech by Linhares).
121. *DCD*, session of 28 January 1859, p. 294.
122. Mendes Leal to the Minister of Foreign Affairs, 10 November 1863 (confidential), AMNE, *cx.* 985; see also opinion of the Conselho Ultramarino (Overseas Council) dated 9 November 1861, *Annaes do Conselho Ultramarino*, March 1862, p. 26.
123. Chamber of Deputies, session of 31 May 1864, *DL*, 2 June 1864.
124. *Revista das Colónias*, 11 December 1863.

– *Chapter 6* –

COLONIAL STALEMATES: 'NEW BRAZILS' OR REAL AFRICAS?

In the mid-1960s Hammond argued that, with the exception of a handful of public figures and a few singular moments when feverish attention might have been paid to African affairs, nineteenth-century Portugal's relationship to its colonies was above all one of indifference. This was why the Portuguese produced an anomalous colonialism, not grounded in clear and consistent material interests: 'no industries seeking overseas markets, no middle class seeking overseas fortunes, no capitalists seeking overseas investments'.[1] Portuguese colonialism had been a reflexive and reactive movement, driven by political and ideological factors, like the need to safeguard the country's prestige, the vortex of international competition—which would later lead to the scramble for Africa at the end of the nineteenth century—and, concomitantly, the almost paranoid fear that foreigners would come and steal what remained of the old empire.

Hammond's view was compatible with the opinions expressed by various leading lights of Portuguese nineteenth-century historiography and was widely accepted, even in Portugal.[2] But, from the end of the 1970s onwards, theories of uneconomic colonialism and of liberal indifference to Africa were challenged by various historians influenced by Marxism, principally by Valentim Alexandre.[3] He identified four or five projects for the development and economic exploitation of the African colonies with which leading figures in the social and financial world—like the count of Farrobo, Pinto Basto and others—were supposedly associated, and saw in these projects revealing evidence that the bourgeoisie in nineteenth-century Portugal had a strong interest in the African possessions. Alexandre recognized that none of these projects had come to fruition but, for him, that failure had to do with external factors—the bourgeois aspiration for Africa was definitely there, if only for reasons deriving from the very logic of the development of Portuguese capitalism, which at that time was operating in the context of the loss of Brazil and the superiority of Great Britain. Given the conditions imposed by such a context, the colonialist path had emerged as the most suitable response: 'nearly all sectors of the Portuguese bourgeoisie were potentially interested in that expansion', and this context would explain, amongst other things, why government intervention had veered towards abolition of the slave trade, which was one of the 'preconditions for reinforcing Portugal's economic presence in Africa'.[4] In other words, for the Marxist historians, the pieces of Lisbon's African policy fell together in a coherent and well-synchronized whole, with the abolitionism recommended by Sá da Bandeira in 1836 'answering to the colonial interests of the Portuguese ruling classes'.[5]

Accordingly, where previously there had been detachment and apathy, recent historians of Portuguese colonialism discovered that the Portuguese ruling classes had had a strong interest in exploiting African potential and that the state had sought to match that interest. These discoveries became a new historiographic orthodoxy that found wide acceptance in Portugal and abroad.[6] However, they are an over-optimistic assessment of the true interests of the Portuguese bourgeoisie in Africa. It is an assessment which, as we shall see, is not grounded in sufficiently solid documentary evidence—especially in connection with the first two-thirds of the nineteenth century, the period that concerns us here. In addition, and in the realm of ideas, this approach values only that current of opinion which was strongly pro-African, ignoring those which diverged from it. In so doing, it conveys a view of the country's attitude to colonial undertakings in Africa that is distorted—because it is unbalanced.

These two reasons would in themselves be sufficient to challenge the new orthodoxy. But there is the additional factor that its way of seeing the relationship of the Portuguese with the African colonies has clear repercussions on the problem of abolitionism in Portugal. In effect, Alexandre's view seems to be incompatible with the information uncovered, in earlier chapters, on Portuguese attitudes to the suppression of the slave trade. Admittedly Alexandre recently revised his earlier interpretation of the nature of the process of abolition in Portugal, dropping the idea of the strict convergence of Sá da Bandeira's abolitionism and the colonial interests of the ruling classes. In his new suggested formulation, quite the opposite is true: abolitionism is reduced almost to a side issue which, 'far from expressing a widespread feeling', represented, according to Alexandre, 'an extreme minority position'.[7] Nevertheless, this recent retargeting of the approach brought with it a new problem in the context of an interpretation which, while severely restricting the sociological significance of abolitionism in Portugal, continues to assert the elites' strong interest in Africa, insisting on the significance the colonial issue had in Portuguese political life from 1820 onwards. If this is the case, it is difficult to understand—and Alexandre does not explain—why political and economic elites that were almost unanimously interested in Africa should have adopted a general attitude of opposition, detachment or silence in connection with the suppression of the slave trade, stubbornly refusing to see the need for that suppression if they were to pursue their supposed political and material purposes.

The fact that there are weaknesses or gaps in the Marxist interpretation does not mean that one should automatically adopt the theories of indifferentism and uneconomic colonialism, as developed by Hammond and others. Admittedly, these theories do not clash with what has already been said regarding the ordinary Portuguese position on abolitionism. However, they are overly schematic and too general. Fixated on the almost total absence of large Portuguese economic undertakings in Africa, they completely ignore—and in ignoring do not assess—projects that did not come to fruition, the different currents of opinion then existing and their meanings. Therefore, faced with two opposing theories that are both unsatisfactory for various reasons, we must revisit the issue of whether Portuguese liberals were or were not interested in the colonies, in order to demonstrate two things: first, that Portuguese involvement in the subjects of colonialism and Africa was far from being as widespread as the Marxist historians claim; and, secondly, that this is one of the reasons—but not the only reason—why no active opposition to the slave trade developed in Portugal.

6.1 Images of Africa

Between 1820 and 1865, with three or four exceptions, which will be analysed in due course, Portuguese capitalists did not carry out a single investment project in Africa. It has been suggested that this reluctance to invest was due to reasons somehow beyond the control of economic actors, in particular obstacles of a political and financial nature. I shall have occasion below to challenge the validity of this kind of justification, as well as to assess the solidity and meaning of the economic projects that did emerge at the time. For the moment, and for methodological reasons, we have to go back briefly to the problem of will and, still further back, to the images nineteenth-century Portuguese had of Africa, given that it is in accordance with their image of reality that men seek to guide their actions. In the realm of images, the documentation shows that, rather than a unanimous sentiment in favour of Africa or of a 'colonial plan' that occupied the attentions of the ruling classes—as the Marxist historians suggest—there was a diversity of approaches to it. We shall examine each of those approaches before looking at the relative significance of each one in giving rise to action or inaction.

6.1.1 'New Brazils'

From 1820 onwards, there was a conspicuous group of Portuguese, which we may call the enthusiasts, who believed that the African colonies could be 'new Brazils':

> There are rich mines of gold, copper, iron and precious stones in the overseas provinces. We can grow in Africa everything we can grow in America; we have more fertile lands in the islands of Cape Verde, in Guinea, Angola and Mozambique, where we can grow rice, indigo, cotton, coffee, and cocoa on a large scale, in a word, all the varieties which are known as colonial, and all the spices. These will be sufficient not only for consumption in Portugal but may also be exported in very large quantities to other markets in Europe.[8]

These projections, which were repeated on countless occasions in nineteenth-century Portugal, were based above all on the conviction that the African soil and sub-soil were amazingly rich. As early as 1822 the Cortes resounded with references to the 'astonishing fertility' of Cape Verde.[9] Of course, it was known that the islands suffered on account of the lack of rainfall but, even so, the enthusiasts never ceased praising the generosity of the Cape Verdean soil, those 'blessed lands where the uncultivated bush produces pulza-oil (from the physic-nut) and the rocks are covered with orchil dye lichen'.[10] And what was said of Cape Verde was repeated in connection with the other colonies, whether choosing one as the pinnacle of tropical opulence or, as more often happened, regarding them all as equally rich. Sá da Bandeira, for example, had absolutely no doubt that all of them could 'perfectly' produce everything that was bought from Brazil.[11] It was normally in this generalized manner that African natural wealth was portrayed in the enthusiast press. *A Revista* (The Review), for example, described all of Portuguese Africa as an extremely fertile land and insisted with merchant organizations that they should look to their enormous natural riches:

> This nation ... may certainly achieve much in the merchandise trade of goods, all of them precious, which are lying abandoned and unvalued in Bissau, Cacheu, Geba and Farim; in the rich wildernesses of Angola and Benguela; and in the still richer lands of Inhambane and Quelimane ... Gold, ivory, tortoiseshell, wax, cotton, rice, coffee, tobacco, hides, indigo and countless drugs of high value ..., will in a few years make wealthy men of the speculators.[12]

The promise of large profits was one of the elements in the enthusiasts' discourse. There were even some who swore that, if they had money, they would invest it in agriculture in Africa because they could earn 'over seven thousand per cent' there.[13] But generally speaking the enthusiast predictions of colonial fortunes tended to go beyond the level of individual gain to encompass the whole nation collectively. The promoters of the 'new Brazil' thought that Portugal was particularly well placed to take advantage of the underlying fertility of the African soil, not only because the Portuguese colonies would yield products that were superior to those of the competition—better sugar than the Brazilian, tastier rice than the Asiatic—but also because they were vast dominions. That was why they thought the African possessions would enable them to obtain better results than foreign lands, and could supply not only Portugal but the whole of Europe. Moreover, for the enthusiasts, the wonder of Portuguese Africa was much more than what the memoirs, notices and reports had already described: to its known production they would add presumed riches, those which were still hiding behind the veil of ignorance: 'chance, mere chance, showed us the treasures which have already been discovered in the African continent; but it holds in its heart many others, hitherto unknown'.[14] By counting in what was still undiscovered, they even went to the extreme of stating that the African possessions would be 'a hundred times' richer than Brazil or Cuba.[15]

It would therefore be in the African colonies, as warranted by Sá da Bandeira, that 'the general prosperity of the whole kingdom' would reside.[16] It was precisely because they were invested with properties that would generate enormous prosperity that many enthusiast politicians and journalists made of them the 'sheet anchor' that would take Portugal out of the precarious financial circumstances it had found itself in since the French invasions and the independence of Brazil. In the 1820s several enthusiasts had already shown the way: to remedy the ills from which the country was suffering, it would be necessary to look to 'African settlements'.[17] Later, all the enthusiasts made the colonies the last hope, 'the last resort' of a Portugal in decline.[18] Some went even further and coloured the idea of salvation in imperial tones, reinforcing it by association with the country's history. We have already seen in chapter 4 how Sá da Bandeira set out that connection as the basis for his abolition decree of 1836. But several other politicians and journalists also tried to do so, and in the wider context of the enthusiast imagination. Lima Leitão, for example, saw the 'new Brazil' as a passport for a return to the 'ancient splendour' of the 'days of heroism'. Without its colonies, Portugal would be at the bottom end of the scale of civilized nations; with them, it would be wealthy and respected, it would become, as Joaquim António de Magalhães said, 'more powerful than it had ever been'.[19]

The belief in African fertility was in no way confined to the enthusiasts. On the contrary, it was a widely held conviction at the time, shared to differing degrees by a large range of people. But in the context of the ideology of the 'new Brazil' the belief took on the strength of a fundamental truth and, above all, it became entangled with other convictions, in a very characteristic mesh.

One of those convictions, which was of a competitive or retaliatory nature—as we have seen in chapter 3—was that, like the pans of a scale, the rise of the Portuguese colonies would correspond to the decline of Brazil. Since it was assumed that the lands of Africa were much more fertile than the already exhausted American soils, and since it was known that slave labour was much cheaper there than in Brazil, the conclusion was reached that the rejuvenated Portuguese colonies would soon rival the old colony. In the mid-1840s, noting a recent increase in Portuguese trade with Angola, Lopes de Lima already foresaw a time 'when the continent of Angola …, from being the slave of the continent of Brazil that it was, would become its export rival'.[20]

Another of the convictions that were part of the enthusiast imaginary was that Africa would be transformed by European capital and European colonists. The emancipation of Brazil had inflicted an undeniable blow on Portuguese foreign trade, and it was assumed that there would be no shortage of businessmen with a strong interest in making up for that blow by investing in Africa. Thereafter it would just be a question of channelling labour to the new tropical sceneries. Once populations and resources had been transferred, the building of the 'new Brazil' would be quick and easy, because in the African lands almost everything grew spontaneously, in 'copious abundance' and 'with no work'.[21] It is true that some of the enthusiasts who had better knowledge of the colonies recommended patience, because nothing could be achieved without it.[22] But the majority were much less cautious. In 1834, Joaquim António Menezes promised that Angola would improve 'in very few years'; at around the same time, Sá da Bandeira was talking of 'a short series' of '10 or 12 years' to derive 'great results' from the African provinces; and, more daringly, Marinho imagined that 'the fortune of Brazil and Havana' might 'immediately' be transferred into Portuguese hands.[23]

The ideas of the Portuguese enthusiasts concerning the speed and ease with which African development would take place coincided clearly with the views that the first generations of British abolitionists had had on the same subject. However, the Portuguese enthusiasts were not as a rule abolitionists: they were generally tolerationists of the more or less obstructive kind. The reason they were not abolitionists lay not only in the politics and ideology we have already discussed in earlier chapters, but also in the fact that their ideas of the speed and ease of the African colonial transformation were based on peculiarly Portuguese notions, which tended to downplay the importance of the suppression of the slave trade. The first of these notions was that Portuguese Africa had not yet developed only because previous governments had passed it over in favour of Asia and later, more glaringly, in favour of Brazil. Already in 1822 José Liberato was of the opinion that 'all the other parts of the realm had always been sacrificed' for Brazil.[24] In mid-century that explanation was insistently repeated:

> When our provinces in Africa were discovered, some agricultural enterprises were established and rapidly prospered, but with the discovery of Brazil, they lost their protection and the care which until then had been bestowed on them … The African provinces were totally abandoned, all the agricultural enterprises were demolished, so that those in Brazil might prosper.[25]

Another significant reason why the African colonies were backward, in the enthusiast view, was the corruption and incompetence of the colonial authorities. That 'is the source of all the misfortune', Menezes proclaimed.[26] All the enthusiasts—even Sá da Bandeira, for whom the abolition of the slave trade was genuinely essential for the progress of the colonies—insisted on stressing the corruption aspect: European nations took the greatest care in selecting their colonial governors; the Portuguese did not, and that was why the colonies were regressing or standing still.[27] At times, the reasoning was more general: some tended to think that the primary cause of African decline was not so much the corruption of men, but the vicious nature of political regimes, whether they took the form of the old absolutism, which had been overthrown in 1820 or, in a more limited and up-to-date version, of the recent despotism of the 1840s.[28] Curiously, and with the exception of enthusiasts such as Morais Sarmento and Sá da Bandeira, for a long time the slave trade was seen as merely a secondary cause of African backwardness, a cause that did not entirely hinder its progress. The slave trade was certainly a negative factor, because it led the inhabitants of the colonies into moral dissolution and ways of enriching themselves that were not to be condoned. But, as Menezes properly stressed in relation to Angola, these were not 'the main causes of the backwardness in which that important possession finds itself'.[29]

These ideas help to explain why most of the colonial enthusiasts felt no obligation to stand up for the abolition of the 'odious commerce'. It was only after the crisis engendered by Palmerston's bill that the idea that suppression was indispensable began to gain ground. But, even so, in mid-century there were still some enthusiasts downplaying, or even criticizing, efforts made by successive governments to suppress the slave trade.[30] And, because, for the enthusiasts, African backwardness should be ascribed rather to a number of erroneous political choices made in the past, there was a need to straighten out the errors of that past and tie together once more 'the thread of African commerce', which had been broken with the colonization of Brazil.[31]

Some of the remedies for this state of affairs would be relatively simple. Since the issue of the political system had already been resolved with the victory of the liberals, the problem of corruption could be solved by employing incorruptible people, a prescription constantly repeated over the years: 'what is missing in those countries, which are so rich in their production? First of all, upright authorities'—*A Revista* put the question and gave the answer.[32] Another type of remedy, which was more all-embracing, demanded a considerable number of men and substantial capital. From the mid-1820s, nearly all the enthusiasts were asking for mass colonization and the promotion of voluntary—and even involuntary—emigration to the Portuguese colonies.[33] As for the capital, some recommended that the government itself should invest in tropical plantations so as to encourage private individuals by its example.[34] State initiative was moreover to provide the engine of development for anything to do with the overseas colonies, particularly the navy. The enthusiasts wanted ships: they regarded steamships as being as important for development of the country as the railways, and argued for the need to channel significant funds into naval construction. Some demanded for the

Navy Ministry a much larger slice of the budget, while others argued for the creation of special taxes for naval development: 'we must convince ourselves that the navy is the nerve-centre of our future prosperity .... I will vote for a tax, of whatever kind, to be applied to the development of the navy'.[35]

In other words, the enthusiasts wanted a state that would spare nothing in order to develop the colonies, a Parliament which, 'with its eyes closed, and with a happy heart', would vote 'large sums' for the colonies every year.[36] If investment by the state was not enough, then the formation of private companies should be encouraged: this was the easiest way of getting around the failings of the exchequer and developing the colonies.[37] The enthusiast press in Lisbon was almost unanimous on this point. *A Revista*, for example, recognized that a colonial chartered company would extract substantial wealth from the concessions granted, 'but would not national industry and trade also grow alongside them? How many hands would not be employed? ... There is no limit to the imagination as one contemplates the rapid movement of such inevitable progress'.[38]

A more indirect but no less significant remedy for making good the mistakes of the past involved public promotion of the colonies. The dissemination of a positive image of Africa was an objective that was expressly undertaken from 1820 and tenaciously pursued in the years following. In 1836 Sá da Bandeira (at the time Minister of the Navy), believing that one of the causes of the decline of the colonies was ignorance of them, had published the *Memorial Ultramarino e Marítimo* (Overseas and Maritime Memorial), which, together with overseas legislation and correspondence, was concerned to describe the colonies as 'a fountain of wealth' that could restore to Portugal much of what it had lost with the independence of Brazil.[39] Only one issue of the *Memorial* was ever published. It did not survive the fall of the left-wing government in April 1836.[40] But in 1840 a similar publication came out, called *Annaes Maritimos e Coloniaes* (Maritime and Colonial Annals), which sought to take up where the *Memorial* had left off. The closing down of the *Annaes* in 1846 was compensated for in the 1850s and 1860s by the appearance of *Boletim* (Bulletin) and *Annaes do Conselho Ultramarino* (Annals of the Overseas Council) and specific publications such as *Revista das Colónias* (Review of the Colonies), *Marinha e Ultramar* (Navy and Overseas) and others. Be that as it may, between 1836 and 1840 the closure of the *Memorial* was made up for by a political press that devoted considerable attention to the idea of the 'new Brazil', publishing memoirs and making suggestions as to the best ways of taking advantage of the riches that abounded in the tropics. In the 1840s there was a clear easing of this promotional fervour, and enthusiast projection of Africa began to appear less frequently in the main Lisbon newspapers (and rarely in those of Oporto). Even so, and despite a very significant reduction in the frequency and even the intensity of the 'new Brazil' arguments, there were still many optimistic projections about Africa circulating in the 1840s. It was during this period that a kind of digest of enthusiast thought was published, entitled *Ensaios sobre a Statistica das Possessões Portuguezas* (Essays on the statistics of the Portuguese possessions), a work commissioned by the government from the deputy and naval officer Lopes de Lima. This document contained an exhaustive survey of vegetable, animal and mineral production in the colonies of West Africa. The author concluded his survey in almost pamphleteer-like style:

> Many other natural riches are perhaps contained in these dense woods and forests, these delightful plains, these rivers and lagoons, these rough mountains, of the interior of Lower Guinea ... But those which I leave detailed here are in themselves sufficient to draw the attention of the Portuguese people—not all of whom will be aware of them—and to excite the well-understood longing of hard-working men who, living in poverty at home ..., may see themselves in a few years' time rich and respected in Africa, as has happened for so many.[41]

Lopes de Lima's work was completed some fifteen years later by another officer of the *Armada*, Francisco Bordalo, at a time when promotion of the 'new Brazil' was once more in evidence in the national press. There were even newspapers that called for at least one article a week (and promised to publish it), in order to convince doubters of the advantages of the African possessions.[42]

To sum up, despite certain nuances, optimistic arguments concerning the potential for colonial development were very common in nineteenth-century Portugal. However, we must avoid a hypnotic fascination with the constant singing of Africa's praises because, alongside it, the press continued to argue in favour of Brazil—the 'land of hope'[43]—and, of course, of Portugal itself. We should also not forget that the promotion of an image of a potentially wealthy and easily exploitable Africa was up against many less enthusiastic views of the African continent—some of them utterly negative.

6.1.2 'The European's Grave'

The dreams of a prosperous black continent had not started in 1820. They went back at least as far as the end of the sixteenth century, but the failure of successive attempts, which often came up against apparently insurmountable obstacles, instilled a degree of pessimism as to the economic viability of the African territories.[44] More inhibiting still was the lack of faith regarding the potential for settlement, a lack of faith that had been a constant of the Portuguese presence in Africa since the beginning of the discoveries. According to João de Barros, the great sixteenth century historian, God had placed on the African coasts 'an avenging Angel with a sword of fire which brought mortal fevers', preventing the Portuguese from penetrating the continent.[45] With some variations this vision of the 'fevers' remained valid in the first half of the nineteenth century. Even though smallpox, tetanus and other illnesses had high mortality rates in Africa, the major threshing-machines of European lives were the so-called 'pernicious fevers', in other words yellow fever and malaria. The first, which is endemic both in South America and in tropical Africa, is a viral infection spread by forest mosquitoes and *Aedes aegypti*. In its most acute form, in which there is jaundice and severe subcutaneous and gastrointestinal haemorrhaging, it generally kills within five to eight days. However, as is usual with virus-borne illnesses, those who survive a first attack acquire permanent immunity. Malaria is more difficult. It is hyper-endemic in Africa, and involves outbreaks of high fever, profuse perspiration and intense shivering. Its principal causes are four types of plasmodium (protozoa) passed on to man by the female of the Anopheles mosquito. As a rule, the first attack of illness lasts a few weeks and is followed by relapses, until such time as the infection ends of its own accord. The timescale varies according to the infectious strain involved. However, even today malaria is still the most lethal tropical illness. Many of the untreated cases tend to persist, with brain and gastrointestinal complications often leading to death on the first occasion a patient is struck by the illness.

Yellow fever was only vanquished in the last third of the nineteenth century when the contagious nature of the disease was established, together with the role of the mosquito in spreading that contagion; these discoveries, and the development of suitable vaccines, made it possible to control the epidemics more effectively. As far as malaria is concerned, it was only with advances in bacteriology and after the discovery of the mechanism whereby the protozoa is passed on to man that quinine and other similar alkaloids could be used properly, whether as prophylactics or as cures.[46] These developments had a substantial impact on life expectancy in the tropics, particularly in Africa. But in the first two-thirds of the nineteenth century the situation was very different. With medicine virtually powerless to deal with tropical illness, living on the African coast was a lottery in which many did not escape. Figanière, who was in Sierra Leone in 1820 as a member of the Anglo-Portuguese mixed commission, left a description of the place and of its people in a series of twelve letters. In them he wrote about how he was constantly under attack from 'fevers' and close to death, giving thanks to the Almighty for having survived another day. For the Portuguese commissioner Sierra Leone was the 'European's grave', a hell with no chance of development where not even the Negroes could live.[47]

The picture given for Sierra Leone applied, in varying shades, to other Africas, including Portuguese Africa. At the end of the eighteenth century the image of Angola was of a region where there were many lethal illnesses—especially in the wet season, during which, as the local proverb said, 'there is plenty of food but no-one to eat it'[48]—and this image persisted throughout the nineteenth century, constantly renewed by the complaints of those who visited or lived in the colony. The image of the islands of São Tomé and Príncipe, of Guinea and even of the 'deadly' island of São Tiago, in Cape Verde, was similar.[49] And the same can be said for the east coast of Africa, which was regarded as 'more sickly' than Angola;[50] in his 'medical topography of the province of Mozambique', published in the *Annaes Maritimos e Coloniaes*, Jacques de Salis Celerina summed up his experience of nine years as chief doctor in the colony in the following sentence: 'this climate is unforgiving: sooner or later, everyone pays tribute to it'.[51] Of course, nearly all the tropics were an epidemiological threat for Europeans. Moreover, yellow fever sometimes went beyond the tropics, giving rise to serious epidemics in temperate zones. Lisbon, for example, was seriously affected in 1857. But in Africa, and perhaps because the more aggressive strains of *Plasmodium falciparum* were prevalent there, the threat was far more extensive than in other places, and produced unusual levels of mortality.[52] Data from British insurance companies on European mortality and morbidity in the tropics show that the death rate for Europeans on the African coast was some four times higher than what prevailed in India or in the Caribbean. At the beginning of the nineteenth century, mortality rates in the region of 20 per cent were common in Africa, and among recent arrivals the rate varied between 35 and 80 per cent.[53]

There are no reliable statistics to assess the overall health situation in the Portuguese colonies during the first half of the nineteenth century, but the available information shows that there were high mortality rates there as well. Bergara, who was deported to Angola in 1830, recounted in the Cortes that almost half his companions in adversity had perished during the first eight months of exile.[54] According to Tams, a doctor who visited Angola in 1841, during the rainy season one-third of white soldiers in Benguela fell victim to the 'climate', and Lopes de Lima recalled that over two years, from 1824 to 1826, fifty-two of fifty-four deportees whom he himself had transported to Benguela had perished.[55] In a plan for the military restructuring of Angola, it was asserted that, according to statistics from the Luanda and Benguela hospitals, mortality amongst European soldiers was over 50 per cent.[56] The image of 'the European's grave' was formed from this sparse but oft-repeated information.

Medicine at the time was as yet unable to associate illness with a specific biological agent, and so tended to explain it by means of false theories. There was a prevalent notion that tropical fevers were caused by a combination of factors, with special emphasis on the miasmas deriving from putrefaction of organic matter and the proximity of the swamps. The term malaria—from the Italian *mala aria*—which was already widely known in the eighteenth century, mirrors faithfully the connection that was held to exist between the air one breathed and the appearance of fevers, and Celerina, for example, thought that the first of the proximate causes of the unhealthiness of Mozambique was 'having to breathe an atmosphere infected with noxious miasmas'.[57] But that was just one explanation. Alongside it there was another that blamed the dampness of the air or bathing in the sea. Pinto de Azeredo, the prestigious Portuguese doctor, who was in Luanda at the end of the eighteenth century, thought that the mere fact of having wet feet might of itself bring on 'pernicious dysenteries'.[58] Another theory, which took its inspiration from the pathology of the humours, focused on the perspiration caused by the African heat. The perspiration was alleged to provoke a malfunction of the liver, which in turn would be debilitating for the whole organism, making it susceptible to illness.[59] Other factors that might encourage illness were excessive evacuation, a dissolute life and excess of food, alcohol or sex. Some attributed yellow fever directly to the slave trade. According to this account, the poor Negroes, packed in and shut up in their 'floating dungeons', were said to poison the air, converting each *tumbeiro* into a true bomb of 'deadly and contagious gas'.[60]

But, while there were differences over the aetiology of the fevers, their consequences were unanimously recognized and justifiably feared on account of the clear difficulty in dealing with them. In fact, there was no specific antidote for viral illnesses like yellow fever, and the only effective solution was to leave the infected areas before the contagion occurred. But malaria could be combated by means of quinquina, a name for various plants whose bark had fever-reducing properties. However, even though quinquina had been used since the middle of the seventeenth century, its utility was far from being universally acknowledged. First, some of the barks used contained few or no antimalarial alkaloids: in these cases expectations of a cure came to nothing. Secondly, quinquina was effective only against malaria, and medicine at the time, which muddled up symptom and disease, made no clear distinction between malaria and other febrile ailments, prescribing quinquina in situations where it was useless. In addition, in order to have any effect, quinquina as a prophylactic had to be taken regularly, and when used as a cure it had to be taken in large quantities—and this rarely happened. Finally, it was toxic and, if taken to excess, might have serious side-effects, like deafness and, it was said, madness. It was therefore strongly resisted by certain schools of medicine, and it was alternately popular and discredited. Pinto de Azeredo, for example, mentioned that in Angola quinquina-based treatment was avoided, on account of its 'caustic' nature. People preferred to use lemonades and other cold drinks instead.[61]

It is true that the Portuguese doctor was writing at a time when quinology was as yet undeveloped. It was only in 1820 that the most useful alkaloid in quinquina, quinine, was isolated. It began to be sold commercially a few years later, mainly in the form of sulphate. Potentially it was the first 'wonder drug', as Curtin calls it, aimed at fighting a specific disease.[62] It was extensively used by the French in Algeria in the 1830s and became common thereafter. In mid-century it began to be used intensively for treatment and even as a prophylactic. The *Pleiad* expedition in 1854 demonstrated its effectiveness: contrary to what had happened twelve years before, there was not a single loss of life among the crew, which went up the Niger.[63] Sulphate of quinine, combined with stricter health measures and with the trend to forgo aggressive or highly toxic treatments like bleeding or the use of mercury, which, in practice, helped to kill off the patient, contributed to reducing European mortality in Africa from the middle of the nineteenth century onwards.[64]

Even so, the use of sulphate of quinine did not radically change the dismal outlook for those who resided on the African coast, because the extent of its use as a cure was limited for several reasons. First, some doctors were reluctant to let go of well-established medical practices. Secondly, the quinine was underused, both as a treatment and, mainly, as a prophylactic. Finally, there was the uncertainty as to the aetiology of the fevers: let us not forget that in the 1860s Europeans were still attributing them to atmospheric pollution, and that most of their efforts at health policies involved draining the swamps or clearing the forested land.[65] The medical scenario of Angola in the 1840s is a perfect reflection of the different fortunes of quinine. The Angola *Boletim* (Bulletin) published tables every month on the numbers going through the hospitals. Sometimes these figures were accompanied by observations regarding treatments, which tended to praise the 'triumph of sulphate of quinine, administered in high doses, for the fevers of Angola' and to destroy 'the fear of a premature death which everyone thought was the most likely fate of all who set foot on those shores'.[66] But the triumphalist tone of those early days of medical euphoria was soon tempered by more cautious and despondent views. At the beginning of 1850, the 'baleful influence (…) of a changeable atmosphere', which gave rise to various diseases medicine found it difficult to keep under control, was already being mentioned, and voices began to be raised against those who had invested excessively in the new drug, giving it miraculous powers and using it indiscriminately.[67] In 1861 some health authorities were still negative in their verdict on the drug, and it was not unusual to believe that some tropical illnesses were incurable, and fatal for Europeans—because they depended on the 'climate'.[68]

In other words, in mid nineteenth century, the Portuguese colonies witnessed a crossfire of optimistic and pessimistic medical reports on the results of the new pharmacology. Behind these differences in the assessments lay, of course, the clash between two different schools of treatment. But there were also the number of cures—which varied according to the time of year—and the relative powerlessness of medicine to deal with the situation. From the summer of 1860 to the end of 1861, the army sent from Portugal to fight in north-western Angola lost around 45 per cent of its men through disease.[69] Moreover, while by that time the outlook for malaria sufferers was slightly improved, yellow fever was still incurable. As the Luanda brigade surgeon wrote in 1861, 'in this climate we know of no fever which is so discouraging'.[70]

So, despite advances in medicine, the image of unhealthiness continued to colour the imagination of all who made reference to Africa, to such an extent that it was rare for anyone to speak of the colonies without making some sort of association with the idea of 'the European's grave'. This almost inevitable association is particularly revealing in the context of the rhetoric of the enthusiasts. As a rule, those who promoted the image of a 'new Brazil' sought to downplay the unhealthiness aspect. They did this in various ways: either by denying outright the dangers of the tropical environment—'Africa doesn't kill anyone, it's those who go there who kill themselves';[71] or, if they did recognize the risk of greater or lesser epidemics, according to the region in question, by playing down their consequences;[72] or yet again, by acknowledging the full extent of the problem, but considering it solvable.[73] Nevertheless, alongside this trilogy of justifications, there was also a dual argument, which was accordingly less reassuring, among those who painted Africa in hopeful colours. At the same time as he argued in favour of potential Mozambican riches, Brigadier Marinho, for example, painted a bleak picture of the region, 'a graveyard' that everyone should 'get out of ... as soon as he could'.[74] The same sort of message permeated the fictional literature that in any way involved Africa. It was to escape the pain of an unrequited love that young Eugénio had decided to swap the mild airs of Europe 'for the arid and deadly beaches of the west coast of Africa' where he would have a strong chance of 'finding his grave'.[75] In Silva Gaio's novel *Mario*, Africa was also ambivalent: on the one hand, it was a splendid region, 'a parade of nature'; on the other hand, it was a land that 'is unforgiving of those who travel it'.[76] These dual arguments also arose in the enthusiast press. Even *O Nacional*, one of the newspapers that most keenly promoted the 'new Brazil', let slip contradictory and pessimistic views now and again: 'for Europeans to be able to develop agriculture on the coast of Africa, our government must decree a reform of the climate, [or else] they will all die, as the experience not of months but of centuries has shown'.[77]

These, then, were the different ways of dealing psychologically with the problem of 'the European's grave' within the enthusiast ideology. They all showed that there was a very thick covering of negative ideas, which alarmist news reports constantly confirmed. We should not forget that the newspapers in Portugal regularly published the lists of Europeans who had died as a result of illness overseas: the burden of these obituary columns, which, as Gomes de Castro acknowledged in 1861, was still 'on everyone's lips', enabled the sepulchral view of Africa to acquire firm roots in Portuguese culture.[78] For this reason, there were people in the Cortes who rebelled against the deportation of prisoners to the overseas possessions: 'to send condemned men to our penitentiaries in Africa, which are precisely the most barren, unhealthy and sickly places in this uncivilized part of the world, is to sacrifice them on the altars of despair and of death; ... Africa is the pit for those unfortunates! It is one vast grave, a horrible graveyard for living bodies'.[79] For the same reason, when rice-growing expanded in the valleys of the major rivers in Portugal, giving rise to strong medical opposition on account of the increase in malaria, there was a general outcry that the inhabitants did not want to see their lands transformed 'into a coast of Africa'.[80]

The sepulchral imagery might well have been behind the categorical refusal to embark on the African adventure, but, for the elites who had never been nor ever intended to go to Africa, it generally served merely to reinforce the disbelief in the 'new Brazil' and the conviction that, at best, the colonies would only be viable in the long term. How long-term was the factor that distinguished the real sceptics from those who merely withheld judgement. But, in either case, the more or less dispirited view led to the colonies being seen more as a heavy burden of inheritance than as an open door to national redemption. For all those who looked to the African colonies as an adjourned promise, they were above all the legacy of a heroic history which, as such, it would be necessary to maintain, even at the price of significant sacrifice.

6.1.3 'Remains of Our Ancient Glory'

In 1839, speaking in the Cortes, the Count of Taipa used an allegory to describe his position on the African colonies:

> When a philosopher told Queen Catherine II that the world's temperature was gradually changing, she said: I am delighted by the idea that in two hundred years' time the fields of St Petersburg will produce orange trees; likewise, I am delighted by the idea of our overseas possessions, but I very much doubt that we are going to load 100 or 200 ships of coffee at the port of Angola.

The Count did not rule out the possibility that Africa might yet yield 'much happiness to the nation' but, for that to happen, it would be necessary 'to invest large sums' and wait a century or more. 'In the meantime, the idea delights me'.[81]

Taipa's position was shared, with greater or lesser intensity, by many who did not believe in the possibility of rapidly improving the African possessions—and therefore were against tying up the sums the exchequer lacked. Tavares de Macedo was perhaps one of those who best and most often set out, both verbally and in writing, his reservations regarding the immediate exploitation of the colonies. His reservations were founded on a melancholic conception of African potential:

> In the current state of the world, what can we expect of Africa? Is it possible to raise our settlements to hitherto unknown levels of prosperity, or will they be condemned by circumstance to remain in the state of near-insignificance which they currently enjoy? It seems to us that the truth lies somewhere between these two extremes, and that the lands of Africa, despite their natural wealth, will never achieve prosperity equal to that of Europe, America or the islands of Asia which are on the same latitude. … the number of European lives sacrificed to the African climate is unfortunately well-known, as is the

> fact that it will not be possible to find a sufficient number of colonists for the labour of the various industries. It would be a criminal barbarity to try to seduce Europeans into embarking on such an unequal struggle.[82]

In other words, it was only by finding a method of civilizing blacks, who were 'climate-resistant', that 'solid industrial progress' would be possible in Portuguese African colonies.[83] This method would be appropriate because, contrary to what slave traders claimed, Africans were not naturally stupid. Nevertheless, it meant that improvement in the colonies would necessarily take a long time, because it depended on the prior civilization of the natives, a process that was waiting on the effective termination of the slave trade.

On the other hand, African development would demand financial resources that went far beyond what a sensible government might make available, and which only capitalist enterprises could command. Tavares de Macedo was not against specially favoured colonial companies; nor were most Portuguese politicians, whether they were sceptics or enthusiasts. If we exclude a few who were firmly opposed to the grant of benefits and protections to colonial entrepreneurs, most members of the government, parliamentarians and journalists, even those who theoretically hated monopolies, accepted that privileges had to be granted, provided that it was in order to look after the colonies.[84] Their differences lay merely in the level of protection deemed acceptable, not only for reasons of sovereignty but also on account of the parlous state of public finances and the potentially antagonistic interests of the various different colonies. As Tavares de Macedo said, the question was 'how far does fair and suitable protection go?'.[85] Within these limits of reasonableness, there would be no objections. Unfortunately, in the practical historical circumstances they faced at the time, it seems there were not enough capitalists interested in investing in the colonies (as we shall see in greater detail below). Despite constant challenges and promises from members of the government—'let the companies come, let them offer reasonable conditions, the government will accept them'[86]—no suitable companies came forward. In 1855 Tavares de Macedo carried out a quick review of all the projects to date, and recalled that some company promoters had lost interest, while others made promises that were so vague and greedy that they were simply unacceptable.

Investments in the colonies would therefore have to be basically state investments and, of course, they would have to be assessed on a scale where the African possessions were low down on the list, since they were not a national priority. In other words, the colonies would have to be self-sufficient and be content with some protection from the metropole, in particular with customs protection. This, for men like Tavares de Macedo, was more than enough.[87] It is true that in general the sceptics wanted investment overseas, but very limited investment, because in their opinion it was not the state's role to waste fortunes on the colonies.[88] They wanted a navy, but only one that was 'absolutely indispensable' for ensuring regular service and maintaining national dignity.[89]

In sum, while the enthusiasts thought that the 'new Brazils' would be created rapidly by transferring men and capital to the fertile lands of Africa, the reticent were relying mainly on civilized natives and a slow process that depended on the effective termination of the slave trade, the civilization of the Negroes and the meagre resources of the Portuguese state. The sceptics also thought that the problem of finding upright men would be very difficult to solve because, given the high health risks associated with residence in Africa, there were no competent and honest people willing to go overseas, unless they were extremely well paid. In actual fact, in mid-century it was still extremely difficult to find qualified people willing to transfer to the African colonies.[90] Moreover, for the sceptics, it was precisely the very unfavourable 'climate', and not, as the enthusiasts claimed, the politics of absolutist governments or the corruptibility of colonial officials, which largely accounted for the backwardness of the colonies: 'let it not be said that Brazil thrived only at the expense of our possessions'—Gomes de Castro warned in 1840—'Brazil thrived on its good climate, which responded better to the efforts of the colonists who moved there'.[91]

The sceptics thought, finally, that African wealth was in part overblown. When at the start of the 1850s the belief was disseminated that Portuguese Africa was full of copper and gold mines, Rodrigo da Fonseca continued to refuse to accept the mirage of a 'new California' and remained modest in his dreams: 'If only there were two coal mines, and good ones'.[92] Likewise, Tavares de Macedo acknowledged that Portugal might 'draw certain resources', but never 'major resources', from its colonies.[93] And Lobo de Ávila went even further: 'it is a serious economic error to say that the whole future of our country lies in the colonies .... I contest the exclusive and exaggerated principle that the future of the country lies wholly in our colonies. It does not. It lies in the development of its internal production'.[94]

The more modest outlook on the extent of African wealth was confirmed by some of the new colonial press. The Cape Verde *Boletim* (Bulletin), which started publication in 1842, helped to establish an image that was rather like the reverse of the enthusiast view. In its pages, the islands of the archipelago were portrayed as arid and rocky places that were regularly ravaged by hunger, and where successive efforts to develop agriculture failed on account of the lack of rain and the high winds. The mineral wealth that some of the enthusiasts imagined to exist under the ground of Cape Verde was nothing more than the 'fruits of Aladdin's enchanted forest'.[95] It should be noted that the sceptical point of view came not only from the Cape Verde *Boletim*, but also from newspapers in Portugal when they printed the dispirited reports by their correspondents in the colonies.[96]

Among those who turned up their noses at the African mirage, there were naturally differing degrees of reticence, which changed in the course of time both in the light of the results of successive experiences and also of the ideas that each person had of the African. Those with a very negative view, like Saldanha da Gama, were very reticent about African prospects. The ex-governor of Angola had been one of the pioneers of the African idea and, as we should recall, had written a *Memória* (Memoir) in 1814 containing various suggestions for the development of the colonies. This work was published towards the end of the 1830s, after the author had revised it and added new material: by now he was frankly doubtful as to the possibility of civilizing Africa:

> We've been there for several centuries and yet the people who deal and are in contact with us are in a state which is little different to that which existed when we first landed on those shores. Where are the brilliant results which were anticipated from the American philanthropists' celebrated Liberia? People with as few needs as those of the majority of the black nations of Africa, are resistant to civilization.[97]

In line with his new scepticism regarding Africa's improvement, Saldanha da Gama decided to supplement the *Memória* with a preliminary essay—which was as long as the *Memória* itself—where he dealt with the problems of the development of Portugal. For him the right way of lifting the Portuguese people out of the sad state they were in could be summed up in two words: industry and roads (the latter being possibly the country's most urgent need).[98]

Given this state of affairs, what then was the ultimate worth of the African possessions for those who were not among the enthusiasts, regardless of how sceptical or reticent they were? As Saldanha da Gama himself stressed, it was a value that could be measured in eminently historical and patrimonial terms. The colonies were a physical and moral inheritance, 'the remains of our ancient glory ... which humiliate us in our smallness and are an insult to our present-day indolence'.[99] As such, they should be preserved, even at the cost of great sacrifice. But Portugal would have to face up to the smallness of its inherent strength and to the fact that it should revise its old imperial plans. The nation had nothing to gain in running after chimeras, in allowing itself to be seduced by the fiery but momentary feelings of past heroism. The Portuguese of the nineteenth century were no longer the heroes of old: 'the springs of their souls were too slack and too rotten for great things'.[100]

All those in the reticent camp saw the colonies, above all, as respectable 'remains of our national glory'.[101] Naturally we find this approach in Tavares de Macedo, for whom the question of the colonies could never be viewed simply from the profit-and-loss angle:

> The place in the history of the world which the ... Portuguese acquired as a result of their discoveries is so beautiful in our eyes, and so envied by foreigners, that the very first way in which any Portuguese looks at our overseas establishments is as an inheritance from our forebears ... So the economic

side, which in other circumstances should be the main aspect of this question, is for us something secondary and subordinated to the other, which is of a higher nature.[102]

In addition to Tavares de Macedo and Saldanha da Gama, several other public figures proclaimed the need to preserve the colonies, mainly for historical reasons, so that, as Alexandre Herculano said, the ghosts of the ancient Portuguese knights should not shout out from distant shores: 'what did you do with the legacy of glory which we left you? What did you do to the edifice which we erected, and which we sweated for with our own blood?'[103] For the sceptics, the colonies were untouchable not because they were profitable, or because it was expected that they would be profitable in the short term, nor yet because they were a 'sheet anchor', but because they were full of history. That was why Lopes de Lima was heavily criticized when he sold a part of the province of Timor to the Dutch. In the words of the deputy Rodrigues Cordeiro, 'he sold up, without taking into account the blood spilled and the exploits performed there by our ancestors'.[104]

Most of those in the sceptical camp who expressed an opinion on the African question saw the colonies, basically, as a remnant of past glory. Of course, they were also the 'remains of ancient glory' for the enthusiasts. There was an area of common ground between the enthusiast and sceptical approaches which made possible a certain shifting of positions from one side of the ideological spectrum to the other, for both personal and political reasons. As an overseas deputy, Fontes Pereira de Melo was an enthusiast; as a member of the government, he tended to be sceptical. But, if we stand back from the personal or party political shifts, if we concentrate on typical speeches and on rhetorical profiles, we can see that, despite the fact that they both wanted the colonies to be a sacred legacy and a potential source of wealth at the same time, the sceptics placed the emphasis on the former aspect while the enthusiasts placed it on the latter. The sceptics wanted to keep the colonies in the best way possible, even if great sacrifice was involved. The enthusiasts, who opposed the resignation and idleness that were taking hold of the country, wanted to invest heavily in them, so as to bring them up to a level of importance and make them the 'sheet anchor' of national salvation;[105] however, for them, as opposed to the sceptics, the colonies were not untouchable and, if the worst came to the worst, they were not averse to selling some of them so as better to take advantage of those which remained. Lopes de Lima was one of the enthusiasts who first argued for this rationalist policy (and implemented it). In the last third of the nineteenth century it was to find greater acceptance and become more widespread.[106]

There were accordingly various approaches to Africa, which, although different, partially overlapped. In their most authentic definitions, the images of the 'new Brazil' and 'the European's grave' were incompatible. But either one of them might converge with the idea of preserving the country's historic heritage. Two distinct attitudes to the colonies emerged from this interplay of opposing and overlapping views: the first was essentially optimistic and voluntarist; the second was dispirited or expectant. Contrary to what the historians of Marxist inspiration claim, there was no near unanimity as far as colonial planning was concerned. At the very least, there were two different plans for the colonies that did not necessarily converge, one of them being basically a plan that focused on the metropole and allocated a very secondary role to the colonies.

We now need to try to identify the relative importance of each of these plans in Portugal from 1820 to 1865. To understand that importance it is not sufficient simply to count the number of opinions expressed. If we could do it in this way, the problem of deciding which plan was most important would be solved forthwith, since the optimistic argument is more frequently found than the pessimist one, both in the newspapers and in other forms of public statements. The verbal comparison is not the only one to be made, however, because the nature of the statements and the channels adopted by the two ideologies are different. Differing behaviours corresponded to each of the views in question. The enthusiasts were active. They sought to make a public impact with their proposals and to motivate people. The sceptics, on the other hand, were passive, discrete and ambiguous, and would only clarify their position when pressed. This reflects once again, but in another context, the problem of silence, which I emphasized earlier in connection with the abolition of the slave trade. For these reasons, a comparison of the specific importance of each of the views of Africa within Portuguese society has to be made principally on the basis of acts and omissions, achievements and opposition to achievements. This takes us directly to the question of practical plans and initiatives for the colonies in the period under review.

6.2 Failed Colonial Plans

This analysis of colonial plans in the period from 1820 to 1865 serves two purposes. On the one hand, it makes it possible to assess the extent to which enthusiast ideas had mobilizing force and sceptical approaches generated inertia. Regardless of the practical results—it is not always the case that faith moves mountains—what I shall seek to do here is to consider the plans that were actually proposed, with or without success. On the other hand, this task is also an opportunity to question how solid an empirical foundation the Marxist historians have for arguing that the ruling classes had a profound interest in Africa. These two purposes demand that we survey and assess the various economic plans that arose in this period. It is a task that has never been carried out in full, either by those who argue for the importance of the interests at stake or by those who doubt it.

6.2.1 *Neither Capital…*

The idea of forming companies to exploit Africa's wealth emerged as early as the 1820s and sometimes came to the attention of the Cortes. At the beginning of October 1822, the deputy Bento do Carmo put forward a suggestion that two trading companies should be developed, one for West Africa and the other for Mozambique and Asia, and requested monopolies for them in various domains.[107] The reports submitted to the Cortes on the state of the colonies also suggested that companies should be formed, one for the fisheries of Cape Verde and another for Mozambique, if the merchants of Lisbon who were traditionally tied to Asian trade were to show an interest in those companies being set up.[108] Later on, in 1828, Lima Leitão argued for a most ambitious project: he sought permission for the formation of a Companhia de Entre-os-Trópicos (Intertropical Company), reserved exclusively for Portuguese shareholders and which should be granted exemption from duties as well as the exclusive right to all colonial trade (except for that of Macao) for a period of 20 years. Lima Leitão's intention was that, as soon as twelve leading businessmen had come forward and expressed an interest in investing in the said company, the government should bring together their suggestions and submit them to the Cortes, so that the Cortes might draw up and approve the future company's articles of association.[109] But his proposal was not discussed before the end of the Parliament, and came to nothing.

These proposals seem to be examples of the voluntarism of some Members of Parliament, but they do not enable us to conclude that there were any clear and strong underlying economic interests involved, and that they did not go ahead only on account of external factors. On the contrary, the available data show that businessmen in Portugal were not much interested in Africa. It should also be mentioned that, in the first place, many of the projects were trial balloons, which it was hoped would fill up once launched. It is significant that the law establishing the Cape Verde fisheries company, the most modest of all these projects, was effectively approved by the Cortes in 1822, despite the fact that, as was said at the time, there were serious doubts whether there was even one individual in Portugal willing to take care of the business.[110] Secondly, at those times when the Cortes were suspended, there was no rush to Africa. In actual fact, at that time it was only very rarely that intentions were transformed into action, and this never occurred spontaneously, consistently or successfully. In 1824–25, following pressure from the government, which foresaw the end of the slave trade, a small group of Lisbon manufacturers and merchants sent some products from Portugal to Angola—alcohols, gunpowder, linen—but the results of the speculation were disappointing. One of the exporters, João Paulo Cordeiro, was allowed to establish a factory in Angola, but very little business passed through it. It only survived by means of 'extravagant privileges', closing down when Cordeiro went bankrupt.[111] In 1825 Vicente Tomás dos Santos obtained from the monarchy the exclusive rights to all trade in the bay of Lourenço Marques, together with the usual exemptions from payment of import and export duties. However, his company never fulfilled its contractual obligations. It took advantage of its exclusive rights to engage in the slave trade, and ended up being closed down in 1834, after a series of ups and downs and complaints.[112]

As had occurred in the 1820s, a number of projects for setting up companies to exploit the African colonies emerged during the period from 1834 to 1850, but they all failed, rarely going beyond the paper they were written on.

The most ambitious of these was the project of the Associação Mercantil Lisbonense (Lisbon Merchants' Association), a businessmen's and manufacturers' organization set up in mid-1834 by the deputy and industrialist José Ferreira Pinto Basto.[113] From the outset the Associação demanded measures in favour of trade and industry and promoted the formation of companies: for the silk trade, for fisheries and one insurance company. In addition to these initiatives, which did come to fruition, the Associação also envisaged forming a Companhia Africana (African Company). The draft provided for the establishment of a company having its head office in Lisbon, open to both Portuguese and foreign shareholders, the objective of which would be trade, agriculture and the mining of all Portuguese Africa. It was hoped that the state would be able to grant tax exemptions, significant concessions such as ownership rights to all the forests and unfarmed lands in the colonies, and also the right to trade directly with foreign ships in African ports (this meant that its business would largely avoid taxation). In return, the projected Companhia Africana would undertake merely to transport some colonists or convicts to Africa free of charge and to hand back to the state, at the end of the concession period of twenty years, the lands it had exploited together with all improvements carried out thereon.[114]

The project was submitted to the government at the beginning of 1836 and Sá da Bandeira, Minister of the Navy at the time, assured the Associação of his support for 'any and every company' that it might propose for the improvement of the overseas possessions.[115] But the undertaking was never approved in the form submitted. Unfortunately that was the only form which the Associação Mercantil Lisbonense wanted, and it turned down an invitation from Sá to take part in less greedy projects—in particular one to set up an agricultural company on Cape Verde.[116]

Since no share capital was ever subscribed, there are no objective data on the extent to which the projected Companhia Africana might have succeeded in attracting the interest of Portuguese capitalists, but the story of the project itself suggests a low level of interest. The members of the Associação who studied the matter in 1835 argued that the project terms should first be submitted to the public for consideration. Only after approval had been obtained in the form of applications for the shares should the company go forward with a request for concessions from the government.[117] The strategy actually adopted was the reverse, the promoters having preferred the state option, which suggests there was little confidence in the colonial enthusiasm of Portuguese investors. Moreover, already in mid-1835 the scheme's promoters had been warned that capitalists in Portugal would not be willing to invest in an African company.[118] For this reason the project, which provided for a share capital of 4,000 *contos*, was also open to foreigners. While this increased the chances of successful fund-raising, it also implied a risk of placing the African colonies under the guardianship of forces and interests outside Portugal. Furthermore, while other projects of the Associação, such as those involving silk and insurance, for example, were enthusiastically received, the projected Companhia Africana made very hesitant progress, on occasion because of delays and carelessness on the part of members of the Associação themselves.[119] This presumed lack of enthusiasm may be due, amongst other things, to the persistence of the 'iniquitous commerce'. The promoter of the African project had worked on the principle that the slave trade had ceased with the entry into force of the Anglo-Brazilian abolition treaty in 1830, whereby agriculture, mining and industry would become possible in Africa.[120] The following months showed how ill-founded such a presumption had been. The idea began to run out of steam, and was finally frozen in 1839.

Portuguese financiers' very likely lack of interest in the African undertaking of the Associação Mercantil Lisbonense is confirmed by other aborted initiatives, which, in certain cases, help to clarify the level of support such projects had at the time. In mid-1837 the articles of a Companhia de Africa Ocidental (West Africa Company) appeared. In July the Associação Mercantil Lisbonense, which operated as a consultative organ of the government, was asked to give an official opinion on the formation of this company: it took almost a year to do so. But, even though the opinion was not a negative one, the company never went ahead.[121] In 1844, Pinto Basto Júnior, son of the founder of the Associação Mercantil Lisbonense, who had in the meantime died, emerged as the promoter of a trading company for southern Angola. He asked for a thirty-year monopoly of trade in salt, orchil dye lichen and all animal substances produced in the territory south of Moçâmedes. He undertook to set up at least three trading posts in the region.[122] But nothing came of this proposal, on which, moreover, the Associação Marítima e Colonial (Maritime and Colonial Association) had given a negative opinion.[123]

The clearest sign of Portuguese financiers' lack of interest in African undertakings came, albeit involuntarily, from the same Associação Marítima e Colonial, an organization which had been formed in Lisbon in 1839 for the purpose of promoting the development of the navy and of the colonies. Its membership included many figures from the Portuguese elites.[124] In its zeal for the overseas provinces, the Associação also tried to encourage the formation of colonial companies. But the project was abandoned for lack of interest or lack of commitment on the part of the members, who did not turn up in sufficient numbers to the session of 18 March 1844, where the subject was to be discussed, and they never again placed the topic on the agenda.[125]

Similar conclusions can be drawn from the initiatives of Jacinto Dias Damásio. At the beginning of 1843, Damásio, who said that he had the personal backing of the Count of Farrobo, went ahead with a proposal to set up a Companhia Africana Portuguesa (Portuguese African Company). This was once again a project to take care of all the African colonies. Its promoters aimed to set up a company that would achieve 'in a few years' what Portugal had not been able to do in four centuries. The share capital was to be 2,400 *contos* and, alongside various fifty-year monopolies, the company was to have the right to choose magistrates as well as civil and military governors for each colony. Having set up a committee to express an opinion on the project, since some of the conditions requested were unacceptable, the government put forward a counter-proposal on terms that were recognized as being advantageous. Despite the fact that the points of disagreement were few, the company turned down the government's counter-proposal because, as Tavares de Macedo would later recall, 'it only wanted what it had imagined'.[126] Damásio would reappear in 1848 with a proposal submitted to the ephemeral Liga Promotora dos Interesses Materiais do País (League for the Promotion of the Country's Material Interests). Putting the failure of his earlier venture down to unspecified 'circumstances', he now wished to set up a less ambitious company, with a capital of 600 *contos* which, amongst other things, would promote wine exports to Africa. But, as with the earlier plan, nothing came of it.[127]

To close this overview of Portuguese intentions of exploiting the colonies in the period before 1850 we should mention the case of the planned Companhia dos Vinhos da Estremadura (Estremadura Wine Company), the express purposes of which included 'tapping copious sources of wealth and prosperity in the Overseas Provinces'.[128] However, this was a marginal objective, which, by evoking a phraseology aimed at dampening political objections, sought to obtain, amongst other things, privileges and monopolies for the introduction and sale of wine, brandies and vinegars into the colonies. The openly conceded central purpose of the plan was to help the owners and farmers of the Lisbon region, who were threatened with financial collapse. Precisely because it involved a variety of elements and motivations, the attempt to set up a Companhia de Vinhos da Estremadura is not a good gauge of the interest of the Portuguese bourgeoisie in African undertakings—just as the similar, contemporaneous plan for a Companhia dos Vinhos do Alto Douro (Upper Douro Wine Company), which also wanted favourable terms and monopolies for introducing wine and spirits overseas, also does not serve this purpose.[129] It is significant in this context that, while Farrobo was initially appointed to the committee that was canvassing subscribers for the

Companhia de Vinhos da Estremadura, he immediately requested (and obtained) dispensation. It is also significant that in a second plan for the company, drafted at the beginning of 1843 by a new committee, of which Farrobo was now indeed part, the colonial phraseology and even any idea of exploiting colonial markets were completely absent.[130]

In theory, from 1850 onwards, the combined effect of the end of the slave trade to Brazil and of the *Regeneração* should have created circumstances favourable to investing in Africa if such a wish to invest had been widespread in the country as a whole. Portuguese capitalists' and merchants' lack of interest in Africa until then was often put down to the political agitation, which lasted until the mid nineteenth century. For this reason the *Diário do Governo* was convinced that, since the country was now living 'under the shadow of order and liberty', the nation would provide the funds to enable colonial development to go ahead.[131] The hope thus founded on political grounds was reinforced by financial reasons, because at the same time, as we have seen in chapter 5, substantial capital was flowing into the kingdom as a result of the return of many Portuguese who had resided in Africa and especially in Brazil. In the 1830s the fight against the slave trade, Palmerston's bill and other reasons had led some slavers to give up the southern hemisphere and move to Europe. This migration proceeded to such an extent that in 1846 the *Revista Económica* (Economic Review) was stressing the crucial significance for the Portuguese economy of the 'large sums' that were coming from Brazil, belonging to merchants who were moving permanently to Portugal.[132] Later, at the beginning of the 1850s, factors such as yellow fever and the final assault on the Brazilian slave trade brought about a sharp increase in this returning migration. In mid-1851 Palmerston, echoing information received through diplomatic channels, assured Parliament that some 140 slavers resident in Brazil had returned to Portugal, bringing their fortunes with them, and that a Lisbon bank had taken in a deposit of one million two hundred thousand pounds sterling.[133] As Palmerston said, many of those coming back or investing were well-known slavers, some of them extremely rich, such as Manuel Pinto da Fonseca, who was perhaps the largest slave trafficker in the 1840s, José António de Sousa Basto and José Bernardino de Sá. But the key point to note is that, whether they had been converted voluntarily or by force, whether they were ennobled or not, these people put their money into industry, land, banking, trade and the public debt, and only rarely into Africa.

This means that, despite the end of the Brazilian slave trade, internal pacification and the influx of capital into the kingdom, the Portuguese capitalist's relationship to the African colonies did not substantially change, even if, for a time, a major colonial project for Mozambique managed to raise some hopes in this regard. But it was a false alarm once again. The project in question was submitted to the government in 1853 by noted figures in Portuguese society (including Pinto Basto Júnior). The signatories of the proposal sought to set up a company to be called Companhia Luso-Africana Oriental (Portuguese East African Company) to administer and exploit the whole of Portuguese East Africa. They requested from the state, amongst other dispensations, ownership and administration rights to those territories for a period of ninety-nine years, during which the Cortes would have no legislative power over them; the right to have land and naval forces, to be paid for by the Exchequer; the right to establish customs posts, levy taxes and mint coin; the right to appoint and dismiss nearly all provincial employees (including churchmen and commanders of military forces); tax exemption for longer or shorter periods of time; their own exclusive courts, for all cases; and, what is more, the possibility of subcontracting to other bodies the concessions and privileges to be obtained from the Crown. For their part, they were willing to do almost everything: abolish the slave trade, civilize the Kaffirs, expel Negro invaders and lay claim to territories usurped by them, to open up roads, unblock rivers, found settlements, cut down forests, drain swamps, cultivate the land, promote the establishment of colonies, build and repair churches, set up schools and maintain ships for coastal trade and for trade with Portugal.[134]

The Conselho Ultramarino was called upon to express its opinion. It concluded that the project was equivalent to a genuine transfer of sovereignty, and as such should be turned down. But in its considerations the Conselho also drew attention to the vague and dangerous nature of the proposal, which offered no guarantees, such as subscription of capital by way of a share issue. The request for subcontracting rights was an open door to possible speculation, because there would be nothing to stop the formation of a ghost company, which would simply sell the concessions obtained. In addition to these objections, the Conselho stressed the megalomaniac and suicidal nature of the project. If authorized, it would rapidly lead potential investors to financial ruin. Accordingly, the majority of the counsellors suggested that the promoters' enthusiasm for colonial adventures should be channelled into other, more limited and more advantageous initiatives, such as the formation of various sectoral companies.[135] Counsellor Almeida Garrett went further along this path of instruction and drew up the general lines of what might be agreed with the company. In his outline he substantially reduced the privileges granted, even though they remained extensive. In 1854 some working meetings took place to reconcile the claims of each side, government and capitalists. The project was briefly discussed in the Cortes. But it never came to fruition,[136] just like other more modest proposals to exploit the districts of Sofala, Quelimane and Tete, submitted in 1858 by the ever-present Pinto Basto Júnior, and a project put forward by the Frenchman Alfred de Courson and deputy Afonseca for setting up a company to build a railway in Angola (and to establish small colonial settlements along the line).[137] One project did go ahead, to form a shipping company called União Mercantil (Mercantile Union), which lasted for a few years.

But, despite the fact it went ahead, or precisely because it did go ahead with special favours and subsidies, this company's story shows not that Portuguese investors wanted to invest in colonial projects, but rather that there was a profound lack of interest on the part of the Lisbon and Oporto marketplace in this type of undertaking.

The establishment of regular shipping lines between Portugal and its colonies had for a long time been one of the main concerns of the enthusiasts. With the development of North American and British steamship companies in mid-century, that concern would grow, on grounds of pure self-defence. In mid-1850 already, alarmed at the entry of foreign shipping into maritime routes that had traditionally been Portuguese, four prominent citizens asked the Chamber of Deputies to encourage the formation of a national company that might compete with its foreign rivals. Moving from words to action, two of the applicants submitted a plan for the formation of a steamship company to operate to and from Brazil, the adjacent islands and West Africa. At the same time they appealed to the Lisbon and Oporto merchants to lend assistance to the plan, because the whole country's survival would depend on it.[138] Two years later a joint Brazilian and Portuguese stock company would effectively be formed, but only for a steamship line to Brazil.[139] As far as Africa was concerned, the situation was much more difficult. This is hardly surprising, given the essentially political nature of the plan. In commercial terms this was a hasty step, as was emphasized in a report in early 1851 submitted by, amongst others, Pinto Basto Júnior. The authors of that document thought it 'premature' to set up a colonial shipping company before there was a rail link to Spain and a major colonial company had been formed: 'to set up extensive means of communication and transport between countries which are remote from each other … before there is anything to trade or exchange, and before commercial relationships and habits have been formed, is to reverse the order and natural sequence of things'; and, because there was such a natural sequence, the committee thought that the African initiative should be relegated to a lower level. It would be better to set up the rail company, because it would have 'a more immediate and direct influence on the agricultural, industrial and commercial prosperity of the kingdom'.[140]

Even though the plan was inopportune, the government persisted in its eagerness to take a steamship line to Africa. A contract with Bernex Philippon (representing Portuguese and foreign investors) was signed in 1856, and was later assigned to the Companhia Real Portuguesa de Navegação a Vapor (Royal Portuguese Steamship Company), which never got off the ground.[141] It was only at the end of the 1850s that the government was finally able to persuade four Portuguese traders, associated with a dozen foreigners, including the Brazilian slave trader Francisco António Flores, to form the Companhia União Mercantil (Union Mercantile Company). Initially aimed at running a steamship service to the Azores and West Africa, the company would also, at a later date, take on shipping to the Algarve. In order to carry out the African part of its operations, the União Mercantil relied on state financial support: apart from an initial grant, it would give the company annual subsidies of 58 *contos* for the whole period of exclusivity (twenty years).[142]

The company started to operate without having obtained the capital required to do so, which obliged it to resort to massive bank borrowing. The management tried to obtain subscribers in Spain and Britain, but without success. In 1860, after two years of effort, the União Mercantil had only sixteen shareholders (of whom more than half were foreigners) and the same share capital it had started out with.[143] In 1861, in an attempt to attract investors and avoid the company going bankrupt, the government and the Cortes accepted an additional contract whereby shareholders were assured a minimum return of 6 per cent on capital. But the results were disappointing: only 55 *contos*.[144] This and other lifeboats allowed the company to carry on for a while, but its situation hardly improved. This was irrefutable proof of 'public indifference' or of what Mendes Leal called the 'ancient and persistent insensitivity of capital'.[145] Some enthusiasts, like Soares Franco, for example, expressed amazement at the complete lack of support from the Portuguese, particularly those who dealt with Africa, for the Companhia União Mercantil.[146] In fact, the main businessmen in Lisbon were willing to invest in a steamship company for the Azores and even for the Algarve, but not for Africa or for the three destinations together.[147]

Despite the favours obtained, the União Mercantil was unable to raise the required capital, and got ever deeper into debt. In mid-1864, with all patience and means of support exhausted, the government closed it down, and immediately opened a more favourably structured tender for the establishment of a new company. But, since no applicants emerged, it ended up contracting directly with Bailey & Leetham, of Hull, a firm which from then on supplied the steamship links with the colonies.[148]

In 1859 a tender was issued for the construction of a railway between Luanda and Cambambe, and a company was even formed for this purpose (which was also to supply a steamship service on the River Cuanza). But the railway was never started, and it was only on 10 June 1865 that a contract would be signed with a Portuguese-American, Archer da Silva, to set up the steamship service on the Cuanza. In the following year Archer assigned that contract to a joint British and North American company established in London.[149]

It was not until the end of the period that interests us here that the Portuguese bourgeoisie gave tangible proof of their intention to risk investing in Africa. As Mendes Leal emphasized, capital seemed 'desirous of rushing overseas *now*, when until now it had been so remiss'.[150] The object of the sudden interest was the formation of the Banco Nacional Ultramarino (National Overseas Bank), set up at the government's insistence in 1864. This was a tax-exempt bank, to which the state granted an annual subsidy of 30 *contos* and which was to operate in Portugal itself and overseas (where it had exclusive banking rights, except in Macao). The initial share capital was to be 4,000 *contos*, but it was envisaged that the bank could start operating as soon as it had obtained a fund of 800 *contos*. In actual fact that sum was not achieved, and Banco Nacional Ultramarino only began operating because a government decree allowed it to do so with only 500 *contos*.[151]

Alongside plans to form colonial companies, which were nothing more than episodes of déjà vu, the prolonging of unfulfilled dreams that had appeared regularly since the beginning of the century, some more modest attempts to develop trade emerged, generally through individual initiative. In 1841, Ribeiro dos Santos organized a trade expedition to Angola: this expedition was a disaster, on account of the illness and death of several of its members (including Ribeiro dos Santos himself).[152] There were at this time a number of trading houses in Lisbon involved in exchanges with Cape Verde and Angola. In the following decades two or three traders also sent their own ships to the east coast of Africa.[153] The Lisbon trading houses involved with Africa were more than 'half a dozen businessmen', as Dias Damásio deprecatingly described them, although they did not exactly amount to the 'enthusiasm for trade' stated, in contrast, by Lopes de Lima. Nevertheless, they did end up being partially responsible for the increase in colonial trade that took place in mid-century.[154] Of course, this increase was far less than that hoped for by those who foresaw that Africa would soon take over from Brazil. In effect, the African trade remained a very small part of total Portuguese trade. At the beginning of the 1840s it represented less than 1 per cent of the total, rising in the 1850s and remaining for many years at around 3–4 per cent. In other words, despite its slow decline, the volume of Brazilian trade, with a percentage of around 12–15 per cent of the total, remained far more significant than the African trade.[155]

There were also some agricultural ambitions. In the late 1830s and early 1840s there were some applications for land grants in the colonies. Rio Tinto (owner of *O Nacional*), José Ribeiro dos Santos and several others applied for and obtained unused lands on the islands of Cape Verde to set up rural and trading establishments there.[156] For a time it was thought that significant capital flows might come into Cape Verde and that these would give agriculture there a considerable boost; but investors from Portugal ended up going elsewhere, and these hopes came to nothing. At around the same time, some businessmen obtained grants of some land in Angola, but here too the results were meagre. The policy of land grants turned out not to be what the state needed in order to get the Portuguese interested in their African colonies. In the mid-1840s, the 'indefatigable farmer' João Pereira Barbosa, who had swapped Brazil for Angola ten years earlier to grow coffee there, was perhaps the only agricultural success story in the colony (for which he was honoured by the Queen).[157] Even so his success was only relative, as he himself recognized: 'Africa is always Africa, and one cannot compare its products with the great gains to be made in America'.[158] Thus, by mid-century, as the then governor of Angola described in a confidential dispatch to the Minister of the Navy, Angolan agriculture was a complete failure:

> Many recommendations are repeatedly made regarding the increase in agriculture, and it would indeed be our salvation; but what has been achieved? Nothing, or practically nothing …; where then is the capital, and where are those white men who want to retreat to the wilderness with the certainty that they will come across dangerous diseases and no means of treating them?[159]

Despite the poor results, the policy of giving land grants was taken up again in following years. In 1854 and 1855 there were a few applications for lands in Cape Verde.[160] But it was in Angola and São Tomé and Príncipe that there was a clear increase in the plantation economy when the slave trade to Brazil came to an end. Some Brazilians and Portuguese were attracted by the low price of labour in Africa at a time when that price was rising in Brazil, so they crossed the Atlantic to take advantage of the situation in Angola. In the 1850s sugar cane plantations began to appear on the coast. There was also a rush for land in the interior to plant coffee, to such an extent that in 1855 there were 321 growers in the district of Cazengo (as against only thirty-six in the preceding year), and that number rose to over a thousand in 1856.[161] However, it was mostly Africans who sought to obtain demarcation and official recognition of their land rights, in response to the recent measures of the colonial government.[162]

In 1856 the Lisbon government enacted a law governing the disposal of unused lands overseas. This was aimed, as Sá da Bandeira admitted, at attracting Portuguese and, especially foreign investors. But these were false hopes (not shared by the sceptics), and despite the fact that foreign investors did make some applications for land, nothing came of it.[163]

At the end of 1861, seeking to take advantage of the cotton crisis that had arisen as a result of the American civil war, the government was willing to make land grants in Angola and Mozambique (and later on in Cape Verde and in India too) on even more favourable terms. Financial incentives were established for the best producers, and duty exemptions were granted on the export of cotton and the import of materials, machinery and tools required for growing and building the plantations. In return, those who received concessions undertook to begin exploiting the lands granted to them within a maximum period of five years, after which the concession would end.[164] The attractive terms drew in a dozen potential investors, who were given large—sometimes very large—tracts of land, and who undertook in exchange to set up agricultural companies with generous funds.[165] Unfortunately, the optimistic expectations did not come to fruition and, as a rule, these major concessions were completely useless, the contracts lapsing with no benefit.[166] Some contracts were signed at the local level, under a law of 1861 that allowed colonial governors to make land concessions up to 1,000 hectares, but these were much more modest undertakings that held out little prospect of the boom in production that had been expected for so long—even though they did lead to a significant rise in cotton production between 1861 and 1865.[167]

Ironically, colonial development policy, which should have sustained gradual abolition, seemed to depend above all on local entrepreneurs, prominent among whom were slavers or former slavers. It was they who had the greatest interest in developing agricultural and trading businesses in the colonies so as in some way to attempt to adjust to the serious threat to their existing business. There follows an account of several schemes mainly promoted by slavers from the colonies. They shed light not only on how such promotion took place, but also on the detachment of the capitalists at home.

At the end of 1822 the deputy for Cape Verde, Manuel António Martins, submitted a plan to set up a company for Cape Verde and Guinea, for which he requested exclusive rights for twenty years, but the proposal came to nothing.[168] Some years later, with government support, he tried to establish a fisheries company in Cape Verde; he invested some money, supplied ships, nets and fish-hooks and built a warehouse, but the scheme failed for lack of interest on the part of the locals, who 'preferred vagrancy and poverty to work and plenty'.[169] In 1831, Martins again took up an idea he had had earlier: together with three of the Lisbon merchants who had then applied for grants of land in Cape Verde, he planned to set up a Companhia de Guiné (Guinea Company), the articles of which were approved by the government in May 1839. The share capital was to be 800 *contos* and the company would be charged with running all state establishments in Guinea. It would be entitled to expand and fortify them. It was granted a monopoly on importing and exporting and duty exemption for a period of ten years. In return, the company was required to encourage missionary activity and promote settlement.[170] However, the scheme never went ahead, despite Martins's renewed efforts to revive it in 1843, when he asked the government to approve new articles.[171] But it went no further, because the shareholders themselves decided that it was not worth their while.[172] Martins died in 1845 and the matter was shelved.

The Companhia de Agricultura e Indústria de Angola e Benguela (Angola and Benguela Agricultural and Industrial Company) was set up in Luanda in 1836, at the instigation of the then governor, Oliveira Daun, brother of the Marquis of Saldanha. In the letter he wrote to his brother, Daun asked him to subscribe to 'a few shares' because the Angolan initiative had been launched only with local investors, who had not been able to raise more than 30 *contos*.[173] In order to raise the rest of the share capital envisaged (80 *contos*), the company's directors were relying on attracting investors from Portugal itself. For this purpose they secured the sponsorship of the Associação Mercantil Lisbonense, which had an advertisement on the formation of the Angolan company published in two of the major Portuguese newspapers, in the hope that businessmen in the kingdom would buy the rest of the shares.[174] The company received the Lisbon government's approval, but it was unable to obtain sufficient capital funding. It ceased trading not only because Daun died (of 'fevers'), but also because the local shareholders continued to opt for the more profitable slave trade.

A similar project emerged in Mozambique, also encouraged by the governor. It even obtained the sponsorship of Sá da Bandeira himself. The project, which required capital of some 200 *contos*, was submitted to the Cortes through the Ministry of the Navy, so that they might approve it 'promptly'.[175] But, as they took too long to do so, the government approved the company's articles by decree on 13 May 1840.[176] However, the project was a failure—and in this case an absolute disaster, as not one investor came forward to buy shares, either in Portugal itself or in the Indian colonies.[177] The resounding failure of the planned Mozambique Company was used by the Associação Mercantil Lisbonense to draw up a dispirited assessment of what might be expected with the formation of trading companies for the colonies: 'to establish a Company in this capital city today is to believe in an illusion, ... especially in such distant parts. Two years ago the articles of an already established Agricultural Company (of Mozambique) appeared here; everything seemed advantageous; public invitations were issued; nobody invested!'[178]

This pattern of initiatives starting out in the colonies and attracting no interest in Portugal would be maintained in subsequent years. Sometimes the initiative was purely African, with the colonial governors trying to attract local capital for legitimate businesses. At other times the initiatives were private undertakings by investors generally involved in the slave trade, and were aimed at European investors. This was the case of Arsénio Pompílio Pompeu de Carpo, who, in 1848, nursed a plan to form a company that would exploit a railway and a steam-driven sawmill in the Cuanza valley. The share capital envisaged was 150 *contos* and the plan, which was dressed up in humanitarian garb, appealing to 'true philanthropists' to buy shares 'in order to improve the lot of the blacks of Africa', promised a return of 10 per cent per annum.[179] But, even though he had credible agents abroad and in Lisbon who were entrusted with canvassing shareholders, the plan did not generate the necessary interest.

The slave traders' projects were open as much to trade as to agriculture and mining. In the latter part of the 1830s, Caetano José Nosolini and his African wife, Aurélia Correia, who were involved in the slave trade until the 1840s, tried to develop plantations in the western part of the island of Bulama.[180] They were probably the first people to grow peanuts for export. However, this was an ambiguous undertaking and may have been just a cover for the continuation of the slave trade since, as was common practice at the time, slaves who worked on plantations could be exported at any time. In December 1838, the Royal Navy brig *Brisk* attacked the plantation, capturing 212 slaves, which it sent to Sierra Leone; it returned in the following year, causing more damage, which led Nosolini to abandon the undertaking.[181] In Angola, Ana Joaquina dos Santos Silva went into partnership with a Frenchman to try to produce sugar in the Bengo. Even though the company was dissolved very early on, Ana Joaquina persevered, though without making much in the way of profit.[182] José Maria Mattoso also tried to invest in agriculture, like Arsénio de Carpo and his partner, Mirandinha, who put a proposal to the government for the colonization of the Huíla region. This proposal was turned down after the Associação Marítima e Colonial had given a negative opinion.[183]

The government's refusal to consider Carpo's plan should not be interpreted as a sign that the authorities were completely averse to slavers and former slavers. The Lisbon government granted them lands, tax exemptions and mining rights, sometimes with positive results. The grant of unused lands to João Maria de Sousa e Almeida in the island of Príncipe, in 1853, launched the plantation economy of the archipelago.[184] Both before and after concessions were granted to well-known slave traders like Jacome Filipe Torres, José Maria Mattoso, Arsénio de Carpo and Francisco António Flores—the same man who would be behind the Companhia União Mercantil mentioned above. The grants made to Flores are the best example of how Lisbon's African policy was tied to initiatives by former slavers, for it is they who were the most amenable recipients and executors of the enthusiasts' message. It was Flores who induced the Portuguese government to occupy the Bembe in 1856 so that he could exploit its copper mines. Flores paid for most of the costs of the military expedition and undertook to build a road within three years and to complete a programme of colonization in exchange for the grant of the mines in perpetuity.[185] This grant of a concession to a Brazilian slaver elicited a strong reaction from the British embassy in Lisbon and a very significant response from Sá da Bandeira, who thought that 'every support should be given to traders in slaves' who wanted to embark on 'honest initiatives'.[186]

The occupation of the Bembe and the grant of copper mining rights to Francisco António Flores were praised in some sections of the press as the dawn of a new era of abundance. The newspaper *Marinha e Colónias* (Navy and Colonies), for which those mines might 'perhaps be the richest in the world', foresaw great changes: 'the example has been given; owners of capital need do nothing more than follow it'.[187] At the time, there was a fashion for mines, in the wake of the Australian and California gold rushes. Portugal too was dazzled, and this enthusiasm overflowed into the colonies. Accordingly, the second half of the 1850s and the early 1860s were a time of many mining concessions, granted both to former slavers like Flores and Carpo and to others.[188] The vast majority of these concessions came to nothing, if only because they coincided with a period of military unrest in Angola and Mozambique. Flores himself ended up assigning his concession in the Bembe to a London company, the Western Africa Malachite Copper Mines Company Ltd., but the mine was never profitable, and it was abandoned at the beginning of the 1870s, having exported a small quantity of copper to Lisbon.[189]

6.2.2 *... Nor Men*

Just as there were not sufficiently vigorous and consistent financial interests in Portugal to encourage the formation of a colonial company and to sustain an anti-slave trade policy, so also there were not enough people willing to seek their livelihood on the shores and in the wilderness of Africa. The settlement of Europeans in the colonies was one of the preconditions for the colonial plan of Sá da Bandeira and other enthusiasts, but here too the intention failed from the start. The salesmen, rural workers and those upon whom fortune had not smiled, attracted by the propaganda of the Brazilian colonizers' associations, which portrayed Brazil as the land of Eldorado, turned down Africa and flocked to Brazil at a rate which the *Diário do Governo*, as early as 1838, judged to be 'astonishing'.[190]

It is difficult to establish the precise volume of this emigration, but there is no doubt that it was substantial. According to data from the Portuguese consulate in Rio de Janeiro, some 25,000 Portuguese arrived between 1853 and 1855.[191] Subsequently, up to 1865, 86 per cent of Portuguese emigrants (equivalent to almost 71,000 people, for this particular period) chose Brazil as their destination.[192] The remainder went to the United States and, mainly, to some British possessions. With emancipation, which had been decreed and imposed in the 1830s, some British colonies in America found that former slaves were reluctant to work as paid labourers in the plantations. The only solution was to promote a wave of immigration that would encourage labour competition, ensuring that there were sufficient hands and forcing wages down.[193] Between 1841 and 1847 some 36,000 Africans freed in St Helena and Sierra Leone were transported to the West Indies. They were joined by nearly 100,000 Asians and a few thousand Europeans, particularly Portuguese from Madeira, where the serious crisis in agriculture was encouraging emigration. In 1841, British Guyana opened its doors to almost 4,300 Madeirans; a further 8,500 arrived in 1845, and this human tide continued under British government encouragement by means of premiums paid to the transporters. While the numbers of migrants did decline towards the end of the 1850s, over 33,000 Madeirans emigrated to the West Indies up to 1865 (of which 27,000 went to Guyana).[194] Far fewer migrated to the United States: some 5,000 Portuguese, mainly Azoreans, up to 1865.[195]

The conditions under which emigrants were transported, whether to Brazil or to the British colonies, were often degrading and reminiscent of the slave trade. In July 1847, the ship *The Loyal*, for example, landed in Demerara with 213 passengers aboard, while its permitted capacity was 54;[196] some years later the *Arrogante*, which was legally allowed to carry

89 persons, took almost 400 to Brazil;[197] in the *Defensora*, which left Oporto overloaded, 35 passengers were lost to hunger and ill-treatment.[198] These conditions and the situation of exploitation that often awaited those who sold their labour in return for food and a free passage to the Americas were called at the time 'white slavery', and led to numerous denunciations and complaints, particularly by the Portuguese community in Brazil, which was shocked at the state of degradation of these victims of a new human trade.[199]

'White slavery' had already attracted the attention of the Portuguese Cortes in 1836, and had justified attempts to restrict the flow of migration or, as an alternative, to channel it to Africa.[200] In 1838, the Parliament even appointed a special commission to study the matter, but there was no time to assess its conclusions. In any event, in 1842 Sá da Bandeira submitted a draft law aimed at making emigration more difficult. He would return to the attack in later years, urging governments to 'do their duty' by directing emigration to Africa so as to establish colonies 'in healthy places'.[201]

The most fervent advocates of the colonies favoured the use of strong measures to prevent emigration. But their efforts were usually in vain, on account of opposition from the moderates. The latter held that, since the country was so poor, emigration would benefit everyone. Moreover, it would be unconstitutional to restrict freedom of movement for men who were legally free. In addition, emigrants entered into free contracts with ships' captains: it was not the government's place to look after each individual, to oblige him to do the opposite of what he judged best for himself. Nor was it convenient to make enemies of the friendly governments of Great Britain and Brazil, which were using perfectly legitimate methods to attract colonists to their lands. Even if none of these reasons had applied, in the last resort any possible diversion of emigration from the Americas to Portuguese Africa would always be contingent on the willingness of the colonists.[202] To the extent that practical circumstances discouraged drastic measures, the government and legislative bodies could do little more than set up the alternatives and use indirect means to encourage settlement in Africa (making the flight to the Americas subject to certain conditions, within the limits of what was legal and suitable). It is in this light that we should interpret the policy of granting free passports for the African provinces, which was implemented right at the beginning of 1837. And we should look in the same light at the rules that placed limits on the number of emigrants transported in each ship leaving Portuguese ports for the Americas. These were rules that also sought to ensure that travelling conditions were minimally humane.[203]

None of these measures, however, was effective. For the poor emigrant, avoiding Africa was justified not only on account of sanitary conditions in the colonies, but also for financial and administrative reasons. There is no doubt that the image of 'the European's grave' was a strong deterrent, but it was more likely to be so for the educated strata of society than for those who were extremely poor, as were the Madeirans, who were willing to go at any cost to Guyana (where health conditions were also not exactly exemplary). Nevertheless, even if conditions or the reputed conditions of public health were similar, Africa would usually be passed over in favour of the Americas, since it had little to offer to those who had nothing more than their own labour. Without capital, without machinery and agricultural tools, the average Madeiran could not even compete in the labour market with over-abundant slave labour, even if he managed to survive the 'climate'.

For medical, financial and even psychological reasons, therefore, Africa was never a sufficiently appealing destination, despite all the incentives and all the propaganda. Even at the end of the nineteenth century, emigration to Africa amounted to no more than 3 per cent of total Portuguese emigration. This puts it on a par with emigration to Hawaii, in the same period.[204] From all the evidence available, the politicians' and journalists' arguments in favour of Africa were not sufficiently captivating and the legislation against 'white slavery' was not sufficiently restrictive to attract the Portuguese emigrant to the lands of Africa. So, as usual, those lands took in the regular supply of exiles, disgraced civil servants and little more. That little more represents mainly limited small-scale attempts at colonization that came to little or nothing.

In 1840 Portugal's consul in Brazil sent some Portuguese vagrants to Angola. They were sent inland, and nearly all died on the way.[205] In the same year a small military fortification was established in Moçâmedes, and another was founded in Huíla in 1845. But the most auspicious attempt at colonization took place in 1849, when a group of 180 Portuguese from Pernambuco were transported to Moçâmedes at their own request. It was a step forward, which was, of course, immediately seized upon by the propagandists for colonization. The Angola *Boletim* immediately opened its pages to 'a colonist' from the recently established settlement at Moçâmedes, who attempted to promote the young colony in regular articles.[206] The first articles were vibrant and enthusiastic and assured the reader that it would be 'a very easy matter' to make the settlement prosper. With such manna from heaven, why go to the Americas to look for a fortune, where one would be insulted and ill-treated?[207] While this was the tone of the early missives, later reports were darker and made no attempt to hide the drama of mortality and the first disappointments in the fields: 'don't expect me to relate only wonders of the colony …; as far as corn and beans are concerned, this is not the right season, and this has upset some of the colonists, who use it to say that the land does not produce …; they thought they were coming to Africa to lie down in a bed of roses'.[208] This excerpt was written at a time when the colonists were expecting the Moçâmedes River to fertilize their lands. But a few months later the very existence of the undertaking was being called into question.[209] In actual fact, the arrival of colonizers in Moçâmedes had coincided with a severe drought, which made agriculture practically impossible. The colony still took in two more batches of emigrants in 1850 and 1851, but then the flow dried up for a time.[210] Some settlers moved to Huíla, but they suffered such hardship there that they moved back to Moçâmedes, and the 'colonist' who had applied his pen to heralding colonization retreated into a lengthy silence. It was ten years before his voice would be heard again in the newspapers.[211]

Despite the failures in southern Angola, in the 1850s the Conselho Ultramarino sought to confront the issue of emigration to the Americas head-on by directing it instead to Africa, where Sá da Bandeira hoped to place three or four thousand colonists.[212] It was in this period, in 1857, that a small colony of Germans settled in the Moçâmedes area, and a little while later a company of European soldiers was established at Huíla as a colony of peasant-soldiers; but both were failures, on account of high mortality, war, abandonment and dispersal of the settlers, who, at Huíla, were not willing to subject themselves to military discipline.[213] The same happened to a group of colonists sent to the bay of Pemba, in northern Mozambique. The colonizer group left in April 1857, but found out on arrival that the place that had been chosen for the colony had no water. Having obtained another location further inland, they brought freedmen and 'coolies' from Macao as labour, but without success. The settlement was soon disbanded, like the one at Bazaruto two years before.[214] Up to 1859, the government made further efforts at colonization in Angola, Guinea and Tete, but 'the same happened to all these colonies as had occurred at Pemba, or worse still, they did not even become established'.[215] The colony of Capangombe, composed of some exiles and Portuguese from Rio, was founded in 1861: years later, this colony was to have some success. Around the same time some Algarve fishermen moved to the Moçâmedes area, and they settled further south, in Porto Alexandre, where a military fort had been built seven years before. Nevertheless, immigration remained low: in the years 1862 and 1863, the number of colonists transported to all the Portuguese colonies at the state's expense was 156 and 213, respectively.[216]

This is a sufficiently detailed survey and assessment of investment plans and colonizing endeavours in the period 1820 to 1865. Having investigated these forty-five years of Portuguese life, this is all I could find on the interest of the bourgeois and the general populace in Africa. These are slim pickings when compared with plans and initiatives for Portugal itself, its adjacent islands, Europe and the Americas, or even the Asian possessions. In the light of the above, it is not reasonable to presume that the Portuguese had a great appetite for the African colonies and to attribute the failure to satisfy that appetite only to external causes or, in other words, not to the will of those involved but to factors that might have existed independently of that will and overcome it. Undoubtedly there were some dreams, and it is even possible to detect a tiny core of persistent believers in Africa, like Pinto Basto Júnior, for example. But it is nothing more than that, which means that, while one must tone down Hammond's theory, its opposite is not acceptable either: the failed plans and their histories can hardly be viewed as evidence of an interest on the part of nearly all sectors of the Portuguese bourgeoisie in African expansion, as Alexandre and other Marxist historians claimed.

To a certain extent, the failure of African development plans reflects the Portuguese bourgeoisie's failure to partake of the optimistic vision of a 'new Brazil', and its greater receptiveness to the pessimistic and reticent approach. Even if this is not usually mentioned, the spectre of 'the European's grave', apart from affecting emigration itself and the viability of agricultural undertakings, also affected the very feasibility of economic plans, as the most clear-headed and best-informed enthusiasts admitted. In 1831 Manuel António Martins, the promoter of the Companhia de Guiné, admitted how difficult it was to organize a company when Portuguese capitalists were so afraid of the African 'climate, they feared that merely touching African products with their hands would be to absorb poison through their fingernails'.[217] Lopes de Lima also confirmed, some years later, that 'the greatest difficulty' facing the operation of potential colonial companies was 'being able to find eight, or ten upright subjects' who were willing to be its directors and agents in the ports of Africa, 'on account of the fear that those unhealthy climates inspire in them'.[218] The relationship between 'fevers' and trade was very well summed up by the Angola *Boletim*: 'so you want Angola … to be a trade emporium? Then reduce its mortality and disease'.[219]

The example of efforts at colonization by other powers also discouraged entrepreneurial initiatives in the African tropics, at least until mid-century, when these clouds began to disperse somewhat. The Bulama Island Association lost more than 60 per cent of its European personnel in its first few months of activity.[220] In Sierra Leone, early settlement had been a total disaster. Disease, conflicts with the natives and desertions caused genuine devastation among the inhabitants of the Province of Freedom, founded on auspicious philanthropic principles in 1787. When Falconbridge reorganized it in 1791, only a small number of the original colonists were left, and the settlement only survived with an injection of private capital and later with the financial support of the British state. Even so, and despite the significant financial investment, results were far from matching up to expectations, and mortality among Europeans remained extremely high.[221] Something similar happened with neighbouring North American Liberia, founded in the early 1820s for the purpose, amongst other things, of taking in slaves freed in the United States or recaptured by the anti-slave trade squadron, which had begun to operate on the African coast at that time.[222]

Portugal was kept informed of the results of its colonial rivals' efforts at colonization, and the *Gazeta de Lisboa*, for example, made no attempt to hide from its readers that 'many lives' were being lost and 'enormous amounts of capital' were being buried in Sierra Leone, in order that the undertaking might 'offer any reasonable prospect of being successful'.[223]

It was known that legal French and British trade was growing auspiciously in certain regions, but the spread of European civilization in Africa was a disappointment. As Tavares de Macedo acknowledged in 1842, 'despite the humanity and intelligence of the Danish government ..., it has been on the point of giving up its possessions, and has probably only not done so because it has been unable to find anyone who will give them any value'.[224]

In the final part of the period that interests us here, the enthusiasts, or at least some of them, understood the decisive importance of ill health as a factor that inhibited any and every African dream. This understanding, by means of which the image of the real Africa began to temper the dreams of a 'new Brazil', brought with it a visible lowering of expectations and implied some strategic changes, which were already obvious, for example, in the draft of an overseas health law, submitted by the then Minister of the Navy, Mendes Leal, in 1862. In the draft's preamble, while continuing to state that the country needed only to 'have faith' in the potential of its colonies for the dreams of greatness to become reality, a colonial 'plan' was created following 'strict logical needs', with the issue of health being placed at the top of the list (tax reforms aimed at facilitating trade were in only seventh place in the list of priorities):

> Because effectively the unhealthy climate ... is the main source of affliction for the natives and, as I have said, it keeps Europeans away from nearly all those provinces ..., it is clear that the urgency of dealing with this evil takes precedence over any other endeavour ... Cultivating the land, prospering, enriching the country, are all just desires and useful purposes, but before anything else, and for everything else, one has to live.[225]

But this moderation on the part of the enthusiasts came rather late in the day. Until mid-century enthusiast propaganda had based itself on the idea of an easily attainable Eldorado. In one sense, the failure of the plans to develop business and settle the colonies between 1820 and 1865 represents the defeat of that propaganda. It was understood in Portugal from quite early on that promotion of the idea of Africa would be fundamental in bringing about a deep-seated interest in Portuguese society. In 1826 deputy Braklami summed up the issue perfectly in a draft law he submitted to the Cortes. He felt that, despite the lack of capital and the demand for sacrifices on the part of both the state and private individuals, colonization in Africa would be both possible and beneficial. The key question was the need to persuade the Portuguese: 'nothing surpasses the will of a nation which has committed itself to any undertaking, the whole task lies in convincing it of the need for that undertaking; the commitment is born out of the conviction and in turn gives rise to enthusiasm'.[226] But, despite the efforts at colonization propaganda, the task of persuasion so desired by Braklami and his peers was a resounding failure in the Portugal of the 1820s, and would continue to be so in subsequent years. In the mid-1850s the newspapers were still appealing to the pride and dreams of Portuguese investors: 'businessmen, rich men and wealthy, everything depends on you! Help the government in the great task of African civilization'. But it was a half-hearted appeal. As the same newspapers acknowledged, contrary to what was happening in Britain, the 'love for their country' that had earlier inspired the Portuguese capitalists was not on show when it came to Africa.[227]

The practical results, or lack of them, and above all the small number of plans and initiatives, in terms both of colonization and of agriculture and trade, are strong indicators of the prevalence of scepticism over enthusiasm. But there is even stronger evidence of this in a theatre where we are able to witness and, up to a point, evaluate the confrontation between the optimistic and the reticent visions of Africa. That theatre is the Parliament, the point where the Portuguese elites were to be found in the greatest number.

6.3 African Issues in the Cortes

Judging by their legislative output, the Cortes paid little attention to African issues. The number of overseas parliamentarians was, of course, small, but they were not the only ones who could legislate for the overseas provinces, and a number of draft bills that were of interest for the colonies were put forward by deputies who represented constituencies in Portugal itself. It is therefore perfectly legitimate to assess the greater or lesser significance of the colonies in the overall context of Portuguese political concerns by the number of bills and debates they gave rise to in the Parliament. As we shall see below, that figure was always regarded at the time as a good indicator of the attention given to overseas affairs, and the Cortes were consistently seen as one of the windows through which it was possible to observe and assess the different interests in play and the hierarchy of political priorities in Portuguese society. From these observations and comparisons we can see that, for the period which interests us here, especially up to the mid-1850s, there was a clear disparagement of colonial issues. It was not that the overseas deputies did not try to put forward draft laws for the colonies. The Chambers usually adjourned them, which suggests that the subject matter was of secondary importance to them. We should add that the study of parliamentary sessions enables us to go beyond this purely deductive assertion and to measure the lack of interest not only in quantitative terms, by the number of drafts submitted and debated, but also in qualitative terms, by the content of the debates—because the arguments that were engendered are at least as significant as the number of drafts considered. Let us therefore take a look, albeit briefly, at what this analysis shows.

In the 1820s, as I have mentioned in chapter 3, the Parliament devoted very little time to African affairs. In any event, the secondary importance of African concerns is shown in the great debate over free trade that took place in 1827. The draft law submitted at that time sought above all to ensure new sources of income for the state and to overcome the decline in dealings with Brazil by encouraging other trade flows, but not particularly those between Portugal and its African colonies. Moreover, the draft set duties on products from the overseas possessions at 10 per cent, which, in Angola's case, was an increase in taxation. It is highly significant that the enthusiasts' suggestion of a duty rate of just 3 per cent on African products, so that they might compete with American products, was turned down without much debate.

After the interlude of the civil war of 1832–34, the overall situation of lack of commitment to the colonies did not change radically. Few admitted that the African possessions were just a minor concern, but they shelved the issues relating to them. As Peres da Silva, deputy for India, observantly noted, the Chambers condemned proposals for the overseas territories to a kind of 'life imprisonment, with no final judgement', instead of killing them off 'publicly, on the scaffold'.[228] Peres da Silva was in fact one of the strongest critics of his parliamentary colleagues' lack of interest in the colonies. At the beginning of 1840 he put a number on that lack of interest: 'from 1834 until now probably over 600 drafts have been submitted to the Legislative Chambers. Not one has dealt with the overseas territories'.[229]

The general attitude reflected in Peres da Silva's figures was far from being the circumstantial result of the troubled times of the 1830s, and it persisted in the years that followed. In 1852, like Peres da Silva before him, Fontes Pereira de Melo did a reckoning of legislative efforts and stressed that up to that time only three laws relating to the colonies had gone through the parliamentary procedures (and, even then, these were of secondary importance).[230] Throughout the period under study, but particularly from 1821 until the mid-1850s, representatives of the colonies often complained that their affairs were treated with the greatest indifference, that colonial issues were 'dragged out forever' in a Parliament that only dealt 'with measures of interest to Portugal', almost never paying attention 'to the wretched state of the overseas provinces'.[231] In these complaints they were joined by a number of parliamentarians from constituencies in the mother country, including Sá da Bandeira himself, who was generally discreet when it came to unmasking the country's hesitations vis-à-vis its colonies.[232] In 1856, Bernardo da Costa suggested that one day per week should be set aside to discuss draft laws for the colonies. This was the revival of a voluntarist intention that surfaced in the Cortes from time to time and which, in José Estevão's opinion, would be a way of compensating for 'the complete neglect of this matter by all Portuguese parliaments'.[233] The proposal was approved but, when the time came, 'everyone was in a hurry to finish the day's business'.[234] Quite clearly, the grandiose rhetoric of Portuguese parliamentarians in favour of the colonies was misleading: 'apparent unanimity of views' but, underneath it all, 'real contradictions and real opposition'; and the simplest form of opposition, one that involved the least political responsibility, was inertia: 'there's no effort involved; inertia is the body's habitual state'.[235]

The Cortes's lack of interest in the colonies may be explained first by low individual involvement of parliamentarians in colonial issues. At the beginning of the 1840s it was clear that most deputies knew little about the colonies, and if we are to believe the speeches made in the assembly, that ignorance persisted.[236] But, behind each individual's lack of interest in the colonies, there were, of course, also national priorities. Vieira de Magalhães acknowledged this openly in 1843: 'we have a lot to do, we will be kept busy for many years just organizing all the branches of the administration in Portugal itself. I do not know when we will have time to concern ourselves with the colonies, in the ordinary course of events'.[237] In order to avoid colonial issues from getting bogged down, as they generally did when they reached the Parliament, Sá da Bandeira suggested as early as 1839 that the Conselho Ultramarino, which had been shut down six years before, should be reactivated. It should engage in consultation, propaganda and the drafting of legislation for colonies.[238] The suggestion was made again several times in subsequent years, but it was not until the end of 1851 that the Council was reborn.

Parliament's relative undervaluation of the African possessions—in other words the prevalence of the sceptics in the Cortes—helps to explain the reluctance to spend money on the colonies. As deputy Arrobas said in 1861, 'foreign possessions are more developed than ours because the respective mother countries spend loads of money on them, which we *do not want to* spend'.[239] The navy's budget, which, as we saw earlier, was a priority for the enthusiasts, is one area where the resistance to public spending on the colonies is best illustrated. Despite much rhetoric in favour of this sector, its budgets were examined down to the last detail and were invariably the first to fall victim to public spending cuts. In line with this progressive reduction in the money available, the naval force, which was voted on year after year, tended to diminish: from the 3,000 naval ratings and twenty-five ships approved in 1846–47 there was a gradual decline to fewer than 2,400 ratings and twenty-one ships in 1852–53, to the dismay of enthusiast parliamentarians.[240] The tendency to put forward and to approve debilitating budgets reflects the tendency to devalue the navy, and through it the colonies, in the list of parliamentary concerns. Carlos Bento emphasized this very point when he noted that in Portugal less than 7 per cent of the budget went on the navy, while Great Britain gave it over 19 per cent, Sweden more than 12 per cent, and Norway and Holland around 11 per cent.[241] Moreover, the mere fact of grouping together, in the same Ministry, the Navy and the Overseas Territories was proof, for many, that Portugal paid 'no attention to the navy, or to the overseas colonies'.[242]

But the low budgetary priority of the colonies was not limited to the sums pledged to the Navy Ministry. It emerged in a number of other financial aspects. The awarding of little over 2 *contos* per annum to finance Welwitsch's scientific expedition to Angola was contested in the Cortes, and even more so in the press, which preferred to see expenditure concentrated in the metropole: 'why should we give a naturalist 200,000 *réis* a month to chase mosquitoes in Angola and squash a few dozen leaves or plant stems between the pages of a herbarium?'[243] Nor did expenditure on colonization go uncommented on. When in 1849 the government sought authorization from the Chamber of Deputies to spend 18 *contos* on founding the agricultural colony of Moçâmedes, several deputies (including two future Ministers of the Navy and Overseas Territories) were opposed to it, basically because they saw no hope of the settlement prospering and because they felt that the amount to be allocated would be missed at home: 'I saw that this Chamber rejected a proposal to award provisions to a few wretched and unhappy nuns; I cannot believe that … it will now allocate 18 *contos* for the establishment of a colony'.[244] In order to overcome the lack of interest and miserliness of the sceptics, the enthusiasts tried to use emigration to the Americas, which they were in any case unable to prevent, to set up a tax on the 'white slavery' agents. They hoped thereby to create a fund for the settlement of Europeans in Africa, but their plan was thwarted by those who saw emigration to America as a positive good for Portugal and by those who were opposed to populating Africa at the expense of depopulating the mother country.[245]

The situation of lack of attention paid to the colonies described above persisted more or less until the mid-1850s, when Parliament began visibly to change its attitude. Several indicators provide evidence of this, including the allocation of more time to the issue and greater speed in approving draft laws relating to the colonies. The change, which was recognized clearly at the time, went beyond oratory and speed, because there was also greater willingness to spend money on the colonies. At the end of the 1850s the Cortes decided to allocate the considerable sum of 800 *contos* to naval construction.[246] To this we may add the 40 *contos* allocated to the establishment of a colony in Tete, 60 *contos* to improve transport facilities in Angola, 200 *contos* to fund military expeditions in that province, and annual subsidies to cover the budget deficit in Mozambique and Angola. This was a step forward that was due, on the one hand, to Sá da Bandeira's prestige and, on the other, to a falling off in the differences of opinion between the enthusiasts and the sceptics on what to do about the colonies. We have seen earlier how the perception of the real Africa clouded the image of the 'new Brazil', helping to put a brake on and reshaping the enthusiasm of the enthusiasts. We should now mention that, at around the same time, there were also changes in the sceptical approach, above all because the war that broke out in Angola and jeopardized security and even the survival of the 'remains of ancient glory', inclined them more readily to accept the awarding of subsidies and other expenditures. Even so, and although they were now less severe, the disagreements persisted. For many enthusiasts the amounts allocated were 'insignificant', and reflected a lack of recognition of the value of the colonies.[247] For the sceptics, on the other hand, and particularly as soon as the military situation calmed down, the subsidies were excessive, especially when they were ongoing: 'we cannot be sending valuable subsidies to the overseas provinces indefinitely. Things have to be arranged so that they are self-sustaining'.[248] The granting of recurring subsidies tended to reinforce scepticism, because it revealed the colonies' inability to become profitable quickly. From being 'sheet anchors' they became, for many, perpetual burdens. As António José de Seixas (deputy for Angola) himself admitted, 'subsidies for the overseas provinces create a bad impression in this Chamber, because it is generally thought that a colony which has to be subsidized by the state, and which is unable to live off its own income, deserves little consideration'.[249]

In sum, the general attitude of the Cortes during most of the period under study shows, just as the analysis of migration patterns and trade and agriculture projects had already shown, that the Portuguese remained aloof in relation to their African colonies. In the first two-thirds of the nineteenth century, the overseas possessions were not a national priority, or, rather, they were only a priority for one sector, the enthusiasts. That sector was not in the majority, nor did it adopt a common front with the sceptics. If it had been and if it had done so, if the ideas of a 'new Brazil' and of an inalienable historical legacy had been the two sides of the same plan for the colonies drawn up by the Portuguese elites as a whole, it would be difficult to explain the lack of overseas investment and the opposition that some enthusiasts—in particular, Sá da Bandeira—faced.

Historians influenced by Marxism did not identify or did not value that duality. On the contrary, they focused exclusively on the enthusiast approach, ignoring the sceptical view and the extent of its influence in Portuguese society, and overestimated the commitment of the Portuguese ruling classes to the African possessions. This led them into an incongruous interpretation because, at the same time as they claimed that the political and financial elites had a strong interest in the development of a colonial plan in Africa, they were forced to admit that commitment to the abolition of the slave trade, which was essential for putting the plan into action, was rare among those elites. This was effectively so for a number of reasons, two of which are of particular interest here: first, because the number of enthusiasts was substantially lower than the Marxist historians imagined; and, secondly, because, even among the enthusiasts, African backwardness was often attributed to a variety of causes other than the continuation of the slave trade.

Notes

1. Richard J. Hammond, 'Some Economic Aspects of Portuguese Africa in the Nineteenth and Twentieth Centuries', in L.H. Gann and Peter Duignan (eds), *Colonialism in Africa, 1870–1960*, vol. IV, Cambridge University Press, Cambridge, 1975, p. 256; see also idem, *Portugal and Africa, 1815–1910. A Study in Uneconomic Imperialism*, Stanford University Press, Stanford, California, 1966; and 'Uneconomic Imperialism: Portugal in Africa before 1910', in Gann and Duignan (eds), *Colonialism*, vol. I, Cambridge University Press, Cambridge, 1969, pp. 352–82.
2. A.H. de Oliveira Marques, *História de Portugal*, vol. 2, Palas, Lisbon, 1978 (1st edition 1974), p. 128.
3. Valentim Alexandre, *Origens do colonialismo português moderno, 1822–1891*, Sá da Costa, Lisbon, 1979; idem, 'O liberalismo português e as colónias de África, 1820–1839', *Análise Social*, 16, 61–62, 1980, pp. 319–40.
4. Alexandre, 'O liberalismo', p. 335.
5. Alexandre, *Origens*, p. 17.
6. Gervase Clarence-Smith, *The Third Portuguese Empire, 1825–1975. A Study in Economic Imperialism*, Manchester University Press, Manchester, 1985.
7. Valentim Alexandre, 'Projecto colonial e abolicionismo', *Penélope*, 14, 1994, p. 125.
8. Report dated 19 February 1836, presented to the Cortes by the then Minister of the Navy, Sá da Bandeira, *Memorial Ultramarino e Marítimo*, 1836.
9. *Diário das Cortes*, session of 28 June 1822, p. 620.
10. José Joaquim Lopes de Lima, *Ensaios sobre a Statistica das Possessões Portuguezas na Africa Occidental e Oriental, na Asia Occidental, na China e na Oceania*, part I, Imprensa Nacional, Lisbon, 1844, p. 13; see also José Acúrsio das Neves, *Considerações Politicas e Commerciais sobre os Descobrimentos e Possessões dos Portuguezes na Africa e na Ásia*, Lisbon, 1830, p. 72 ff.; Sebastião Xavier Botelho, *Memória Estatistica sobre os domínios Portuguezes na Africa Oriental*, Lisbon, 1835, p. 30; and, in the press, *A União*, 26 June 1850; *A Revolução de Septembro*, 17 June 1851. There are many other documents that provide evidence of the enthusiasts' views of Cape Verde, but it seemed unnecessary to list them all. This principle of simplification will be applied, for the same reasons, to subsequent notes, in which I shall limit myself to two or three documentary references (even though the main characteristics of the currents of opinion analysed in this chapter are abundantly illustrated both in the press and on the parliamentary platform).
11. *DCD*, session of 13 February 1839, p. 246; and Chamber of Peers, session of 24 May 1848, *DG*, 25 May 1848.
12. *A Revista*, 15 April 1836. Among many other examples of enthusiast projections in the press, see *O Nacional*, 27 August 1838; *O Patriota*, 11 April 1845.
13. *DCD*, session of 28 January 1840, p. 201 (speech by Manuel António de Vasconcelos); see also session of 20 July 1850, p. 249 (speech by Fontes Pereira de Melo); the *Revista das Colónias* (30 October 1863) promised interest as written of in 'the holy scriptures: one hundred to one'.
14. Sebastião Xavier Botelho, *Escravatura: benefícios que podem provir às nossas Possessões d'Africa da prohibição daquele Tráfico*, Lisbon, 1840, p. 17; Lima, *Ensaios*, p. 30.
15. Joaquim Pereira Marinho, *Memória contra a facção dos negreiros, dedicada ao Illmo. E Exmo. Senhor Visconde de Sá da Bandeira*, Lisbon, 1842, p. VII.
16. *DCD*, session of 13 February 1839, p. 246.
17. *DCD*, session of 11 December 1826, p. 155 (speech by Braklami); and session of 8 February 1827, p. 278 (speech by Francisco António de Campos).

18. *DCD*, session of 29 July 1940, p. 438 (speech by Joaquim António de Magalhães). For other examples, see session of 14 April 1849, p. 139 (speech by J.I. Guedes); session of 23 May 1859, p. 343 (speech by Rebelo Cabral).
19. *DCD*, sessions of 21 February and 8 March 1828, pp. 586 and 732, respectively (speeches by Lima Leitão); session of 9 February 1839, pp. 240–41 (for the speech by J.A. de Magalhães).
20. Lima, *Ensaios*, pp. 66–67. For similar projections see Joaquim António de Carvalho Menezes, *Memoria Geografica e Politica das Possessões Portuguezas n'Affrica Occidental, que diz respeito aos Reinos de Angola, Benguela e suas dependencias...*, Lisbon, 1834, p. 33; O Estandarte, 26 August 1848.
21. *DCD*, session of 10 February 1827, pp. 294 and 296 (speech by the bishop of Cape Verde); for identical projections, see *O Nacional*, 27 August 1838; *A União*, 26 June 1850; *A Revolução de Septembro*, 17 June 1851 and 14 September 1854.
22. *DCD*, session of 4 March 1828, p. 675 (speech by Chapuzet).
23. Menezes, *Memoria*, p. 34; *DCD*, session of 13 February 1839, p. 247 (speech by Sá da Bandeira); Marinho, *Memória contra*, p. VII.
24. *Campeão Portuguez em Lisboa*, 11 May 1822, p. 91; for other examples in the same period, see *Diário das Cortes*, session of 28 June 1822, p. 620 (report on Cape Verde); *DCD*, session of 4 March 1828, p. 675 (speech by Chapuzet).
25. *DCD*, session of 28 January 1840, p. 199 (speech by Manuel António de Vasconcelos); and also session of 4 July 1848, p. 11 (speech by Fontes Pereira de Melo); *A Restauração*, 9 August 1842.
26. Menezes, *Memoria*, p. 13.
27. Chamber of Senators, session of 26 April 1839, *DG*, 2 May 1839; in 1858 Sá was still explaining the backwardness of Mozambique by reference to successive bad governments and administrations (*DCD*, session of 28 July 1858, p. 334); *O Patriota*, 27 January 1848 and 16 February 1850, and *A Revolução de Septembro*, 2 January 1851.
28. *DCD*, session of 8 March 1828, p. 732 (speech by Lima Leitão); Menezes, *Memoria*, p. 11; for an ascription of colonial decay to the despotism of Costa Cabral, see, for example, *O Patriota*, 1 February 1850.
29. Menezes, *Memoria*, p. 10.
30. See, for example, *A Revolução de Septembro*, 31 December 1845; *DCD*, sessions of 20 January and 16 May 1849, pp. 152 and 279 (speeches by Lopes de Lima).
31. *Memorial Ultramarino e Maritimo*, March 1836, p. 23; identical views on the simple ways of changing direction in *A Restauração*, 9 August 1842; and Francisco Maria Bordalo, *Ensaios sobre a Estatistica das Possessões Portuguezas na África Occidental e Oriental, na Ásia Occidental, na China e na Oceania*, Imprensa Nacional, Lisbon, 1859, p. 69.
32. *A Revista*, 14 April 1836.
33. *DCD*, session of 11 December 1826, p. 156 (speech by Braklami); session of 8 March 1856, pp. 84–85 (speech by Pinto de Magalhães); sessions of 9 January and 2 August 1858, pp. 59 and 8, respectively (speeches by Soares Franco).
34. Lima, *Ensaios*, p. 49; Barbosa Leão wanted the state to set up model farms in the valleys of the Cuanza and Zambezi Rivers (*A Revolução de Septembro*, 1 July 1851).
35. *DCD*, session of 2 June 1855, p. 24 (speech by Alves Martins); see also session of 8 February 1836, p. 375 (speech by Leonel Tavares); and Chamber of Peers, session of 28 March 1863, *DL*, 21 April 1863 (speech by Soares Franco).
36. Chamber of Deputies, sessions of 23 February and 6 August 1861, *DL*, 26 February and 9 August 1861 (speeches by Pinto de Magalhães); see also sessions of 5 and 6 August 1861, in *DL*, 9 August 1861 (speeches by Afonseca).

37. Among many other arguments in favour of the formation of colonial companies, see *Diário das Cortes*, sessions of 27 April and 8 June 1822, pp. 980 and 385–88, respectively (speeches by Soares Franco, Vaz Velho and Morais Sarmento); *DCD*, session of 9 February 1839, p. 241 (speech by J.A. de Magalhães); session of 18 July 1860, p. 189 (speech by Soares Franco).
38. *A Revista*, 14 and 15 April 1836; see also *Miscellanea Politica*, 18 August 1838; *O Estandarte*, 4 February 1848 and 3 August 1849.
39. *Memorial Ultramarino e Marítimo*, 1836, pp. 3–4, 11–15 and 21–23.
40. According to *O Nacional* (26 April 1836), the publication was suppressed by the new Navy Minister, Manuel Gonçalves de Miranda, who was less interested in the colonies.
41. Lima, *Ensaios*, pp. 30–31.
42. *A Revolução de Septembro*, 14 September 1854. Note that this journalistic militancy was far from being consistent and that by 1857 *A Revolução de Septembro* was mentioning the subject of the colonies less and less.
43. *O Panorama*, 20 December 1837, p. 279; see also *A Revolução de Septembro*, 2 December 1854.
44. Luiz Felipe de Alencastro, *O Trato dos Viventes. Formação do Brasil no Atlântico Sul*, São Paulo, Companhia das Letras, 2000, pp. 34–35.
45. *Da Ásia*, Década Iª, Livro III, Chap. 12.
46. Philip D. Curtin, *Death by Migration. Europe's Encounter with the Tropical World in the Nineteenth Century*, Cambridge University Press, Cambridge, 1989, pp. 65–66; for the advances in hygiene and tropical medicine at the end of the nineteenth century, see chaps. 5 and 6.
47. J. César de Figanière e Morão, *Descripção de Serra Leoa e seus contornos. Escripta em doze cartas à qual se ajuntão os trabalhos da Comissão-Mixta portuguesa e inglesa estabelecida naquela colónia*, Lisbon, 1822, pp. 12–14, 16, 22, 32, 36 and 38. The expression 'the European's grave' was apparently invented by Figanière himself and was to have a great future in its English version (the white man's grave). It became popular as a result of the book by F. Harrison Rankin, *The White Man's Grave: a Visit to Sierra Leone in 1834* (see Christopher Fyfe, *A History of Sierra Leone*, Oxford University Press, London, 1962, p. 151; and Philip D. Curtin, *The Image of Africa. British Ideas and Action, 1780–1850*, University of Wisconsin Press, Madison, 1964, p. 179, note 4).
48. José Pinto de Azeredo, *Ensaios sobre algumas Enfermedades d'Angola, dedicados ao Serenissimo Senhor D. João, Principe do Brazil*, Lisbon, 1799, p. 49.
49. Lima, *Ensaios*, p. 9.
50. Ibid., p. 50.
51. *Annaes Maritimos e Coloniaes*, no. 2, 1846, p. 54. Celerina's 'topography' was probably the first extensive description, in Portuguese, of the diseases of that coast.
52. Philip D. Curtin, 'Epidemiology and the Slave Trade', in *Congrès International des Africanistes*, Présence Africaine, Paris, 1972, p. 106 ff.
53. Curtin, *Image of Africa*, pp. 71 and 433–87, and idem, *Death by Migration*, pp. 7–8 and 18.
54. Chamber of Senators, session of 26 February 1839, *DG*, 4 March 1839.
55. George Tams, *Visita às Possessões Portuguezas na costa Occidental d'Africa*, 2 vols., Porto, 1850, p. 111 (see also p. 38); *O Estandarte*, 26 January 1848.
56. *DL*, 18 June 1861.
57. *Annaes Maritimos e Coloniaes*, no. 2, 1846, p. 53 (see also pp. 45, 48 and 50).
58. Azeredo, *Ensaios*, p. 50.
59. Tams (*Visita*, p. 203) was one of those who believed in the ill effects of perspiration.
60. *Gazeta de Lisboa*, 28 February 1825 (summary of the theory of Dr Audouard, a doctor in the military hospitals of Paris).

61. Azeredo, *Ensaios*, pp. 84–85.
62. Curtin, *Death by Migration*, p. 62.
63. Curtin, *Image of Africa*, p. 311; Howard W. Temperley, *White Dreams, Black Africa: The Antislavery Expedition to the River Niger, 1841–1842*, Yale University Press, New Haven, 1991, p. 170.
64. Curtin, *Death by Migration*, p. 62.
65. Ibid., pp. 66–67. In Portugal, memoirs on the improvement of colonial settlements insisted on the idea that draining the swamps and cutting down forests, followed by cultivation of the drained and cleared lands, would be sufficient to dissipate the pernicious air (see, by way of example, *O Independente*, 21 January 1822; for similar recommendations at a later date, see *A Revolução de Septembro*, 8 September 1851). However, the African *Anopheles* were insensitive to such environmental changes, since they only required small puddles of water exposed to light in order to survive and reproduce. Moreover, *Anopheles gambiae* tended to make its ecological nest next to man, so the clearing and cultivation of new open land actually helped it to propagate (Curtin, *Image of Africa*, p. 81).
66. *BOGGPA*, 13 March 1847 (report of the chief medical officer Manuel Rodrigues de Bastos); see also *BOGGPA*, 10 April 1847.
67. *BOGGPA*, 26 January 1850, p. 3 (report by J. Vieira de Carvalho, acting chief medical officer in Angola).
68. *BOGGPA*, 4 May 1861, p. 7 (report by Faustino José Cabral, in Angola).
69. René Pélissier, *Les Guerres grises. Résistances et révoltes en Angola (1845–1941)*, Pélissier, Montamets, 1977, p. 108; Jill Dias, 'Angola', in Valentim Alexandre and Jill Dias (eds), *O Império africano, 1825–1890*, Estampa, Lisbon, 1998, p. 425.
70. *Relatórios sobre a epidemia de febre amarella em Loanda no anno de 1860*, Imprensa Nacional, Lisbon, 1861, pp. 47–48. For the alarm generated by the major epidemic that occurred in Cape Verde in 1845, see *Boletim Official do Governo-Geral de Cabo Verde*, 14 February 1846, pp. 509–11, and subsequent issues.
71. Jorge Faro, 'Os problemas de Bissau, Cacheu e suas dependências, vistos em 1831 por Manuel António Martins', *Boletim Cultural da Guiné Portuguesa*, XIII, 50, 1958, p. 214; see also *Paquete do Ultramar*, 4 September 1839, and *BOGGPA*, 28 December 1861, p. 3 (for Welwitsch's view).
72. Lima, *Ensaios*, p. 31; see also DG, 16 October 1838.
73. Botelho, *Escravatura*, p. 26.
74. Marinho, *Memória contra*, pp. 63 and 94.
75. Francisco Maria Bordalo, *Eugénio. Romance Marítimo*, Lisbon, 1854 (2nd edition), pp. 21–22, 70 and 89.
76. António da Silva Gaio, *Mario. Episódios das luctas civis portuguezas de 1820–1834*, Guimarães eds, Lisbon, 1924 (1st edition 1868), pp. 82, 96 and 154.
77. *O Nacional*, 23 February 1839; see also *O Nacional*, 1 July 1839 and *Paquete do Ultramar*, 20 August 1839.
78. Chamber of Deputies, session of 27 July 1861, *DL*, 30 July 1861.
79. *DCD*, session of 2 December 1844, p. 276 (speech by Vasconcelos e Sá); for a further example, see Chamber of Peers, session of 12 February 1848, *DG*, 15 February 1848 (speech by Bonfim).
80. *DCD*, session of 19 February 1859, p. 121 (speech by Melo Soares).
81. *DCD*, session of 9 February 1839, p. 242.
82. *Annaes Marítimos and Coloniaes*, no. 3, 1842, pp. 128–29.
83. Ibid., pp. 128, 130 and 136.
84. There was near unanimity on this point, as acknowledged by Gomes de Castro, a well-known opponent of chartered companies (*DCD*, session of 15 October 1840, p. 328).

85. *DCD*, session of 17 April 1855, p. 140.
86. *DCD*, session of 18 April 1855, p. 141 (speech by Atouguia, Minister of the Navy); see also session of 15 April 1859, pp. 187–88 (speeches by Silvestre Ribeiro and Ferreri, respectively).
87. *DCD*, session of 17 April 1855, p. 140.
88. *DCD*, sessions of 9 January 1858 and 18 July 1860, pp. 58 and 189 (speeches by Soares Franco, which mention that line of thinking generally); Chamber of Deputies, sessions of 8 and 9 April 1863, *DL*, 10 and 12 April 1863, speeches by Ferreri); session of 5 May 1865, *DL*, 8 May 1865 (speech by Garcês, who stated, amongst other things, that he feared Africa would be a factor in the 'disgrace' of the country, if successive governments, dragged on by the 'burning imagination' of the enthusiasts, invested too much in it).
89. *DCD*, session of 22 April 1839, p. 184 (speech by Manuel António de Carvalho, Minister of Economy); session of 15 May 1848, p. 6 (speech by Gomes de Castro); session of 22 April 1850, p. 271 (speech by Carlos Bento).
90. Chamber of Peers, sessions of 6 March 1851 and 17 June 1854, *DG*, 10 March 1851 and 24 June 1854 (speeches by Rodrigo da Fonseca and Atouguia, respectively). On the relationship between 'climate' and the difficulty in obtaining qualified candidates for overseas posts, see *DCD*, sessions of 16 and 28 July 1860, pp. 163 and 374 (speeches by José Estevão and law on navy doctors).
91. *DCD*, session of 28 January 1840, p. 202; session of 25 November 1840, p. 375 (speech by Rodrigo da Fonseca).
92. Chamber of Peers, session of 6 March 1851, *DG*, 10 March 1851; see also *DCD*, session of 25 November 1840, p. 374, for an explanation by the same Rodrigo da Fonseca, downplaying the supposed wealth of the Benguela sulphur mine.
93. *DCD*, session of 17 April 1855, p. 140.
94. *DCD*, session of 1 June 1855, p. 18; for other examples of this type of judgement, see session of 1 February 1849, pp. 6–7 (speech by Ferreri); Chamber of Deputies, session of 5 May 1865, *DL*, 8 May 1865 (speech by Garcez).
95. *Boletim Official do Governo-Geral de Cabo Verde*, 4 June 1844, p. 244.
96. *A Revolução de Septembro*, 5 November 1845 and 27 February 1846, for example.
97. António Saldanha da Gama, *Memória sobre as colónias de Portugal situadas na costa Ocidental d'Africa, mandada ao Governo pelo antigo Governador e Capitão-Geral do Reino de Angola… em 1814, precedida de um discurso preliminar, augmentada de alguns additamentos e notas,…*, Paris, 1839, p. 111.
98. Ibid., pp. 2–7.
99. Ibid., p. 1.
100. Ibid., p. 2.
101. *DG*, 18 October 1851 (preamble to the decree establishing the Conselho Ultramarino); Chamber of Peers, sessions of 23 May and 14 August 1853, *DG*, 31 May and 16 August 1853 (speeches by José Maria Grande and the Minister of the Crown, respectively); and *DCD*, session of 2 May 1860, p. 13 (speech by Carlos Bento).
102. *Annaes Maritimos e Coloniaes*, no. 2, 1842, pp. 71–72; for a similar speech by Tavares de Macedo see *DCD*, session of 18 April 1855, p. 151.
103. *DCD*, session of 6 July 1840, p. 65. Among other similar views see session of 14 October 1840, p. 313 (speech by Gomes de Castro); session of 22 April 1850, p. 268 (speech by Rebelo da Silva); session of 24 March 1852, p. 304 (speech by Xavier Cordeiro); *O Correio Portuguez*, 21 December 1844.
104. *DCD*, session of 27 March 1852, p. 334.
105. Chamber of Deputies, session of 23 April 1862, *DL*, 25 April 1862 (speech by Mendes Leal).

106. Lopes de Lima was reportedly one of the authors of an article published in *A União* (26 January and 19 February 1848), that advocated the partial sale of the colonies. For arguments in favour of similar positions by other enthusiasts in the 1860s and 1870s, see, for example, *Jornal do Comércio*, 31 August 1868 and 12 March 1869, and J.B. Ferreira de Almeida, *Portugal e os seus Domínios Ultramarinos. Memória apresentada à Commissão de Exploração Africana da Sociedade de Geografia de Lisboa*. Lisbon, 1877.
107. *Diário das Cortes*, session of 2 October 1822, pp. 656–67.
108. Ibid., sessions of 19 April and 28 June 1822, pp. 888 and 621, respectively.
109. *DCD*, session of 8 March 1828, pp. 732–34.
110. *Diário das Cortes*, session of 8 June 1822, p. 388 (speech by Vasconcelos).
111. Neves, *Considerações*, pp. 240–41.
112. Tito Augusto de Carvalho, *As Companhias portuguesas de colonização*, Lisbon, undated, pp. 72–73; Alexandre, *Origens*, p. 328.
113. Vasco Pulido Valente, *Os Devoristas. A Revolução Liberal, 1834–1836*, Quetzal Editores, Lisbon, 1993, p. 58.
114. J. Roque da Fonseca, 'A Associação Comercial de Lisboa e o Império (1834–1900)', in *Primeiro Congresso da História da Expansão portuguesa no Mundo*, Ministério das Colónias, Lisbon, 1938, pp. 12 and 42–46).
115. António Pedro de Carvalho (secretary to the Minister of the Navy) to the Associação Mercantil Lisbonense, 12 January 1836, *A Revista*, 16 January 1836.
116. Pinto Basto to Sá da Bandeira, 13 February 1836, AGM, *cx*. 50. See also government order of the Minister of Economy, 15 December 1837, and the reply by the Associação Mercantil Lisbonense, in J. Roque da Fonseca, *Cem anos em defesa da Economia nacional, 1834–1934. História da Associação Comercial de Lisboa*, Lisbon, 1934, pp. 79–81.
117. Fonseca, 'A Associação Comercial', p. 53.
118. Ibid., p. 59.
119. By way of example, see Associação Mercantil Lisbonense to Tomás Ramos da Fonseca, 26 April 1838, Associação Comercial de Lisboa, Minute book of the Associação Mercantil Lisbonense.
120. See Fonseca, 'A Associação Comercial', p. 42.
121. Fonseca, *Cem Anos*, p. 80; see also Carvalho, *As Companhias*, pp. 84–85.
122. Proposal submitted by Pinto Basto Júnior as attachment to dispatch from Falcão to Gomes de Castro, 13 January 1844, ANTT, MNE, *cx*. 385.
123. *Annaes Maritimos e Coloniaes*, nos. 5 and 6, 1845, pp. 223 and 260, respectively.
124. Members of the Associação included well-known officers of the *Armada*, creditworthy businessmen, and several men who had been, were or would be governors, colonial deputies, ministers, heads of government and, of course, Sá da Bandeira (*Annaes Marítimos e Coloniaes*, no. 1, November 1840, pp. 52–55).
125. Ibid., nos. 10, 11 and 12, 1843, and no. 3, 1844, pp. 524, 571–73, 637–38 and 145–46, respectively (minutes of sessions of the Associação Marítima e Colonial); see also Carvalho, *As Companhias*, pp. 88–91.
126. *DCD*, session of 17 April 1855, p. 140. For the project, opinions and negotiations between the parties, see documentation attached to dispatch from Falcão to Gomes de Castro, 15 May 1843, ANTT, MNE, *cx*. 384.
127. *A Liga*, 11 November 1848, pp. 15–16. The Liga Promotora dos Interesses Materiais do País in a way reflects the level of importance colonial issues took on in the spectrum of Portuguese concerns at the time. The purpose of the association—which had members such as Farrobo, Terceira and other notables—was, as its name implies, to promote the development of the physical wealth of the country; in theory, developing the colonies was one

of the association's targets. The editor of the newspaper *A Liga* (4 November 1848, p. 3) promised to give close attention to the matter. But the promise remained just a promise, because the journal ended up devoting itself entirely to political economy, industry, the reorganization of the mails and, in a broader sense, roads and agriculture—but not to the colonies.

128. *DG*, 2 January 1839.
129. *DCD*, 12 March 1839, p. 543.
130. *DG*, 2 January 1839; *O Correio Portuguez*, 18 and 20 February 1843.
131. *DG*, 5 March 1850. For similar subtleties see also the editions of 10 and 26 October of the same year.
132. *Revista Económica*, 24 April 1846, p. 164.
133. *BOGGPA*, 24 January 1852, p. 3 (summary of speech by Palmerston, delivered on 14 July 1851). See also Charles Vogel, *Le Portugal et ses colonies. Tableau politique et commercial de la Monarquie Portugaise dans son état actuel*, Paris, 1860, p. 116.
134. *Boletim do Conselho Ultramarino*, August 1854, pp. 53–54.
135. Ibid., p. 55–62.
136. Carvalho, *As Companhias*, pp. 101–04; *DCD*, sessions of 17 and 18 April 1855.
137. Carvalho, *As Companhias*, pp. 105–06; for Courson's project, see *DG*, 12 September 1857.
138. *A Revolução de Septembro*, 11 July 1850, and *O Patriota*, 2 December 1850. For evidence of concern of a similar nature in the press, see *A Nação*, 2 and 17 January 1851.
139. The company in question was the Companhia Luso-Brasileira (the Luso-Brazilian Company). It had no state aid and was in direct competition with a British company, and so faced great difficulties; it made attempts to obtain a subsidy, in exchange for extending its services to West Africa, but in the end it was dissolved (João Pedro Marques, 'Penosa navegação: Portugal e as carreiras a vapor para África, 1850–82', *Anais de História de Além-Mar*, 2, 2001, pp. 278–83).
140. Report of 6 March 1851, *A Revolução de Septembro*, 2 June 1851.
141. For the contract with Philippon and the role played by this French capitalist, see *DG*, 28 June 1856; and Chamber of Peers, session of 27 June 1863, *DL*, 5 October 1863 (speech by Miguel do Canto).
142. See *BOGGPA*, 9 October 1858, pp. 5–8; *DG*, 8 September 1858.
143. *DL*, 18 August 1863 and 28 June 1864.
144. For the hope that these new circumstances would quickly lead to a demand for the company's shares, see Chamber of Deputies, session of 26 February 1861, *DL*, 28 February 1861 (speech by the Minister of Public Works, Tiago Horta).
145. Chamber of Deputies, session of 28 April 1864, *DL*, 30 April 1864; for the expression 'public indifference' in the inquiry into the activities of the Companhia União Mercantil, and for the table of shares issues and dealings over time see *DL*, 5 and 8 July 1864, respectively.
146. *DL*, 5 October 1863, Chamber of Peers, session of 27 June 1863.
147. Marques, 'Penosa navegação', p. 283 ff.
148. Ibid., pp. 291–96.
149. Manuel J. Pinheiro Chagas, *As colónias portuguesas no século XIX (de 1811 a 1890)*, Liv. A.M. Pereira, Lisbon, 1890, p. 164; Dias, 'Angola', p. 369.
150. Chamber of Deputies, session of 28 April 1864, *DL*, 30 April 1864 (italics in original).
151. *DL*, 19 August 1864. On the formation of the bank see Braga Paixão, *Cem anos do Banco Nacional Ultramarino na vida portuguesa, 1864–1964*, vol. I, Academia das Ciências de Lisboa, Lisbon, undated, p. 5 ff.
152. Tams, *Visita*, pp. 45 e 149.

153. Bordalo, *Ensaios*, p. 70.
154. *DCD*, session of 20 January 1849, p. 152 (speech by Lopes de Lima); for the deprecating remarks by Dias Damásio, see documents attached to dispatch from Falcão to Gomes de Castro, 15 May 1843, ANTT, MNE, *cx*. 384.
155. Clarence-Smith, *Third Portuguese Empire*, pp. 24–25 and 64; for the percentages of Brazilian trade in the period from 1839 to 1851, see Maria de Fátima Bonifácio, *Seis estudos sobre o liberalismo português*, Estampa, Lisbon, 1996, p. 131
156. *DG*, 5 January 1839, and *DCD*, session of 7 March 1839, p. 497 (report by the Minister of the Navy); for contracts signed with some dozen and a half interested parties, see *Boletim* and *Annaes do Conselho Ultramarino*.
157. It was Lopes de Lima who described him as the 'indefatigable farmer' (*Ensaios*, p. 48). In the report read out to the Cortes in August 1840, Bonfim, then Minister of the Navy, was already praising João Guilherme Pereira Barbosa as 'the only man who has devoted himself to agriculture (in the colonies)' (*Annaes Marítimos e Coloniais*, no. 4, 1841, p. 164).
158. Letter from José Pereira Barbosa to the governor of Angola, 17 October 1845, *DG*, 6 January 1846. For Barbosa's life history in the colony of Angola, see Aida Freudenthal, 'Arimos e Fazendas. A transição agrária em Angola, 1850–75', Universidade Nova de Lisboa, 1989 (unpublished master's degree thesis), p. 102 ff.
159. Attachment to dispatch from Vila Nova de Ourém to the Minister of Foreign Affairs, 30 May 1849, ANTT, MNE, *cx*. 387.
160. *Annaes do Conselho Ultramarino*, July 1854 and June 1855, pp. 411 and 155–56, respectively.
161. *DG*, 30 April 1857.
162. Freudenthal, 'Arimos', pp. 75 and 99 ff.; Dias, 'Angola', pp. 441–42.
163. In 1858, Carlos Bembé, an agent for a German company, applied for lands on the banks of the Zambezi, Count Henrique d'Arpoire applied for land in the Cuanza area and, at around the same time, a Manchester company was said to have been interested in developing cotton in Angola (*Annaes do Conselho Ultramarino*, July and December 1858, pp. 605 and 675, respectively). For the general scepticism on the practical results of the legislation, see Chamber of Deputies, sessions of 19 and 20 January 1863, *DL*, 21 and 23 January 1863 (speeches by Ferreri and Carlos Bento).
164. *BOGGPA*, 22 February 1862, pp. 60–61 (decree of 4 December 1861).
165. In Angola the largest concessions, of around 170,000 hectares of land, were given to the Englishman John Beaton, the Frenchman Jean de Bellegarde and the Fonsecas, Santos e Viana company; most of them, however, were of much smaller tracts of land, of around 5,000 to 10,000 hectares (and the funds contractually required were correspondingly lower); for a listing of concessions made at this time, see *BOGGPA*, 16 September 1865, p. 347; there were also one or two applications for lands in Cape Verde and Mozambique (see *Annaes do Conselho Ultramarino*, January 1862, November 1863 and March 1864, pp. 2, 88 and 30, respectively).
166. Chagas, *As colónias*, pp. 117–18, 123, 155–56, 160 and 163. The exception to the rule was the concession of over 9,000 hectares given to Teresa Barruncho, who would become the major exporter of cotton from Benguela in 1863–64 (see Dias, 'Angola', p. 435).
167. For details of the approx. 29 concessions given at this time, see *BOGGPA*, 10 October 1863, 23 April 1864, 18 March and 9 September 1865, pp. 340, 138, 109–10 and 335–36, respectively. For the increase in cotton production in the districts of Benguela and Moçâmedes in the period immediately before 1865, see Dias, 'Angola', pp. 435–36.
168. *Diário das Cortes*, session of 20 December 1822, p. 216; José Gonçalo Santa Rita, 'As questões coloniais nas Cortes Constituintes e na Segunda Legis-

latura (1821–1823)', *Revista da Faculdade de Letras de Lisboa*, XIV, 3, 1949, pp. 85–87.

169. A posteriori judgement of the *Boletim Official do Governo-Geral de Cabo Verde*, 29 June 1844, p. 260.
170. Carvalho, *As Companhias*, pp. 86–88; for the company's articles, see *Annaes do Conselho Ultramarino*, April 1855, p. 92 ff.
171. *A Revolução de Septembro*, 11 March 1843.
172. *DCD*, session of 17 April 1855, p. 140 (speech by Tavares de Macedo).
173. Oliveira Daun to marquis of Saldanha, 7 March 1836, in *Documentos àcerca do Tráfico da Escravatura extrahidos dos Papéis relativos a Portugal apresentados ao Parlamento Britannico*, Lisbon, 1840, p. 5.
174. *O Nacional*, 24 August 1836.
175. Sá da Bandeira to the Minister of Marine, 7 February 1838, ANTT, MNE, *liv.* 316.
176. Carvalho, *As Companhias*, pp. 75–76.
177. For the refusal by Goa, Damão and Diu to take part in the share issue of the company, see the account by deputy Peres da Silva (*DCD*, session of 15 October 1840, p. 319); on the city of Oporto's total lack of interest in the plan for the Mozambique Company, see José Capela, *A burguesia mercantile do Porto e as colónias (1834–1900)*, Afrontamento, Porto, 1975, p. 17.
178. Opinion on the formation of a Company for the *Estado da Índia*, 3 July 1840, Associação Comercial de Lisboa, minute book of the Associação Mercantil Lisbonense, pp. 250–51.
179. For the so-called Companhia Africana Ocidental Portuguesa (Portuguese West African Company), see Arsénio Pompílio Pompeu de Carpo, *Projecto d'uma Companhia para o melhoramento do commercio, agricultura e industria na Provincia de Angola, que se deve estabelecer na cidade de S. Paulo d'Assumpção de Loanda*, Lisbon, 1848, p. 7.
180. António Carreira, *O tráfico de escravos nos rios de Guiné e ilhas de Cabo Verde, 1810–1850. Subsídios para o seu estudo*, Junta de Investigação Científica do Ultramar, Lisbon, 1981, pp. 42–44.
181. Ibid., pp. 32–33; G.E. Brooks, 'A Nhara of the Guinea-Bissau Region: Mãe Aurélia Correia', in C.C. Robertson and M. Klein (eds), *Women and Slavery in Africa*, The University of Wisconsin Press, Madison, 1983, p. 314; the growing of peanuts for export was later carried on by António Ferreira and João Marques de Barros (see *Boletim Official do Governo-Geral de Cabo Verde*, 25 May 1852, pp. 377–78).
182. Jackson and Gabriel to Palmerston, 14 February 1848, PRO FO 84/719; *BOGGPA*, 12 September 1846; Freudenthal, 'Arimos', p. 93.
183. *Annaes Maritimos e Coloniaes*, no. 11, 1845, pp. 456–67. Carpo and Mirandinha had earlier suggested forming a mining company in Massangano, and a colonizing company in Lobito (*A Revolução de Septembro*, 1846).
184. Sousa e Almeida, who was born on the island and made a fortune with the traffic in Benguela, was one of those who encouraged the growing of coffee and cocoa. For this he was rewarded with honours and the title of Baron of Agua-Izé. For the grant of lands on the island of Príncipe, see *O Portuguez*, 22 November 1853.
185. *BOGGPA*, 14 February 1857, pp. 1–3.
186. Howard de Walden to Sá da Bandeira and his response, both dated 16 October 1856, AHM, Sá da Bandeira archive, *cx.* 5; from London, where he was posted as ambassador, Lavradio was also surprised at the grant made to a man like Flores (Lavradio to Atouguia, 16 March 1856, AMNE, *cx.* 985).
187. *Marinha e Colónias*, 1 February 1857, pp. 5–6.
188. *Annaes do Conselho Ultramarino*, February 1857, p. 566; *Boletim do Governo-Geral da Provincia de Moçambique*, 12 June 1858; for the concessions in Angola,

see *BOGGPA*, 14 February, 11 July 1857 and 25 July 1857; 9 April 1859; 1 and 22 February, 24 May and 6 September 1862; 17 January and 26 September 1863.

189. Pélissier, *Les Guerres*, p. 103; on the Western Africa Malachite Copper Mines Company Ltd., see *BOGGPA*, 9 April 1859, pp. 1–2.
190. *DG*, 13 January 1838.
191. Jules Duval, *Histoire de l'émigration au XIXe siècle. Europeènne, asiatique et africaine. Ses causes, ses caractères, ses effets*. Paris, 1862, p. 165.
192. Joel Serrão, *A emigração portuguesa. Sondagem histórica*, Horizonte, Lisbon, 1977 (1st edition 1972), pp. 42–43; Miriam Halpern Pereira, *A política portuguesa de emigração 1850–1930*, A Regra do Jogo, Lisbon, 1981, p. 15.
193. W.A. Green, 'Was British Emancipation a Success? The Abolitionist Perspective', in David Richardson (ed.), *Abolition and its Aftermath. The Historical Context, 1790–1916*, Frank Cass, London, 1985, p. 188; Seymour Drescher, *The Mighty Experiment. Free Labor versus Slavery in British Emancipation*, Oxford University Press, Oxford and New York, 2002, pp. 158 ff.
194. W.A. Green, 'The West Indies and British West African Policy in the Nineteenth-Century. A Corrective Comment', *Journal of African History*, XV, 2, 1974, p. 257; idem, *British Slave Emancipation: The Sugar Colonies and the Great Experiment, 1830–1865*, Clarendon Press, Oxford, 1976, p. 287.
195. Duval, *Histoire*, p. 168; Serrão, *A emigração*, p. 42.
196. Green, *British Slave Emancipation*, pp. 286–87.
197. Chamber of Peers, session of 3 April 1854, *DG*, 24 April 1854 (information supplied by Gomes de Castro); *A Revolução de Septembro*, 13 February 1854.
198. *DCD*, session of 7 July 1855, p. 112 (speech by Justino de Freitas). Of the 35 emigrant ships that entered Rio harbour between 1855 and 1861, coming from Portugal, 32 had an excessive number of passengers, carrying more (or far more) than their tonnage allowed (see the list in *DL*, 24 October 1861).
199. *O Nacional* (Porto), 13 July 1846; *O Patriota*, 13 October 1851.
200. *DCD*, sessions of 18 January and 5 February 1836, pp. 117–18 and 349–50, respectively (speeches by Leonel Tavares and Passos Manuel).
201. *DCP*, session of 26 April 1843, pp. 354–55. For similar opinions, see speeches by Lavradio and Linhares in the same session. In his constant insistence that emigration should be diverted to the African colonies, Sá sometimes used the paradoxical argument that emigrating to Demerara led to death, on account of the unhealthiness of that British colony (Chamber of Peers, sessions of 3 July 1849 and 26 April 1850, *DG*, 4 September 1849 and 30 April 1850, respectively).
202. *DCP*, session of 26 April 1843, pp. 353–55 (speeches by Vila Real, Gomes de Castro and Ornelas). For an even stronger argument in favour of Madeiran emigration, see Chamber of Peers, session of 3 July 1849, *DG*, 4 September 1849 (speeches by Palmela and especially the Baron of S. Pedro). See also *O Puritano*, 18 September 1846.
203. For the debate on the law of 1855, see *DCD*, session of 11 July 1855, and Chamber of Peers, session of 13 July 1855, *DG*, 9 August 1855.
204. Vitorino Magalhães Godinho, *Estrutura da Antiga sociedade portuguesa*, Arcádia, Lisbon, 1977 (1st edition 1971), p. 49.
205. Lima, *Ensaios*, p. 47 (n. 1); *DCD*, session of 14 June 1849, p. 168 (speech by Lopes de Lima).
206. The columnist-colonist was Bernardino Abreu e Castro, the head of the colony; for echoes of Moçâmedes colonization propaganda in the press in Portugal, see *DG*, 7 November 1849, 5 March, 19 April, 10 and 26 August 1850.
207. *BOGGPA*, 6 October 1849, p. 3.
208. Ibid., 16 February 1850, p. 3.

209. Ibid., 20 July 1850, p. 3.
210. Even though more colonists arrived later, in 1857 Moçâmedes had only 213 white inhabitants (*Boletim do Conselho Ultramarino*, August 1858, p. 497).
211. *BOGGPA*, 22 January 1859, p. 9.
212. *DCD*, session of 26 January 1858, p. 212.
213. Dias, 'Angola', p. 426. For the two colonies' regulations, see *Annaes do Conselho Ultramarino*, December 1857, pp. 509–10.
214. Chagas, *As colónias*, p. 130. The government launched a public offer to raise funds for the Pemba colony, but the results were poor: less than 2 *contos*, most of which came from a small group of 30 enthusiasts in Lisbon, which included, of course, businessmen with interests in the area, former colonial governors, former slavers (like Flores), enthusiast deputies and, needless to say, Sá da Bandeira, the idea's main mentor (*DG*, 20 March 1857).
215. Chagas, *As colónias*, p. 132.
216. *Annaes do Conselho Ultramarino*, January 1863 and March 1864, pp. 13 and 30, respectively.
217. Faro, *Os problemas*, p. 214.
218. Lima, *Ensaios*, p. 48.
219. *BOGGPA*, 9 February 1856, p. 7. For the relationship between the 'climate' and people's reluctance to commit capital to agricultural and commercial undertakings in Angola see *BOGGPA*, 5, 12 and 19 November 1864, pp. 404–05, 416–18 and 432–33, respectively.
220. Curtin, *Image of Africa*, p. 177.
221. Temperley, *White Dreams*, p. 45.
222. John D. Hardgreaves, 'African Colonization in the Nineteenth Century: Liberia and Sierra Leone', in J. Butler (ed.), *Boston University Papers in African History*, vol. 1, Boston University Press, Boston, 1964, pp. 59–60.
223. *Gazeta de Lisboa*, 12 February 1824, p. 157.
224. *Annaes Marítimos e Coloniaes*, no. 3, 1842, p. 139.
225. Chamber of Deputies, session of 23 April 1862, *DL*, 25 April 1862; see also *O Progressista*, 18 and 24 October 1863, for the definition of a similar programme.
226. *DCD*, session of 11 December 1826, p. 156. For a later view on the importance of propagandising in favour of the colonies, see *DCD*, session of 18 July 1860, pp. 188–89 (speech by Soares Franco).
227. *A Revolução de Septembro*, 6 December 1854; see also ibid., 18 January 1855, and *A Pátria*, 21 December 1855
228. *DCD*, session of 25 November 1840, p. 373.
229. *DCD*, session of 21 January 1840, pp. 112–15.
230. *DCD*, session of 27 March 1852, p. 328.
231. *DCD*, session of 29 July 1840, p. 440 (speeches by Menezes and Trindade); for similar assessments and complaints, see session of 12 June 1853, p. 178 (speech by Simão da Luz); session of 4 February 1857, p. 12 (speech by Bernardo da Costa).
232. Chamber of Peers, session of 24 May 1848, *DG*, 25 May 1848; see also session of 9 July 1857, *DG*, 8 August 1857 (speech by Atouguia); *DCD*, session of 16 June 1860, p. 224 (speech by Sousa Machado).
233. *DCD*, session of 28 January 1856, p. 40.
234. *DCD*, session of 13 February 1856, p. 95 (the expression is Afonso de Castro's); see also session of 16 July 1860, p. 164 (speech by Afonseca). For press comment on the episode, see *A Revolução de Septembro*, 30 January and 13 February 1856.
235. *DCD*, session of 2 June 1855, p. 25; for similar assessments see Chamber of Peers, session of 28 June 1849, *DG*, 24 August 1849 (speeches by Gomes de Castro and Palmela).

236. *DCD*, session of 11 January 1841, p. 15; see also sessions of 20 April 1859 and 6 March 1860, pp. 248 and 43, respectively (especially the speech by Afonseca); and Chamber of Peers, session of 22 June 1863, *DL*, 10 September 1863 (speech by Soares Franco).
237. *DCD*, session of 17 March 1843, p. 282 (see also p. 272 of the same session); further examples in session of 17 March 1843, pp. 274–75 (speech by Gomes de Castro); Chamber of Deputies, session of 6 August 1861, *DL*, 9 August 1861 (speech by the minister of the Navy, Carlos Bento).
238. Chamber of Senators, session of 26 April 1839, *DG*, 2 May 1839.
239. *DCD*, session of 16 January 1861, p. 55 (italics in original); for similar considerations, see session of 19 July 1850, p. 237 (speech by Lopes de Lima); Chamber of Deputies, session of 6 August 1861, *DL*, 9 August 1861 (speech by Pinto de Magalhães).
240. *DCD*, session of 1 June 1853, p. 16 (speech by Arrobas). For protests at the slimness of the navy budget, see Chamber of Peers, sessions of 25 June and 14 August 1853, and 14 March 1854, *DG*, 29 June and 16 August 1853, and 18 April 1854 (speeches by Lazarim); *DCD*, session of 30 May 1857, pp. 432–33 (speech by Fontes Pereira de Melo).
241. Chamber of Deputies, session of 25 July 1861, *DL*, 29 July 1861.
242. *DCD*, session of 15 May 1849, p. 251 (speech by Lopes de Lima); for the political reasons for the decline in the *Armada*'s ratings, see, among others, *O Ecco Popular*, 23 May 1848.
243. *A Revolução de Septembro*, 22 July 1850. Some days later the same newspaper published a long article in which no fewer than 77 measures to improve the country were announced; significantly, the few measures applicable to the colonies—a mere eight out of the total of 77—appeared at the end of the list (ibid., 19 August 1850).
244. *DCD*, session of 14 June 1849, p. 171 (speech by Antunes Pinto); see also session of 12 June 1849, pp. 154–58 (speeches by Pereira de Melo, Rebelo da Silva and Carlos Bento).
245. See *DCD*, sessions of 11, 23, 26 and 27 January 1858. A colonization fund had already been set up in 1852, using duties levied on alcoholic beverages exported to Africa, but it proved to be inadequate.
246. *DCD*, session of 30 May 1857, p. 422 ff.
247. *DCD*, session of 15 April 1859, p. 189 (speech by José Estevão); for a similar view in the press see *Revista das Colónias*, 18 and 28 September 1863.
248. Chamber of Deputies, session of 1 April 1865, *DL*, 4 April 1865 (speech by Loulé).
249. Chamber of Deputies, session of 11 April 1864, *DL*, 13 April 1864; see also, in the same session, the speech by Mendes Leal and, in the session of 27 April 1864, *DL*, 29 April 1864, the speech by Sá Nogueira.

Conclusions

There were two different reasons for the relative silence that reigned over the history of the abolition of the slave trade in Portugal. From the outset there was the typical silence surrounding a subject that had not been studied sufficiently, but this was not based on any serious lack of public statements on the problem of the 'odious commerce', or even on their extreme rarity. Over the first two-thirds of the nineteenth century such statements on the slave trade were many and varied, and sufficient material was available to give the subject the resonance it lacked. But another type of silence had fallen on the issue of abolition, an intrinsic silence that reflected not just the country's aseptic detachment, but also a form of resistance to the advance of abolitionism. It was a silence that carried a load of different meanings and which had been adopted voluntarily, and was therefore of historic significance and could never be avoided or ignored. On the contrary, a complete understanding of the Portuguese position on the abolition of the slave trade demanded that this silence should be interpreted and assessed. The work I carried out on these two types of silence enabled me to ascertain that resistance to abolition in Portugal was in effect strong and persistent, both before and after Brazilian independence. On the ideological level, this resistance took the form of tolerationism; on the practical level, its preferred manifestation was inaction.

As the eighteenth century moved into the nineteenth, the Portuguese remained essentially detached from the problem of abolitionism. This does not mean that there was a complete void in relation to the issue. In fact, there were two ways of viewing the slave trade. One of them, which I have called the tolerationist perspective, was critical of the injustices and inhumanities of that trade, but was prepared to countenance its continuation, if only temporarily, for political and economic reasons. The other, the pro-slavery view, was an older point of view that justified the slave trade and the ownership of men in terms of the salvation of souls and the lesser evil for the Africans.

Tolerationism and pro-slavery were different conceptions, but they were not antagonistic and not even mutually exclusive. There was even a key point of convergence between them, in so far as both had as an immediate aim the maintenance of the status quo, even if only by way of silence or omission. This veil of silence, partially imposed by the censor, was in large measure responsible for keeping the Portuguese in ignorance, for a very long time, of the directions in which abolitionism was going in the outside world (above all, in Great Britain). This ignorance explains the ease with which, in 1810, the Portuguese government agreed to be coupled to the British abolitionist locomotive, committing the country to a way of thinking that was alien to it and to actions that were frankly contrary to its immediate material interests. It also explains the feeling of having been cheated that took hold of the nation as the first arrests of slave ships were made by the Royal Navy, a feeling that was moreover constantly exacerbated, because those arrests were nothing more than the beginning of political pressure that would continue to manifest itself, in this and in other ways, throughout the nineteenth century.

Initially, Portuguese governments managed to resist the first wave of British abolitionist pressure, even if they had to give some ground in order to preserve essentials, namely supplying Brazil with slave labour. In any event, at the beginning of the 1820s Portugal was the only colonial nation that still had a legal slave trade (even though only south of the equator). However, the long-drawn-out dispute with Britain affected the way abolitionism was thereafter viewed in Portugal. To the extent that the attack on the slave trade was seen as foreign interference, abolitionism took on from the outset a negative connotation vis-à-vis sovereignty and national independence. In other words, it became part of a wider political controversy that necessarily affected it, limiting its future scope and confining it to particular channels of expression. These channels, which tended to become constricted and more rigid in periods of greater foreign pressure, made it more difficult for an independent and outspoken abolitionism to emerge.

This was first of all because British pressure and the corresponding Portuguese resistance narrowed the ideological spectrum. As far as ideas were concerned, the most interesting characteristic of the 1810s was the complete disappearance of public manifestations of pro-slavery thinking, or, rather, the dissimulation of this type of ideology in tolerationist arguments. Because of the amalgam thus produced, tolerationism, the only remaining form of non-abolitionist thinking, which from then on existed in both the sincere and the dissembled version, usually became a means of obstructing abolition.

The dissembled version of tolerationism, which emerged in the first half of the 1810s with the slave traders, some members of the government and, above all, the press, persisted over time, adjusting to new developments and challenges and parroting the changes in the opposing ideology so as to absorb and neutralize it. At times when the controversy died down somewhat, this obstructive ideology tended to evaporate and was barely noticed. In contrast, at times when controversy was greatest or when British pressure for abolition increased, it came out into the full light of day, sometimes very virulently. This happened from 1838 to 1840, a time when strong arguments against abolition appeared in the voices of the slave traders, inundated the pages of the main newspapers, led to articles in its defence and found echoes in the Cortes and in the *Septembrista* government itself. The end of the 1830s was the period in which there was the clearest evidence of the strong opposition that suppression of the slave trade generated in Portugal. Later on, this opposition receded and was once again submerged in relative silence. But the obstructive ideology remained alive and adaptive, re-emerging strongly from the end of the 1850s onwards, both in the newspapers and in the Cortes, at the time when the issue of the transport of freedmen to São Tomé and Príncipe arose.

Much of the strength of this disguised ideology of slavery derived from its proximity to the sincere version of tolerationism, which was based on a number of shared concepts. Admittedly, the sincere tolerationist, as a rule, did not see the slave trade as a lesser evil, nor did he assume that the African was intrinsically barbarous. But everything else —the denigration of British philanthropy, the fear of financial collapse and the loss of the colonies, the arguments in favour of gradualism and national honour in its struggle against foreign interference—took him ideologically closer to the position of those who were in the obstructionist camp. And the positions became even closer whenever outside pressure was greatest and suppression imminent. The sincere variant of tolerationism was a way of thinking that expanded and contracted according to the extent of and variation in British interference. When confronted by practical measures or unexpected difficulties, it tended to resort to obstruction, instead of advancing firmly and perseveringly in favour of abolition. It was voluble and inconsistent and, as with retaliatory abolitionism, it depended on an improbable combination of circumstances, in particular on the abandonment of Brazilian markets in favour of a firm commitment to Africa. The tendency of these pro-abolition ideas to recede is particularly marked at the end of the 1830s, a period when the increase in British pressure and the imminent end of the slave trade led to an exponential growth in fears of losing the colonies and desperate arguments in favour of gradualism—even though, paradoxically, the slave trade had already been prohibited by law—that is to say, it led to the re-establishment of a common front with the obstructivists.

The ideological promiscuousness between sincere and dissembling tolerationists would only unravel in the 1840s, when the function of the idea of national honour within the tolerationist ideology was reversed, and defence of the nation's dignity required a frontal assault on the slave trade (rather than giving sustenance to obstinate resistance to British abolitionist pressure). The conviction that national decorum demanded effective suppression was not new, but it was only from 1839–40 onwards, in the time preceding Palmerston's bill and in its aftermath, that this idea became generally accepted among the political elites and the journalists and helped decisively to overcome the country's resistance to suppression. From then on it became the main engine of what would be Portuguese action against the slave trade.

Until then, Portugal's action had been nothing more than an accurate reflection of the realm of ideas: action—or, more accurately, inaction—that accepted the continuation of the 'iniquitous commerce'. Even though Portugal had signed various international agreements on abolition and established its own anti-slave trade legislation, Portuguese governments did little or nothing to prevent the trade in slaves. Up to 1822, they invoked the interests of Brazil to justify this paralysis. Later on, it was the interests and the survival of Africa—as well as the lack of material resources—which allegedly made it difficult to put its own laws into effect. For a time, in the 1820s, it seemed that Portuguese journalists, parliamentarians and ministers had come together to form a consensus on abolition. However, that consensus was circumstantial: different ways of thinking had momentarily converged, and it all fell apart. In 1826 Morais Sarmento did put forward a draft law for the abolition of the slave trade, but nothing came of it. And, as the years passed, Sarmento lost most of his initial enthusiasm.

The manoeuvrings of Sá da Bandeira in the second half of the 1830s were more persistent, but also much more complex. Having sponsored an unsuccessful abolitionist bill in the Cortes at the beginning of 1836, Sá took advantage of the period of the *Septembrista* dictatorship to have a law passed that totally abolished the Portuguese slave trade. However, this law, which did not reflect any true commitment on the part of the country, was not immediately applied, and would even come to be the foundation for tenacious resistance to signing an abolition treaty with Britain. It was, as we have seen, one step forward and two steps back.

Historians have attributed the failure of *Septembrista* abolitionism to factors that were external to the Portuguese 'will', mainly the opposition the law of 1836 faced in the colonies. I believe I have successfully established that the major obstacle to suppression, in the period under study, lay in Portugal itself. Essentially, it was the build-up of internal opposition to the immediate suppression of the slave trade (centred, as usual, on the imagined loss of the colonies) which led Sá to embark on a duplicitous policy: on the one hand, he sought to encourage the abolition of the traffic in slaves and, on the other, he resisted signing an Anglo-Portuguese treaty (without which it would be difficult to end that trade). This duplicitous policy in essence sought to encourage abolition at a pace that was compatible with Portuguese interests and feelings, at the same time providing a legal umbrella against British abolitionist pressure. It might have succeeded if it had achieved practical results and had been backed by a solid interest in Africa. But the emigrant and the capitalist remained aloof from the attractions of African shores, and the authorities continued to tolerate the slavers. With the failure of his ambivalent policy, and being unable to sign the treaty on account of pressure from the slavers, from those hostile to the British and, above all, from sincere tolerationists, who were alarmed at the possibility of losing the colonies—a coalition of ill will that was too broad to be confronted by the *Septembrista* government—Sá was left with no way out and, from 1838 onwards, became entangled in a labyrinth of argument and legal minutiae.

It was the violent action by Britain in 1839 and the sharp blow it inflicted on national honour, as well as, more remotely, the risk that blow entailed for holding on to the colonies, which forced Portugal to undertake steadfast anti-slave trade measures. From 1839 onwards, Portugal's governments sought to align themselves unambiguously with British abolitionist policy. To this end, they placed most of their warships in African waters, and this brought the first tangible results: the seizure of slave ships. With the advent of Anglo-Portuguese naval (and land-based) action, the Portuguese flag ceased to be sought after by slave traders, and the trade declined, or moved to areas outside Lisbon's jurisdiction.

At the end of thirty years of hesitation and subterfuge Portugal had finally joined the 'cause of humanity', not because there had spread throughout the country a consistent condemnation of the slaver or because there were strong economic interests pressuring for a different way of exploiting Africa, but because national honour was at stake. In the years that followed, in between the usual concessions to the slavers, there was also a definite effort to cut back the slave trade, which resulted in the capture or destruction of over 120 slaving ships. Slowly, dragged up by force, Portugal acquired the legitimacy to claim a place among the abolitionist nations and to cash in on the corresponding political dividends.

APPENDIXES

The sources for the Appendixes are as follows: *BOGGPA* (various editions); annual reports of cases tried by the mixed commissions of Luanda and Cape of Good Hope; table of captures drawn up by Gomes de Oliveira, 13 April 1844 (PRO FO 84/521); report by Gabriel to Palmerston, 5 August 1850 (PRO FO 84/792); *Memória àcerca da extinção da escravidão e do trafico de escravos no território portuguez*, Ministério da Marinha, Lisbon, 1889, pp. 85 ff.; António Esparteiro, *Três séculos no mar (1640–1910)*, 32 vols., Ministério da Marinha, Lisbon, 1974–86.

APPENDIX A. Number of days that ships of the *Armada* suitable for combating the slave trade were immobilized in Lisbon, from 1/1/1835 to 31/12/1840

Ships Name		1835	1836	1837	1838	1839	1840
Schooner	*Faial*	152	245	196	320	157	174
	Amélia	227	265	85	365	366	167
	Maria Isabel	177	298	365	365	366	365
	Algarve[1]	131	74	339	109		
	Esperança[2]	228	188	279	304	296	260
	Boa Vista[3]				0	51	53
	Cabo Verde[4]			0	118	106	
Brig	*Audaz*	148	89	0	0	153	365
	Tejo	174	242	306	175	0	0
	São Boaventura	366	365	184	231	277	242
	Conde de Vila Flor	120	0	56	365	217	365
	D. Pedro	200	84	168	193	153	255
	Liberal	273	199	242	365	148	195
	Faro	186	180	0	233	131	264
Corvette	*Urânia*[5]				161	0	133
	Galateia[6]	282	229	106	214		
	Elisa[7]	160	321	154	334	79	
	Dª. Isabel Maria	228	126	365	82	0	0
	D. João I	48	301	273	365	276	166
	8 de Julho	366	365	365	365	366	83
Total		204	210	205	253	175	188

Note: the corvettes *Infanta Regente* and *Damão* were not taken into account here. They were permanently stationed in India during this time.

1. The schooner *Algarve* was judged unfit for service in July 1838.
2. Came into service in March 1835.
3. Schooner arrested in Bissau, came into service in mid-1838.
4. Schooner arrested in Cape Verde, came into service in mid-1838.
5. *Urânia* was under arrest in Brest, and only returned to Lisbon on 14 May 1838.
6. Caught fire in the Tagus and sank on 3 February 1839.
7. *Elisa* was scuttled as useless at the end of 1839.

APPENDIX B. Number of days that ships of the *Armada* were at sea and in the colonies of Africa, from 1/1/1835 to 31/12/1840

Ships Name		1835	1836	1837	1838	1839	1840
Schooner	*Faial*	116	58	0	0	187	176
	Amélia	0	0	255	0	0	0
	Maria Isabel	0	0	0	0	0	0
	Algarve[1]	59	254	0	76		
	Esperança[2]	0	0	0	0	0	70
	Boa Vista[3]				181	297	300
	Cabo Verde[4]				184	230	240
Brig	*Audaz*	200	228	215	365	182	0
	Tejo	110	0	0	0	122	365
	São Boaventura	0	0	160	119	75	100
	Conde de Vila Flor	0	0	0	0	60	322
	D. Pedro	0	0	0	145	200	0
	Liberal	0	0	0	0	0	0
	Faro	0	0	0	0	0	30
Corvette	*Urânia*[5]				51	366	221
	Galateia[6]	0	102	242	138		
	Elisa[7]	0	0	0	0	50	
	Dª. Isabel Maria	0	0	0	28	275	365
	D. João I	0	0	0	0	0	0
	8 de Julho	0	0	0	0	0	60
Total		28	38	51	72	114	132

Note: the corvettes *Infanta Regente* and *Damão* were not taken into account here. They were permanently stationed in India during this time.

1. For calculating the average, and given that it was judged unfit for service in July 1838, the *Algarve* counts as half a unit only.
2. Came into service in 1835.
3. Came into service in mid-1838.
4. Came into service in mid-1838.
5. Was under arrest in Brest, and only returned to Lisbon on 14 May 1838.
6. Sank on 3 February 1839.
7. Scuttled as useless at the end of 1839.

APPENDIX C. Arrests, demolitions and sinkings of slave ships, carried out by the Portuguese *Armada*, between 1839 and 1867

Cape Verde/Guinea area				
Date	Ship arrested	Flag	Arresting vessel	Location
? / ? /1839	Brigantine *Ensaiador*	Spanish	Schooner *Cabo Verde*	?
06/09/1840	Schooner *Nova Constituição*	Portuguese	Schooner *Boa Vista*	Island of Praia
11/07/1841	Schooner *Dª Maria II*	Portuguese	Schooner *Boa Vista*	Bissau
São Tomé/Angola area				
Date	Ship arrested	Flag	Arresting vessel	Location
17/03/1839	Brig *Maria Virgínia*	Portuguese	Schooner *Faial*	High seas
23/03/1839	Schooner *Paquete Portuguez*	Portuguese	Corvette *Urânia*	Mouth of the Zaïre
25/09/1839	Schooner *Dª Clara*	Brazilian	Brig *Tejo*	Island of Príncipe
19/01/1840	Schooner *Nereide*	Portuguese	Corvette *Urânia*	Mouth of the Dande
03/02/1840	Schooner *Águia*	Portuguese	Brig *Tejo*	S. Tomé
03/02/1840	Schooner *Nova Madalena*	Portuguese	Brig *Tejo*	S. Tomé
05/02/1840	Brig *Caçador*	Portuguese	Corvette *Urânia*	South of Luanda
10/07/1840	Brigantine *Nereide*	Portuguese	Brig *Tejo*	Luanda
03/01/1842	Schooner *Virtuosa Maria Aldina*	Brazilian	Corvette *8 de Julho*	Benguela
26/03/1842	Sumacca *Amizade*	Brazilian	Corvette *8 de Julho*	Benguela
07/07/1842	Sumacca *Maria Rosa*	Brazilian	Schooner *Conselho do Governo*	?
07/07/1843	Sumacca *Rio Tâmega*	Portuguese	?	?
07/07/1843	Brig *Paquete de Benguela*	Portuguese	?	?
07/07/1843	Brig *S. Manuel Augusto*	Portuguese	Corvette *8 de Julho*	Benguela
15/05/1844	Launch ?	Portuguese	Corvette *Urânia*	Buraco
27/05/1844	Brig *Caçador*	Brazilian	Corvette *Urânia*	Mouth of the Dande
24/06/1844	Brig ?	?	Corvette *Urânia*	Mouth of the Dande
11/09/1844	Brig *Jupiter*	Brazilian	Launch no. ?	Buraco

Date	Ship arrested	Flag	Arresting vessel	Location
11/09/1844	10 Launches	Portuguese	Launch no. ?	?
15/12/1844	Brig *Bom Sucesso*	Brazilian	Launch no. ?	Cape Ledo
02/01/1845	Brig *Despique da Inveja*	Brazilian	Schooner *Ninfa*	Mouth of the Cuanza
31/01/1845	Brigantine *Canário*	Brazilian	Corvette *Relâmpago*	Quicombo
04/05/1845	Launch ?	Portuguese	Schooner *Ninfa*	Benguela Velha
15/05/1845	Brig *Constante Amizade*	Brazilian	Corvette *Relâmpago*	Mouth of the Cuanza
15/05/1845	Brig *Lealdade*	Brazilian	Corvette *Relâmpago*	Mouth of the Cuanza
22/05/1845	Brig *Cacique*	Brazilian	Corvette *Relâmpago*	Cape Ledo
05/06/1845	Galley *Primavera*	Brazilian	Corvette *Relâmpago*	Ambriz
06/06/1845	Schooner *Gago*	?	Launch no. ?	Mouth of the Cuanza
04/08/1845	Brigantine *Favorita*	Brazilian	Corvette *Relâmpago*	Loacho
27/10/1845	Brig *Lady Sale*	British	Schooner *Constituição*	Ambriz
17/02/1846	Sumacca *Boa União*	Brazilian	Corvette *Urânia*	Ambriz
10/04/1846	Sumacca *Lealdade*	Brazilian	Corvette *Relâmpago*	Ambrizete
11/04/1846	Brigantine *Espírito Santo*	Brazilian	Corvette *Relâmpago*	Ambrizete
23/05/1846	Brigantine *Felicidade*	Brazilian	Corvette *Relâmpago*	Ambriz
19/08/1846	Brig ?	?	Schooner *Ninfa*	Ambriz
17/09/1846	Sumacca *Nova Trindade*	Brazilian	Cutter *Príncipe Real*	Mouth of the Dande
19/09/1846	Yacht ?	?	Schooner *Ninfa*	Ambriz
30/10/1846	Sumacca *Flor de Campos*	Brazilian	Brig *Tâmega*	Benguela
08/07/1847	Launch ?	?	Launch no. 5	Mossulo
27/07/1847	Sumacca *Bom Fim*	Brazilian	Schooner *Ninfa*	Benguela Velha
08/08/1847	Sumacca *Paquete de Itagoahy*	Brazilian	Corvette *Relâmpago*	Ambriz
01/09/1847	Brig *Paquete Portuense*	Brazilian	Cutter *Príncipe Real*	Mouth of the Dande
13/12/1847	Sumacca *Amor de Pátria*	Brazilian	Corvette *Relâmpago*	Ambriz
24/01/1848	Schooner *Emília*	?	Brig *Mondego*	Loacho
20/02/1848	Launch ?	?	Schooner *Ninfa*	South of Luanda
24/02/1848	Launch *Fortuna*	?	Schooner *Ninfa*	Benguela Velha
27/02/1848	Brigantine *Aurora*	Brazilian	Schooner *Ninfa*	Benguela Velha
06/04/1848	Brig *Dois Amigos*	?	Corvette *Relâmpago*	Corimba

Date	Ship arrested	Flag	Arresting vessel	Location
16/05/1848	Brigantine *Voador*	Brazilian	Yacht *15 de Agosto*	Novo Redondo
22/05/1849	Brig ?	?	Schooner *Ninfa*	Benguela
07/11/1849	Polacca *Esperança*	Brazilian	Brig *Corimba*	Benguela Velha
17/06/1850	Schooner *Rival*	?	Yacht *15 de Agosto*	Mouth of the Dande
18/02/1856	Brig ?	North American	Brig *Serra do Pilar*	Benguela Velha
20/10/1856	Launch ?	?	Schooner *Conde do Tojal*	Mouth of the Loge
18/07/1857	Barque *Velha Anita*	Spanish	Schooner *Cabo Verde*	Benguela Velha
? /09/1860	6 Launches	?	Yacht *D. Pedro V*	Zaïre
02/09/1860	Brigantine *Equimina*	Portuguese	Brig *Pedro Nunes*	Luanda
21/01/1861	Brig *Lord of the Isles*	British	Schooner *Cabo Verde*	Moçâmedes
10/02/1861	2 Launches	?	Yacht *D. Pedro V*	Zaire
26/02/1864	Brigantine *Virgen del Refugio*	Spanish	Schooner *Napier*	Rio Tapado
24/10/1864	Launch *Foguete*	?	Schooner *Napier*	Benguela
?/10/1864	Launch *Sensível*	?	Schooner *Napier*	Benguela

Mozambique area

Date	Ship arrested	Flag	Arresting vessel	Location
25/03/1841	Brig *D. Manuel de Portugal*	Portuguese	Corvette *Real Príncipe D. Pedro*[1]	Lourenço Marques
23/06/1841	Brigantine *Paquete da Madeira*	Portuguese	Corvette *Real Príncipe D. Pedro*	Lourenço Marques
17/06/1842	Polacca *Ignez*	Brazilian	Brig *Gentil Libertador*[2]	Quelimane
07/07/1843	Yacht *Philantropico*	Portuguese	? ?	
26/08/1845	Brig *Montevideu*	?	Brig *D. João de Castro*	Island of Macaloé
07/09/1845	2 Dhows	?	Brig *Conde de Vila Flor*	Pemba
08/09/1845	Dhow?	?	Brig *Conde de Vila Flor*	Pemba
07/07/1845	Galliot ?	Dutch	Cutter *Andorinha*	Fernão Veloso Bay
28/11/1846	Dhow?	?	Brig *Tejo*	Ibo
03/03/1847	Brig *Commerce of Providence*	North American	Brig *D. João de Castro*	Quelimane
24/03/1847	Polacca *S. Francisco II*	Sardinian	Schooner *Infante D. Henrique*	Angoxe

Date	Ship arrested	Flag	Arresting vessel	Location
21/11/1847	Brig *Magoum*	North American	Brig *D. João de Castro*	Angoxe
07/06/1849	Dhow *Uxar*	?	Yacht *Voador*	Cabo Delgado
07/07/1857	Dhow ?	?	Yacht *19 de Maio*	Chicoma
29/11/1857	Barque *Charles et Georges*	French	Brigantine *Zambeze*	Conducia
31/12/1859	Dhow *Fatol Her*	?	Schooner *Angra*	?
25/02/1860	Dhow *Ganima*	?	Schooner *Angra*	Chicoma
14/08/1860	Dhow *Zagalle*	?	Schooner *Angra*	Pemba
01/08/1861	Dhow	?	Schooner *Angra*	Mocambo
07/01/1865	2 Dhows	?	Schooner *Barão de Lazarim*	Conducia
07/01/1865	Dhow *Toba*	?	Cutter *Andorinha*	?
17/01/1865	Dhow?	?	Steamship *Maria Anna*	Mozambique
30/03/1866	2 Dhows	?	Schooner *Barão de Lazarim*	River Sto. António
17/03/1867	3 Dhows	?	Schooner *Barão de Lazarim*	Mocambo
07/12/1867	2 Dhows	?	Corvette *Infante D. João*	?

Notes
1. Would later be called *Relampâgo*.
2. Would later be called *D. João de Castro*.

APPENDIX D. Arrests of slave ships carried out by various administrative and port authorities between 1837 and 1870

Date	Ship arrested	Flag	Arresting person	Location
		Cape Verde / Guinea area		
?/04/1837	Schooner *Esther*	Portuguese	Governor of Cape Verde	Bissau
?/09/1837	Schooner *Funny Buttler*	North American	Governor of Cape Verde	Cape Verde
?/09/1837	Schooner *Roberto*	Portuguese	Governor of Cape Verde	Cape Verde
?/09/1837	Schooner *Constituição*	Portuguese	Governor of Cape Verde	Cape Verde
?/ ?/1844	Schooner *Fortuna*	Brazilian	Governor of Bissau	Bissau
		São Tomé / Angola area		
Date	Ship arrested	Flag	Arresting person	Location
27/04/1842	Brig *Rosa*	Brazilian	Governor of Angola	Luanda
?/03/1844	Cutter *Red Rover*	British	Governor of S. Tomé	?
?/11/1844	Schooner *Ninfa Catalana*	?	Governor of S. Tomé	?
		Mozambique area		
Date	Ship arrested	Flag	Arresting person	Location
13/07/1840	Brig *Importador*	Portuguese	Governor of Mozambique	?
27/07/1840	Galley *D. Maria II*	Portuguese	Governor of Mozambique	?
31/07/1840	Barque *Maria da Glória*	Portuguese	Governor of Mozambique	?
14/11/1840	Brig *Fortuna de África*	Portuguese	Governor of Quelimane	?
28/05/1842	Dhow *Mossumgario*	Portuguese	Governor of Mozambique	?
14/11/1842	Dhow *Nagar*	Portuguese	Governor of Mozambique	?
28/02/1846	Brig ?	?	Governor of Mozambique	?
?/ ?/1861	Dhow *Sabala*	?	Governor of the Ibo	Ibo

APPENDIX D (CONTINUED)

The following slave ships were captured with slaves on board:

1. In the São Tomé/Angola area: Brig *Rosa*, arrested by the Governor of Angola with 68 slaves on board; Schooner *Nereide*, arrested in January 1840 with 92 slaves; Brig *Caçador*, arrested in May 1844 with 844 slaves; 10 Launches arrested in September 1844 with a total of 95 slaves; Launch arrested in May 1845 with 92 slaves; Sumacca *Flor de Campos*, arrested in October 1846 with 195 slaves; Launch arrested in July 1847 with 3 slaves; Launch arrested in February 1848 with 20 slaves; 6 Launches arrested in September 1860 with a total of 65 slaves; Brigantine *Equimina*, arrested in 1860, with 11 slaves on board; Launches arrested in 1861 with a total of 33 slaves.
2. In the Mozambique area: Dhow arrested in July 1857 with 20 slaves; Barque *Charles et Georges* arrested in November 1857 with 110 slaves; Dhow arrested in 1861 by the Governor of the Ibo with 9 slaves; Dhow arrested in January 1865 by the Cutter *Andorinha* with 160 slaves; and Dhow arrested in the same month by the steamship *Maria Anna* with 61 slaves.

These tables do not take into account arrests made by naval forces on land, in search-and-destroy missions to the barracoons and other slaving establishments. Nor do they take into account the arrests and scuttlings undertaken in the Indian Ocean between 1868 and 1880 (19 Dhows and 2 Launches).

APPENDIX E. Total arrests up to 1867

Year	Cape Verde/ Guinea area Ships	São Tomé/ Angola area Ships and Launches	Mozambique area Ships
1837	4	0	0
1838	0	0	0
1839	1	3	0
1840	1	5	4
1841	1	0	2
1842	0	4	3
1843	0	3	1
1844	1	17	0
1845	0	10	5
1846	0	8	2
1847	0	5	3
1848	0	6	0
1849	0	2	1
1850	0	1	0
1851	0	0	0
1852	0	0	0
1853	0	0	0
1854	0	0	0
1855	0	0	0
1856	0	2	0
1857	0	1	2
1858	0	0	0
1859	0	0	1
1860	0	7	2
1861	0	3	2
1862	0	0	0
1863	0	0	0
1864	0	3	0
1865	0	0	4
1866	0	0	2
1867	0	0	5
Totals	8	80	39

Bibliography

MANUSCRIPTS

Academia das Ciências de Lisboa
'Diccionário jornalístico Portuguez' (Manuscrito Azul, *cota* 445–47)

Arquivo Geral de Marinha (AGM), Lisbon
Caixas 50 and 311
Livros 32 and 135

Arquivo Histórico Militar (AHM), Lisbon
Arquivo Sá da Bandeira, *caixas* 1–21

Arquivo Histórico Ultramarino (AHU), Lisbon
Papéis Sá da Bandeira, *maço* 824

Arquivo Nacional da Torre do Tombo (ANTT), Lisbon
Real Mesa Censória
Caixa 142
Livro 12

Ministério dos Negócios Estrangeiros (MNE)
Caixas 35 (*maço* 10), 43 (*maço* 6), 53 (*maço* 2), 223, 224, 229, 382–87, 461, 464, 481, 485, 492, 496, 707–11, 732–33, 930 and 961.
Livros 47, 113–14, 179–85, 315–17, 535–36, 565–76, 583 and 592

Ministério do Reino
Livro 1

Arquivo do Ministério dos Negócios Estrangeiros (AMNE), Lisbon
Caixas 985 and 1150–53

Associação Comercial de Lisboa
Livro de Actas da Associação Mercantil Lisbonense (minute book)

Biblioteca Nacional (BN), Lisbon
Reservados: *livros* 4710 and 9049–93

Public Record Office (PRO), London

FO 84 (Foreign Office, Slave Trade): 10, 31, 41, 54, 72, 103, 140, 155, 178, 202, 215, 248, 249, 250, 251, 281, 282, 283, 284, 320, 321, 322, 361, 362, 403, 404, 436, 464, 517, 521, 569, 579, 626, 631, 671, 676, 719, 724, 757, 762, 763, 764, 792, 793, 798, 799

PRINTED SOURCES

Journals and other Periodical Publications[1]

(O) *Amigo do Povo*, Lisbon (1820–21)
Annaes das Sciências, das Artes e das Letras, Paris (1818–22)
Annaes do Conselho Ultramarino, Lisbon (1854–65)
Annaes Maritimos e Coloniaes, Lisbon (1840–46)
Astro da Lusitania, Lisbon (1820–23)
(O) *Athleta*, Porto (1838–39)
Boletim do Conselho Ultramarino, Lisbon (1854–65)
Boletim do Governo Geral da Província de Moçambique, Mozambique (1854–58)
Boletim Official do Governo-Geral de Cabo Verde, Boa Vista (1842–62)
Boletim Official do Governo-Geral da Província de Angola, Luanda (1845–65)
Campeão Lisbonense, Lisbon (1821–23)
Campeão Portuguez, London (1819–21)
Campeão Portuguez em Lisboa, Lisbon (1822–23)
(O) *Compilador*, Lisbon (1821–22)
(O) *Constitucional*, Lisbon (1839)
Correio Braziliense, London (1808–22)
Correio da Tarde, Lisbon (1823)
Correio de Lisboa, Lisbon (1837–42)
(O) *Correio Portuguez*, Lisbon (1841–45)
(O) *Democrata*, Lisbon (1839–40)
Diário da Câmara dos Deputados, Lisbon (1826–65)
Diário da Câmara dos Pares, Lisbon (1835, 1842–43)
Diário das Cortes, Lisbon (1821–23)
Diário de Lisboa, Lisbon (1859–65)
Diário do Governo, Lisbon (1835–59)
(O) *Director*, Lisbon (1839–40)
(O) *Ecco*, Lisbon (1835–40)
(O) *Ecco Popular*, Porto (1847–49)
(O) *Estandarte*, Lisbon (1847–50)
Gazeta de Lisboa, Lisbon (up to 1828)
Gazeta de Portugal, Lisbon (1822–23)
Gazeta Universal, Lisbon (1821–23)
Idade d'Ouro do Brazil, Bahia (1813–19)
(O) *Independente*, Lisbon (1821–22)
(O) *Investigador Portuguez em Inglaterra*, London (1811–18)
Jornal da Sociedade Literária e Patriótica, Lisbon (1822)
Jornal do Comércio, Lisbon (1865–69)
(A) *Lança*, Lisbon (1840)
(A) *Liga*, Lisbon (1848–49)
(The) *Lisbon Chronicle*, Lisbon (1839)
(The) *Lisbon English Journal*, Lisbon (1836)
(The) *Lisbon Mail*, Lisbon (1836–37 and 1840)
Marinha e Colónias, Lisbon (1856–57)
Memorial Ultramarino e Marítimo, Lisbon (1836)

Microscópio de Verdades, London (1814–15)
Miscellanea Politica, Lisbon (1836–38)
(*A*) *Nação*, Lisbon (1847–65)
(*O*) *Nacional*, Lisbon (1834–42)
(*O*) *Nacional*, Porto (1846–53)
Observador Luzitano em Paris, Paris (1815)
(*O*) *Panorama*, Lisbon (1837–42)
Paquete do Ultramar, Lisbon (1839–40)
(*A*) *Pátria*, Porto (1849–55)
(*O*) *Patriota*, Lisbon (1843–50)
(*O*) *Popular*, Lisbon (1836–37)
(*O*) *Portuguez*, London (1814–25)
(*O*) *Portuguez*, Lisbon (1853–54)
(*O*) *Progressista*, Porto (1846–47 and 1863)
(*O*) *Puritano*, Porto (1846–48)
(*A*) *Restauração*, Lisbon (1842–46)
(*A*) *Revista*, Lisbon (1833–36)
Revista das Colónias, Lisbon (1863)
Revista Económica, Lisbon (1846)
(*A*) *Revolução de Septembro*, Lisbon (1840–60)
(*O*) *Templo da Memória*, Lisbon (1820)
(*O*) *Tempo*, Lisbon (1838–39)
(*A*) *União*, Lisbon (1848–50)
(*A*) *Vedeta da Liberdade*, Porto (1835–40)

Note

1. The titles of periodical works, which are all in the Biblioteca Nacional, Lisbon, are given in alphabetical order (taking into account also the first date of publication).

Legislation and Official Documents

Albuquerque, J., *Indice Alphabetico e Remissivo dos trabalhos Parlamentares das Cortes Geraes da Nação portuguesa*, 4 vols., Imprensa Nacional, Lisbon, 1901–07.

Biker, Julio Firmino Júdice, *Suplemento à Colecção de Tratados, Convenções, Contratos e Actos Públicos celebrados entre a Coroa de Portugal e as mais Potências desde 1640 até ao presente*, vols. XVII– XXVIII, Lisbon, 1879.

Castro, José F. Borges de, *Collecção dos tratados, convenções, contratos e actos públicos celebrados entre a Coroa de Portugal e as mais Potências desde 1640 até ao presente*, vols. IV and V, Imprensa Nacional, Lisbon, 1857–58.

Documentos àcerca do tráfico da escravatura extrahidos dos papéis relativos a Portugal apresentados ao Parlamento Britannico, Lisbon, 1840.

Documentos Officiais sobre a negociação do Tratado para a Supressão do Tráfico da Escravatura, mandados publicar por ordem da Câmara dos Senadores, Lisbon, 1839.

Documentos relativos à negociação do Tratado entre Portugal e a Gram-Bretanha para a abolição do Tráfico da Escravatura, mandados publicar por ordem do Governo de Sua Magestade em aditamento aos que a Câmara dos Senadores mandou imprimir, Lisbon, 1939.

Relatórios sobre a epidemia de febre amarella em Loanda no anno de 1860, Imprensa Nacional, Lisbon, 1861.

Repressão do Tráfico da Escravatura. Extracto de Documentos Officiaes, Imprensa Nacional, Lisbon, 1888.

Silva, J.J. de Andrade e, *Collecção Chronologica da legislação Portuguesa*, Lisbon, 1859.

Vasconcellos, J.J. Reis e, *Despachos e Correspondência do Duque de Palmela*, 4 vols., Imprensa Nacional, Lisbon, 1851.

Other Publications

Augustine, *City of God* (Portuguese translation by J. Dias Pereira, *A cidade de Deus*, Gulbenkian, Lisbon, 1995).

Almeida, J.B. Ferreira de, *Portugal e.os seus Domínios Ultramarinos. Memória apresentada à Comissão de Exploração Africana da Sociedade de Geografia de Lisboa*, Lisbon, 1877.

Amorim, Francisco Gomes de, *Ódio de Raça*, Lisbon, 1869.

Aristotle, *Politics* (Spanish translation by Julian Marias y Maria Araújo, *Politica*, Instituto de Estudios Politicos, Madrid, 1951).

Azeredo, José Pinto de, *Ensaios sobre algumas Enfermedades d'Angola, dedicados ao Serenissimo Senhor D. João, Principe do Brazil*, Lisbon, 1799.

Bandinel, James, *Some Account of the Trade in Slaves from Africa, as Connected with Europe and America. From the Introduction of the Trade into Modern Europe, down to Present Time, especially with Reference to the Efforts made by the British Government for its Extinction*, Frank Cass, London, 1968 (1st edition 1842).

Barros, João de, *Da Ásia*, Década 1ª, Livro III, Lisbon, 1778.

Beaver, Philip, *African Memoranda: Relative to an Attempt to Establish a British Settlement on the Island of Bulama, on the Western Coast of Africa, in the Year 1792...*, London, 1805.

Benci, Jorge, *Economia cristã dos senhores no governo dos escravos*, Livraria Apostolado da Imprensa, Porto, 1954 (1st edition 1700).

Benezet, Anthony, *Some Historical Account of Guinea, Its Situation, Produce, and the General Disposition of Its Inhabitants with an Inquiry into the Rise and Progress of the Slave Trade, Its Nature and Lamentable Effects*, London, 1788 (1st edition Philadelphia, 1771).

____, *A Caution to Great Britain and Her Colonies in a Short Representation of the Calamitous State of the Enslaved Negroes in the British Dominions*, London, 1784 (1st edition Philadelphia, 1766).

Biancardi, Theodoro José, *Cartas americanas*, Lisbon, 1820.

(Blanco White), *Bosquejo sobre o commercio em escravos. Reflexões sobre este tráfico, considerado moral, política e christãmente*, London, 1821.

Bordalo, Francisco Maria, *Eugénio. Romance Marítimo*, Lisbon, 1854 (2nd edition).

____, *Ensaios sobre a Estatistica das Possessões Portuguezas na África Occidental e Oriental, na Ásia Occidental, na China e na Oceania*, Imprensa Nacional, Lisbon, 1859.

Bosman, William, *Voyage en Guinée, contenant une description nouvelle et très exacte de cette côte, ou l'on trouve et ou l'on trafique l'or, les dents d'éléphants et les esclaves*, Utrecht, 1705.

Botelho, Sebastião Xavier, *Memória Estatistica sobre os Domínios Portuguezes na Africa Oriental*, Lisbon, 1835.

____, *Escravatura: benefícios que podem provir às nossas Possessões d'Africa da prohibição daquele Tráfico*, Lisbon, 1840.

Breve resumo sobre a natureza do commercio da escravatura e das atrocidades que dele resultam, London, 1821.

Brito, João Rodrigues de, *Cartas económico-políticas sobre a agricultura e commercio da Bahia*, Lisbon, 1821.

Buxton, Thomas F., *The African Slave Trade*, London, 1839.

____, *The Remedy: Being a Sequel to The African Slave Trade*, London, 1840.

Carpo, Arsénio Pompílio Pompeu de, *Projecto d'uma Companhia para o melhoramento do commercio, agricultura e industria na Provincia de Angola, que se deve estabelecer na cidade de S. Paulo d'Assumpção de Loanda*, Lisbon, 1848.

Carvalho, José Liberato Freire de, *Memórias da vida de José Liberato Freire de Carvalho*, Assírio e Alvim, Lisbon, 1982 (1st edition 1855).

Chagas, Manuel J. Pinheiro, *As colónias portuguesas no século XIX (de 1811 a 1890)*, Liv. A.M. Pereira, Lisbon, 1890.

Clarkson, Thomas, *An Essay on the Impolicy of the African Slave Trade*, London, 1788 (French translation, *Essai sur les désavantages politiques de la traite des Nègres*, Neufchatel, 1789).

____, *History of the Rise, Progress, and Accomplishment of the Abolition of the African Slave Trade by the British Parliament*, London, 1839 (1st edition 1808).

____, *Os gemidos dos africanos por causa do traffico da Escravatura, ou breve exposição das injurias e dos horrores que accompanham este traffico homicida*, London, 1823.

Costa, João Severiano Maciel da, *Memória sobre a necessidade de abolir a introdução dos escravos africanos no Brasil*, Coimbra, 1821.

Coutinho, D. José Joaquim da Cunha de Azeredo, *Ensaio económico sobre o comércio de Portugal e suas colónias*, Lisbon, 1794.

____, *Analyse sobre a justiça do commercio do Resgate dos Escravos da Costa de Africa, novamente revista e acrescentada por seu author*, Lisbon, 1808.

____, *Concordância das leis de Portugal e das Bullas Pontificias, das quaes humas permittem a escravidão dos pretos d'Africa, e outras prohibem a escravidão dos Indios do Brazil*, Lisbon, 1808.

Cugoano, Ottobah, *Thoughts and Sentiments on the Evil and Wicked Traffic of the Slavery and Commerce of Human Species*, London, 1797.

Dias, L.F. Carvalho, *Algumas cartas do Doutor António Ribeiro dos Santos aos seus contemporâneos*, Coimbra, 1975.

Duval, Jules, *Histoire de l'émigration au XIXe siècle. Europeènne, asiatique et africaine. Ses causes, ses caractères, ses effets*, Paris, 1862.

Equiano, Olaudah, *The Interesting Narrative of the Life of Olaudah Equiano, or Gustavus Vassa, the African: Written by Himself*, London, 1789.

Faro, Jorge, 'Os problemas de Bissau, Cacheu e suas dependências, vistos em 1831 por Manuel António Martins', *Boletim Cultural da Guiné Portuguesa*, XIII, 50, 1958, pp. 202–14.

Figanière e Morão, J. César de, *Descripção de Serra Leoa e seus contornos. Escripta em doze cartas à qual se ajuntão os trabalhos da Comissão-Mixta portuguesa e inglesa estabelecida naquela colónia*, Lisbon, 1822.

Franco, Francisco Soares, *Ensaio sobre os melhoramentos de Portugal e Brazil*, Lisbon, 1820.

Freire, José Joaquim, *Projecto para a abolição do tráfico da escravatura*, Lisbon, 1840.

Fronteira, Marquês de, *Memórias do Marquês de Fronteira e d'Alorna, D. José Trazimundo Mascarenhas Barreto*, 4 vols., Imprensa da Universidade, Coimbra, 1929.

Gaio, António da Silva, *Mario. Episódios das luctas civis portuguezas de 1820–1834*, Guimarães Eds., Lisbon, 1924 (1st edition 1868).

Gama, António Saldanha da, *Memoria historica e política sobre o commercio da escravatura, entregue no dia 2 de Novembro de 1816 ao Conde Capo d'Istria, Ministro do Imperador da Russia*, Imprensa Nacional, Lisbon, 1880.

____, *Memória sobre as colónias de Portugal situadas na costa Ocidental d'Africa, mandada ao governo pelo antigo Governador e Capitão-Geral do Reino de Angola... em 1814, precedida de um discurso preliminar, augmentada de alguns additamentos e notas,...*, Paris, 1839.

Labat, Jean-Baptiste, *Voyage du Chevalier Des Marchais en Guinée, iles voisines, et à Cayenne fait en 1725, 1726, 1727*, Paris, 1730.

Lima, José Joaquim Lopes de, *Ensaios sobre a Statistica das Possessões Portuguezas na Africa Occidental e Oriental, na Asia Occidental, na China e na Oceania*, Imprensa Nacional, Lisbon, 1844.

Macedo, José Agostinho de, 'O Preto Sensível', *Minerva*, Lisbon, II, 1836, pp. 99–115.

Marinho, Joaquim Pereira, *Memória Official em resposta às acusações dirigidas a Sua Magestade contra o Governador Geral da Província de Cabo Verde, o Brigadeiro Joaquim Pereira Marinho*, Lisbon, 1839.

____, *Memória contra a facção dos negreiros, dedicada ao Illmo. e Exmo. Senhor Visconde de Sá da Bandeira*, Lisbon, 1842.

Memória àcerca da extinção da escravidão e do tráfico de escravos no território portuguez, Ministério da Marinha, Lisbon, 1889.

Memorial aos habitantes da Europa sobre a iniquidade do Comércio da Escravatura, London, 1824.

Mendes, Luís António de Oliveira, *Memória a respeito dos escravos e tráfico da escravatura entre a costa d'Africa e o Brasil, apresentada à Real Academia das Ciências de Lisboa em 1793*, Pub. Escorpião, Lisbon, 1977.

Menezes, Joaquim António de Carvalho, *Memoria Geografica e Politica das Possessões Portuguezas n'Affrica Occidental, que diz respeito aos Reinos de Angola, Benguela e suas dependencias...*, Lisbon, 1834.

Neves, José Acúrsio das, *Considerações Politicas e Commerciais sobre os descobrimentos e Possessões dos Portuguezes na Africa e na Ásia*, Lisbon, 1830.

Oliveira, Fernando, *Arte da guerra do mar*, Arquivo Histórico da Marinha, Lisbon, 1937 (1st edition 1555).

Pereira, J. Silva, *O jornalismo portuguez. Resenha chronológica de todos os periódicos portuguezes impressos e publicados no Reino e no estrangeiro, desde o meiado do século XVII até à morte do saudoso Rei Senhor D. Luís I, bem como dos jornais em língua estrangeira publicados em Portugal durante o mesmo tempo*, Lisbon, 1895.

Raynal, Guillaume-Thomas, *Histoire philosophique et politique des établissements et du commerce des Européens dans les deux Indes*, Paris, 1770.

Rocha, Manoel Ribeiro da, *Ethiope resgatado, empenhado, sustentado, corregido, instruido e libertado. Discurso theologico-juridico em que se propoem o modo de comerciar, haver e possuir validamente, quanto a hum e a outro foro, os Pretos cativos africanos, e as principais obrigações que correm a quem deles se servir*, Lisbon, 1758.

Rousseau, Jean-Jacques, *Du Contrat Social, ou principes du droit politique*, Neufchatel, 1762 (Portuguese translation by L.M. Brum, *O contrato social*, Pub. Europa-América, Mem Martins, 1974).

(Rosas, Sebastian Charles), *Breves Reflexões àcerca do estado actual do Trafico da Escravatura, em relação ao Progresso da Civilização Europea*, Lisbon, 1839.

Sá da Bandeira, Visconde de, *Diário da Guerra Civil (1826–1832)*, 2 vols., Seara Nova, Lisbon, 1975–76.

____, *O tráfico da escravatura e o bill de Lord Palmerston*, Lisbon, 1840.

Saint-Pierre, Jacques-Henri Bernardin de, *Voyage à l'Isle de France, à l'Isle de Bourbon, au Cap de Bonne Espérance ... par un officier du Roi*, 2 vols., Paris, 1773.

Sanches, António Ribeiro, *Cartas sobre a educação da mocidade*, Imprensa da Universidade, Coimbra, 1922 (1st edition 1760).

(Sarmento, Alexandre de Morais), *Russell de Albuquerque. Conto moral por um portuguez*, Cintra, 1833.

Sequeira, António d'Oliva de Sousa, *Projecto para o estabelecimento político do Reino-Unido de Portugal, Brasil e Algarves*, Coimbra, 1821.

Silva, Innocêncio Francisco da, *Diccionario Bibliographico Portuguez*, various volumes, Imprensa Nacional, Lisbon, 1860.

Snelgrave, William, *Nouvelle relation de quelques endroits de Guinée et du commerce d'esclaves ...*, Amsterdam, 1735 (1st edition 1734).

Stedman, John Gabriel, *Narrative of a Five Years' Expedition against the Revolted Negroes of Surinam*, London, 1796 (excerpted in I and J.L. Vissière, *La Traite des noirs au siècle des Lumières*, A. M. Metaillé, Paris, 1982, pp. 133–44).

Tams, George, *Visita às Possessões Portuguezas na costa Occidental d'Africa*, 2 vols., Porto, 1850.

Tocqueville, Alexis de, 'On the Emancipation of Slaves', in Seymour Drescher (ed.), *Tocqueville and Beaumont on Social Reform*, Harper & Row, New York, 1968, pp. 137–73

Vieira, António, 'Sermão vigésimo sétimo', in *Sermões, problemas raciais e políticos*

do Brasil, Ed. Cultrix, São Paulo, 1975, pp. 57–87.
Vilhena, Luis dos Santos, *Recopilação de notícias soteropolitanas e brasilicas, contidas em vinte cartas …*, Bahia, 1921.
Vogel, Charles, *Le Portugal et ses colonies. Tableau politique et commercial de la Monarquie Portugaise dans son état actuel*, Paris, 1860.
Voltaire, François-Marie de, *Candide ou l'optimisme*, Paris, 1759.
Zurara, Gomes Eanes de, *Crónica de Guiné*, Livraria Civilização, Lisbon, 1973.

BOOKS AND ARTICLES

Alencastro, Luiz Felipe de, *O Trato dos Viventes. Formação do Brasil no Atlântico Sul*, Companhia das Letras, São Paulo, 2000.
Alexandre, Valentim, *Origens do colonialismo português moderno (1822–1891)*, Sá da Costa, Lisbon, 1979.
____, 'O Liberalismo português e as colónias de África, 1820–1839', *Análise Social*, 16, 61–62, 1980, pp. 319–40.
____, 'Portugal e a abolição do tráfico de escravos, 1834–51', *Análise Social*, 26, 111, 1991, pp. 293–333.
____, 'A desagregação do império: Portugal e o reconhecimento do Estado brasileiro (1824–1826)', *Análise Social*, 28, 121, 1993, pp. 309–41.
____, *Os sentidos do Império. Questão nacional e questão colonial na crise do Antigo Regime português*, Afrontamento, Porto, 1993.
____, 'Projecto colonial e abolicionismo', *Penélope*, 14, 1994, pp. 119–25.
Anstey, Roger, *The Atlantic Slave Trade and British Abolition, 1760–1810*, Macmillan Press, London, 1975.
____, 'The Pattern of British Abolitionism in the Eighteenth and Nineteenth centuries', in Christine Bolt and Seymour Drescher (eds), *Anti-Slavery, Religion and Reform: Essays in the Memory of Roger Anstey*, Dawson, Folkestone, 1980, pp. 19–42.
____, 'Religion and British Slave Emancipation', in David Eltis and James Walvin (eds), *The Abolition of the Atlantic Slave Trade. Origins and Effects in Europe, Africa and the Americas*, University of Wisconsin Press, Madison, 1981, pp. 37–61.
Aron, Raymond, 'Comment l'historien écrit l'épistémologie: a propos du livre de Paul Veyne', *Annales*, 26, 1971, pp. 1319–54.
Austen, Ralph A., 'The Trans-Saharan Slave Trade: A Tentative Census', in H. Gemery and J. Hogendorn (eds), *The Uncommon Market. Essays in the Economic History of the Atlantic Slave Trade*, Academic Press, New York, 1979, pp. 23–76.
____, 'The Mediterranean Islamic Slave Trade out of Africa', *Slavery and Abolition*, 13, 1, 1992, pp. 214–48.
Bastos, José Timóteo da Silva, *História da censura intelectual em Portugal*, Imprensa da Universidade, Coimbra, 1926.
Behrendt, Stephen D., 'Crew Mortality in the Transatlantic Slave Trade in the Eighteenth Century', *Slavery and Abolition*, 18, 1, 1997, pp. 49–71.
Bender, Thomas (ed.), *The Anti-Slavery Debate: Capitalism and Abolitionism as a Problem in Historical Interpretation*, University of California Press, Berkeley, 1992.
Bethell, Leslie, 'The Mixed Commissions for the Suppression of the Transatlantic Slave Trade in the Nineteenth Century', *Journal of African History*, 7, 1, 1966, pp. 79–93.
____, *The Abolition of the Brazilian Slave Trade. Britain, Brazil and the Slave Trade Question (1807–1869)*, Cambridge University Press, Cambridge, 1970.

Bonifácio, Maria de Fátima, 'Os arsenalistas da Marinha na Revolução de Setembro (1836)', *Análise Social*, 17, 65, 1981, pp. 29–65.

____, '1834–42: a Inglaterra perante a evolução política portuguesa', *Análise Social*, 20, 83, 1984, pp. 467–88.

____, 'Comércio externo e política pautal na 1ª metade do século XIX', *Ler História*, 10, 1987, pp. 75–108.

____, *Seis estudos sobre o liberalismo português*, Estampa, Lisbon, 1996.

Booth, A.R., 'The United States African Squadron, 1843–1861', *Boston University Papers on Africa*, Boston, vol. 1, 1964, pp. 77–117.

Brooks, G.E., 'A Nhara of the Guinea-Bissau Region: Mãe Aurélia Correia', in C.C. Robertson and M. Klein (eds), *Women and Slavery in Africa*, University of Wisconsin Press, Madison, 1983, pp. 295–319.

Capela, José, *Escravatura: a empresa do saque. O abolicionismo, 1810–1875*, Afrontamento, Porto, 1974.

____, *A burguesia mercantil do Porto e as colónias (1834–1900)*, Afrontamento, Porto, 1975.

____, *As burguesias portuguesas e a abolição do tráfico da escravatura*, Afrontamento, Porto, 1979.

____, 'Abolicion y abolicionismo en Portugal y sus colonias', in Francisco de Solano and Agustín Guimerá (eds), *Esclavitud y derechos humanos. La lucha por la libertad del negro en el siglo XIX*, CSIC, Madrid, 1986, pp. 577–603.

Carreira, António, *O tráfico de escravos nos rios de Guiné e ilhas de Cabo Verde, 1810–1850. Subsídios para o seu estudo*, Junta de Investigação Científica do Ultramar, Lisbon, 1981.

Carrington, Selwyn, 'The State of the Debate on the Role of Capitalism in the Ending of the Slave System', in H. Beckles and V. Shepherd (eds), *Caribbean Slave Society and Economy*, IRP, Kingston, 1991, pp. 435–45.

Carvalho, Tito Augusto de, *As Companhias portuguesas de colonização*, Lisbon, undated.

Chatillon, Marcel, 'La diffusion de la gravure du *Brooks* par la Société des Amis des Noirs et son impact', in Serge Daget (ed.), *De la traite à l'esclavage*, vol. 2, CRHMA/Société Française d'Histoire d'Outre-Mer, Nantes, 1988, pp. 135–47.

Clarence-Smith, Gervase, *The Third Portuguese Empire, 1825–1975. A Study in Economic Imperialism*, Manchester University Press, Manchester, 1985.

Coughtry, Jay, *The Notorious Triangle: Rhode Island and the African Slave Trade, 1700–1807*, Temple University Press, Philadelphia, 1981.

Coupland, Reginald, *The British Anti-Slavery Movement*, Frank Cass, London, 1964 (1st edition 1933).

Curtin, Philip D., *The Image of Africa. British Ideas and Action, 1780–1850*, University of Wisconsin Press, Madison, 1964.

____, *The Atlantic Slave Trade: a Census*, University of Wisconsin Press, Madison, 1969.

____, 'Epidemiology and the Slave Trade', in *Congrès International des Africanistes*, Présence Africaine, Paris, 1972, pp. 87–114.

____, *Death by Migration. Europe's Encounter with the Tropical World in the Nineteenth Century*, Cambridge University Press, Cambridge, 1989.

Daget, Serge, 'A Model of the French Abolitionist Movement and its Variations', in Christine Bolt and Seymour Drescher (eds), *Anti-Slavery, Religion and Reform: Essays in Memory of Roger Anstey*, Dawson, Folkestone, 1980, pp. 64–79.

____, 'France, Suppression of the Illegal Slave Trade, and England, 1817–1850', in David Eltis and James Walvin (eds), *The Abolition of the Atlantic Slave Trade. Origins and Effects in Europe, Africa, and the Americas*, University of Wisconsin Press, Madison, 1981, pp. 193–217.

____, 'The Abolition of the Slave Trade by France: the Decisive Years, 1826–1831', in David Richardson (ed.), *Abolition and its Aftermath. The Historical Context, 1790–1916*, Frank Cass, London, 1985, pp. 141–67.

____, 'Armateurs Nantais et trafic illégal: une histoire sans petite boîte verte', *Enquêtes et documents*, XIII, 1987, pp. 69–98.

____, 'Les croisières françaises de répression de la traite des noirs sur les côtes occidentales de l'Afrique (1817–1850)', *Enquêtes et documents*, XIV, 1988, pp. 25–35.

____, 'Tactiques, stratégies et effets du droit de visite', in Serge Daget (ed.), *De la traite a l'esclavage*, vol. 2, CRHMA. / Société Française d'Histoire d'Outre-Mer, Nantes, 1988, pp. 343–58.

Davis, David B., 'The Emergence of Immediatism in British and American Anti-Slavery Thought', *Mississipi Valley Historical Review*, 49, 2, 1962, pp. 209–30.

____, *The Problem of Slavery in Western Culture*, Cornell University Press, Ithaca, NY, 1966.

____, *The Problem of Slavery in the Age of Revolution, 1770–1823*, Cornell University Press, Ithaca, NY, and London, 1975.

____, *Slavery and Human Progress*, Oxford University Press, Oxford, 1984.

Dias, Jill R., 'Angola', in Valentim Alexandre and Jill R. Dias (eds), *O Império africano, 1825–1890*, Estampa, Lisbon, 1998, pp. 321–556.

Drescher, Seymour, *Econocide: British Slavery in the Era of Abolition*, University of Pittsburgh Press, Pittsburgh, 1977.

____, 'The Slaving Capital of the World. Liverpool and National Opinion in the Age of Abolition', *Slavery and Abolition*, 9, 2, 1988, pp. 128–43.

____, 'The Ending of the Slave Trade and the Evolution of European Scientific Racism', *Social Science History*, 14, 3, 1990, pp. 415–50.

____, 'The Decline Thesis of British Slavery since Econocide', in H. Beckles and V. Shepherd (eds), *Caribbean Slave Society and Economy*, IRP, Kingston, 1991, pp. 136–49.

____, 'Whose Abolition? Popular Pressure and the Ending of the British Slave Trade', *Past and Present*, 143, 1994, pp. 136–66.

____, 'Capitalism and Slavery after Fifty Years', *Slavery and Abolition*, 18, 3, 1997, pp. 212–27.

____, *The Mighty Experiment. Free Labor versus Slavery in British Emancipation*, Oxford University Press, Oxford, 2002.

Eltis, David, 'The British Contribution to the Nineteenth Century Transatlantic Slave Trade', *Economic History Review*, 32, 2, 1979, pp. 211–27.

____, 'Abolitionist Perceptions of Society after Slavery', in James Walvin (ed.), *Slavery and British Society, 1776–1846*, The Louisiana State University Press, Baton Rouge, 1982, pp. 195–213.

____, 'Slave Departures from Africa, 1811–1867. An Annual Time Series', *African Economic History*, 15, 1986, pp. 143–71.

____, 'The Nineteenth-Century Transatlantic Slave Trade: An Annual Time Series of Imports into the Americas, Broken Down by Region', *The Hispanic American Historical Review*, 67, 1987, pp. 109–38.

____, *Economic Growth and the Ending of the Transatlantic Slave Trade*, Oxford University Press, New York, 1987.

Esparteiro, António, *Três Séculos no Mar (1640–1910)*, 32 vols., Ministério da Marinha, Lisbon, 1974–86.

Fonseca, J. Roque da, *Cem Anos em defesa da Economia nacional, 1834–1934. História da Associação Comercial de Lisboa*, Lisbon, 1934.

____, 'A Associação Comercial de Lisboa e o Império (1834–1900)', in *Primeiro Congresso da História da Expansão portuguesa no Mundo*, Ministério das Colónias, Lisbon, 1938.

Freudenthal, Aida, 'Arimos e Fazendas. A transição agrária em Angola, 1850–75',

Universidade Nova de Lisboa, 1989 (unpublished master's thesis).

Fyfe, Christopher, *A History of Sierra Leone*, Oxford University Press, London, 1962.

Geggus, David, 'Haiti and the Abolitionists: Opinion, Propaganda and International Politics in Britain and France, 1804–1838', in David Richardson (ed.), *Abolition and its Aftermath. The Historical Context, 1790–1916*, Frank Cass, London, 1985, pp. 113–40.

Godinho, Vitorino Magalhães, *Estrutura da Antiga sociedade portuguesa*, Arcádia, Lisbon, 1977 (1st edition 1971).

____, *Os descobrimentos e a economia mundial*, vol. 4, Ed. Presença, Lisbon, 1983 (2nd edition).

Green, James, 'The Publishing History of Olaudah Equiano's Interesting Narrative', *Slavery and Abolition*, 16, 3, 1995, pp. 362–75.

Green, W.A., 'The West Indies and British West African Policy in the Nineteenth Century. A Corrective Comment', *Journal of African History*, 15, 2, 1974, pp. 247–60.

____, *British Slave Emancipation: The Sugar Colonies and the Great Experiment, 1830–1865*, Clarendon Press, Oxford, 1976.

____, 'Was British Emancipation a Success? The Abolitionist Perspective', in David Richardson (ed.), *Abolition and its Aftermath. The Historical Context, 1790–1916*, Frank Cass, London, 1985, pp. 183–202.

Green-Pedersen, Svend E., 'Slave Demography in the Danish West Indies and the Abolition of the Danish Slave Trade', in David Eltis and James Walvin (eds), *The Abolition of the Atlantic Slave Trade. Origins and Effects in Europe, Africa, and the Americas*, University of Wisconsin Press, Madison, 1981, pp. 231–57.

Hall, Catherine, *Civilising Subjects. Metropole and Colony in the English Imagination, 1830–1867*, Polity Press, Cambridge, 2002.

Hammond, R.J., *Portugal and Africa, 1815–1910. A Study in Uneconomic Imperialism*, Stanford University Press, Stanford, California, 1966.

____, 'Uneconomic Imperialism: Portugal in Africa before 1910', in L.H. Gann and P. Duignan (eds), *Colonialism in Africa, 1870–1960*, vol. 1, Cambridge University Press, Cambridge, 1969, pp. 352–82.

____, 'Some Economic Aspects of Portuguese Africa in the Nineteenth and Twentieth Centuries', in L.H. Gann and Peter Duignan (eds), *Colonialism in Africa, 1870–1960*, vol. 4, Cambridge University Press, Cambridge, 1975, pp. 256–80.

Hardgreaves, John D., 'African Colonization in the Nineteenth Century: Liberia and Sierra Leone', in J. Butler (ed.), *Boston University Papers in African History*, vol. 1, Boston University Press, Boston, 1964, pp. 57–76.

Honour, Hugh, *L'image du noir dans l'Europe Occidental. De la Révolution Américaine a la Première Guerre Mondiale*, Vol. 1, Gallimard, Paris, 1989.

Jennings, Judith, 'Joseph Woods, Merchant and Philosopher: the Making of the British Anti-Slave Trade Ethic', *Slavery and Abolition*, 14, 3, 1993, pp. 162–84.

Jennings, Lawrence C., 'The French Press and Great Britain's Campaign Against the Slave Trade, 1830–1848', *Revue Française d'Histoire d'Outre-Mer*, 67, 246–47, 1980, pp. 5–24.

____, *French Anti-Slavery. The Movement for the Abolition of Slavery in France, 1802–1848*, Cambridge University Press, Cambridge, 2000.

Johansen, Hans Christian, 'The Reality behind the Demographic Arguments to Abolish the Danish Slave Trade', in David Eltis and James Walvin (eds), *The Abolition of the Atlantic Slave Trade. Origins and Effects in Europe, Africa and the Americas*, University of Wisconsin Press, Madison, 1981, pp. 221–30.

Karasch, Mary, 'The Brazilian Slavers and the Illegal Slave Trade, 1836–1851', University of Wisconsin, Madison, 1967 (unpublished master's thesis).

LeVeen, E. Philip, *British Slave Trade Suppression Policies, 1821–1865*, Arno Press, New York, 1977.

Lloyd, Christopher, *The Navy and the Slave Trade. The Suppression of the African Slave Trade in the Nineteenth Century*, Frank Cass, London, 1968 (1st edition 1949).
Macedo, Jorge Borges de, 'Real Mesa Censória', in Joel Serrão (ed.), *Dicionário de História de Portugal*, vol. IV, Figueirinhas, Porto, 1981, pp. 276–77.
____, *História diplomática portuguesa. Constantes e linhas de força. Estudo de geopolítica*, Instituto de Defesa Nacional, Lisbon, 1987.
Marques, A.H. de Oliveira, *História de Portugal*, vol. 2, Palas, Lisbon, 1978 (1st edition 1974).
Marques, João Pedro, 'Uma revisão crítica das teorias sobre a abolição do tráfico de escravos português', *Penélope*, 14, 1994, pp. 95–118.
____, 'A Armada portuguesa no combate ao tráfico de escravos em Angola (1839–1867) ', *Anais de História de Além-Mar*, 1, 2000, pp. 161–93.
____, 'Uma cosmética demorada: as Cortes portuguesas face ao problema da escravidão (1836–1875) ', *Análise Social*, 158 / 159, 2001, pp. 209–47.
____, 'Penosa navegação: Portugal e as carreiras a vapor para África (1850–82)', *Anais de História de Além-Mar*, 2, 2001, pp. 273–98.
____, 'Arsénio Pompílio Pompeu de Carpo: um percurso negreiro no século XIX', *Análise Social*, 160, 2001, pp. 609–38.
Midgley, Clare, 'Slave Sugar Boycotts, Female Activism and the Domestic Base of British Anti-Slavery Culture', *Slavery and Abolition*, 17, 3, 1996, pp. 137–62.
Miller, Joseph C., *Way of Death. Merchant Capitalism and the Angolan Slave Trade, 1730–1830*, University of Wisconsin Press, Madison, 1988.
Murray, David R., *Odious Commerce: Britain, Spain and the Abolition of the Cuban Slave Trade*, Cambridge University Press, Cambridge, 1980.
Oostindie, Gert, 'Voltaire, Stedman and Suriname Slavery', *Slavery and Abolition*, 14, 2, 1993, pp. 1–34.
Paixão, Braga, *Cem anos do Banco Nacional Ultramarino na vida portuguesa, 1864–1964*, vol. I, Academia das Ciências de Lisboa, Lisbon, undated.
Pélissier, René, *Les Guerres grises. Résistances et révoltes en Angola (1845–1941)*, Pélissier, Montamets, 1977.
Pereira, Miriam Halpern, *A política portuguesa de emigração, 1850–1930*, A Regra do Jogo, Lisbon, 1981.
Rawley, James A., 'London's Defense of the Slave Trade', *Slavery and Abolition*, 14, 2, 1993, pp. 48–69.
Rice, C. Duncan, 'Literary Sources and the Revolution in British Attitudes to Slavery', in Christine Bolt and Seymour Drescher (eds), *Anti-Slavery, Religion, and Reform. Essays in Memory of Roger Anstey*, Dawson, Folkestone, 1980, pp. 319–34.
Rizzini, C., *Hipólito da Costa e o Correio Braziliense*, Companhia Editora Nacional, São Paulo, 1957.
Santa Rita, José Gonçalo, 'As questões coloniais nas Cortes Constituintes e na Segunda Legislatura (1821–1823)', *Revista da Faculdade de Letras de Lisboa*, XIV, 3, 1949, pp. 7–91.
Serrão, Joel, *A emigração portuguesa. Sondagem histórica*, Horizonte, Lisbon, 1977 (1st edition 1972).
Silva, Maria Beatriz Nizza da, 'A repercussão da Revolução de 1820 no Brasil. Eventos e ideologias', *Revista de História das Ideias*, 2, 1978–79, pp. 1–52.
Temperley, Howard W., 'The Ideology of Anti-Slavery', in David Eltis and James Walvin (eds), *The Abolition of the Atlantic Slave Trade. Origins and Effects in Europe, Africa and the Americas*, University of Wisconsin Press, Madison, 1981, pp. 21–35.
____, *White Dreams, Black Africa: The Antislavery Expedition to the River Niger, 1841–1842*, Yale University Press, New Haven, 1991.
Tengarrinha, José, *História da imprensa periódica portuguesa*, Lisbon, undated.

Thomaz, Luís Filipe, 'A escravatura em Malaca no século XVI', *Studia*, 53, 1994, pp. 253–316.

Tise, Larry E., *Proslavery: A History of the Defense of Slavery in America, 1701–1840*, University of Georgia Press, Athens, Georgia, 1987.

Turley, David, *The Culture of English Antislavery, 1780–1860*, Routledge, London, 1991.

Valente, Vasco Pulido, *Os Devoristas. A Revolução Liberal, 1834–1836*, Quetzal Editores, Lisbon, 1993.

Verger, Pierre, *Flux et reflux de la traite des nègres entre le golfe de Bénin et Bahia de Todos os Santos du XVIIe au XIXe siècles*, Mouton, Paris and The Hague, 1968.

Verlinden, Charles, *L'esclavage dans l'Europe Médiévale*, De Temple, Brugge, 1955.

——, *The Beginnings of Modern Colonization. Eleven Essays with an Introduction*, Cornell University Press, Ithaca, NY, 1970.

Veyne, Paul, *Comment on écrit l'histoire. Éssai d'épistémologie*, Ed. du Seuil, Paris, 1971 (Spanish translation by M.M. Alonso, *Como se escribe la historia. Ensayo de epistemologia*, Fragua, Madrid, 1972).

Walvin, James, 'The Rise of British Popular Sentiment for Abolition, 1787–1832', in Christine Bolt and Seymour Drescher (eds), *Anti-Slavery, Religion and Reform: Essays in Memory of Roger Anstey*, Dawson, Folkestone, 1980, pp. 149–62.

____, 'The Public Campaign in England against Slavery, 1787–1834', in David Eltis and James Walvin (eds), *The Abolition of the Atlantic Slave Trade. Origins and Effects in Europe, Africa, and the Americas*, University of Wisconsin Press, Madison, 1981, pp. 63–79.

Williams, Eric, *Capitalism and Slavery*, Andre Deutsch, London, 1964 (1st edition 1944).

INDEX